Judy Metliss

LIFTING THE STONE AND OTHER ADVENTURES

AUSTIN MACAULEY PUBLISHERS
LONDON * CAMBRIDGE * NEW YORK * SHARJAH

Copyright © Judy Metliss 2024

The right of Judy Metliss to be identified as author of this work has been asserted by the author in accordance with sections 77 and 78 of the Copyright, Designs and Patents Act 1988.

All rights reserved. No part of this publication may be reproduced, stored in a retrieval system, or transmitted in any form or by any means, electronic, mechanical, photocopying, recording, or otherwise, without the prior permission of the publishers.

Any person who commits any unauthorised act in relation to this publication may be liable to criminal prosecution and civil claims for damages.

The story, the experiences, and the words are the author's alone.

A CIP catalogue record for this title is available from the British Library.

ISBN 9781035848423 (Paperback)
ISBN 9781035848430 (ePub e-book)

www.austinmacauley.com

First Published 2024
Austin Macauley Publishers Ltd®
1 Canada Square
Canary Wharf
London
E14 5AA

Table of Contents

1. Roses in Cyprus 9
2. Sadness in Seville 26
3. A Moment in Istanbul 33
4. Breakfast in Bilbao 46
5. Muck in Marrakech 66
6. Nuts in Naples 89
7. Bananas in Tenerife 107
8. Angst in L'Ile Rousse 128
9. Traipsing through Copenhagen 149
10. Door Slamming in Dublin 168
11. Oysters in Antwerp 182
12. My Day Out 200
13. Lifting the Stone 208

Roses in Cyprus

Well, here I am in cloudy Crete, Corsica? – no, it's Cyprus, the birthplace of Aphrodite, the island where the ancient Greeks came because of copper – hence the name of the island which is like 'copper' in Greek – and latterly the Turks, to the anger and distress of those who were uprooted and driven from their homes and the rest of the islanders too. The Turks would say that all is fair in love and war.

Protaras (pronounced with the emphasis on the last syllable) is about eight miles from Ayia Napia, and is a purpose built tourist resort with even less charm than its sister resort down the road, which at least has a monastery surrounded by cypress trees. But there is a small church on a hill over the road from a massive 'McDonalds', its gigantic yellow 'M' serving as a useful landmark. Behind a stone wall surrounding the small park which leads up to the church are beds of roses, deep red and deeply fragrant. In goes my nose, checking that a bee hasn't got there first. But as you leave this spot and walk down the High Street, which is called 'The Strip' you could just as well be in Newmarket High Street where the pubs also are covered with signs and are brown all over. This is a long way from the image of the almond-eyed goddess arising from the wine dark sea. But escaping from a cold, wet, rain soaked early May in the U.K. it's hard not to be blown over by the sight of all the Mediterranean flowers – pink oleander and red hibiscus hedges lining the slope to the hotel, bushes of wild jasmine growing by the bus stop, red geraniums and mauve petunias in wooden tubs outside supermarkets.

I browse around one such supermarket which seems less garish and plastic than the others – one which is selling vacuum packed green and black olives, sachets of herbs and spices all neatly packed together and nut bars, drenched in syrup, hard enough to break your teeth on. You can buy packets of sticky sweet baklava for your relatives back home but even the thought of the caloric and fat content would send their cholesterol soaring. There are tins of Greek chocolate cigars called 'Caprice' which I already have in my kitchen cupboard and shelf loads of spirits to get you in the groove. I'd love to buy a bottle of sweet red Cypriot wine but who am I going to drink it with? Mr. Noone. I start chatting to a young Scottish couple whom I remembered seeing at the 'Welcome Meeting' at the hotel and the young lad said that he couldn't abide the taste of olives. I tell him that all you need to live on is bread and a handful of olives and he doesn't seem to mind my high-minded Mrs Thatcherish take on things and smiles cheerfully, displaying his gleaming white strong innocent teeth. I have a hang-up about my teeth which were destroyed in the 1950s by daily doses of all the chocolate that money could buy. All that is left are ugly black stumps, hideous to behold, the detritus of war.

There is also a section of the supermarket which sells souvenirs like tea towels stamped with a cluster of grapes and 'Cyprus' in lemon yellow and other such stuff for the kitchen to which I give no more than a fleeting glance. I need a new wallet – one which separates the wheat from the chaff or rather separates all your cards but the ones on display are of shoddy, inferior quality. And what a nuisance it is to have to carry around all those cards which don't exactly get you through the pearly gates into Heaven. I suppose the AA breakdown card, a distinct yellowy orange, is a necessity saving you from the horror of being stranded on the motorway (rule number one, as in a Maths exam is to keep a clear head and not to panic) but the blue Tesco points card is hardly a life saver. Actually I'm always a little ashamed by the fact that I never forget to hand it over to be swiped by the cashier. The Tesco tag of 'Every little helps' could be transposed into Macbeth's final famous soliloquy prompted by news of the death of his greedy possessive wife when he considers the slow and petty crawl 'from day to day/ to the last syllable of recorded time;' This is life devoid of spirit. Then there is the National Trust card (which now has to be swiped) the never used library card (who bothers with libraries since the advent of 'Amazon') and, when abroad, the pale spotty E11 which will save you paying an arm and a leg if you have to be hospitalised (God forbid). However, this was my experience in Rome and Corsica and there was no protective card but the hospital food was guaranteed to make you feel better, more alive. And last and not least is the Visa Debit Card which never lets you down; you give it, they take it and sometimes it spares you the pinch of paying for something you don't really want or is possibly over-priced. I compliment the proprietor on his nice little shop and ask him where he was born and raised. 'See you again' he says, with a big smile on his face, as I depart with my purchases.

I make my way back to my purpose-built touristy hotel which nevertheless has a lovely lounge where nobody sits but I. The sofas are upholstered in chocolate brown leather and the huge cushions are lime green. This extremely elegant colour combination is carried over into the curtains. The view is of an attractive outside terrace with round tables and chairs with orange cushions and beyond that is the pale cloudy sky and the rain wet sea. Yes, it's raining, just as it is in the U.K., and that's why I'm going to have to sit indoors. All the other hotel guests avoid this section of the lounge – maybe because it is an invitation to stimulating conversation. I suppose they are too involved in getting married – counting the bridesmaids and seeing that the table is properly laid. It seems to be the in thing for young people to tie the knot under the wide open sky in the sunny climes of Protaras, courtesy of the 'Sunrise Beach' Hotel, surrounded by their loving relations.

What would have been a decent night's sleep (in spite of what feels like a straw filled mattress) was disturbed by someone knocking on my neighbour's door, getting them to open it because they didn't have the key card. What do they care that it's two or three o'clock in the morning. If you gotta get in you gotta get in. For me being brutally woken up when I'm fast asleep is the worst thing in the world. It's worse than the plane landing in the sea or a delayed take-off. I finally doze off again but awake feeling as if I've been stoned in the head. I tell Maria at reception that the mattresses are too hard. She tells me that no one has EVER complained – the reverse in fact. I say that I like a firm mattress but this is like sleeping on the floor. All the listening attendants, porters and such like hear 'foam' for firm and throw their hands up and make eye contact with one another as if to say 'she is used to cheap foam and has no experience of our high quality mattresses'. 'No, you stupid idiots, I said FIRM – do you think I'd sleep on bloody foam...?' They soon withdraw into their customary facial passivity and realise that their English isn't as good as they thought. Maria, the head receptionist, assures me that all the beds in the hotel are identical. When I change rooms on the sixth day it transpires that she was not telling the truth.

She's one of these over confident people of fixed horizons who love their job and would never beat themselves up over anything. At the end of my stay when she charges me double what had been agreed for the last two nights in a sea-facing room she just says, 'oh yes, I remember' (and it's signed, on paper) without a tremor of an eyelash.

She sends me to a town called Paralimni in order to find my 'Fresh Look' products from the Dead Sea, which are imported into Cyprus by a company called 'Vanguard'. Since I pay a lot to have them sent over to the U.K. I thought I'd try to find them at their source. On the bus I chat to a couple of Pakistani lads from Islamabad studying leisure and tourism in Larnaca. Actually Larnaca is where the Vanguard office is but it's a very long bus ride (with all the frequent stopping). In Paralimni I get a bit lost and never have I encountered such indifferent souls – are they half-asleep or what. Nobody has heard of the 'Main Street' let alone 'Fresh Look'. You'd think that a man in a wheelchair would be friendlier. I pop into a small pharmacy to ask the way and a young man with horribly chapped lips, who is obsessively creaming his hands, comes out of the shop, blinks in the light of day and tries to point me in the right direction. Nobody speaks any English and I'm beginning to feel a bit nervous. With a combination of aplomb and revulsion I enter a shoe shop selling hideously vulgar shoes and can hardly wait to get out because of the strange stink of leather. Oh please don't have a staff meeting about it – it's obvious that you've never heard of 'Fresh Look' or the 'Big Pharmacy in Paralimni' Finally I find the Main Road, along which I walk for about twenty minutes arriving at a large pharmacy which sells only conventional brands like Helena Rubenstein (nice name that) and Estee Lauder. There isn't a tree or a café in sight, just a dreary stretch of road and pavement and D.I.Y. shops. A couple of nurseries, ablaze with summer colour, enliven the dreary street and there's a nice-looking school with a sign outside saying that knowledge is freedom and power. At least I'm not wasting precious sunny weather because the sky is thick with clouds. When I finally meet Mr. Vanguard in person, an exiled Cypriot from Famagusta, he tells me that Paralimni is for 'hillbillies'.

On the way back I decide, on account of the overcast skies, to kill two birds with one stone and stop off at Ayia Napa just to see how awful it really is. I want to stare awfulness in the face and not drop down dead. It's a fairly long bus ride because there are stops every hundred metres (can't people just walk a bit further?) We pass a Nature Reserve called 'Cap Greko' on the outskirts of Ayia Napa where the birds fly freely without danger of being shot and I wonder when the real horror of the alcohol fuelled resort will begin. We are dropped off in the centre where there is an oval lawn surrounded by a flower bed sporting little flowers and behind that is a monastery which was obviously here before all the hotels, pubs and souvenir shops. A Russian group are being shown around by a Russian priest and I've never seen anyone with such a rosy pink fresh complexion. I doubt that he uses 'Fresh Look' products. He's probably very pure in thought. I walk through the monastery garden and then have an expensive (four euros) cappuccino at a nice café (i.e. the chairs are comfortable) facing a fountain. But I can see that there is absolutely nothing else to see in the 'Devil's Playground' so I wait for the bus back to Protaras. On reflection I reckon that Protaras has even less to offer than Ayia Napa so the devil is on my doorstep. Looking at the faces of the chaps in the windowless pubs watching football on the TV accompanied by patient submissive wives I realise that the 'devil' is in the lack of imagination. I shock the rep by telling him that Paralimni is a 'soulless dump' but he can't help but laugh as he imagines himself relaying this information to potential visitors.

Back in my room I sit on the balcony overlooking what is in fact a building site although I think it's a disused car park and feed off stuff that I've nicked from the breakfast buffet. I make the effort to swim ten lengths in the hotel pool and then push myself into the sea, which is mighty cold at first. But the water is clear and beautiful and salty. I wonder what is going through the minds of the folk who lie around a pool all day long. Mind you, that's what I used to do as a teenager. I had no interest in history or culture because image, turning into a date, was the thing. I always enjoy dressing for dinner, gives me a chance to air my pretty dresses, and outside the restaurant I enjoy a nice chat with an intelligent waiter from Salonika (he has lovely blue eyes and a cheeky grin) who tells me just how bad it is in Greece – everyone is leaving. He reckons that China, the alpha male of the twenty-first century, is not a trouble maker as the United States was. What a pity that he can't join me at my dinner table so that we can continue the conversation. All the hotels present the same sort of buffet fare which is tasty and varied although the second course meats all seem to be swimming in some sort of dubious sauce. The desserts are exquisitely made cakes which possibly all share the same ingredient – custard cream. As they say in the classics 'a moment on the lips is an inch on the hips' and this is true when the creamy moments are multiplied ad infinitum.

The after dinner entertainment consisted of a man showing off his performing macaws from Venezuela with their brilliant green plumage. He'd taught Joey to ride a bike, play basketball and lie on a sunbed. This last feat seemed really strange – birds aren't meant to lie on their backs – but it was greeted with huge uproar from the crowd who love to see animals mimicking humans. I thought it was very weird indeed. But the piece de resistance came when the trainer asked anyone to call out two numbers between one and ten and somebody (who is going to be the first to call out?) said 'five' and 'six'. The bird, with a look of real concentration on its bigly beaked face, proceeded (having looked at its protector/tormentor raise five fingers and then six) to ring the bell eleven times. Behind all these doings the bird would hear a continuous light refrain of 'good boy, good boy, good boy' which kept it on task and is probably something we all need. I told Angelo, the young Italian guy from Taranto in southern Italy, that that bird would get its revenge and swoop down on humans, pecking out their eyes. Had he seen Alfred Hitchcock's 'The Birds'. 'But that's only a film,' he replied, 'how absurd! That's just one hell of a clever, well-trained bird.' All the kids were having photos taken of themselves with Joey gripped to their forearm.

Oh God, am I cursed or what? I'm fast asleep in the middle of the night when I'm rudely, brutally awakened by the sound of a chair scraping across the floor. Who, in God's name, has decided to move the furniture around at 2 a.m. I could scream, I could kill but I just lie still and register my disappointment and pain. Being woken up like that when you're so beautifully asleep is a minor trauma. My old friend Macbeth knows that through his violent deed he will never sleep again – he has separated himself from God and nature, the deep relaxing therapy of SLEEP. And how can I go back to sleep when I'm expecting a shrill wake-up call at 7a.m. because I've booked an excursion to the Troodos Mountains. It's like awaiting a grim knock on the door. I manage, sometime or rather a long time later, to drop off only to be disturbed by the noise of drunken youngsters cruising along the corridor. They couldn't care less, the jolly bastards. I'm now in a sort of twisted mess. I probably doze again and wake up at six. So it's me phoning reception to tell them that they don't need to wake me up. As is self-evident I am wide-awake. I swear to myself that I'll never stay in a hotel again.

The day is bright and sunny and warm and this is what dispels misery and fatigue. I'm all set to hit the road. On the coach I tell an Indian couple from Leeds about my bad night. I say that I am going to stick notices on the neighbouring doors telling the occupants to be aware of other people who are sleeping. She says that she has had the same experience in her hotel but thinks it's a better idea to get reception to ring the rooms rather than directly confront people. We mull all this over at some length but I know that nobody is going to lift a finger to help … But the thing about sharing problems is that you create a bond, a friend. Her turbaned husband is very nervous and insecure, taking photos of literally everything in sight. They were exiled to Kenya by the British and then came to Britain in the 1970s where they worked around the clock in a corner shop.

The tour guide, who is Cypriot born but grew up in London, is called Stavros but says that we can call her Lola or Lulu, has been a guide for umpteen years and certainly knows her stuff. She's very upset and distressed by what happened when the Turks invaded in 1974 and points out the shacks where the refugees still live, rent-free. The Turks had a bit of a nerve; I suppose they reckoned that the 300 year old Ottoman residency should never have come to a close. The Troodos Mountains are quite magical and you can well understand why Daphne du Maurier wrote 'Rebecca' in a mountain village rather than down by the seaside. Apparently, they're restoring the oldy worldly famous hotel where she, and other notable personalities, stayed during the pre-war years. It's lovely to see the olives, the cherry trees on which the cherries are just beginning to ripen and, as you climb higher, the different varieties of pine. I also notice that the coach load of people only starts to relax after a joke or two. En route to the Kykkos monastery we stop off at a café where I have a glass of fresh orange juice. I sit myself down to a girl who has managed to escape her two friends who don't want to go anywhere and drive her mad by arguing as to which of the two snores the loudest. The monastery is typically ornate and dripping with gold as is the Byzantine fashion and the chandeliers crammed into such a small space are something to behold. It is our guide's theory that the original earth goddess of fertility became Aphrodite who then morphed into the Virgin Mary. People are lighting candles and saying a prayer for a loved one, or someone who is sick and dying. Mother Mary heal us all! The thing is that it's so difficult to remember all the stuff you are told when so much is crammed into one day. I do think that it is a wonderful thing to be a monk or a nun. No one can shift you from your place of knowledge and faith.

We visit the tomb of Archbishop Makarios (1913-77) and hear his story. I'm good at remembering dates due to revising for history exams at school. I also remember seeing him on television in his distinctive black gear. His massive statue captures his facial expression entirely and his tremendous poise. Apparently, what is written in the black tomb is that wherever he is he will always be with his people and the country he loved.

The next stop is lunch in the village where Stelios, the founder of EasyJet, was born and grew up. His parents have provided the village with a cultural centre and other amenities. The Indian lady beckons me to join her and her husband at their table where we have a direct view over the village. The son of the cook comes to take our order and I can't help but notice the thick rims of dirt beneath his fingernails and his bad skin and greasy hair. His sister also looks unclean, as does mum and I realise that we are our parents really. We were all looking forward to a nice Greek meal and so the disappointment is all the more when I am served a lukewarm moussaka topped with a thick wadge of pale béchamel sauce that doesn't look too fresh. It is, as you might expect, over-priced. That's what comes from being tied to a group. Over the meal, talking enthusiastically about the plight of the euro, a woman from the next table, part of a marriage party group from St. Neots, turns round and looks at me with scorn and disapproval because I am expressive and emotional. Her son, who is in the military, is tattooed to bits and they all sit tightly together, with no space between them whatsoever. They are comparing the sizes of respective wedding rings. I think of what my son (and I too for that matter) say about educated people who have no insight but to have no culture whatsoever is maybe even worse. It's probably due to generations in the factories or the fields just as Jews are what they are through generations of rootlessness and insecurity. God I hated that look she gave me. Or maybe I was exaggerating her animosity and she was just wondering who was being noisy at the next table.

Our next stop is another village high up in the mountains where we are going to be able to sample all the nuts in the world and taste a fiery liqueur. As we get off the coach and walk towards the mountains of nuts and dried fruits people are getting heavily into a discussion as to the pros and cons of self-service check-outs in Tesco. This is obviously of real and meaty interest to all. In order to perhaps curtail the discussion I say, 'well, there are far too many people around anyhow' but nobody is listening. I make my way to the awaiting thimblefuls of red dessert wine. It's nice but not as sweet as the dark red 'Kiddush' wine I remember from childhood. I was always allowed a second glass. On top of each nut mountain is a small plate with samples to try and I walk along the line tasting the honey coated cashews, the almonds in rose water, the dried kiwi fruits and tiny white figs. A woman from the coach samples the 'eau de vie' and says that it is 'disgusting' and nothing like saltimbocca. I'm expecting something which sets your windpipe on fire but it's hardly blindingly potent. I'm not sure whether to buy the dried strawberries but they really are something special, full of concentrated sweetness, and hemming and hawing, unable to make up my mind because who is going to eat them other than me I finally make up my mind and make the purchase. The gypsy looking vendor is amused by my indecision and my questions and so pops in a few more for good luck. I always feel obliged to buy stuff (it's the same with the fishman who comes all the way from Lowestoft in his fish van) to keep the poor man in business.

Back on the coach we learn how religious the Cypriots are and how a Cypriot wedding is a momentous occasion. Sometimes the whole village or three thousand people are invited and money is sewn onto the bride and groom so that at the end of the evening they are covered in notes. It is an honour to be a godparent but an expense too because the godparents have to buy all the child's clothes – three of everything. Male and female children have to have different godparents to prevent incest (?) There are other rituals pertaining to funerals. The Cypriots seem a trifle conservative. But it's certainly better to snack off dried fruits and nuts rather than Toblerones and Kit-Kats. We also learn about their tax and social security benefits and what happens if there is a drought.

Ah, how I enjoy a cup of tea in my room far from anyone. It's the bliss of solitude and reflection. And it's so nice drinking out of a cup and saucer rather than a mug. At dinner I bring in my own bottle of water and get told off by the wine waiter. I have to buy <u>their</u> water which is twice the price (or thereabouts) of what you pay in a shop. But I suppose that by taking in my own water I am downgrading the establishment like going for dinner in shorts and a T-shirt. There have to be boundaries. Every evening the buffet is 'themed' and this evening it is Italian Night. Some of the salads are delicious, principally potato salad with fried courgettes, cherry tomatoes, and pesto (glorious fresh pesto) and one with Parma ham, rocket leaves and shavings of parmesan. The main courses are, as usual, a bit on the mucky side and unmemorable but the guests seem to be piling their plates high, putting quantity before quality. I certainly don't mind eating alone in my silent bubble, unnoticed but noticing.

After dinner the children's 'entertainer' the young Angelo from Taranto drags me into some childish dance in which we all go round in a circle to the rhythm of some child's song (which obviously does the rounds because I remember hearing it in the hotel in Sharm-el-Sheikh, Egypt) making faces at one another, pretending to play the piano and the trombone, jumping from side to side and flapping our wings, like chickens. After the dance (was anyone watching and laughing at me?) I chat to Angelo who says that he must hurry to the bathroom to wash away the sweat. Next on are a dance troupe consisting of three girls (who look like triplets because of their identical build) and a guy. The girls have tiny waists, ultra slim legs and beautiful round buttocks and breasts. They obviously get that way through daily training. They couldn't be lighter on their feet, execute more intricate steps and, above all, expend more energy. 'Look how slim they are,' I whisper to the lady on my left and she replies, 'yes, sickening, isn't it!' She and her husband were on the trip to the Troodos Mountains and we'd compared notes as to how we'd ruined our skins when young through excessive sunbathing. 'Look at my old ladies hands covered in liver spots' said I with a grunt of disgust whilst she showed me a mole on her back which looked crustily suspicious but apparently had been checked out and given the all-clear. These girls are dancers from heaven and they also have a mime act. After the acclaimed performance, I see a little boy of about eight or nine years of age watching them with rapt attention, they emerge from the changing room in tight denim jeans and high heeled shoes and short denim bomber jackets which all serve to emphasize their oh so slim shapely legs and miraculous little asses. They are heavily made-up. I approach the guy and ask him where they come from because their dances seem to have a Russian flavour. They are from Bulgaria. 'Ah, I know Bulgarians, such lovely people,' say I. 'But don't you get really tired, with all that dancing?' And what he replies is this: 'You are born to dance or not dance. You want to give to others and when you enjoy what you do you are not tired. Only your muscles get tired.' He shook my hand warmly and was gone.

    I go out for a walk with the 'how sickening' lady and her husband. They have recently moved to Northamptonshire and can't settle because they were in their old house in Cambridgeshire for thirty odd years. But Northamptonshire has hills and sheep … I am surprised when they tell me that they go on rock and rolling weekends in Wales and Spain. Good for them – perhaps I should do the same. The truth is, the absolute God-given truth is that you can't be unhappy when you're dancing. We walk down 'the strip' and I start singing ''77 Sunset Strip, click click' vaguely remembering a snazzy, sexy TV show in the 60s which they remember well. Now I know where the night music is coming from (another less intimate disturbance which I failed to mention) as we pass karaoke bars and pubs and eating joints and supermarkets. He leads us to a bar at the end of the strip, near McDonalds where a guy in drag is putting on a show. It's all a bit much and we shudder to imagine what this place is like in high season. I'm interested in checking out the Greek restaurant 'Kykkos' where you can eat of an evening as a change from the hotel although I expect it provides inferior stuff for fools. I am surprised when the guy insists on accompanying me down the road … but that's what gentlemen do. He reckons that the strip is no place for ladies out on their own. Back in the hotel we meet one of their four sons who is over here for his wedding. Going to up to his room he calls out, 'see you in the morning, mum', with a naturalness and grace that is alien to my experience. My father couldn't even look at his mother; he was so furious with her. The dad wants me to join him and his wife for a drink and, as usual, I hum and haw, worried about overshooting my bedtime and putting them to extra expense. In the end I partake of an orange juice and we chat about the usual stuff – probably my worries and disappointments. How come that I then find myself chatting to the son – he must have come downstairs again – who contradicts a lot of what his dad had said about him and tells me that he could never travel alone, although he's forty tomorrow, because he's far too nervous. He lives in St. Neots and has a very ordinary sort of job. I like him.

Can you believe it, God almighty, God on high, I actually enjoyed a good night's sleep, probably because I was too tired to be woken by anything. So the day is one of enjoying swimming in the beautiful turquoise blue sea and sitting with my book ('Salmon Fishing in the Yemen' which is well worth not reading) in the attractive bar area overlooking swimming pool, beach and sea. It's as good as having your own personal villa. But sometime during the afternoon, maybe on account of observing couples together with their physical connection I get overwhelmed by a sense of feeling totally unwanted and alone. It's so bad and awful that you could do away with yourself altogether and I realise, I know, that my mother too was a poor child, a poor girl, a poor woman whose needs had never been met and who could only escape from herself into material objects. So this was the flatness, the total lack of emotion and response. It's easier to cut out the feeling. No wonder she couldn't bear to see me flower. 'I'll nip her in the bud as sure as my name is Anita'. My role is to be a doll and wear pretty flowery dresses. I am her compensation package. But when you know and are right in there in the sense of never having been seen there is no more blame which is not to condone another's filthy behaviour. I'm determined not to sink under this weight of unhappiness, of being a reject, an outcast but get myself down to the sea where I put my face in the cold water and swim for the life of me. Coming out I lie down on a sunbed wrapped in a towel and take pleasure and sustenance from what is going on around me. On one side an attractive group of bronzed, bearded Cypriot men in their early to middle twenties are joking and laughing amongst themselves. On the other a group of girls, about sixteen or seventeen years old are stretched out on sunbeds, sunbathing and licking ice creams coated in chocolate. One checks her bikini line to see how her tan is getting on. It's all so normal and natural as in boy meets girl. A bit of retail therapy follows – buying presents for my daughter. That night I am woken up, unpleasantly, by the dream of a child running down a corridor. Or did it really happen?

In the morning I am determined to enjoy my breakfast and drive away the blues. God how furtive am I making up my little serviette parcel of a cheese cucumber and tomato roll with a few black olives thrown in. A couple of hard boiled eggs will be useful to stave off the hunger pangs and a tiny Cypriot banana (or two). Mass produced imported bananas are rubbish as are the cucumbers and tomatoes from Tesco. Far too weak and watery. As I'm popping my lunch into my bag I half expect the policeman's hand on my shoulder asking me to come down to the station to answer a few questions. The police are always low-key, undramatic and sans imagination or flair. 'I'm just doing my job miss'. 'Well, do it somewhere else mate far away from me!' Anyway if I was arrested for this misdemeanour I would just tell them the truth: 'it's my lunch cos I don't really eat breakfast'. However, I enjoy my dish of pink grapefruit, followed by thick Greek yoghourt. But what I really love and what is guaranteed to lift my spirits are the mini 'pains aux raisins' which are exactly as they are in a French boulangerie. I eat two with my coffee (which is passable because it is 'different' but you wouldn't want to drink it in a café) and then a few chopped baby figs. As I wait for the lift to go to my room (Go to your room!! Is something that gypsy children never hear) Maria calls to reception (bad news?) telling me that there's a message for me from 'Vanguard' and I should ring them. I'd rung them late the previous afternoon asking them if they had a representative who visited the area with the products. I speak to Lola the secretary and before I can say that it's a bit far for me to come on the bus she tells me that she and the boss's son will pick me up in half-an-hour, take me to the office where I can choose my stuff, then take me out to lunch, and before I can say that I'll get the bus back, she tells me that they'll drive me back to the hotel. How nice is that? Wow, people to speak to – a day out!

At the stated time Lola and the boss's son Andonis arrive to pick me up. I'm not in the reception waiting for them because I've been told that if I want to upgrade my room (it was on the advice of new arrivals in the next room who, being asked by me in the lift whether they had slept well replied explosively in the negative and couldn't believe that I'd put up with the BUILDING SITE and the karaoke blast for so long) I have to move all my stuff (the Bulgarian porter helps, with a rail) tout de suite! I'm a few minutes late for hosts and I always feel it is a great disrespect to keep anyone waiting. They too look a bit agitated. Andonis drives the ladies to his father's office in Larnaca where I am treated to traditional Greek (not Turkish!) coffee ('yes, I will dare another cup') and a helluva lot of salesman's talk. No wonder his son is so quiet. I think that I too used to overwhelm my daughter with my spiel, not letting her find her own voice. I purchase a ton of products and he knocks 30% of each one because, I suppose, I am a guest in his office. He then drives us to a beach restaurant where you choose the fish you want them to cook for you. For me it was a perfect meal from the bread to the taramasalata to the salad and the fried fish because it was totally FRESH. Fine dining is something else. But a meal like this flowed. We even had little cakes stuffed with white cheese and dusted with flour that had just been cooked. With coffee there was a platter of peeled and sliced pears, bananas, and kiwi. This is grace from heaven. The white wine was locally produced.

Mr Yiallouros changed through the course of the meal. The pushy salesman was replaced by a real, intelligent person. We talked about national stereotypes and how much truth there was in truisms. He liked doing business with the French, the Scandinavians ('they are so innocent and trusting') and the Israelis ('once they shake your hand and have given their word, they never go back on it') All the rest, from the Italians to the Bulgarians and the Arabs were untrustworthy. He'd had a lot of experience of the Israelis (Israel is only a thirty minute flight away) because his wife had been ill with ovarian cancer for five years and had been treated in Jerusalem. He said that Israel was economically strong because they exported medical knowledge (they're at the cutting edge) and medical instruments. After the war his family let a room in Famagusta to a Jew en route for the newly formed state of Israel and in 1974, when Danny heard that the Cypriot Greek inhabitants of Famagusta had lost their homes, he was really concerned and managed to trace Mr. Yiallouros through the Red Cross and they've remained great friends ever since. I thought that that was a really moving story. The businessman has now altogether taken a back seat as he says that soon, one day, he will get a boat and go fishing at dawn. 'The sea is milky pale and the atmosphere is so still and …' and I butt in and provide the final word, the one he was looking for which is 'holy'. I can see that he wonders how I know. I don't – I enter his experience and imagine. Lola also lost her husband to the nasty disease and now lives in Larnaca with her daughters and their families living next door. I felt sorry for silent Andonis and made efforts to include him in the conversation. Lola asked me about my family (and the songs we shared!) and I told her that I was an orphan. 'Ha! Only kidding BUT you don't want to hear any more!' Evangelos, the dad, drives me back to the hotel after I share fond goodbyes 'and I'm so pleased we've met' with Lola and twenty year old Andonis. In the car I'm aware that he's aware of my knees and the fact that we're both single although he is probably still mourning. His face is blotchy with rough red patches so he obviously doesn't use his own skin nourishing products.

Back in Protaras (why on earth did I go there and not Paphos?) Evangelos shows me the pharmacy situated about a hundred yards from the hotel, next to a pub called 'Cheers' where they sell all his products. This pharmacy was chosen above all others because he knows the family and can rely on being paid. Next time I visit Cyprus he says that he will show me places. I like him and thank him warmly for his hospitality.

I'm now installed in a new room overlooking the swimming pool, beach and beautiful sea and as I drink my English tea, I see a little girl in the swimming pool screaming for joy as she rides on her father's back. But my, how different I feel in this room. Formerly I felt poked, 'cabin'd, cribbed, confin'd, bound in …' (like Macbeth) a prey to saucy fears but now, as I contemplate the wide horizon of sea and sky, I feel calm and serene. Nature is God's gift to us as the fluffy white bathrobe and towelling mules are the hotel's gifts when you pay for a superior room. Being up is better than being down because no one is on top of you. The new room boasts turquoise velvet cushions on the bed and heavy turquoise curtains. The walls are a delicate cream rather than a dreary beige.

In the evening I try the Greek restaurant down the road as a change from the crowded buffet restaurant in the hotel. 'Kykkos' is a plain establishment with an adequate distance between the tables and the Greek music is unobtrusive and pleasant, like birdsong. Following my large lunch I don't have that much of an appetite and so fail to do justice to the fried octopus followed by grilled sea bass, and roasted whole red pepper, aubergine, courgettes and lemony potatoes. It's so tasty and delicious and it's good to be away from the canteen atmosphere of the hotel. Who is the cook? He obviously has some secret up his sleeve. Back at the hotel I am accosted by Angelo who wants me to help him with 'Bingo' and then join in the kiddies dance. Hmm. He also asks me to recommend books for him to read and I suggest 'Macbeth' for starters. He's impressed that I'm familiar with 'La Divina Commedia' and tests out my Italian. I understand his simple questions but I can't speak a word. I am mute, silent. He tells me how you learn nothing at school because you are too young and just want to see your friends and have a good time. I've heard that before! However, I don't turn up for 'Bingo' because I'm too tired and can't face the crowd but feel impelled to go downstairs and seek Angelo out to offer my apologies. Back in my room I'm aggrieved to find that I have lost my grey 'Per Una' linen jacket with the diamond buttons but the search will have to wait till tomorrow.

I am awake at 5.30 a.m. the next day in order to let reception know that I don't need their wake-up call at seven. Next time I'll travel with a small clock. Amazing that I didn't hear a peep from the karaoke but I still heard a door slam somewhere in China. It's the day of excursion number two – this time to Nicosia, the exciting dynamic capital of Cyprus. Not. On the coach our guide, the same one as before, gives us the lowdown regarding 'crossing the line' and makes it sound like climbing the Berlin Wall or escaping from Colditz so that we all feel a little nervous. Biros, for filling in the visas, get hastily passed around. She warns us against not smuggling goods back from the Turkish side since they search your bag and if they find anything they'll put you in jail. In the event 'crossing the line' is no more than joining a queue to buy a train ticket, albeit waiting under a hot sun. Earlier in the morning we'd visited the Presidential Palace and seen the two black chevvies which Jack Kennedy had given to Archbishop Makarios as a present. We visited the tiny cathedral of St. John, which resembled the one at Kykkos with its lashings of gold and ornate chandeliers and paintings of stories from the New Testament, and then me and this couple from Sunderland (who have visited Cyprus nineteen times) get lost and can't find the red coach. The guy is very worried about getting separated from the herd and ashamed of his lack of direction. Our next stop is the main shopping street and Lola, in her measured tone, is sure that we'll never be able to drag ourselves away from its fabulous offerings. Well, on the Turkish side it's a load of old crap and in Cypriot Nicosia it's a load of boring rubbish. However, the museum was interesting. The early pots are painted with dancing girls and there are fertility goddesses with tiny waists and ample breasts and hips. I think it's the case that when you are locked away (like Rapunzel et al) it's a big NO to your rosy vagina – that's the truth of it. You can't speak, let alone scream, shout or laugh because nature has to be dominated. We learn about Caterina, the first Queen of Cyprus, who was used by the Venetians and then forced to renounce her crown. She lived a sad, lonely life and died young. There's a painting of her by Titian. Before I came I knew nothing about Cyprus during the medieval period (we saw the walls built by the Venetians to keep out the terrible Turks although that was a bit later). Richard the Lionheart owned Cyprus for a bit but was too busy with his crusading venture so sold it to his cousin who had a French wife. Cyprus became very poor under the Turks (unlike the Greek Cypriots, Turks have big round eyes) and when they couldn't pay their taxes they preferred to give their land to the Church rather than the Turks. The Church got rich at their expense. Women were poor workers but every woman had a piece of jewellery to wear on her wedding day that had been given her by her mother. I spot an identical pair to my own, with hanging gold drops and three small rubies. What sort of mother is so bound into hatred and envy that she can't give to her own daughter? Why should she? The cathedral of St. Sophia has been converted into a mosque and outside I chat to a whirling dervish in his high cone of a hat who tells me that they will be performing at 2 pm. Unfortunately I will be in the big red coach. For my money the most fetching place was the square where travellers used to come to sell their produce in the sixteenth century. It was built in 1571 and seems very Renaissance to me with its arched gallery. I get someone to take a photo of me under the bright pink pot of bougainvillaea but he's a very odd guy, a care worker, and I wish I'd kept my distance. Maybe he felt the same because he takes the photo from about a mile away. This would have been the place to have enjoyed a Greek coffee but the coach calls. The guide is annoying me now, speaking to us as if we were little children, repeating the directions to 'Rimis', our lunchtime watering-hole, over and over again. Her nightmare is that someone will get lost.

I tag along with the wife of the care-worker (how does she suffer her husband?) and we walk past the turning to Rimis but can't miss Lola waving her white flag. I want to get away from her. I can't look at her. We're now stalled in the old city at two long tables. The bread is lovely and the hors d'oeuvre of tahini, tzatziki and a green salad mixed with red cabbage, celery and black olives. The colour combination is striking. The meat rissoles which are served as the main course are really tasty but I see that some of my neighbours have left theirs. I am rebuked for digging into foreign food. The woman next to me from Bristol, on holiday with her friend, tells me that I look the spitting image of her next door Pentecostal neighbour, Susan Walker, who is mean and horrible. They talk about their children, grandchildren, great grandchildren and recently deceased partners. 'Of course I'll join my daughter and the grandchildren at Butlins. I'm not going to stay at home on my own for five days.' The women are good, kind, simple people. At the poncy Japanese style hotel in Protaras they paid £20 for two sandwiches. I tell them that they need a good solicitor. 'In future,' they laugh, 'we'll stick to the café in Fig Tree Bay' Funnily enough, on my visit to this lovely beach I had spotted a café at the end of it which I reckoned deserved to be checked out. I make a mental note to revisit it tomorrow, my last day, when I will have plenty of time on my hands once I am evicted from my room. Some man or other makes silly jokes which gets everyone rolling around in laughter. I go to the loo and then disappear. Later on, back in the car park the lady from Bristol (with the onset of diabetes) tells me she wondered where I had gone. I thanked her for thinking about me and she looks a bit confused. That's a bit heavy, innit?

The last stop on the itinerary is a trip to the top of the Debenhams Tower (on the spectacular main shopping street) where, apparently, you can see a spectacular view of the city. My new companion is the wife of the care worker who is also irritated by the guide: 'you've said it once, now leave it – we're not two years old' and less than impressed by the view but she wouldn't have said it first. Still, I point out an old shack where a woman is putting out the washing and a monastery in the distance surrounded by trees. But otherwise it seems like a city without design. Loads of white apartment blocks. Nicosia is so uninspiring because it is basically a place for conferences and seminars. There don't seem to be many people around. I'm pleased when the tour is over and I'm dropped back at the hotel. I advise others not to go to Nicosia. The best thing was the meatballs.

That evening I eat my fill in Kykkos but I can't finish a whole leg of pork in filo pastry. The young waiter is very friendly and tells me what to order but the fat boss is ignoring me and I realise it's because I'm buying neither wine nor water. I don't blame him. (The next day, walking past his restaurant I think about apologising but decide to leave it.) Back in the hotel I see Angelo and ask him to tell me what I was wearing last night. 'A pink dress,' he replies. I think he wonders where this is leading. 'And was I wearing a jacket?' 'No,' he says with total confidence and conviction. Ah, so I'm not mad and I don't have to continue looking in the wardrobe. It must be in the hotel because I didn't leave it in the restaurant. I find myself sitting at a table with Angelo listening to a couple of mediocre self-loving musicians or rather one of them is. They're playing old songs and I beckon to Angelo to get up on to the dance floor. Someone has to start things off. We do our disco stuff and are joined by a Scottish couple who are very elegant and accomplished ballroom dancers and a young pregnant German couple who are dancing ceroc at a slow measured pace on account of her bump which actually looks very charming in her tight black dress. A woman from Linton, Cambridgeshire not far from me struts her stuff uninhibitedly and good luck to her really. When the entertainment starts to get crude and touristy I make a quick getaway.

A waiter found my jacket and gave it to the housekeeper and a nice receptionist (who hunts in the nature reserve?) is pleased to present it to me folded up in a bag. It's my last day and I'm not going back to the U.K. without one last swim in the wide open sea. I also sunbathe a little in my bikini. I buy a lovely hair ornament studded with pearls in a pharmacy and then wait for the Ayia Napa bus which takes in Capo Greko en route. Guess who should be there but Angelo, the hotel entertainer. Of course I hadn't said goodbye, hadn't told him that I was leaving today so I'm really pleased to see him. We chat as we wait for the late bus and I decide not to go to Capo Greko because it's midday and you know what they say about walking about in the midday sun. The bus finally arrives (to Angelo's relief – he's off to find an internet café in Ayia Napa) and we kiss and say our goodbyes. As he's mounting the bus I suddenly change my mind and run after it … Angelo pays my fare which is very kind of him. When I get off at Capo Greko we kiss again on both cheeks (it's the done thing, isn't it?) and he says, 'ciao bella' … Now, ain't that nice … Capo Greko is a beautiful nature reserve with an old church and caves and a spot where you can sit under eucalyptus trees and gaze at the stunning blue sea. Towards the end of the afternoon I seek out the café at Fig Tree Bay which is great and it's a pity I only found it on my last day. And the last day of my life – will that be the one when my dream is realised?

Sadness in Seville

I parachute into Seville at about 10 am. I am wearing my "Per Una" shocking pink linen dress with the ruffled hem and mushroom patent leather sandals decorated with turquoises. I land softly on the grass in the Maria Luisa Park and hope that my dress isn't smeared with grass stains or my shocking pink toenails chipped. I go in search of a cup of delicious coffee but it's Sunday in a Catholic country and everywhere is closed. Heavens, they sleep late in Spain, the lazy buggers!

I wander up and down the gravelly aisles of this beautiful park admiring the garden features though not knowing who built and designed what in which century. I'm charmed by the canopy of tall trees such as eucalyptus, tulip, pine and cypress and a host of others. This is a city in which the creation of shade is number one priority since summer heat is stupendous. How on earth do they cope?

I could do with a guide book (there were none available in Waterstones in Cambridge) directing me to an important palace to visit in this unknown city. In the event of having neither book nor map I sit myself down on an old stone seat decorated with mosaics and set myself to worrying about my nearly twenty three year old son and his brokenness. You only have to go into his room and see the pile of papers and clothes littered all over the floor to know that this isn't evidence of a cool, calm, contained individual. Most of the papers relate to the Law and the Bank coming down hard with warnings, penalties and notices as well as hospital recommendations and reports ("you lost a fair amount of blood in that stabbing incident and that collarbone isn't mending as it should"). In the centre of this pile of paper is a battered passport and a birth certificate. He knows what his name is. But what about the wound that is invisible. Will that ever be faced? A boy without a male in his midst is a boy without a firm framework and structure. Rules keep things in place.

So much worry and distress that my eyes are sinking further and further into my head and I think to myself that most people would be aghast at this holiday activity of mine. "She can't let it go – not for a minute, an hour, a day. She'll worry herself into an early grave. Be like us, making the most of our money, travelling all over the world." I get up with a sigh and walk around. It's certainly sad when suffering prevents you from enjoying beauty and love.

Some big sporting event is taking place in this ancient park and a voice is booming out instructions through a loudspeaker. (His problem at primary school was always with following instructions). Everywhere young runners are revving up and raring to go. It's 2011 and running has replaced flamenco. Girls of thirteen in vests and running pants with long thick ponytails flex their muscles and are light years away from the iron brace which says NOOOO to woman as the inheritor of the earth and its life blood. Woman is life's lining – without her, her freedom, there is the empty shell of male control and exploitation. He is no longer the guardian of the good but the filthy desecrating pig. She sits alone at home and mourns her excess baggage, the rolls of fat around her waist. Flank after flank of runners make it to the finishing line, huffing and puffing and sweating and doing their best. Two unselfconsciously pretty girls cheer for their beau as he careers past. You wouldn't expect them to cheer for the hunchback and scarface. Like attracts like and life is about reaching for the stars.

I stumble upon a leafy enclosure which is home to several skinny cats. They have such delicate bodies and tiny faces. They don't look as if they would scratch your face to shreds but I wouldn't touch them; who know what germs they are carrying. A middle-aged hippy looking guy in a pink T-shirt with long thickly matted brown hair is sitting in a corner making a roll-up, focussing on the delicate concentration that this task requires. He sees me looking at the stray cats and tells me that they're 'abandonados'. Poor kids! I wonder what happened to his teeth since most of them are dark stumps. Fancy-free and without an itinerary and extremely friendly there's nothing to stop me passing the time of day in his company.

When I say I'm from the city of Cambridge in the U.K. people invariably look awed and impressed as if I've told them that I'm a distant relative of the Queen. In the collective unconscious learning and being considered clever has its halo of nobility. If I'd said I was from Hull or Staines or Newport Pagnell they might see me as an obscure nobody. Or perhaps it's just the clunky sound of these names. He himself is a pure Sevillano who has lived in Seville all his life. He doesn't look particularly Spanish. Middle-aged drop-out hippies probably look the same the world over. He has a big nose and small dark eyes which don't look unkind.

I can't understand much of what he says but we bungle through some dialogue and he takes me to a water fountain "where you can drink for free". I attempt to fill my water bottle and he shakes his head sternly, wagging his finger, indicating that you can't mix the different waters. Something terrible will happen. Obviously the locals know best. In another part of the park is the Plaza

America inhabited by pigeons. On a plaque I start to read about the place, its history etc. but "Palma" as he is called ("what, the capital of Mallorca?") is telling me about a market where you can eat cheaply and well. With other people you never know exactly what is going on in their minds. I know that I'm a sucker for good food and drink that doesn't cost the earth. But somehow I can't imagine where this market could be, where he's taking me. By this time I have showed him a dog-eared photo, now two and a half years old, of me and my offspring. "Guapo!" he exclaims, a big smile spreading from ear to ear, causing him to brighten up considerably. I think he has three children and three dogs and I get the sense that the children aren't his concern. "Estoy libre" he says; "silly fool" I think to myself. Everyone is impressed by my children's exceptional good looks but I don't show the photo in order to show off but to give myself some legitimacy, put myself on the map so to speak. I have done something with my life you know. And I'm too aware that behind the handsome exterior is someone with crippling OCD (some people haven't even heard of this disorder), who is too dependent on me. And now he has a broken collar bone which might, as the consultant indicated, require surgical intervention if he doesn't want to be stiff and deformed for the rest of his life. Looking at my daughter's beauty you'd never know that she's worked her fingers to the bone, and flown. Photos don't tell you where a person's at. Look at Marilyn. Supremely gorgeous precisely because she'd sold herself to the camera lens. To ensure the happiness and safety of your children you'd willingly sacrifice an arm or a leg (though not both I'm afraid; even my masochism doesn't go that far!). Probably it's the total maternal giving which prevents a boy growing up and standing on his own two feet.

With a stick I write my name in the dust so that he'll get it right. I tell him that "Judy" was such a popular name after the war and in the early fifties on account of the American singer and movie star Judy Garland. He has never heard of her, to my irritation and surprise. "What planet are you on then mate?" However, like an ultra polite oriental person I never show what is going on in my mind. We're heading towards a bus stop which will take us to the market and we don't have to wait too long for the bus to arrive. On we get and he swipes his card. (At the fountain he had thrown five cents over his shoulder into the water. "For good fortuna?" I enquired casually.

"No," he replied with a great air of wisdom, "for health and happiness, not for money."

"Of course, of course," was my response to this fool.)

Who in this scenario is Don Quixote and who is Sancho Pancha? He jabbers away to the bus driver who responds amicably enough. After a few stops we get off, cross the road and wait for the next bus outside the gold and white Lope de Vega theatre. Waiting at bus stops is tedious at the best of times and a question mark over the location of the market is starting to grow in my head. His mobile phone rings and it's his dad asking why he isn't at Sunday lunch with the rest of the family. He tells him he's with an English woman.

On the bus we sit at the back and he tells me that his father is eighty four and his mother is seventy eight. He himself has a room in Triana – across the river. Triana was the poor and romantic cradle of great toreadors and flamenco singers and dancers. Their energy is a fire in their blood. No such fire in anybody's blood sitting at the back of a bus passing through the flatlands of the outskirts of Seville with the usual shops, roads and apartment blocks. Nothing to inspire, stimulate or encourage. His phone rings again and this time it's his friend to whom he says the same thing; "I'm with una inglesa". We've been on the bus for ages and he's jabbering more than ever and I don't understand a word he says. On the other hand all I can say is "Esta lejos?" and he assures me, in a tone of total casual indifference, that the market will soon appear. It's all very queer. Big open markets serving the people aren't usually miles from anywhere.

We get off the bus and stand facing huge corporate buildings and green fields stretching to the horizon. No one is out and about because it's Sunday. In genuine puzzlement I turn to him and express my doubt that the market exists. "Look, there's nothing for miles around!" This is expressed through gesture and tone of voice rather than precise words. The market is, apparently, at the end of a very long embankment, fields on one side, the road on the other. Mad dogs and Englishman go out in the midday sun and indeed the sun is beating down on the back of my neck. He's clad in brown boots so can walk comfortably but my fancy sandals are letting me down. One of the straps is digging in, cuttingly, but on I march. We see an elderly man carrying a big brown paper bag full of peaches coming from the other direction and he tells Palma that the market is indeed there but "esta terminando". "Well, what's the good in that then", I attempt to say; "we should turn back". "And my feet are beginning to hurt" I mutter to myself, too proud to admit need or pain.

(I recall a home movie of us in Pompei in August 1965. My father films me mouthing the words "I'm <u>so</u> thirsty" as my head leans to one side in desperation. Those were the days before bottled water. Tough endurance. No charity).

I suspect his intentions and he shoves his dinky red mobile phone under my nose, no doubt suggesting that I'm free to call for help. He looks surprised when I stop a couple of chaps to check that something exists at the end of the path. They answer affirmatively and one of them is from Hong Kong and speaks English really well. Palma turns around and says "agua?" as in "give me a swig of water from your bottle?" I look at him blankly and he repeats the vital word for me. I don't want to be mean and I feel a bit mean but no way am I going to share the rim of my bottle with his cavernous cadaverous mouth. Anyway, he's not dying.

We've reached an open expanse of rocky ground strewn with plastic bottles and other stuff. Two girls, clad in jeans, T-shirts and trainers, appear from the right and ask Palma if they're on course for the market. We cut through a stony alleyway (I watch my step in case I step on anything mucky) and emerge into a human encampment. Small nylon tents, packed with belongings, are sweltering in the sun. Roundabout is an eyesore of rubbish – from broken dolls to kitchen waste. It's a heap of unidentifiable crap. Beyond the crap is more crap – only this time it's laid out as bric-a-brac. Stall after stall displaying stuff no one would ever buy and perhaps that's why they're all packing up. Where are the stalls selling creamy spring onions as big as your fist, broad beans in their blankety beds, glistening local strawberries and dark fulsome luscious cherries ... We pass a shellfish eaterie operating from a white van but I don't fancy sitting down. It's British equivalent would be the hotdog stand. Palma obviously isn't hungry. He turns to me and says "estas contenta?" with a sort of smirk. "No," I reply. He's looking around and suddenly he sees a group of people he knows and explodes into ebullient mirth. He hugs two of the guys and one showers him with water. These fellows and a young woman as well are from the north of Portugal and seem very cheerful and pleasant. I'm introduced as English and they take an interest. Prompted by something or other I express a desire to return to Seville. Palma waves his hand in the direction of the road and turns his back on me, as if to say go find it then. His friends seem genuinely shocked at this rudeness towards a foreigner. He shrugs. He couldn't care less. Without more ado I take my leave in order to start the long trek back into Sevilla.

I can't deny that I'm a bit nervous since it's a known fact that I have very little spatial sense; but on the other hand I'm damned brilliant at accosting people and asking them if I'm OK, going in the right direction. The thing is that I haven't eaten anything since my handful of luxury dried fruits and nuts brought with me from the U.K. in case of an emergency. I sat on a stone step which had the word FASCIST daubed all over it in black and red. Ah, can one ever forget?! I espy a fruit and vegetable stall manned by someone hunched over his wooden boxes. I ask if I can have one single banana and without turning to face me he says "No" in a grim tone such as you don't associate with warm Mediterranean types. I offer one of his young sons fifty cents for a banana and the boy has more sense than his father and accepts it. Things are obviously hard for this family. I applaud the boy's spirit, going against his father. Well, I have my banana and won't die of starvation. I've already died of the other kind.

It's now incumbent on my to navigate cautiously if this trip isn't to end disastrously. I'll have to ask the way more than ever and risk making a bloody fool of myself. A guy (also in a pink T-shirt) points out a shortcut through the "travellers" encampment bypassing that long path. As I pass through the dump I call out "Hola" to a teenage girl standing by a tent. She calls back "Hola, que pasa?" Teenagers are always looking for a way out. A naked toddler is sitting in the dirt crying and the fat mother is powerless. When mothers are on their own, receiving no support, they lash out.

    I scramble over the embankment bit and take some steps down to the road. At the pedestrian crossing I feel a soft pinch on my bottom which is a very strange sensation. Perhaps I imagined it. But lo and behold the guy in the pink T-shirt is at my side and CREEP is written all over him. This is the ghost train in which huge spiders and rattling skeletons with leering grins jump out at you in the dark cobwebby tunnel, making you scream. Dirt and dishonesty, the refusal to take up your cross and suffer, is not a good thing by any stretch of the imagination. I don't fancy waiting at a deserted bus stop – a gay couple (gay in that they seem bright and open) tell me that it's possible to walk back to Seville "it won't take longer than twenty minutes". I'm not so sure about that but I feel safer stepping it out, escaping the clutches of fate. My feet hurt but I walk fast, energised by the banana (or fear) and pass rectangular pools of water surrounded by wide pedestrian walkways. The Spanish certainly have excellent design ideas. I glance behind me and he is still around, he's popped out from one of the bushes. Luckily I see a woman washing her dogs; she takes a breather in order to assure me I'm walking in the right direction. She's friendly as friendly can be not like 'mother' who'd turn to me on the way to the synagogue, her hair a nest of snakes dripping venom, numbing any response at all due to the bitterness and malice embedded in her "can't you keep up with ME!" You're squashed underfoot like a louse. Just at this point I reach a roundabout and the gay couple have caught up with me. They roll down their window and gaily ask if I want a lift. (I thought they said it was only a shortish walk into town). I don't dare say yes. They drive on not hearing or understanding that I have changed my mind ... Walking over the bridge I meet two nice girls from Santander who are on holiday; we discuss the difference in weather between north and south and the respective problems with learning English and Spanish. "At least you try", they say; but I don't think I try very hard at all. I like adjectives, not verbs. One of the girls seems to be very sure as to the direction of the cathedral. We part company since they are going elsewhere and I go into a bar where people are drinking beer and peeling prawns. Shall I join in, I ask myself. Na, too messy. But the scene is so friendly and relaxed – people meeting their friends before they go home to lunch. Anyway a woman tells me that I'm going in the wrong direction and I need to take a bus.

    Finally I find the C3 bus stop and sit myself down, watching the endless traffic stream by. A bossy young woman tells me that it ain't the right bus stop;

the C3 is around the corner. Around the corner a group of young teenage boys standing outside a bar direct me back again (what sort of crazy dance is this?) and the girl knew nothing because she's waiting for her boyfriend who pulls up in his car. Eventually I see the C3 and breathe a sigh of relief, as we all do when our bus finally comes. The driver informs me and a couple from Barcelona that he only goes NEAR the cathedral. Near is good enough for me. I recognise the route from the voyage out and I wonder why the hippy guy took two buses.

    The whole experience has been a shoddy dismal waste of time. Lying in my bed at night I realise that I have learnt at first hand the real meaning of the expression 'foot sore'. My blisters are bad. I am furious with myself because I missed the only opportunity available to see the paintings of Murillo and Zurburan in the Museum of Beautiful Arts. If only I'd found a guide book in Cambridge. Why did I speak to a stray dog amongst the abandoned cats? I should have concentrated on the young runners, fighting their way to the finishing line, doing the best that they can. Observing them Palma said with his usual casual indifference: "that looks like hard work".

A Moment in Istanbul

I'm out of school. I don't want to be in a box like a battery hen. I don't want to be subject to innumerable commands and take endless exams. So I stay at home and stare at the living room walls which gets me nowhere at all. It's not exactly profitable. In Shakespeare's play 'Macbeth' his lady wife makes it clear that she would have bashed out the baby's brains if she'd known that he wasn't going to drive ahead and get, get, get but, instead, hold fast to his manhood, devoting his life to service. She's a predatory black bird if ever there was one.

I decide to pay a visit to Istanbul. Istanbul, like Florence or Venice, is one of those magical cities that are so packed full of treasures that a single visit is insufficient and you have to return to get more deeply into their groove. But you have to start somewhere and I do my homework – reading from cover to cover an 'Insight Guide' to the magical city.

I cross the seas with Air Turkey and I'm very impressed by this plane with turquoise velour upholstered seats. The interior of a plane that is decorated in turquoise and white, with a rose that is presented to the ladies, can never fall out of the sky or suffer mechanical problems. Somebody, somewhere, is taking care. I'm very surprised to be handed a luncheon menu by a Turkish air hostess in a smart turquoise uniform. I can't believe that Turkish wine is provided gratis – but it is. Halfway through the flight I partake of a meal of stuffed aubergine, my favourite vegetable, and other Mediterranean fare. With a dignified gesture I lift my cup to the passing lady and she fills it with scalding hot coffee.

I'm sure that air hostesses have the best manners in the world – they're always calm and smiling and they never press you to buy a drink, a scratch card, a newspaper. They don't cry/lose their temper if you refuse the invitation. If, walking down the aisle, they see that someone is out of order because their seat isn't in the upright position or their seat belt isn't correctly fastened, they don't point the finger, scream and shout, hit them with a hammer or order them off the plane. In such a scenario the pilot would emerge from the cockpit to see what all the fuss was about and feel sorry for the traumatised passenger who was trying to hide under the seat. No, bullying isn't allowed.

As the plane comes in to land it seems to me that we're going to hit the sea, not the runway. I have to tell myself that the pilot knows what he's doing, that he wants to live as much as me. Of course he lands the machine beautifully – the wheels gently gracing the tarmac – and we're back in the dull prosaic world of the everyday and making one's own way. One has to contend with getting a visa (who knows why for a flying visit?) and queuing to get through passport control. Why does the passport officer never ask me why, in my passport photo, I look like someone who is about to be shot in the head? Resigned terror is writ large on my face. Anyway, out of the airport melee I'm on my own and I have the subway route to my hotel mapped on my mind. I'm approaching its entrance when a burly man hovering on the threshold of his car hire/taxi business place stops me in my tracks and asks me where I'm off to with my purple suitcase and then proceeds to persuade me not to go down into the underground where pregnant women with pushchairs are screaming to get onto the train (his wife belongs in this group) and people are pushing and shoving and there's no air and do I know how many people there are in Istanbul and they'll all be there at this time of day and that's why I should take one of his taxis. I wonder if he's making a monkey of me but his offer sounds sensible so I agree. I baulk at the price and then realise that Turkish pounds go much further than their British equivalent.

I'm taken to my hotel in the Sultanahmet District of the city where most of the top ten sights are situated. Minutes after arrival I'm on the streets checking out the local shops. My daughter, who makes bespoke ladies shoes, has asked me to look out for beautiful trimmings so that's something that's on my mind. My feet lead me to Hagia Sophia which is floodlit at night. I'm a bit nervous about losing my way so make a mental note of landmarks. Here I am, just me, as I stand outside and gaze up at the deep walls with their massive buttresses. I can just make out the rosy red hue of some of the flattish domes. Actually, I could just as well be outside the orthodox synagogue in London, the place I went to, as a child, to show off my clothes. Thick walls repel anyone who is not of the faith, who has other ideas. I wonder what the Emperor Justinian was like, the guy who consecrated the Eastern Church. And what was life like in 537 A.D.? Did the mass of people live in wooden huts or hovels? There was no central heating, no internet dating, no 'American Dream'. There were no cars or washing machines. God only knows how the architect, builder of one hundred and forty four mosques and two hundred and twenty one other buildings, lived to the age of ninety nine? Michelangelo was made of the same ultra tough material. Generally, I guess, people knew their place and there was no escaping your fate. Whatever happened was the will of God. Sunday afternoon's entertainment was to go and laugh at mad people with their wild gesticulations, distorted grimaces and incomprehensible utterances – people not realising that these poor souls had been driven mad through being locked away. The interior of this great church will be my first stop in the morning.

I never sleep well and especially not on my first night abroad. How lucky are normal folk who sleep all through the night without waking up even once and have sweet dreams of everything cosy and nice. How do they do it? I expect as babies they spent a lot of time strapped to their mother's back as she laboured in the field, and they'd absorb her sweet melodic singing. Following a breakfast of bread and olives, cucumber and tomatoes (these big fat Mediterranean tomatoes are of a different breed to the homegrown British varieties) I set out for the church, joining quite a long queue although it's early in the morning. A Turkish lad approaches a young woman in front of me, saying smarmily: 'You are very rich and beautiful – will you buy my postcards?' She is embarrassed and he moves on, in search of another tourist. I can't help but mimic his flat expressionless tone of voice with a follow-up of 'and *you* are very stupid' drawing a laugh from an American couple who I then get talking to. As we enter the Imperial Gate and climb over the thick wooden step, he waxes enthusiastically about this great fish restaurant in Beyoglu which is over the bridge, behind a fishmongers and next to an amazing baklava shop. His wife silences this nice man, who is in full flow, and we part company.

It is dark within but there are windows beneath the dome which let in light and the flat oval chandeliers are anointed with candles. I walk about getting the feel of the place. I probably should have picked up a pair of earphones at the entrance but I know that I'm really too tired to concentrate on the information. I'll have to do my best by reading inscriptions and overhearing snippets from tour guides or people reading out loud from their guide books. What a sad scavenger I am! The main point of the place though is that it was converted into a mosque in 1453 and a lot of the artefacts relate to this changeover. You can't miss the Emperor's Throne which was considered to be the centre of the world, the Weeping Pillar where Justinian was miraculously cured – and the calligraphic roundels beneath which are wonderful Byzantine mosaics, only discovered in the 1930s. Hovering on the edges of a young all male American group – I remembered two of the lads from the passport queue at the airport – I learnt a bit about the mosaics which include local heroes flanking the Virgin Mary and the Infant Christ with or without John the Baptist. Over hundreds of years no one ever got sick of depicting the holy trio – Mother Mary the epitome of placidity, baby Jesus with his halo and John the Baptist – all perhaps symbolising hope over despair. Nobody has really understood the saviour's mysterious humanity (can you believe it he rose from the dead) or doubted the sacredness of the Mother.

Outside, into the light of day, I cross the road to visit the vast underground water cisterns built by the Byzantines. I'd heard a prominent radio broadcaster talk about this place as the real marvel of Istanbul so I had to make a beeline for it. NOT TO BE MISSED. I wander through the dark grotto, along with everyone else. We are respectfully silent when we find ourselves before some revered relic. So human beings really were here all those years ago and left their mark in stone. There's a small cafe near the exit and a shop with an assortment of tacky jewellery such as you see in shops all over Istanbul but there is one ring which takes my fancy. It is a miniature mosque in beaten bronze surrounded by a ring of diamonds topped with a small jade stone. I haggle a bit over it with the vendor and tell him I'll think about it. He thinks it's just words – I'm not serious – and he won't see me again. But I have to decide if the thing is a passing fancy or a real expression of my personality. It's a bit pathetic really if that's the full extent of your self-expression and creativity.

Out in the open once again the next stop is The Blue Mosque. En route, a stone's throw away across Sultanahmet Square I buy a glass of pomegranate juice. Such is the colour of the pomegranate skin, pink like a hibiscus flower, that one can only wonder at it, wanting to caress its smooth roundness. And everywhere there are stalls selling corn-on-the-cob cooked in tanks of boiling water, roast chestnuts served in brown paper bags and pretzel beigel type things costing one Turkish lira strung over a pole like a string of bracelets. You could never starve on the streets of Istanbul. Someone is at my side asking me to buy something and because I don't ignore him and walk on by, like a robot, he talks some more and accompanies me to The Blue Mosque because he'd like to show me around and get a chance to practise his English. He's a Kurd, he tells me, and has been working since the age of twelve. We approach a lengthy queue but my new Kurdish friend tells me that we can be fast tracked because he knows the man at the door … I hardly believe him but in we go with no fuss at all. I want to feel more appreciative than I do but the fact is that I'm not feeling too well which is very unusual for me and a bit scary. I know it's because I've been driving myself too hard and feeling aggrieved about a son who is tense and anxious beyond belief and won't receive the therapy which might help him get away from me or at least help him to understand his deepest fears. Why can't you make people act in their own best interests especially when it's your nearest and dearest? Perhaps we all carry within us a hurt child. Well, I'm feeling dizzy and faint and ask if it's ok to leave the mosque, with its famous blue Iznik tiles, and sit outside. The reaction I expect is one of anger: 'we're here now and you'll have to stay put and put up with it' i.e. 'put up and shut up and you're not allowed to be ill anyhow'. But the reality is that he's kind and sympathetic, understanding that stress can have this effect on the body, and he says that I need to sit down outside and drink some apple tea. Sitting on a bench near a newspaper kiosk I tell him something of my story plus recent domestic history, and he listens and wants me to come to his cousin's carpet shop, which is opposite the police station on Divanyolu, a busy street that leads to Suleymaniye Mosque, which is actually *the* mosque to see.

Without further ado I'm introduced to his cousin and receive a glass of lovely apple tea. The cousin, also a Kurd, is divorced, with a son whom he never sees and his own mother died when he was young which was a blow indeed. He also worked from a young age (Oh Lord, I think to myself, they're not going to want to hear about my offspring who is on the soft side and more interested in his social life than earning a living) carrying carpets on his back and collecting wood for the fire to cook on and generally being discriminated against. 'How awful it is,' he laments, 'waking up in the morning on your own without the embrace of a woman …' I spill out my worries and once again I suspect that the son is going to be belittled as a mummy's boy and mum is going to be categorised as over emotional and protective. But he just seems to have a sense of human suffering and the necessity of human solace. He comments on my pretty sandals and my youthful legs and imagines taking me out to dine and dance although hard facts creep in here because this offer is dependent on me purchasing a carpet. I don't blame him one bit. I feel truly grateful for his advice which centres on not making it my business if my child doesn't deal with official correspondence or check the pressure on his tyres and how relieved and surprised I am to be restored to health and sanity. Just as he needs the plump cushion of a woman so I need the firm hold of a man. As much as I've been told that I need to develop the measured male external side, the fact is that I'm not a man and I'd like to have one around as much as I try my best to be a hermaphrodite. You can have the best therapist/analyst in town, the one with the deepest heart, the soundest head and the most experience but everyone is flawed and incapable of total objectivity and selflessness or knowing another entirely so don't expect miracles. But I'm talking about myself here. It is my belief that, in the last analysis, the patient has to minister to himself. He has to "pluck from the memory a rooted sorrow/Raze out the written troubles of the brain." (Macbeth 5.3.41-42) Personally, I'm not the crying type. As I leave he advises me to take care and not to be too friendly with people. He genuinely wants me to be safe.

Finding the recommended restaurant is no easy task but the sun is out (it's late September) and the weather is nice. Every child draws a blue sky and a yellow sun and a smiling face until they need to hide away. I follow the tramline to the Galata Bridge, which is further away than I expected and, frightened mouse that I am, I continually stop poor people in their tracks and check that I'm going in the right direction. The male gesture which means 'straight ahead' is a sharply inclined hand to the left. I pass a cafe near the harbour – the windows of which are filled with piles of baklava – a sweetmeat one should try accompanied by a tiny cup of black Turkish coffee, just the once. I grew up on a diet of fat and sugar and I can't afford to become, as I once was, a mountain of miserable flesh. I've now arrived at the Galata Bridge and I could fall in love with this bridge just as I fell in love with the Pont Neuf in Paris when I was nineteen, employed as an au pair, attempting to escape the family cage. Power gets its own way but always crashes in the end. Behind me, as I walk across, is the view of Suleymaniye Mosque on its hill with its towering domes dominating the skyline and in front, on the other side, the Galata Tower built by the Genoese in 1348. Such a long time ago that was – way before the 20th century and the crimes of the Nazis. Is a criminal someone who has fallen out of the living universe into a needy, greedy hell? All along the bridge men are fishing, hoping for a catch – that ravenous tug at the end of the line. They might get a man-eating shark and then they'd be done for. A young man of twenty three tries to sell me perfume – successfully. Who else except me would buy two bottles of 'J'adore' from a man in the street who tells me that I am a fine human being because I listen to him speak. I wish my son was standing on the Galata Bridge selling something. At the end of the day he could present his mother with a silver coin which would help pay for the groceries. He wouldn't be like the lazy son in 'Jack and the Beanstalk' or those kids in the TV show 'Young, Dumb and Living off Mum' which I never watched just in case I saw my own child writ large. Back in the U.K. I give one of the bottles to my daughter but she notices the faulty packaging and misspelling of 'Christian Dior'. Diluted with water is the verdict. I did wonder why the perfume evaporated so fast. My children poke fun at my gullibility; in fact it makes them angry.

    The restaurant is proving a devil to find. I'm tempted to buy a tasty looking grilled mackerel baguette from an old man standing by the water's edge. The locals seem to know him and he's probably been in that same spot for a hundred years. Someone leads me through a maze of narrow streets lined with tons of shops selling batteries and electrical equipment until we reach a dark old building. 'But the American told me that it was a tent – I'm sure he said that' I say out loud. It's no tent but a narrow three storied edifice and the price of the food goes up the higher you climb. I settle on the ground floor and make myself comfortable. A half-German Turk (as many of them are) speaks English (how do they all pick it up so easily? Is it because English is associated with American movies, affluence and prosperity?) and really wants me to visit another great fish restaurant which is some way away up the Bosphorus coast, at a place called Yenikoy. He draws a map for me on the serviette. I can imagine myself sitting on some lovely terrace sampling bitter, black, gleaming shrivelled olives (just as I love 'em) and looking out over the blue sea across to the Asian side of Turkey. A delectable moment to remember, a moment wholly fresh and sweet. Such is a first kiss or salt beef from 'Blooms' (long gone), the Kosher restaurant in

London's East End. I tell the German guy that I'll give it a try. He tells me that he's been sitting in this same place, 'Tarihi Karakoy' for twenty odd years. There's another man cheerfully enjoying his lunch – he's a civil servant with four children. He is replaced by a guy (a waiter) who is as ugly as in – he resembles Punch of 'Punch and Judy' fame who casually asks me, in front of all, to accompany him for dessert. The cashier and the chef look distinctly uncomfortable, hoping that I'll abstain from entrusting myself to Willy the Waiter. Abroad, people do idiotic things they'd never do at home. Thank goodness for me my good sense prevents me from jumping in.

Nevertheless loneliness and isolation suddenly engulf me. I better get on with the job of seeing the sights which entails a long walk back to the Sultanahmet district and the Topkapi Palace, home of the sultans since 1459 until Abdul Mecit 1 moved to Dolmabahce Palace in 1856, a luxurious pad that was modelled on Versailles. I could have taken the tram but that involves not angst but practical steps which seem complicated and isolating but actually are just a matter of putting money into a machine, receiving a token and taking the tram that's going in the right direction. I don't get on well with machines! I'm sure they're going to hit me! So on I trudge through the desert, passing restaurants, jewellery shops and yet another carpet shop where the employees are standing around the doorway enjoying each other's male company. They ask me if I'm looking for a carpet. 'Only a magic one' I reply and tell them that I'm on my way to Topkapi Palace where the sultans kept their women and the soldiers used to train. One of the guys (none of them are particularly good-looking) says, in a decisive tone, that he'll accompany me to show me the way. This seems perfectly natural and as we walk he also says that he needs to practise his English.

His name is Abdullah and he looks the spitting image of an Ottoman Sultan with his fine red lips, massive build and thick black eyebrows. He seems far older than his twenty two years. I can't imagine him swilling pints at his local trough, stinking of aftershave, and then staggering home in a mindless state, totally out of it. He's stable, sane and sober – a law student at Istanbul University. Guiding is his hobby. How has he found the time to work eighteen hours a day on cruise ships? 'It's very hard work' is all he says.

In the gardens of the Palace he guards my perfumes as I go to the 'ladies' and looks slightly suspicious when I extol my beautiful perfumes which I got at such a bargain. Maybe he decided not to say anything – not wanting to deflate my enthusiasm. I also decide not to say anything when it comes to claiming my concessionary entrance fee – I don't want him to know that I am sixty; he might gasp in horror, turn tail and run away. I come from a place where looks were everything. Every single hair had to be in place, If you happened to be ugly/stupid/poor you were ignored, judged wanting, or institutionalised. Being old was a disgrace. Faith, hope and charity belonged to another planet, millions of light years away.

Abdullah probably looks so much older than he is on account of his size. He has broad shoulders and legs like tree trunks. Together we view the exhibits, methodically going from showcase to showcase, marvelling at the jewelled throne, the royal robes with their tiny neck space, huge shoulders and sleeves and, last but not least, the splendid jewel-encrusted Topkapi Dagger. These jewels are the most brilliant you are likely to see outside of Aladdin's Cave and even the chain mail looks pretty – unlike anything they were wearing in Britain at the same time. Fairy fingers produced these artefacts, fingers that were highly trained and skilled. Sounds like my daughter who makes shoes which are the footwear equivalent of haute couture. You cannot help but marvel at the Topkapi Diamond; it emits rays of yellow and white, it is a living, changing thing. I express my desire for it and Abdullah quips 'I'll try and get a good price for you' and he's chuffed when the people around us chuckle. We view the Imperial Bed, big enough for an army and his conservatory overlooking gardens and pavilions. The thing about these palaces is that there was always someone in the wings plotting to murder you. In the company of Abdullah I don't feel that there's someone behind me wanting to get their claws into my neck or a faceless beater threatening to bang my head against the wall if I don't read fast enough or understand mental arithmetic problems. Here's just another person, using his eyes to see and his lips to speak. In a glass case we look at the red hairs of the Prophet's beard – one of Islam's holiest relics. On the other side of the room an Iman is reading out loud from the Koran and Abdullah tells me that this reading goes on for twenty four hours. I ask him what makes people bad. Without hesitation he replies: 'they lie'. We agree that most obey the letter of the law not the spirit and that the former observance depends on outward show. I tell him that it's the same in all religions. I wouldn't tell him or anyone else for that matter that I'm of the Hebrew persuasion because everyone knows that the Jews are a stubborn, stiff-necked people with, understandably, a persecution complex.

Outside he insists on taking wind-swept photos of me leaning on the balustrades. He's concerned that the batteries are defunct preventing him from taking more photos. Leaving the palace I mention with a note of regret that I haven't seen the harem but he says, somewhat emphatically, that it's closed and that the harem in the Dolmabahce Palace is far more interesting. We pass the Archaeological Museum – hmm, I think to myself, it looks BORING but Abdullah maintains that it's well worth a visit. Reading up about it later I learn that the building contains the world's oldest peace treaty and all sorts of pagan idols. Christians, and rightly so, pray to be delivered from temptation … I vow that next time I visit this city I'll take my time and not dash around like a hunted animal.

I ask him to come with me to the cistern place to check out the ring in the form of a mosque. There's a bit of argy bargy because the guards say that I have to buy another ticket to get into the shop but we protest and they rest their case. Having become enamoured of the Topkapi Diamond the circle of diamonds around the ring look repulsively fake – like something you'd get out of a Christmas cracker. However, Abdullah is as enchanted with the piece as I am and the deal is done. I'm then invited to the family shop to take tea.

On arrival I'm taken upstairs, seated on the viewing throne (in order to view the carpets) and introduced to his uncle, Lord Sin. He doesn't realise that I'm not there as a customer but as a tea-drinking guest of his nephew. Another nephew, Abdullah's cousin, is called on to throw carpets and he is certainly someone who is seen, not heard. Abdullah is obviously the brains of the family. Earlier, on the street, we had bumped into his father (a striking absence of family resemblance) with whom he had shaken hands formally. He, the father, couldn't have been much older than forty. But I guess that age is irrelevant when it comes to parenting. Some respect and guide others and some don't and will actually feed their offspring poisonous substances and spoil them utterly. Uncle Sin has no children and is really ugly with his fat mouth and pock-marked skin. He asks me to guess his age and when, tentatively, I suggest fifty four he and Abdullah look taken aback indeed because he is only thirty eight. His talk is divided between women and carpets. His wife lives in Japan and they do a lot of business with the Japanese. His woman talk is unsavoury but I notice that Abdullah laughs at his jokes and reveres an older family member. Uncle appears thoughtful when I tell him my age and his deduction is that western women are sporty – a fact that he seems to find both admirable and unsettling. How are women really meant to be? He keeps on getting up and leaving the room and each time he does I inadvertently turn to Abdullah for some normal conversation and my preference doesn't go unnoticed. There's one silk carpet which I admire and although I say repeatedly that it won't go in my living-room because the dark red centre will clash with the pink and green wallpaper he's got his hook in and won't let go. He won't listen to a thing I say because his mind is geared into selling mode. What he doesn't realise is that the more he pushes and prods the more I am turned off and indifferent to his every word and moreover it does occur to me, when I leave the shop, that I could never buy that beautiful carpet because every time I looked at it or stood on it (in my slippered feet) I'd remember his ugly face. When he is out of the room Abdullah kneels down on the floor and points out the religious symbolism of the carpet's patterning. Reaching God is a stern ascent. Outside the Topkapi Palace I was impressed that he was able to read the age-old sundial accurately. Why am I so stupid, never understanding external phenomena. What I'm into is interpreting shadows …

I suppose we got onto the subject of dancing because Lord Sin said that if I bought the carpet us three could all go out dancing. Abdullah looked doubtful. Uncle gets up and proudly demonstrates his 'camel' (an Arabic dance move which consists of rolling the tummy muscles) boasting that this never fails to impress the women. I myself hate dancing for show. Suddenly, without warning, he pulls me onto the floor and grabs me around the waist with one hand, letting his other hand savour my flesh. Yuk, yuk and yuk again! But I'm aware that I'm a guest and as usual I keep my emotions under strict control in case I antagonise the beast. Abdullah looks a trifle confused – is this how liberated and civilised women behave? Sound instinct tells him that Uncle is a bit out of order – why is she going along with it? I do wriggle out of his slimy embrace and return to my comfortable golden throne. The wallflowers at the back of the room don't bat an eyelid and just do Uncle's bidding … Disappearing behind the scenes in order to make tea Uncle disappears again and I wonder whether Abdullah will have to be assassinated as a dangerous rival. Or is he too useful in his present role …?

With Uncle out of the room I get onto the subject of the Beatles and dancing material. I loved this 60s group with all my heart, mind and soul (as one is meant to love God in the Bible) probably because they sang about LOVE LOVE LOVE – and boys boys boys were my raison d'etre. It wasn't possible not to love the Beatles unless you were the grimmest killjoy who ever walked the earth, a monster of nothingness. Without making any effort whatsoever I knew every word of every song that they ever recorded. Abdullah eagerly and anxiously locates the songs on his phone and scrolls down until something comes up that I can dance to. I only have to hear the opening chord to identify a song. 'Eight days a week' will do and I'm up on my feet singing and dancing, clicking my fingers and shaking my hips. When I'm dancing I'm on Cloud nine and space and time cease to exist. In other words I'm free and happy! And I'm back in the magical world of 1964/65 which, in spite of the Beverley, the best friend turned cold bitch who led a cruel campaign against me, and the cold blanking out at home, was better than anything today because I was young and looked great in Mary Quant gear and the boys would queue up to dance with me. Mr Right is going to appear on the horizon, wiping out all sorrow, loving you till the cows come home. I can inhabit my narcissistic bubble for ever and ever. Yet it was still better in those days because an egg was still an egg, an apple an apple, a spade a spade. I can't get on with the metallic speed at which everything moves today and the increasing divorce from reality. As I dance alone Abdullah is gazing at me with rapt delight.

Lord Sin is back in the room telling me that if I pay £500 the next day I can pay the rest later (the total cost of the carpet is £1,500). Does he really think that I'd part with so much money at the drop of a hat? But he doesn't see me as a real person at all but an instrument of commerce. I've told him for the millionth time that the dark red won't go with my cushions and can't we change the subject and talk about something interesting like 'Mothers and Sons'? Of course I flog this topic to death and become an absolute bore but WORRY keeps on rearing its ugly head. No one in the world except your truly would expose their troubles to total strangers but there's sanity in my madness because deep down I'm testing to see if 'others' will give me the family, the loving response – which is normal and natural – or the one that I know, the slow 'gloom and doom' shake of the head from side to side with the voiceover of critical, negative input: 'you've got a problem son. You should have sent him to boarding school – forced him into line. What a low-life he is, swilling beer with his low-life mates. My sons never gave me the grief you get from yours. When is he going to grow up and take responsibility for himself? Is he going to be a parasite like his own father who never ever comes to see him?' She, mother, the spouter of toxic waste, deserves an almighty punch in the cakehole but such an attack on an elderly person would probably kill them. Old people must be protected. BUT, to my surprise and relief no one, but no one, is like that in the outside world – all ready with their battery of stones – so quick to crucify. 'Stone her, stone her, stone her,' was the scream when, aged twenty two, (hardly a minor) I wanted to spend the weekend in Brighton with my boyfriend who was actually more of a friend than a lover. Like Samson, who pulled down the stone pillars and destroyed all his enemies and himself, I can take the assault. Or can I? How my skull aches after my father has beaten it with his fist. But it's still in one piece so it's a wonder, I tell myself, how much punishment the body can take. So when my partner whacks me around the head repeatedly when I am pregnant my stance is one of sheer martyrish defiance: 'I can take it and the baby is safe because he's hitting my head, not my stomach.' Why did I sympathise so much with his bewailing difficulties in the job market, his resentment of me as a stay at home mum? Why did I take on board his vicious hatred of the Jews: 'You lot had it easy, you took all the gold that was meant to come my way …'

So I expect the look on Abdullah's face, when I tell him about my son being drunk and knocked over by a car, will register disgust, but the opposite is the case. He thinks carefully and offers the same advice as the Kurdish clan in the other shop. 'Leave him alone'. And then he adds, after a pause, 'but he needs to calm down a bit'. I bring out my battered photo and he, like everyone else, can see that 'he's a good boy'. Being my son, his heritage, I suppose, has to be one of pain and stress. At the age of two or three, perceiving my nervousness in the driver's seat, the sweetness emanating from the child's seat behind me were the words, 'I love you mum'. My mother, (who declared herself 'the best driver in the world') was at my side; she abruptly turned her head and said in her denigrating, carefully enunciated critical tone of voice: 'Does he know what that means?' The child has no voice, no value. Nobody ever shut her up let alone strangled her. But to stand up and speak is to burst the bubble and break free.

During my 'spiel' Uncle looked flat and indifferent, wanting to get back to business and speculation as to his future possibilities with females. A while earlier I had raised the issue of slave labour in relation to the carpets (something you're expected to do) and I received a barrage of information as to how the female weavers are highly trained and well-paid. Perhaps it's true. It's agreed that if I want the carpet, which is undeniably lovely, I'll return the next day with the loot. On this note Uncle disappears and Prince Abdullah soberly informs me that if I pay tomorrow they'll be able to pay their girls. He escorts me out of the shop and we say our farewells. He thanks me for a wonderful afternoon. If he had invited me onto his magic carpet I'd have said, 'yes, yippee' without a moment's hesitation and would have rejoiced in the Lord for having given me a man to love and cherish, a man with gleaming white teeth and cherry red lips who would have taken me to heaven and back. Of course Abdullah, sooner or later, will marry a nice, educated Turkish girl from a good family (all good families see that their daughters receive a proper education) and they'll have a handful of children whom they'll love dearly and who will be blessed with security and happiness. He's bound to be a good lawyer. Maybe if man loved his neighbour as himself – if he loved truth more than the protective power of gold – there'd be peace on earth and support for all.

Alone I walk back to my hotel past the yellow wooden police station (like something out of 'Noddy') and hope that they've finally managed to unblock the sink. It ain't nice to come back to a sink full of dirty water. The smart besuited smarmy receptionist seems to enjoy not calling in a plumber and will only do so if I shout and scream. My basement room is ok but what I like best is the cosy corridor lined with gilt-edged full length mirrors, which leads to the breakfast cafe where the yoghurt is heavenly and bears no comparison to the stuff labelled GREEK which you can buy in the UK supermarkets. In the evening I take my pick of the restaurants in the old part of the city. There is always one which is less flashy, attracting a quieter, more reverential type of person. It doesn't bother me to eat alone although sometimes you feel the pinch when everyone around you is laughing and gay. A lovely waiter presents me with a basket containing strips of pitta bread which I devour ravenously. In England they never give you bread for free. The waiter lays my place with careful precision and is very busy, running from kitchen to table. He's about thirty three, bald, and has an attractive gap between his two front teeth. Waiting on a retired English couple he heats a clay pot directly in the flame and then smashes it to relieve its saucy contents. The English woman gets everyone to observe this marvellous happening and takes a photo of the waiter and the dish to record the event for posterity.

I finish my sea bass and the waiter asks if I'd like a drink. I decline, because, I guess, I have no one to drink with. Who wants to drink on their own? Maybe I'm like the poor, wretched 'Haversham' in Carol Anne Duffy's poem, punishing herself for her fate, unable to transcend guilt and revenge. Biting a corpse won't get her anywhere. The waiter, bless his heart, asks me to accept a drink from him. I accept graciously. Oh what a pity I'm flying away the next day and will never see him again, never find out about his mum and dad in Bulgaria or Anatolia, his grandma who always used to read to him and has a special place in his heart … I'll never see him again. I'm going back to the UK, to a world which is on its knees because what comes first is money.

Breakfast in Bilbao

Why on earth do I go on these random trips, these one man journeys into the unknown? As my son says to me, en route to the airport at 7a.m. 'why exactly are you going to Bilbao?' and the honest reply is: 'well, actually there's no reason except that I'd like to see the Guggenheim Museum'. I feel somewhat nervous, as you would do before some reckless act of daring and I'd just passed one of the worst nights in living memory as regards fitful sleeping and waking and dreams of dread, which always occur when I have to do something new.

    A little drama occurred as, along with the herd, I made my way through security. My purple case comes out of the checking tunnel on the wrong roller and the guy next to me mutters 'Bad News'. I'd already expressed my concern to his wife that my toiletries were in a Tesco freezer bag and not the small plastic bag sold on site. I fret over the instructions; surely 'a bag …' means any old bag'? And stuff like deodorant and savlon and insect repellent cream (some nasty insect bit me in Cyprus and the barman gave me a lemon to apply to the swelling) and E45 lip salve I leave in my case. Oh God, I've set off the alert and all the cops in uniform have come running over … They pin me to the ground, bind my wrists together with rope and bundle me into the awaiting police car. I'm too shocked, to intent on wondering what I've done wrong to shout and scream. In reality quite a nice fellow comes over, opens my case, and investigates all its contents. He scans my mobile phone and digital camera and puts them to one side. He tells me that all toiletries (deodorant is liquid isn't it?) have to go into the prescribed bag and it has to be able to shut properly. He passes over my pink panties and espies my new white 'per una' handbag with the big bow, at the bottom of the case. 'That's empty', I say, with a faint air of exasperation, and so it is. Nothing in my case other than two dresses and a pair of shoes. Ah, he's discovered the secret pockets inside the cover of the case and draws out a Spanish phrase book and George Eliot's 'The Mill on the Floss'. Hmm. Underneath the tiger skin toiletries bag (a present from my daughter) he glances at the A5 Tesco Notepad, with its pure white pages and looks a little perplexed. Perhaps she's a spy. (No, I'm just away on a note-taking exercise which I'll write up properly when I get home). The deodorant won't fit into the prescribed bag and has to be 'chucked' as my mother would say. The bag still won't close and I bemoan my sensitive skin necessitating hand cream, foot cream etc. etc. 'OK, you can go, I'll be lenient with you but the bag is meant to close.' God, I'll certainly know for next time. I think he realised that I wasn't quite sure about the rules.

Following this brush with authority I'm all flummoxed and flustered; however, it must be said that for the first time ever I didn't set off the alarm when I walked under the arch because I'd removed my heavy metal diamond encrusted watch (purchased from Oxfam) and my beautiful silver ring from Jordan, with its silver petals embedding a chic green stone. I'm always amazed at the light-handed way in which the security woman runs her hands all over my body, under my bra and along my thigh feeling for the hidden knife. My case firmly zipped shut (just about) I glance at the departure board and see that the 8.05 has already departed. 'Oh my God' (i.e. what has happened? what have I done?) is my silent panicked utterance and then I realise that my flight is at 10.05; 8.05, or thereabouts, was the time set for leaving the house. Oh my God, I'm like the character in the TV comedy sitcom 'Outnumbered' who is accused of having a brain like cheese. 'Cheesy Brains' is what her husband calls her.

I buy a new deodorant in Boots and suggest that this one could contain a lethal dose of whatever they use to blow up planes. 'Oh no,' the saleswoman assures me 'our products are all specially checked beforehand'. The good thing about the stop and search interruption is that it has used up boring waiting time. It seems to me that unless you have your own independent means of getting from A to B travel consists of a helluva lot of waiting time and anticipation of things not going to plan. Jumping into the queue to board the plane (how is it that some people just know when to start queuing and are the first jumpers) I get into conversation with a girl who is doing a Ph.D. on bird migration up in Durham and is going to Bilbao to a wedding and it's also where her mother lives. I tell her the story of the confiscated deodorant and can't believe that I've lost the new one – although I remember slipping it into my case. 'Am I going mad or something?' I beseech the heavens until I finally locate the misplaced object. I'm ashamed of how untogether I am and feel the need to confess that I was thumped around the head as a child and nearly suffered a broken skull. But back to birds. I ask her whether birds are ever upset by the noise of planes and if their flight paths ever clashed and then I realise of course that birds fly at a lower altitude … She looks at me strangely, not knowing how to answer because obviously this isn't an academic question. She takes her leave of this madwoman to enter the plane from the rear. Some people say that flying at the back of the plane is safer but the roar and thunder of the engines on take-off and landing is definitely louder. I don't know why I describe myself as a nervous flier because take-off is actually rather thrilling and the plane *never* shatters into a million pieces or bumps down to the earth again, too heavy to fly – like a peacock or an ostrich.

Prior to landing the pilot informs us that there are strong winds around and true to his word we experience some turbulence. All the children are laughing (it's a fun day out on the roller coaster) but the woman next to me is clutching her mobile phone to her chest as if it were a crucifix. I tell her that at least the luggage isn't falling out of the overhead lockers which is what happened to a Spanish friend and his mum when they flew from England to Spain. The possibility of a worse situation comforts and consoles and by then the worst is over and we delicately touch down on Spanish soil. How great it must be to kiss your native soil (like Anwar Sadat when he alighted from his plane in Cairo) because your motherland is so much a part of you. Religious Jews have also been known to do it when they make contact with the land of their forefathers, Abraham, Isaac and Jacob. 'This is the place where we feel safe, where we belong, where no one can attack us'. Oh for God's sake, get real …

Talking in substandard Spanish I locate the bus stop outside the airport and am aware that it's a bit chilly and there are patches of blue sky between clouds as well as some sunshine. Soon the sun disappears, the clouds thicken and that is that for the next four and a half days. It's a good thing that I brought my rolled up black umbrella and a cardigan to wear under my jacket. Alighting from the bus in the Plaza Frederico Moya I ask for directions and arrive at my hotel which is a sort of secret place down one of the old medieval streets in the Casco Viejo (the old city). It's as old as the hills and as dark. There are bars here, there and everywhere with cool stone walls and wooden features. Next door to the hotel is a tiny booth where a cobbler still cobbles and, interspersed with modern pharmacies, are tiny baby clothes shops with exquisite little dresses in the window, which were probably the sort my mother dressed me in. I wonder who can afford such expensive clothes. Entering the gates of the hotel from the street you find yourself in a smelly sort of stable with a stone floor, a model goat and some broken wooden benches and chairs. I think nothing but just make my way up the stairs although an American lady, arriving in the middle of the night, told me that she wondered what on earth the room was going to be like and was ready to make her escape. The reception area is dark and the walls are hung with cloth and there's a tiny courtyard with a palm tree from where you can hear the drip drop of the intermittent rain. There is a small area with about six round tables with old-fashioned tablecloths and upholstered chairs. That's how they lived in the old days; no self-respecting woman would live in a house without lace curtains and paintings of the Virgin Mary with the baby Jesus on the wall and huge wooden chests containing bed linen that would last forever. It's all a bit musty and fusty but for some reason I don't feel downhearted. I'm shown my room (number five) which is a pleasant surprise because it's so pleasantly old. The first thing that catches my eye is a real old desk – a bit like the elegant desk/writing table which belonged to my father with all its tiny compartment for different items of stationery and leather blotter – and there's an old cupboard sporting gay paintings of a bunch of purple grapes and a pineapple. It looks friendly, along with the teak wardrobe. Everything is clean and fresh and the double bed feels OK – sometimes it's nice to sleep in the old-fashioned way with sheets and a couple of cosy blankets. Hmm – there is no bath, no place for a long hot soak before getting into a cold bed but the shower will have to do.

I am given three keys attached to a keyring which has a snazzy, lime green snake- like thing hanging from it and instructed as to which one opens which door. The outside of this typical Basque townhouse is painted blue and yellow and there are pots of geraniums and other pink and red trailing plants attached to the railings of the narrow balconies. These pots of trailing petunias (the tough variety) and geraniums give the place its sweet enticing identity. I always look up and wonder who the lady is who waters these pots devotedly and enables them to grow so vigorously and yet keeps them so contained. So it is with young girls who have thick lustrous pony tails which swing from side to side as they walk, run and jive. (Perhaps I'll never get over the fact that I was sent to the local barber once a month for a short back and sides). Without my small wheely case I am free to explore and clutching my guide book, like an open bible, I try and orientate myself as best I can. Am I by any chance walking around in circles? I stumble on the Bar Motrikes on the Calle Somero which is advertised in the guide book as situated in one of the oldest streets in Bilbao. It certainly seems very quiet (siesta time I guess) but sitting on the steps of the bar and crowded around the open door are young people who look like total hippies in torn jeans, spiky multi-coloured hair dos and of course tattoos. I go in and order a beer and manage to tell the chap serving me that he's in the guide book and it says that 'the grilled mushrooms are delicious' so I better order some. He presents me with one grilled mushroom on a small piece of bread which tastes like a grilled mushroom on a small piece of bread. Nevertheless I express my wonder and gratitude. I hope the beer doesn't make me woozy because I have to look after myself and get to places. I am about to move on when he indicates that he's got to get something from a side room leading off the bar. I wait for a moment or two and then think that perhaps it has nothing to do with me and am about to disappear forever when he runs after me and presents me with a little present in the form of a key ring to which is attached a poppy red cork on which is printed the name and address and email address of the establishment. Don't get taken in by the wine-stained walls and the stone floors. Everyone has to move with the times and embrace technology.

I go back to the river and admire the picturesque old buildings alongside the River Nervion, especially the old train station which has 'Bilbao Santander' written across the semi-circular arch in blue and terracotta mosaics. I could stand and look at that arch forever as it harks back to a time when people spoke to one another and weren't selfishly eaten up by their own concerns. This is pure wishful thinking of course. It's nice wandering through the old medieval streets but the Plaza Nueva, once the life and soul of the city, seems as if it's seen better days. It seems grey and dismal as does the Catedral de Santiago. I notice that there seem to be a lot of people walking dogs, some on leads but mostly not. Outside a small greengrocers are boxes of lumpy, bumpy tomatoes, so different from those that are on display in British supermarkets. I can't resist the fat dark red cherries and subtle toned pink/orange apricots. Indecisive about the amount I want, the proprietress gets irritated. Two euros twenty six cents is nothing by English standards but she should still have given me my change when I gave her two euros forty cents. The look on her face, 'I can't be bothered to mess around with such small amounts with people who take up so much time' said it all. I should have gone to the greengrocers down the road where there was no bitter 'madame' and you could freely feast your eyes on the mountains of apples, pears, peaches and nectarines and green-red tomatoes. It's as if these piles of natural produce correspond with the way people stand in the street, outside the bars, with their glasses of wine and plates of pintxos, talking their heads off. I wonder what they're talking about so forcefully and at such high volume. It's probably not the recession and the economic power of Germany, all set to give Greece and Spain a kick in the bum.

 I sit down on a bench in the Plaza de Miguel de Unamuno, opposite the Museo Vasco and can't resist biting into the luscious apricot. Damn! The juice squirts all over my pistachio green trousers and cream lace top. Typical – now I have to go around with apricot splashes all over me … It's not that bad actually but I go into the nearest café and ask if I could have some cold water and a J cloth – or whatever. The kindly faced barman presents me with a glass of hot water and a serviette and hey presto the stains are out. I never knew that the secret to removing a fresh stain was hot water. I return to my room in the B&B, lie down on the bed, and fall into a sort of heavy drugged doze which leaves me feeling groggy. I go out again although it has begun to rain. I'm very impressed by an open air gym on the riverfront where a woman is exercising her legs – a much pleasanter option it seems to me than the rigours in the horrible grey windowless cage that people seem to thrive on. I buy a new black wallet, (with proper compartments for cards) because the old one, with its motto of 'Je t'adore' is falling apart, and then stumble into the beautiful Biblioteca Municipal de Bidebarrieta where you can sit comfortably for ever, ensconced in your book. This building dates from the end of the nineteenth century and used to be home to the Sociedad El Sitio, a society established in 1975 by liberals, following the death of Franco. It's a good shelter from the rain but it's 7.30pm, closing time, so I have to leave. The rain isn't heavy and doesn't last very long but it's a general indicator of not very seasonal weather. What was I thinking of packing my suntan lotion and summer dresses? I'm not sure where to have my evening meal and an elderly gentleman recommends a bar/ restaurant at the end of Calle Jardines (which seems to be the liveliest street all round) where you can eat typical Basque food. The trouble is that it is expensive and frequented by elderly gentlemen. I find another place that looks OK but they haven't removed their 'Menu del dia' from the window and in the evening it's the less economic deal- having to choose dishes from the leather bound menu book. I wait about half an hour for a very mediocre fish soup (no fish in it that I can see) and then about an hour for a squid, bacon and artichoke stew which is tasty but not what I imagined and not a lot of it. The waitress is kind and friendly (after the long wait I was given squid rings by mistake) but the waiter, about my son's age, is cold and impersonal and I don't like him at all. As I leave the restaurant I brush the dust off my heels. I can't believe how quiet my room is – facing an inner courtyard and not the street. Surely after such a long day I should sleep well but I don't because I'm not relaxed and early in the morning I hear them crashing around in the kitchen area, getting the tables ready for breakfast.

At eight o'clock on the dot, when breakfast is served, I appear in the table area and am surprised to find the tables beautifully laid with serviette lined baskets full of croissants and biscuits and another containing baguettes. The coffee, served with a jug of hot frothy milk, is excellent. Potent coffee is for me what heroin is for others – something which provides an adrenaline rush, a little high which drives your cares away. The front of your brain feels sharper, if not the back. I start on one of the croissants which is in the form of a Catherine wheel dusted with icing sugar (disgusting, childish stuff). Little thief that I am, I pop two croissants into my bag because I might get peckish later. By this time I am joined (at the next table) by an American couple from Oxford, Mississippi who are without their companions because the woman lost her passport and had to go to the Embassy in Madrid to get a new one. Talk about hassle. The upshot is that they offer me her ticket for the Guggenheim. We go together with me searching through the guide book to give Anne (from Oxford) information about the 'Teatro Arriaga' which opened in 1890 and resembles the Paris Opera House. Americans love anything that looks lavishly baroque or hauntingly gothic. Her husband Dale, I can see, is not the slightest bit interested; he's just had gallstones removed, surgery on his spine and a pacemaker fitted and is finding the fairly long trek, along the river, to the Guggenheim, a little bit arduous. He has to sit down en route, on a bench, for a little rest. The Guggenheim finally appears around a corner and it really is a sight to behold. The sun, unfortunately, isn't shining but the titanium architecture still glows and is a miracle of execution, a dream realised. Louise Bourgeois's massive bronze spider sculpture 'Maman' stands in the foreground, making one aware, as one positions oneself beneath her egg sack, that mothers have huge looming power and are threatening even when they are benevolently protective. (I can't imagine what it could feel like to have a mother who cared for you, wanted the best for you and wasn't a dark envious harpy) I make some reference to this and Dale gives a little chuckle of assent. Once we're in the museum Anne is bothering herself over God knows what and I'm aware that time is passing and the crowd of tourists is increasing. Dale tells me to do my own thing, go at my own pace, which I appreciate. And so we part company.

Actually I'm pretty well dead on my feet and when you're that tired it's best to keep moving. The first thing on the agenda is a first floor gallery full of what look like vast copper vats. Without guilt, I give it a miss – I lack the mental energy to peruse stuff of doubtful interest. There are only three floors in the building and you can take the glass lift or climb the spiral staircase. I heard something about the interior being modelled on the human heart and the staircases being the arteries. I couldn't concentrate on what the headphones were telling me in the introduction because it was in the foyer and I wasn't sure what was happening with Anne and Dale. To my utter surprise I find that the David Hockney exhibition, which I missed in London (too busy, too much bother) was here now, at the Guggenheim – all of it. I did feel guilty about missing it so now I've been given the chance to catch up. Cor, you have to marvel at the man's skill and ingenuity and the colours of his Yorkshire fields are stunning beyond belief. However, watching the film of the countryside from six cameras filming simultaneously makes me feel a bit dizzy (isn't it obvious that we're always moving through space and time or maybe I didn't quite grasp the point) and at one point during the hour long documentary about his life the interviewer suggests that there is a certain emptiness in the paintings. Hockney replies that this couldn't be because he had painted them. The interviewer then deduced that no painting could be 'empty' if someone had painted it. Hockney then said, 'what about an empty room, then – huh? (as if prodding the interviewer, or God, to explain this non-sequitur). A painting I found interesting was that of a couple in a car speeding through a grim grey mountainous countryside from Switzerland to France. The man and woman in the car look terrified in the midst of this barely signposted nightmarish landscape. I checked to see that it really was a David Hockney – perhaps a painting by another artist had found its way in accidentally – upsetting the marvellous vitality and expertise of his work but it had indeed been executed by the master himself. I loved his charcoal drawings of trees. I'm very into words of wisdom and I wasn't convinced by his dictum that if this life is a mystery the next one must be one too. He doesn't paint mystery.

Enough, enough, time for a break, time to check out the Guggenheim café. It serves dainty little tapas, a couple of anchovies and a slice of tomato on a piece of baguette, slices of potato omelette on bread (that's a popular one) and under a plastic dome are delicate multi-layered white bread ham and cheese sandwiches with a sprinkling of grated egg yolk on top. These tapas and pintxos are often, it must be said, a work of art. The coffee is not too bad but eating and drinking outside under thick grey clouds in a chill wind isn't too pleasurable. But the wind and the sprinkling of rain pass and it's generally warmer than it is in the U.K. but still not typical of the usual June weather. I walk over to 'Puppy' Jeff Koon's flower sculpture and take a picture which I promptly delete because you can't see the colours.

I go back into the museum and make my way to the third floor, getting into the lift as Anne and Dean are getting out. She is obviously dragging him around, doing the whole museum from bottom to top, and doesn't see me although he, the dragee, does. They've done David Hockney (they've never been to Yorkshire so it was interesting) and have just seen all the paintings on floor number three from the Spanish Civil War. I stick my head in this gallery, see messy daubs of purple and brown, and withdraw immediately. Too tired, not for me. Outside the museum I bump into an English couple whom I'd asked for directions when I couldn't locate the lifts and the man asks me where I'm off to. Well, guide book to hand, my plan is to visit the Museo de Bellas Artes', which is near a park, somewhere in the vicinity. We discuss the David Hockney exhibition and the wife says, somewhat spitefully, that all his work is infantile. She only likes representational art. 'Well you might as well take a photograph' I politely suggest. When people are angrily opinionated it's hard to stand up to them (you might get a thwack on the back) but stand up to them you must. The husband is keen to direct me to the fine arts museum and she tells him to leave me alone: 'she knows what she wants to do'. The wife doesn't think much of Bilbao; San Sebastian is better and the view from the funicular is superb. I think they come from Worcestershire or some other beautiful county in the west country. In my guide book it says that the museum houses works by Goya, Zurbaran, El Greco, Gauguin, Bacon, as well as Basque artists. The one and only Goya is at the cleaners, the Gauguin is one of his early Brittany paintings lacking the lovely mauve and pink palette of his Tahitian works, and I can't find any El Grecos, Bacons, although there are loads of Zurbarans. One painting which arrests me is that of a milkmaid with a white face making her way to the cows. She's no happy servant, skipping through the wild flower meadows, singing 'Glad that I live am I for the sky is blue/ glad for the country lanes and the fall of dew …' The painter has shown all her tackle in the back of her head and her body including tin pails and cloths and mops, all her burden of heavy work. Her face is faceless, blank, unsmiling. 'That's my poor mother' I think to myself. No wonder she had nothing to give to anyone. I have a chat with one of the gallery attendants, telling him that I did the same job at the Fitzwilliam Museum in Cambridge. He agrees that it's boring but he's pleased to have a job, something to get up for in the mornings, in this dire economic climate. I wander through the museum and take a rest on one of the sofas in a small ante-room overlooking the courtyard where a tramp is asleep on the ground, on the hard concrete, dead to the world. Such a sight always makes me think of Roger, my ex-'partner' and it ain't a happy thought. I certainly wouldn't be surprised to see him begging in the street with his long white beard or asleep in some doorway. It's no surprise that my daughter works so hard, takes so much control; this is what happens when there's no father. He was a liar, a woman exploiter and a weirdo. And the lesson is that you can be too kind and sympathetic to other humans, embracing those from whom you need to keep a distance. They get under your skin and do damage.

I find myself in the midst of an exhibition which is a record of the Spanish Civil War, through the photographs of Robert Capa, David Chim and Gerda Taro. Rolls and rolls of negatives were accidentally discovered somewhere or other. Robert Capa died young and by the sound of it was a brave man, as was David Chim. Tired as I am, I look closely at these photos which really bring home the awfulness of that conflict and the suffering of ordinary people. The old and the sick are made to walk miles to internment camps and the beautiful young men have their precious lives stolen from them. War is a horrible beastly bully and will always be with us so long as man refuses to dance, and perceives Mother Earth as a force to be dominated and straightjacketed and exploited rather than celebrated. Woman is blood and blood is life! The good thing about man is his passion for adventure, exploration, knowledge; the bad thing is his bucket load of vanity, pride and self-love. Ego will always hold you back. Emerging into the busy Plaza del Museo I eat, not the Spanish croissant, but the British mango and Brazil cereal bar tucked into my bag as an emergency ration, as I make my way to the Parque de Dona Casilda Iturrizar which is pleasant to behold. I then tramp down the Gran Via de Don Diego Lopez de Haro (whoever *he* was?) en route for the old city and its dark medieval streets which were once lined with butchers and fishmongers shouting their wares. Now they are all established in the Mercado de la Ribera which is the largest covered market in the country dating from 1929. The 'Haro' street is the shopping and business centre of Bilbao, resembling shady tree lined grand boulevards all over Spain and halfway along this grand boulevard is the Plaza Moyua, a large roundabout with flower gardens at its centre and an attractive geometric layout. The Hotel Carlton, (built 1927) where the Basque government had its headquarters during the Civil War looks unprepossessing and dilapidated. It's an important landmark because it's where you get the bus back to the airport. (Mustn't forget). On and on I tramp until I locate the Café Exquisita in the Calle Tenderia, opposite the covered market which is exactly as described in the guide book (although there's no sign of the famous 'Carolina meringue named after the Confectioners daughter because she was so sweet and gorgeous'). It's packed with women drinking their drinks and chatting animatedly to one another. It's a good place to rest my weary feet and enjoy a very acceptable cup of coffee, although it's tea-time.

Back in the dark mute reception area of the hotel the lady who runs this unusual abode is doing her accounts, answering emails and other necessary office stuff. She's always present in the morning, putting the hot coffee jug on your table and her reticence and discretion make her guests feel comfortable. I've told her that she has exactly the same accent as my near neighbour in Cambridge who comes from Madrid. She wears a long skirt and her hair is totally covered by a scarf. She tells me that she's run the hotel for sixteen years. To another guest I heard her mentioning a lovely country house and two children so there was obviously a (lovely) husband. As regards my forthcoming trip to San Sebastian she's advised me to take the train from the bus station which departs on the hour. (They don't and they didn't so it's best not to believe what people say and get yourself a timetable prior to travel.) Since she's a native Basque person and knows what's what, I ask her to recommend a nice restaurant in the area, not too pricey. You only need to go to a really classy place if you have someone to share it with. She names some restaurant on the Calle Jardines and reminds me that they don't open their doors before eight thirty because this is gay Espana and not church mouse Bottisham, UK. But nowhere is gay when it's grey and raining. The place is ridiculously easy to find – it's just across the road from the Calle Santa Maria and is better than the joint I visited the night before in that I don't have to wait years for my meal. There are two other people at single tables – one of whom is playing with his mobile phone. The asparagus soup is fine (I need warming up) and the warm cod salad is very Spanish/Basque, arranged decoratively with chicory leaves and pine nuts and some brown sauce drizzled all over. I'm a bit annoyed because they charge me one euro for a stale piece of bread which I never ordered. Sometimes you just can't be bothered to say because it seems too petty, trivial and mean, damaging your reputation and doing nothing to inflate your heart strings. The meal is bloody not worth twenty odd euros so I don't leave a tip and I'm sure I haven't imagined the angry look I receive from the middle-aged waiter (with a family to feed) as I walk out the door. The whole experience was a bit miserable and I burnt the roof of my mouth on the piping hot soup. I walk around the streets a little, joining in the general crush and throng and marvelling at the tiny cheese shop, like a hole in the wall and another which specialises in 'Jamon, Jamon'. There's always the same matriarch within supervising the slicing of the dark leathery looking ham. She's short, broad, with short grey hair and she knows her bacon when it comes to ham. Wandering around in the rain isn't so pleasant so I spend the rest of the evening in my room, lying on the bed attempting to get into 'Mill on the Floss' and listening to the news and the weather forecast on Spanish television. I'm sure that English TV is the best in the world. Continental TV produces what seems to me to be cheap crap.

This is only my second night so I still haven't relaxed and so pass another bad night. Am I accursed or something? At breakfast the next morning Dean asks me where I'm gallivanting off to today and the answer, of course, is San Sebastian! I am advised to take the tram to the bus station, which takes about fifteen minutes but I prefer to walk, enjoying the fresh air and the overhead arcade of leafy branches … The proprietress makes no comment but she's no doubt thinking: 'but Bilbao is a city, a place where you wear shoes and cover your flesh as you go about your business'. With some trepidation I set out (will I find the bus station which is near the football station?) but there's always someone to ask once I get to the Plaza de Sagrado Corazon (where a statue of Jesus or one of his mates is gazing down and protecting me) and fall upon the ugly bus station area. I even have a pleasant conversation with a Bilbaon woman in which we discuss our relative climates and the present bewildering unpredictability of the weather. At the ticket kiosk I discover that I am queuing for the wrong bus company and time is getting short – the next bus is about to leave and the ticket woman tells me 'anden' (platform) 234 and bus number two. I'm in a bit of a panic now ('anden' means bloody platform not 'bay' as we say in English) and where is platform '234'? As I'm looking hard, with a fixed stare for platform two hundred and thirty four, a young man takes me by the hand (metaphorically speaking) and points out that the bus comes in at either bay 2, 3, or four and there it is, where people are getting on. God, I'm so relieved and grateful to him. I find my seat, number forty four, and just as the bus is about to go the young man sits next to me, his seat number being forty three. Our expressions say: what a coincidence! As we get into our journey I decide not to engage the poor boy in conversation – it's always a bit of an effort to talk – it's nicer sometimes to be quiet and rivet myself to the window and the wonderful green hills of the Basque country. I don't know though it comes to a point where it's rude not to communicate and I ask him if he lives in Bilbao. It's a bit like the old Cilla Black routine on 'Blind Date' (ghastly programme!) which began with: 'what's your name and where do you come from?' As you might imagine our conversation progresses and I find out all about him. His English is excellent although he never studied in England but attended a private school in Bilbao. He tells me about Newcastle, Plymouth and Glasgow – as is often the case he's been to more English cities than I have and I make a vow to experience Glasgow in all its wonder and beauty. He points out a village in a valley which is crammed full of apartment blocks housing forty thousand people. People say that it's the ugliest village in the Basque country but he thinks it's the most beautiful. His mother is Basque and his father is Spanish and he considers himself Basque. He locates my daughter's beautiful hand-made shoes on her website and is as impressed as he should be! The journey goes quickly and I give him my email address in case he ever comes to Cambridge and needs a contact. Once off the bus he shows me where the ticket office is to purchase my return ticket and tells me which way to walk to get into the centre of town. It's miles! His name is Michael and suddenly he sees his sister and brother-in-law who are going to give him a lift to their hometown, about eight miles away. As he says goodbye his face is no longer that of a blank person in a queue but that of an eager wide-eyed human being.

If only the weather were a bit warmer and sunnier – it's not really very nice at all and so I feel a bit of an idiot as a tourist. The trouble is that I'm off the map, literally, and the first landmark I can ask to be directed to is the Catedral del Buon Pastor (Cathedral of the Good Shepherd) at which I eventually arrive. It is closed but it's situated in a square with nice gardens, weather permitting. I mess around in a bag shop for a bit, trying on sun hats which reach my nose, in order to take the edge off the long walk. The assistant doesn't mind that I don't buy a bag, a hat or a wallet and tells me to keep right if I want to get to the sea-side. It's always a miracle when you reach the sea (even if the umbrellas are going up only to come down again five minutes later which is the way on the Basque coast) and the sea in question is the 'Bahia de la Concha'. The beach, the 'Playa de la Concha' is a golden swathe of sand bordered by the 'Paseo de la Concha' (the promenade) and in the distance is the Palacio Miramar Maria Cristina which was built as a summerhouse for the Spanish Royal Family. I start to walk towards it to get a closer look but it really is too far away for someone as tired as me. I decide to walk in the other direction, past the magnificent town hall, towards the old city. A young woman who is meeting up with her parents (a jolly affectionate greeting ensues) tells me that France is just around the corner, so to speak. You take a twenty minute train to Ermeo on the border and then you can catch a train to Biarritz. How nice it would be to do this – coffee in Biarritz – but I know that I'm too tired and with all the waiting time in between trains I might miss the last bus back to Bilboa, and I don't know when that is. But I like the idea of crossing borders, showing my passport, making a great escape, like something out of a thrilling war movie. My energy is returning a little as I find myself in the sturdy old harbour away from the promenade where the houses are old and weather beaten and you can really smell the sea and imagine the lives of the people whose existence for centuries were totally dependent on her vagaries. After lunch I will visit the Aquarium, which, according to the guide book, is a must.

I really should find out who St. Sebastian was and how he died – a Christian martyr no doubt. I'm looking for the restaurant in the Calle Mayor which delivers tasty tapas when I'm drawn to a golden baroque church, with an ornate façade, (the Basilica de Santa Maria del Coro), at the top of a flight of steps. In the olden days it must have been at the heart of the community. I don't know why people hate religion so much when it is religious organisations who feed the hungry, clothe the naked, and tend to the sick and dying. A nice elderly man tells me that 'Ubarrechena' is not as good as 'Beti Jai' on the Calle Fermin Calbeton which is where all the locals go. I find it and step aside and gaze at the mouth watering selection of seafood tapas on the counter which all look plump and fresh. I choose the tuna topped with a green olive and an artichoke, tomato and sardine delight accompanied by a beer. This is my first real experience of a tapas bar and I like it here because the barman is totally unassuming and modest even as he pours white wine into a glass from on high, deliberately not looking at what he's doing. In San Sebastian you hear a bit of French as well as Spanish and some of the pastry shops (oh that warm vanillary smell!) are distinctly French. I order a potato omelette on bread – always a safe bet and it fills you up more than a fish. The octopus looks enticing but I had my fill of octopus in Cyprus. Well, I enjoyed that and pay my bill and leave. Someone else can take my tabletop space. The guy next to me was totally absorbed in the local rag, consuming his tapas, before going home to lunch.

I wander around the old city a bit, the streets of which are far more crowded (tourists?) than those of Bilbao. There are also more souvenir shops selling sea shells. Back down at the harbour side I buy a postcard to send to my daughter who has just moved to Cornwall. It will be nice for her to receive a postcard rather than bills. The entrance fee to the Aquarium is quite expensive but I have nothing better to do so I pay and pass through the barrier. There's so much on the history of the people of San Sebastian and the sea and I don't have the mental energy to read. I love the photos showing men and women of character and vitality. Surely the two go together. There are umpteen models of boats and ships and you can learn about the evolving science and tools of navigation. All this reading is a bit of a job … Eventually I come to the fish which begins with the skeleton of a whale, his bones are clean and bleached white (like my son's hands from so much washing) and on display, in glass cabinets, you can see the skeletal jaw and teeth of a variety of sharks. What is so astounding, if you look up close, is the perfect alignment of these tiny, or not so tiny, fangs – each one being perfect and suited to purpose. I wish my teeth were like that. Following the yellow arrows on the floor I come to the fish themselves in tanks which are a faithful replica of their native habitat and the world you see is silent and wondrous beyond belief. I like the pretty jellyfish with their delicate pulsing dance and the water daisies gently waving their petals, begging for forgiveness. Not! Then there are the milk white and yellow fish whose mouths are permanently pursed in a kiss. When I was about eleven I had a grey summer shirtwaister dress, obviously the fashion in 1962, which sported a pattern of seahorses in bold squares. I loved that dress and here are the real thing, so tiny and sensitive, and as we all know the males get pregnant and give birth to their young. What does it really do to babies to have a mum who isn't in tune with her offspring, who in fact makes the baby respond to her and not the other way round? No wonder such a mother weighs a ton. I pass into an amazing underwater sea corridor where you can get up close and personal with a variety of fish, including two massive sharks. They have the most miserable awful mouths on them and I'm sure they don't have a brain in their head, they don't deliberately and maliciously attack humankind. I'd like to take photos of the vivid tropical fish darting around but I don't know how to turn the flash off on my camera – (the flash blinds the poor fish). How does everyone else know these elementary things and me not. (??)

The walk back to the bus station, along the river is well sign-posted and I pass attractions such as the 'Teatro Victoria Eugenia' and the 'Maria Cristina' bridge (now who was she, the name seems to pop up a lot') which was inspired by the Pont Alexander the third in Paris and is richly decorated with dragons and coats of arms. I'm tempted to stop off at some famous park but it's a bit of a detour and I don't want to lose my way. And anyway this Paseo Republico Argentina is wide and sandy and beautiful and before cars came along to disturb the peace, it must have been divine. All the houses are tall and elegant and I stop before one in order to gaze over the high gate where I can see a shower of red roses and trailing red geraniums and a gilt garden table and chairs. Inside the house a group of four elderly people are enjoying their lunch. The house has probably been in the family for generations. What's wrong with not being a peasant? At the bus station there is the usual hoohah about which bus is really going to Bilbao and when it is established, beyond all reasonable doubt, that we're in the right place at the right time, we all clamber on and look for our seat numbers. The journey seems longer when you've no one to talk to. Michael from Bilboa had overruled the advice of my 'landlady' as regards getting to Santander, my planned excursion for the following day. 'Why would you want to sit in the train for three hours? You can take a bus like this and it takes about an hour and a half'. Arriving back at the grungy station I pick up a timetable for the morrow so as to be prepared. I arrive back at the hotel, trek trek trek down the 'gran via', and decide to do without dinner, to make do with my stash of croissants, apricots and cherries and big bag of assorted nuts and dried fruits. Hopefully I'll survive the night and won't wake up starving with hunger. I watch TV, read my book, and endure the ennui which is more difficult in a small room that isn't your own. Thankfully I sleep well and deeply and wake up feeling like a human being rather than an untogether ant.

 The whole thing about going to Santander is the fact that an ex-student of mine, Javier, lives there and we've kept up sporadic emails for about a year, since he returned to Spain. I texted him to say that the bus would arrive at the bus station at 11.30 a.m. and he replied that 'this time was perfect for him.' We enjoy quite an emotional rapport since he's the quiet, thoughtful type. He has an engineering degree and because of the dearth of jobs in Spain is currently tutoring youngsters in Maths and Physics. Needless to say, like most continentals, he lives at home in the heart of a strong, supportive family (although his mother has been on antidepressants as of late and his brother, a philosophy graduate, is profoundly anti-social. His paternal grandfather was in the Spanish civil war and had a rough time so maybe there is distress in the family after all and maybe this is why we have an unspoken bond). The bus draws into a deserted underground car park and with some nervousness I wonder if we'll find each other and whether I'll have to call him to tell him where I am. As this worry is probably registering on my face I catch sight of him striding towards the bus, feet slightly turned out because he is a sportsman, a hockey player. It's as if I'm a teenager again, being met in the Hilton Hotel, Tel Aviv, by my handsome he-man Israeli paratrooper boyfriend. It's the beaming smile on their face. However, I am taken aback when he starts to speak Spanish as if to say 'Now you're on Spanish soil …' and I reply that I can't. He is also trying perhaps to put a distance between himself and this woman whose intentions/attentions might be a bit much. Maybe part of him wishes that I'd stayed at home. I'm probably older than his mother. He's about twenty six years old. He leads me to a big black four wheel drive and here proceeds our tour of Santander. (God knows what I would have done if I'd come here alone since Santander isn't in the guide book).

 He takes me for a walk along the promenade overlooking the beach and the clear waters of the sea, with mountains as a backdrop in the far distance. I can't get over the cleanliness of the orange sand and the deliciousness of the Atlantic waves as they pound the beach. He says that it's a pity it's so cloudy (yes, what a pity!) because you can hardly see the mountains (where he goes hiking with his brother). Apparently everyone does a lot of sport in Santander, a city which has no crime at all (except for the suicides who throw themselves into the sea from the area around the lighthouse where you see the smashed wall through which a desperate couple drove their car …) Today is Sunday and so many people are taking a pre-lunch stroll and they all look quite reserved and northern. Everywhere is so clean and open and even the balustrade is ornamented and painted mermaid green. He points out the house where the banking boss of 'Santander' lives, a very strange house on a hill with lots of turrets. 'He's sticking his neck out and angering the natives because of his intended location for the building. It won't be like the Guggenheim which was built on waste ground and revitalised the city'… I don't take in everything Javier tells me because I'm a bit overwhelmed by his generosity and hope that I'm not encroaching on his Sunday. He keeps on saying, 'and now I want to show you …' In this way we drive everywhere (past the famed casino) and see everything. All that remains of the zoo are the seals, lifting their sweet faces out of the water and a few bedraggled penguins. We climb the very steep hill to the palace which was given to the King as a present and which he 'rudely' sold back to the city. I am told that Santander is about the same size as Cambridge but it seems much bigger. The main street on sea level reminds me a bit of Brighton with every steep street leading down to the sea. He drives me to one of his favourite beaches which is totally private and enclosed by huge boulders. I keep telling him that he's so lucky to live in such a place and indeed he can't stand to be in Madrid or any stultifying inland place where you can't breathe. He shows me three expressive sculptures of children in various postures of diving or jumping into the sea and the story behind these works is that visitors used to throw their money onto the sea bed and then be entertained by the sight of the poor, local children diving to retrieve the coins. I sigh in moral outrage and empathy whilst he points out that the sculptures are also meant to show how much the sea is part of everyone's lives. 'Yes', I assert, 'the sea is your subconscious mind'. I stroke the head of one of the children and he follows suit. Whenever I speak, and I speak a lot, he listens and smiles. I can see, by the expression on his face, that the day is turning out to be pleasurable, not an ordeal.

'Are you feeling hungry?' he asks me. Dead right I am! We're on route to the best fish bar in town which isn't all wood, as in Bilbao, but glass and chrome. This is where he comes with his mates. As we enter I sense that he might be worried about bumping into one of his friends (he has six close friends and the nice thing is that their parents are all friends) but any fear on his part ('what, has he become a gigolo?!') is superseded by his pride and desire to show me the best that Santander can offer. I would have fancied oysters, they were being 'chucked' a plenty by a guy at a table, but you can't buy them individually. We enjoy mejillones (mussels) in a tomato sauce as well as fish balls, plus beer of course, at a table on the street. I'm a bit worried about spilling tomato sauce on my beige linen jacket with the diamond encrusted buttons. He's already told me in Cambridge, at Sevinos, the Italian café where we used to meet when I was more into learning Spanish, that I am a bit nervous, like his mother. From various comments I have made about my accommodation I reckon that his parents, or rather his mother, has said to him, 'why don't you ask your nice teacher to stay here, in our flat?' (he has in fact showed me the steep leafy road where his apartment block is and the one they lived in previously) and I'm sure his answer would have been: 'you don't speak English and she only speaks a little Spanish so it wouldn't work and anyhow I think she likes her independence'. Nevertheless I can see he feels a bit guilty which of course is absurd but understandable when you come from a people centred hospitable family.

He takes me to the monastery, commenting wryly that that's where his brother should be. I say that I can understand the appeal of the contemplative life and he, surprisingly, agrees. This place is right by the sea and is now open to the public which must affect the atmosphere somewhat. From here we go to the Cathedral which he likes so much because it is dead plain, without any fancy ornamentation. As we walk I tell him, with some passion, about the 1971 Australian film 'Walkabout' (I not too successfully explain the term 'walkabout') and its tragic outcome. He silently absorbs everything I say. So we move from tragedy to light-hearted comedy as I have to tell him about the series entitled, 'An Idiot Abroad' with Karl Pilkington. He gets the message of how funny it is and we agree that seeing sights around the world can be pretty meaningless. The plain cathedral has a romantic inner courtyard which is more akin to southern Spain. Oh, if only the sun was out and it was a bit warmer! And I'm surprised that there are so few people around. I do get the impression that Santander is quite a genteel, conservative place even though he's told me that his parents sometimes go clubbing! He has told me more than once that his grandmother crosses the road if she sees a black person walking towards her. I mention something about the funicular in Bilbao 'for those who are staying for more than a day or two' and he promptly takes me to the highest point in Santander where we discuss the breakdown of society, the disadvantages of too much choice and gaze at an old man's cottage with its vegetable patch showing masses of potato plants and lettuces. He shows me where the gypsies live. The last stop on the itinerary is the university complex adjacent to a new, artificial park (the Spanish have great design ideas) and a whole other city of functional apartment blocks which aren't ugly at all. From here we drive down to the best beach of all, passing little fields, bordered by handmade stone walls redolent of Wales, where horses and cows are peacefully grazing. You wouldn't believe that high rise apartment blocks and these intimate little fields could lie together so closely. He drives over boulders and stones and God knows what and we're almost on the beach where frothy green waves crash over the rocks. He stops the car and I extol the wild (and indeed unforgettable) beauty of the place. This is where he comes when he wants to be alone, to think. A trembly sensation travels up my legs.

We look at the timetable and decide that I'm on cue for the five o'clock bus. He drives me to the bus station and says there is just time for a coffee in a café opposite. It's quite a nice little place and he says that he knows really nice places further out of town where he goes with his friends but of course we don't have enough time. We sit face to face and talk about plane travel and his discomfort with flying. He says that he'd prefer to drive four hours to Madrid rather than take the plane. He had this experience some years ago when there was so much turbulence that the overhead lockers fell open and all the luggage was falling out onto people's heads!! His mother was with him and she vowed never to fly again. It was pretty tough for him when he was in Cambridge because he was always having to fly back and forth for hockey matches. He consults his mobile phone and, just as I thought from watching TV, there's going to be a thunderstorm the next day, at lunchtime/early afternoon, the time of my flight. We have to laugh at ourselves but his eyes are wide with anxiety and his mouth looks child-like, vulnerable. He's looking at me very closely. I need to visit the 'ladies' and he looks embarrassed; he doesn't seem to want to connect me with natural functions. We pay the bill, me throwing in a euro, and walk over to the station. In the underground car park there's the usual mix up over the buses (who is changing all the numbers?) and he says it was the same when I arrived; there was no sign of the Bilbao bus on the board … But at least I can leave it to him to sort things out in Spanish at the ticket office. We locate the right bus and it's time to say goodbye. I tell him how much I've appreciated the day out and how kind he has been. He is amused because a Spanish person would just say 'Muchas Gracias'. He kisses me so warmly on the left cheek and then on the right and then is impelled to do it again, on the left and the right, and I'm aware of my hand on his back, sliding up, which is what always happened when we said our goodbyes outside Savinos in Cambridge, before he unlocked his bike. It's simple affection really. I get a vibe which says: 'I like you so much and I really wish you were more my own age because then something could happen between us.' Once or twice he's casually mentioned his new girlfriend from New Jersey and her 'rude' but ebullient Irish father. In Cambridge he had a Spanish girlfriend called Martha. Well, such is life and as Blake wisely said it's best to kiss the joy as it flies … The bus driver won't let me on the bus for some invalid reason and so I have to fly up the escalator to the ticket office to get the ticket stamped with the hour of travel. I fly down again in order not to miss the bus. All the way back to Bilbao I entertain myself singing old love songs. How pathetic am I! I spend another evening in my room feasting on nuts and raisins and reliving that wild rocky place at the water's edge.

Not a good night since I am disturbed by the crashing of saucepans in the kitchen and although I'm well ready to go home – can't wait to enter the silence of my bedroom and luxuriate in the space of my living room (watching Shakespeare on TV and not having to worry about the vagaries of travel) – I'm not looking forward to the various stages involved in getting there. I wish I could fly! Because I have a couple of hours to kill (this is the ultimate crime apparently) before getting the airport bus I walk in a new direction, up the Paseo del Arenal and through a small park where a beautiful sweet smell wafts over me. Elderly retired men are sitting around or maybe just people who are out of work. I pass the handsome old Bilbao Bank Building, founded in 1857. I find nineteenth century monuments very reassuring and friendly, unlike the impersonal business blocks of today. Opposite is the Church of San Nicolas de Bari, dating from the mid eighteenth century but I haven't got time to explore it today. I have to go all the way back to the hotel to get my case and then back to the Plaza Federico Moya, where the airport bus stops. I'm held up at the traffic lights and the bus slowly pulls away just as I get to it and the driver looks the other way. I then have to wait half-an-hour for the next one. The timing is higgledy-piggledy and not what I was told by those in the know. I still arrive at the airport (it's only a fifteen minute ride) with bags of time which I pass in a café drinking coffee and eating a cold spinach slice of omelette on bread. As we get into position to board the plane the dreaded thunderstorm crashes down, complete with thunder and lightning.

I start chatting to a cool looking young couple from Stoke Newington, voicing my fears. I had spotted the girl earlier because she was wearing a black trilby hat and dark purple trousers and had a tattoo on her foot which matched her T-shirt. He is really nice-looking and every now and again strokes the tip of her nose. She tells me that they were once surrounded by lightning on a night flight over Guatemala and it was utterly beautiful and striking (!) and she wasn't frightened because there was no turbulence, no rocking of the boat so to speak. Apparently they stayed in San Sebastian, hired a car and visited all the little medieval villages off the beaten track, experiencing noisy fiestas and carnivals … 'you don't want to hear the noise bouncing off the walls when you're drunk …' I liked them so much and wished them good luck. They reckoned that by the time the plane actually took off the storm would have passed. I sit in the middle of the plane, they sit at the front. A guy says to me 'this is rotten luck' and I tell him that by the time everyone is seated it will have passed. He is really grateful for this comforting offering and indeed by the time we take off the heavens are smiling. This young man had been staying with a friend in Avilas and the previous summer had busked around northern Spain with a group of mates earning as much as 1000 euros in two days. They made a killing in Biarritz in the expensive restaurants and even got as far as Pamplona, where there is the famous bull running. They slept in campsites. He really was trying to learn Spanish. He said he'd see me on the northbound train (another long wait and this time in the cold and rain) but of course he got into a different carriage. How I admire these adventurous souls in their jaunty gear. What they express is an innocence, a desire not to win, but to live.

Muck in Marrakech

How do you beat depression, boredom, whatever? Well, you certainly don't go on a pilgrimage to Mecca or the Holy Land or start running up and down the stairs to increase your aerobic capacity and flood your brain with life-enhancing chemicals. No, you book yourself onto a convenient flight from Stansted Airport, buy a 'Top 10' guide book and study it hard to ground yourself in the reality of the place and get high on the idea of novelty and change, if not exploration. Wasn't Marrakesh a hippy destination in the 60s and wasn't there some wild song about taking the road to Marrakesh? Surely I'll discover the pure blue skies of deep belief and the joyous profusion of pink and purple bougainvillea. Marrakech is, after all, North Africa.

A week before the trip I've done my homework but I'm getting decidedly nervous. It was the same before I was due to travel to Verona from Cambridge Airport but then a good excuse came up to cancel – the safety concerns about the airport (although no mid-air collisions have yet to materialise) and an unprecedented heat-wave that was sweeping across Northern Italy). I just couldn't see myself taking trains to Milan, Brescia, Bergamo, Lake Garda in my beautiful pink and orange dress. The 'Top Ten Milan and the Lakes' was returned to the bookshelf, to nestle against 'Top 10 Copenhagen and Naples and the Amalfi coast. So, I know I've got to go (my self-esteem would plummet if I didn't) and I make a conscious effort not to let fear invade my bones and drive me insane.

The day of departure dawns and my beloved son drives me to the airport. In the car I tell him that I couldn't decide whether to paint my toenails shocking pink or poppy red and in the end I left them boring and bare (and slightly discoloured I might add) – left them both behind. 'What a self-punisher you are' he declares, 'you should have taken them with.' Arguments are always the same and are usually about wanting the other to change. Outside the airport with a catch in my voice I tell him that I hope he knows how much I love him. He gets into his car and then gets out again to check what day I'm coming back. Us and our damn checking!

Stansted isn't like the other London airports – it has a nice, friendly feel. NOT ANY MORE. Where is that open walkabout central area looking out onto the tarmac? It's been converted into a rabbit warren of shops and god knows what. What was once a few casual security gates has become thirteen lanes packed with grim-looking fliers and guards. I had to speak, to assert my separateness from this long miserable queue. I asked one of the security men how he felt about all the extra lanes. He didn't relish it one bit but added that they're doing more than one hundred and sixty flights a week more than before. You can go to Posnan or Katowice (I had a boyfriend from there in 1978) every day of the week. We should be asking more basic questions such as what is the meaning of life, why are we here at all? Where does the materialism end? We are supposed to respect and celebrate our planet, not use it for our own selfish ends.

One woman before me in the queue is giving me the heeby jeebies, causing me to shut down although I stand up for myself and prove her wrong (ha!) when she loudly and blatantly insists that Marrakesh is two hours ahead and I'll have to find my hotel in the dark. She is fat, blonde and vile (although also God's child) boasting that this is her fifth trip and she's not a fool like me paying £36 for storing baggage in the hold. 'I don't want to be rude but can you tell me how much you paid for your flight?' she mischievously inquires. Of course it's not rude to ask in this competitive impersonal business environment which we all inhabit but the words are shot out like a hard bullet. I could happily shoot her dead. However, this know-all of Marrakesh was really put out about the time issue (that's pretty basic isn't it?) and boards the plane at the rear end. She is rear end and I hope that I'll never see her again. My prayer is answered. My travelling companion is a nice woman from St. Ives, although an itsy bitsy small-minded. She's travelling with hubbie and four friends, one of whom (their leader) suggests going around in identical kit to serve as camouflage. I voice my apprehensions about changing money (the Moroccan dirham is a closed currency) and she stops the EasyJet hostess and asks her about currency exchange at the airport. (Of course I am worrying for nothing – they must change money at the airport – and it really is advisable to keep your petty fears to yourself). It doesn't surprise me when the EasyJet worker replies that she knows nothing about Marrakech – as soon as they land they turn around and fly back to base).

My baggage appears straight away (God's wonders never cease) and I'm out of the terminal asking about the No. 19 bus which goes into central Marrakech. Unlike the bus the taxis are all in place. After some inevitable haggling (just as the guide book says the cost of an airport taxi can hit the roof) and the lucky appearance of an Italian couple who are going the same way I arrive at the edge of Jmaa El Fna Square, the must-see, all-happening 'Assembly of the Dead' which used to be a place of public execution. I realise that without French in this part of the world you'd have a pretty hard time of it. I've mislocated the 'Dabachi' area of the hotel or rather had no idea as to how the city was laid out. (I felt a bit miffed on the plane when I heard more than one person saying that their riad was sending a taxi to the airport to pick them up. Lucky beggars!) I espy a nice, educated-looking. young man walking across the square and I ask him the way to my riad. He's from Rabat and insists on wheeling my suitcase as he asks the locals for directions. I so appreciate his help that I engage him in conversation. We make our way past the raffish 'Café de France' (a useful landmark), into the Souq Al Kessabia and down a narrow, bustling road until we see an unobtrusive sign – Derb el Hajra – on the wall of a secluded street, which is where I get off, so to speak. He, I forget his name, escorts me down this dark residential typically Moroccan alleyway until we get to No.29 which is a heavy oak brass-studded door. He gives his phone number and tells me to call him if I need help with anything.

I ring the bell, relieved that I've safely arrived. I continue to ring and rap the heavy lead knocker but nobody comes. I realise now why I was asked to state my time of arrival. Alert to possible delays I casually typed in 5.30p.m. It's only 4.30p.m and I'm standing, with a slight feeling of panic in my stomach, (perhaps they've forgotten me altogether?) in this old deserted alley full of lovely old houses in that pinky brown colour. I knock on the door of the house opposite and explain my predicament to 'the lady of the house' or is she the cleaner since she has a scarf around her head. She is nice, sympathetic and invites me in. I guess that this place is another riad. It is very elegant. I am served coffee in a lovely Arab pot accompanied by Moroccan biscuits. I recline on the couch and bide my time, enjoying the peace and quiet after the hubbub of the world outside.

Finally the concierge or 'le guardien' as he is called arrives at my hotel and I am let in. I enter what seems like a palace, a virtual Aladdin's Cave of antique objets d'art, quality baroque furniture, rare embroideries and luxurious textiles. There are secret alcoves lined with books and lit with ornate brass lamps and my room on the ground floor, opening onto the lounge area, boasts a gorgeous glittering chandelier, all pale green and white cut glass with thousands of droplets. It resembles the chandeliers in the Brighton pavilion, hanging above the sumptuous dining table. With pride the gardien shows me the massive bathroom (although the wooden door leading to it is a bit makeshift). He tells me that I have the best room – the amethyst suite – but the bed is far too big – he didn't realise that I was coming on my own. In the central living area you look up and see the gallery (housing the other four bedrooms) and the glass panelled roof is well high and can be opened onto an electric blue sky. Not a sound from the outside enters the metre thick walls (except for the faint constant drumming from the square and of course the 5a.m call to prayer). The people had to turn inwards to protect themselves from the ferocious beat of the sun. Anything else would be suicide.

Le gardien (I never found out his name) is sorry that I was locked out. I ask if I can have a key but he says that there isn't one. He looks at me with a certain admiration as I 'hit the town' in order to get some supper. At the end of the quiet dimly lit alleyway is the bustle of daily life. There are tables packed high with jumble and a mass of women searching for jumpers and jackets. The bra table is particularly popular though these young women can't be too fussy about fit and size. Stalls abound selling bananas, green grapes, pomegranates, and the ubiquitous strings of figs and mountains of dates. Walnuts are spread out on a mat on the ground. In booths along the road are grey-haired men busy on their sewing-machines surrounded by gaudy fabrics. They must wonder why the foreigners come; haven't they enough to do at home. Nobody is isolated and alone except perhaps the woman draped in brown cloth from head to toe, her hand open in begging position, a great wart above her nose, immobile like a brown rabbit. I bet nobody celebrated her much when she was young. There are men beggars as well, down on the ground. It's amazing what some find to sell. Teenage girls in close chattering intimacy drink milkshakes and eat pastries in one of the cafes; this is their bounded home for ever and a day. Groups of young men, standing outside, physically bonded, receive disdainful glances. Mothers gaze on sternly as their young sons get a haircut in one of the hole-in-the-wall barbers. As you get nearer 'La Place' there are exits into the souqs. No such thing here as private space. You have to make way for people on their scooters and donkeys pulling carts laden with bananas. There are piles of shoes for sale – from flip flops to boots – 1950s style and jewellery of the utmost tackiness. A long way this from my hotel of too much space which used to be the residence of a very important Moroccan family.

Darkness has fallen and 'La Place' (the place where traitors met their end) becomes an open kitchen. Out are the brightly coloured iron barrows selling fresh orange juice for four dirhams – about 30p – and in are the eateries, each one numbered, offering a menu of brochettes (meat on skewers), spicy sausages, Moroccan salad, olives and the like. Bread comes free. There is a stand selling eggs and onion in pitta bread and the air is smokily pungent with the smell of barbecued meat. (It reminds of Guy Fawkes Night – the only night when my father became excited and alive). I am dragged into eaterie no. 34 – I'm advised not to go next door – and I happily sit down and engage my neighbour in conversation because what he's eating looks nice. He's very nice, looks Moroccan, and tells me that he and his two friends (one of whom is a silent woman) are from Marseilles and are en route for the Sahara, having hired a car. He is a ski instructor and expresses his concern about decreasing amounts of snow in the French Alps. (I must have alerted him to the dire state of the planet!) We part extremely amiably. I enjoy my skewered meat and then wander around the square noting the entertainment on offer. A crowd has gathered around some 'men from the hills' banging their drums and singing their songs. They seem closely in tune with one another, bonded like brothers. Tribal loyalty, and the thickness of blood is sort of in the genes in these parts and history bears this out. They were governed not by obedience and other tame attributes but by ambition and rage.

I walk around the square a couple of times before I recognise the minaret beside 'Al Kessabia' turn-off. I'm going to have to remember that name. I make it to Derb el Hajra, which is written oh so lightly on an inside wall, and ring the bell of no. 29, the Dar Al Assad hotel. To my severe consternation nobody answers yet again – and this time I have absolutely no idea where he's gone and what time he'll be back? God this is my childhood nightmare revisited (and perhaps finally put to rest) when my parents went out on a Saturday night, and most other nights, leaving me to look after myself – overwhelmed with sobbing loss. As I bang on the door in adult righteous indignation a group of little girls gather around, all messy brown hair and poor cotton dresses, sharing my angst. One little girl looks up at me with huge brown eyes becoming deadly serious as somehow she becomes aware of how she'd not survive if separated from her clan. Luckily for me the neighbouring house opens its door and a stout Frenchman emerges. Once again I am invited in, seated and offered a glass of fresh orange juice. The lady of the house tells me that she is an actress. The rescuing man says that he'd never turn his pad into a riad due to the unreliability of staff. I tell my story to two Danes (are they guests or friends?) and they think the concierge's continuing absence is preposterous. My host telephones the guy next door who soon returns. I thank my neighbours for their liberal hospitality and kindness. I tell le gardien that I'm going to be nervous whenever I go out, for obvious reasons. Can't I have a key? He insists that there isn't one. He tells me that his not being around was just an unfortunate mis-timing – he'd gone to get provisions for my breakfast in the morning. From where? There's no supermarket or egg stall around the corner. I am the sole occupant in the sumptuous mansion and perhaps he just got fed-up holding the fort for no one.

He tells me again that my room is choice but the way that it opens onto the lounge, the thoroughfare for all, is a bit strange. I have to let down heavy satin drapes over the stained glass windows. There is no lock on the door to make me feel extra secure but I'm very relieved not to be out on the street, to have my new bed for four days. Le Gardien directs me to one of the cosy alcoves lined with bookshelves where I can sink into the silk and velvet and read my book. I find myself stroking the smooth deluxe satin of a cushion and feeling soothed. Oh, is this why people keep a pet? No problem sleeping when the time comes but it is annoying to be woken up at 5a.m by the wailing call to prayer. No direct mention of this alarum in 'Top 10 Marrakesh'.

I think it's a bright warm day but it's difficult to tell when you're shut away. A huge round table is set up outside my room and the Moroccan cook/housekeeper (the other resident member of staff) sets down plate after plate of beautifully prepared food which actually consists of bread presented in different ways. There is a butter fried egg and pancakes cooked in a funny oil, very sweet yogurt and fresh, flaking pain au chocolat. This, with the coffee, and the freshly squeezed orange juice is the best. I wonder what he does with the nibbled pancakes. A bit of a waste. I slip a couple of triangles of bread into my bag for later, just in case.

Armed with my guide it's time to see the sights. The weather is warm and I'm determined to wear my pink, orange, green and turquoise pleated crepe dress from 'East' together with sandals that are not ideal for traipsing around Marrakech. But anything else would look ridiculous with the loose, floaty dress. I also have a white cotton cardigan, again – just in case. As Freud said: 'there is never the wrong weather, only the wrong clothes'. Down the street everyone is set up for the day's business and the men call out to their mates across the way. Young women, sensibly dressed, are off to work. Emerging into the square I see a man, in a long brown djlaba, (a sort of kaftan) with a tumour on his neck the size of a tennis ball. One of the booths along the way is a proper-looking pharmacy but I've not seen a doctor's surgery. I hope the poor man is OK. The orange men are all in place having replaced the smoky al fresco restaurants with their tables and benches from the night before. They all seem cheerful enough so I expect they earn a living wage. There are a few 'gerrab' (water sellers) in their colourful costumes and tassel-fringed hats floating around but they aren't selling water (brass cups for Moslems, white metal cups for the rest) but doubtless looking for photo opportunities. I pop into a souvenir shop and buy postcards and stamps from a bad-tempered young man. Is it possible that a stamp to the UK could cost £1.60? Maybe. It occurs to me that if you travel alone you must have your wits about you. On the far side of the square, diagonally opposite my turn-off, stand a line of droshkeys, no doubt awaiting a steady stream of tourists. The horses seem in good nick. What is it about this place? Nothing really – just another day in Marrakesh.

The Koutoubia Minaret was built in 1158 and it rises above the city dominating the skyline and creating its character, like the Eiffel Tower in Paris or the Colosseum in Rome. The guy who built it went on to build the tower of the Giralda in Seville and they do look remarkably similar and a lovely sight to behold. Non-Muslims are not permitted entry but through an open door I catch a glimpse of the arcades of horseshoe arches just like the ones in the great mosque in Granada, southern Spain. To the south of the mosque (though what do I know of the points of the compass or locating myself in real space?) are gardens divided by topiary hedges and planted out with roses. There are rose gardens galore and you wonder how they survive the intense heat of the summer months. Only the week before I arrived the temperature was up in the thirties. I'm really grateful that the weather is just fine for walking around.

I'd always wanted to visit the Mamounia Hotel, one of the world's oldest and greatest, and frequent haunt of Sir Winston Churchill. I can't believe it's just over the way and like all the buildings here is pinky brown, not grey. I always check just to make sure (a neurotic habit that irritates my daughter) and then get netted by a taxi-driver guide who gives me the low-down on all the countries he's worked in etc. and how he'll take me to see all of Marrakesh for 10 dirhams an hour. When I talk to people I never suspect they have an ulterior motive which is, for the male of the species, making money. I find out, a greenhorn youth on the door, that the hotel doesn't open its doors to the public until 11am so I make my way to the Saadian Tombs which is within the Medina, flanked on each side by sober cemeteries. A fact of life that everyone dies but the righteous get to sit by God's side and the faithful Christian is resurrected to eternal life, so long as he believes in Jesus Christ, lover of humanity. Because we're so mired in everyday shit we cannot conceive of this. Talking of which – to get to it you have to cross 'La Place des Ferblantiers' which is a hive of open workshops full of bits and pieces of metal and wire whilst cars and motorcycles tear around which makes crossing the road a precarious feat. But gainful occupation takes place out of doors on the street whilst in the UK people sit alone in their own homes watching TV including poor little me! The streets around the Royal Palace (the residence of the present ruler Mohammed the sixth, a kind man, presumably, unlike some of his forebears, mentioning no names, who ruled with an iron fist and performed acts of unspeakable cruelty.) are taken up with young men passionately absorbed in fixing their motorbikes. Who cares about oil, grease and dirt? Sitting on the pavement in any which way position they are totally absorbed and devoid of hang-ups and obsessions. I chat to the young guards outside the palace who ask me about Cambridge and find my presence infinitely amusing. The ugliest among them, with huge teeth, and acne ridden skin, doesn't stop laughing. I ask them if they like their king.

The city walls date from the 1120s when the ruling Almoravid sultan was under threat of attack from the Almohads of the south. Threat of attack I know all about that – it paralyses your very life blood. The scream is never released. The walls were punctuated by towers and gates and are largely still intact and I gaze up in admiration, before entering the dark corridor leading to the tombs, at the 'Bab Agnaou', the "Gate of the Gnawa" which has that distinctive pinkish hue (due to pigments in the native earth) and a decorative workmanship which is eternally beautiful. I'd like to hold the beautiful stone in my hands and kiss it. The guy from the pottery shop who is chatty and friendly – he really does want to share his love of his native city – points me in the direction of the best shop in Marrakesh, a treasure trove of herbs and spices and all things to cure all ailments and diseases. I promise to pay a visit and would feel guilty about breaking my word.

The presence of other tourists makes me want to cry, throw stones, shout obscenities? Can't they put their cameras away for one second? Can't they just look and remember? Or forget, most likely. Maybe they are gathering material for a research project? Maybe they feel obliged to use the latest magical technology which has the bonus of both feeding their self-importance and proving that they are in fact here and in control of their environment. The burial chambers are ranged around a small garden with all sorts of scrubby bushes, white roses and the odd stray cat. The exquisitely carved cedar wood and the Alhambran style decoration, the pillars and general majesty of the place makes you wonder about their ideas on death and the afterlife; no, not really; I'd love to see them in the flesh, talk to a Saadian who was around in Shakespeare's day. I guess they wouldn't have heard of the Tudor and Stuart dynasty.

Having ticked off a major tourist attraction I, true to my word, enter the herb and spice emporium. A young Moslem lady with a cold who speaks English takes me through all the marvellous herbs, spices and oils, explaining their wondrous potencies. I have my lips smeared with beetle juice, or whatever it is, but I forbid her to line my eyes with kohl 'because I am too old for all that'. I've had my time in the sun (to the detriment of my skin actually). The bait having been sprung I could have bought out the whole shop but I don't lose my head and buy a little bottle of argan oil for my daughter (it wards off headaches), real mint tea (excellent for upset tummies) a ginger mix for coating chicken thighs and some black herb which, when sniffed, eliminates the aftermath of a cold and snoring. (My snoring, in Tenerife, drove my daughter to sleep on the living-room sofa. She's generally in life a non-complainer. Accepts what life has thrown at her and does her best with it.) Oh, I couldn't resist a pot of special hand cream composed of green tea which will remove the ugly liver spots (all that sunbathing on the beach in Riccione) on my hands. She asks me if I want to see the bank of grateful letters from customers far and wide. No thank you. When it comes to the bill I deliberately swipe my mind. Too expensive of course but all my own fault. When I come out I espy the elderly man who ushered me in and told him that I actually bought stuff. He laughs. Only later it occurs to me that he must work on commission. It's as if there's a flipping mafia network that works around the city luring foreigners to visit, taste, buy.

Where is my next stop? It's almost lunchtime but there's no 'Pret a Manger' where you can buy a lovely sandwich. There are no sandwiches at all. There are a couple of cafes in 'Place des Ferblantiers' frequented by men sitting alone at tables. I'm certainly not going to join them. The morsels of bread in my bag come in useful. I decide to visit the 'Mellah', the old Jewish quarter which is just outside the Kasbah. I am fascinated by these pre World War Two Jewish communities, these vibrant ghettos, but here in Marrakesh Jews lived peacefully alongside their Arab brethren (as they did in Southern Spain) because they looked almost the same! I pass a hole in the wall full of bits of hardware, from rubber tubing to bicycle guards, hammers and nails and ask the guy if he could direct me to the Mellah. I know that he is Jewish (it's a certain 'look' which is the 'badge' of 'suff'rance') and he (knowing that I know) asks a wizened old grey beard who is standing around outside to escort me to the old synagogue. It's a fair walk and sometimes since there are no pavements we have to mount a high step by a wall. He waits for me outside whilst I scrutinise the turquoise tiled synagogue from the 16th century. I peruse all the photographs outside and indeed all these Jewish people look Jewish Moroccan or Moroccan Jewish. The Moslem concierge asks me if I want to blow the shofah (the ram's horn that is blown in the synagogue on the high holy days (the heavy Day of Atonement when God decides who is to live and who is to die in the year to come; who will wax rich and who will get poor, losing all they have … But constant prayer can tip the balance and alter the final decree. I decline. I'm not the rabbi. Jauntily he takes up one of the many shofas on display and blows it to his heart's content and laughs. That's the spirit man! Then he asks me if I can make a donation. The once thriving community has shrunk to almost nothing.

Walking back through old narrow streets and stony courtyards I ask my 'guide' if I can see how a family lives. We enter a courtyard and an opening in a rocky wall. In a room the size of a bathroom a family is living together. Granny sits in pride of place holding a sickly looking baby, mum is sitting close by and dad stands near the TV set. The Grandma is fat and motherly. There's a white tablecloth on the table and wooden furniture. No room to walk around though and who knows where they sleep. They bring me mint tea, Moroccan biscuits (which are dry like pebbles), pitta bread and a plate of oil. I ask them about their life and they ask me about mine. Women are lovely everywhere. The elderly guy pops his head in and says that he has to be getting back since the shop is closing for lunch. Outside in the street the dad puts out his hand and asks for a present for the child (his daughter had just come home from school and was happily smiling) giving me that 'poor little me' look. Less than graciously I give him less than a pound and he is obviously dissatisfied. What can he do – shoot me? When we arrive back at the shop the 'guide' also puts out his hand and I give him considerably more – something to do with my confusion with the loose change. He is obviously pleased but I expect it was the wrong way round. But all this begging on account of services rendered leaves a bad taste in your mouth.

The next must-see stop is the Badii Palace, which, like the Saadi Tombs is within the Kasbah. I'm not expecting anything and am amazed to discover a ruin that was once a world in itself. (Do I really care about this place, can I be bothered to read all the information – I just want to get round as fast as possible!) The palace was built by Sultan Ahmed El Mansour after the Battle of Three Kings (1578) in which the Moroccans vanquished the Portuguese. It took armies of labourers and craftsmen 25 years to complete. (Always the same scenario). I compare these massive pools (now empty) and sunken gardens, summer house and harem with England in its heyday – all woods and streams and vibrant green and Elizabeth Tudor in her royal regalia inspiring her troops at Tilbury before the Spanish Armada. Never share your fears, only your courage.

I tag onto the tail of an American group from Kansas City but they're proceeding very slowly and because they're mostly elderly they have difficulty clambering over the stones. A nice man asks me if I'm joining them and I honestly reply, 'not really'. We all enter the mosque 'minbar' which the Americans can't help refer to as the 'minibar'. Actually this ten foot high intricately carved pulpit is something to behold, a true work of art. The iman could not sit on the top step because that is reserved for Mahomet. All this religion is something more than mere fantasy and wishful thinking as some would have us believe. Love is a depth of truth, honesty, commitment. Storks have made their nests in the protrusions along the crumbling walls and they stand in majestic silence. One of the guards tells me that they are here on account of the free food and easy living. On the rooftop terrace surveying the whole complex I share a sense of wonder with some French tourists, a friendly big-nosed woman who might be Jewish. The sky is blue and the weather is warm.

My feet are now hurting me, as any sensible person would expect, as I trek back towards the Mamounia Hotel – on and on and on. Not a sandwich bar in sight. No manna from heaven. The traffic is very noisy and I pop into a covered market to gawp at the fresh meat and the displays of black olives and pomegranates. Two guys are busy arranging bouquets and one of them gives me a long-legged red rose. I wonder why he did so and I hold it with pride. I am a latter day hippy, advertising flower power. The Mamounia Hotel is a bit disappointing inside – it's obviously been renovated since Churchill's day. It's very posh and grand and there's a deserted shop selling dull-looking Dior bags. The terrace garden is very nice but the price of a sandwich is astronomical. I sit myself down and look around. There's an elderly gay couple with a dog – quite a few well-behaved dogs actually. I can't help thinking of Dorothy Parker's quip: 'If you want to know what God thinks of money just look at the people he gave it to.' Ugly and hideous enough to make you turn away. I self-possessedly walk through the lunch restaurant in order to explore the environs and speak to the head waiter. He is surprised that I am on my own. Well I certainly am. We have a nice civilised chat and he carefully helps me on with my cardigan. I proceed to walk down the manicured paths which separate the extensive rose gardens – there are seventeen acres of them. The hotel dates from the 19th century, it was a palace for the crown prince of Morocco but was converted in 1923 by the French as a hotel for the railways. I ask to see Churchill's paintings in his old suite but it is out of bounds/occupied by some faceless nonentity or two. It looks like rain and I'm concerned about getting back to base pronto. On my way out through the delightful front garden I see a group of Italians stepping off a tourist coach. I s'pose it's not ideal to be on your own but to be holding onto a group rope, spouting infantile inanities, 'what's the money they use here?' would impel me to burst the bubble, cut loose and run. See yer!

The sky is darkening considerably – I don't know why – and my red umbrella is hanging up in the wardrobe. My left foot is hurting but I have to press on regardless. I reach Jemaa El Fna and am surprised to see a man covered in a veritable cloak of dead birds. A couple of men with pipes are inducing some docile looking snakes to do their stuff. A third man is running after the babies who are keen to escape, covering them with a saucer. I ask if the snakes are dangerous. He answers in the negative and asks me whether I have a husband. I answer in the negative and he turns to me, smugly grinning and says 'Moroccan men beaucoup fuck fuck.' Needless to say I walk away but I should have finished his sentence with 'comme les chiens' (like dogs). Once again I've gone the wrong way – there are two minarets which look the same – but I backtrack and use the 'Café de France' as a landmark. It is tatty and beguiling – with a kind of old world charm but I wouldn't sit down – too many seedy-looking men around and an absence of privacy. It's just not a place where a woman can tuck herself into an inconspicuous corner and read the paper. I enter Souq El Kessabia and recognise the sausage stands and the café selling pastries, thick with cream. When I arrive at the Dar Al Assad and ring the bell and, to my relief, someone opens the door.

My foot was hurting for good reason; there's a mighty blister on the bunion area but at least my dress got an airing and tomorrow it's back to crepe soled sandals. It seems that I am no longer the sole occupant of this riad. Three ladies from Casablanca are seated on the sofa. I never really understood the purpose of their visit and they probably wondered about mine. The aunt was small, plump and pretty (originally from Tunis)) and liked to talk. Her sister sat in silence with a disapproving look on her face (possibly due to the quality of my French). Her daughter, who looked the split image of my next door neighbour, ignored her mother and was constantly on the phone to her husband back home. A cold and condemnatory brace of females. The daughter was complaining about the long drive from Casablanca due to the heavy traffic. (Same the world over). The plump aunt expressed her liking for this hotel – they've stayed here many a time – and the deep armchairs support her collapsed back. She's a sad widow – garnering great comfort from her beloved grandchildren and I can see how pretty she must have been as a young bride of twenty one. Her husband operated in diplomatic circles and they lived in Knightsbridge for four years. Amongst themselves the three women spoke expressively in Arabic.

By now it has started to rain and soon it's coming down in buckets. Talk about 'a hard rain gonna fall'. In fact buckets have to be placed at strategic points in the lounge since the beating sun has melted the joins in the roof, as Le Gardien explains. I bet all the tourists all over Marrakesh are wondering if the day ahead will be fair or foul. I imagine that the main square is empty of people – no open kitchens in this weather. I bet they're cursing the loss of livelihood. The ladies have retired to their rooms and Le Gardien offers to cook me dinner. A table is laid next to the library alcove and he lays before me an exquisitely cooked omelette with a triangle of Dairylea in its centre followed by a salad of minutely chopped beans and cucumber. He says that it is what he eats himself because he has something wrong with his stomach. When I've finished he tells me, smiling from ear to ear, that it has given him great pleasure to cook for me. (It must be so indeed because I was never charged for this meal). I go to my room to grab a tangerine from a bowl and he is amused at how I've supplied my own 'dessert'. He brings mint tea. Doubtless it was his way of saying sorry.

And then something dreadful happens during the course of the evening which shames me to this day. It is deadly quiet in the hotel in spite of the unremitting rain. I wonder what the streets are going to be like in the morning. I'm nestled into the alcove, reading my Isaac Bashevis Singer novel, a family saga set in pre-war Warsaw. Good job that he was awarded the Nobel Prize for literature. I hate crowds and noise but this degree of mute is a bit oppressive. I wonder where Le gardien is. Does he live in? I'm not sure. And then I see him creeping past the alcove and imagine that he has turned back to leer at me – I'm laid out in a relaxed and somewhat unlady-like position on the dark red velvet sofa. I'm sort of sprawling. I should have been sitting bolt upright. Did I imagine it or not? I'm like Macbeth with his flipping dagger. I suddenly feel very unsafe with my unlocked bedroom door and a strange man on the premises. It is time for bed and I'm scared. If he burst in my room and murdered me in the night nobody would ever know. Oh God in heaven what am I to do? I can hear female voices from the gallery – obviously the women are still up and conversing. I know I'll go up and knock on their door and find out more about him. I'm sure they'll reassure me. I have my doubts about this move (I'll probably make a total fool of myself) but I'm well and truly spooked. I can't go to bed in this state. I climb the old staircase and knock on a door, asking to speak to someone. There is silence and then a great commotion as the cold-faced mother opens the door in her long white nightgown and asks what is wrong. The sweet-faced aunt hovers in the background totally bewildered. I think they'd been asleep and I'd woken them up. The voice(s) I heard was probably that of her daughter on the phone to her husband. But I certainly heard voices. I apologise profusely and rush downstairs, not fully aware of the damage I've inflicted but aware enough to know that I've inflicted on others the very thing that has so threatened and enraged me in the past. Bloody hotel guests coming in late and slamming their doors or mother banging on mine urging me to 'rise and shine' – calling me a lazy, hostile, selfish bitch. She was good with adjectives.

I sleep well and next morning I receive cold glances from the table opposite. En passant the bony-faced mum asks me if this is the first time I've travelled alone and suggests, coldly, that I read too much fiction. It is incumbent upon me to apologise and explain. I insist that if I hadn't heard voices I wouldn't have disturbed them. Later in the day I tell my story so dramatically that the sweet aunt can't help but laugh. What a lovely nature she has because she is still talking to me in spite of the fact that my 'break in' so scared her that she was shaking and couldn't get back to sleep for hours. She then shows me how to use the shutters which shut from the inside, keeping out psychic intruders. Ah, there's a trick! And of course le gardien is no threat at all, quite the reverse. He's recently married and has a small baby. She tells me the history of how she has suffered with her back, what she likes to eat 'chez elle' in Casablanca, and reminiscences about a Tunis that no longer exists (surprise, surprise) and I am touched by her ability to forgive. Would I, who value sweet sleep so highly, have been so forgiving?

I always admired the French fashion designer Yves Saint-Laurent, a highly gifted and sensitive man, and was sorry when he died. He lived in Marrakech for a long time and loved the place. The Majorelle Gardens were created by the French artist Jacques Majorelle as a botanical sanctuary around his studio and the property fell into disrepair until it was rescued by Yves and his partner Pierre Berge. How do I get there? That's the question but I have a vague sort of map. After the deluge of the night before the streets aren't as muddy as you'd expect and everyone is going about their daily business. Skirting around the Koutoubia Mosque and attempting to cross the busy thoroughfare I ask someone the way and then this guy pops up out of nowhere and offers to show me the short cut. The short cut seems a long cut indeed as we pass seedy looking bathhouses (I'm sure they are very nice but I'm reluctant to try one I'm not really in the mood) and lots of butcher outlets selling stuff that you'd rather not see, let alone eat. He keeps on pointing out shops selling toilets and baths for rich people. It's all a bit muddy and rough and claustrophobic and I start to tell him that I'm Ok on my own – I don't need his guidance. He insists that I do. He's an evil looking bastard in red jeans and a dirty purple jacket and I can't shake him off. I lag behind and ask another passer-by if I'm proceeding in the right direction and it seems that I am.

When we get to the bus stop area, frequented by working folk, I firmly take my leave. He asks for money and when I refuse starts swearing at me in Arabic, calling me a whore, no doubt, and more. I lose him in the crowd and approach a nice policeman and report him. He asks me what he was wearing and seems genuinely concerned and embarrassed. But hey, kick off the dust and onwards march.

The day is a little overcast and drizzly but still warmish. Because it is reasonably early a horde of tourists haven't descended on the place but there are still some looking at all the marvels through their lens finder. They don't look and decide what to capture i.e. making a beeline for a pool filled with golden carp or a pot in Majorelle's signature shade of electric cobalt blue but simply photograph the whole bloody lot. I complain to an attendant who listens and then 'shuts down' in bewilderment. There is a cactus garden and bamboo garden with plants taken from all over the world but what is most beautiful are the bright warm terracotta paths and the preponderance of that amazing blue. You can see all of Yves Saint-Laurent's 'Love' posters which were sent as New Year greeting cards to his fashionable friends and clients. There is a shrine to his memory in the gardens.

I decide to explore the New City, known as Gueliz, and I need the map for this. You just have to check you're going the right way otherwise you've walked a mile for nothing. Best to accost a policeman or a respectable member of society. A little way up from the gardens is the villa where Yves lived, set of course in beautiful gardens of flowering pink and purple bougainvillea. It is closed to the public. The view from his gate is a dusty main road full of noisy traffic beyond which are scrubby fields and derelict buildings, and I wonder why he and his partner loved Marrakesh so much. Is the noise of the traffic so loud due to the flatness of the city; one can imagine it as a trading oasis in the Middle Ages. Armed with my guide book I make my way down the Avenue Yacoub el Mansour, passing lots of cafes which are the hang-out of pasty-faced, middle-aged men. Do they have a wife at home or an unpaid slave, such as my grandmother was. I am pleased to actually discover a restaurant recommended in my guide book; it is called 'Al Fassia' and it is totally run by women. Anyway, I go in, check the place out and say I'll be back. But I know that when I start to wilt nothing happens; I just can't be bothered. And then there is the anticipated hassle with the taxi-driver.

It was early in the 20th century that Marrakesh (due to the French) broke out of the wall of the medina and who can blame anyone wanting to escape a backward world of no plumbing, no electricity, no cars. I fall into the Boulevard Zerktouni and Mohammed the Fifth and search out the Rue de la Liberte with its French style buildings and exquisite Moroccan patisserie. I can't help noticing a deranged local, obviously mentally ill, walking up and down. Not a pretty sight. I find the Hotel Renaissance, built in 1952, and frequented by hippies in the late 1960s. I go in and explain my interest but no one is aware of the history of the place, the fact that it's an iconic building. From the rooftop terrace you have a great view of Marrakesh, its total flatness with the Koutoubia Minaret rising up as a landmark and the peaks of the Atlas mountains in the distance. Aren't they meant to be snow-covered to complete the romantic image? I don't expect I'll take a day trip to visit them. I chat to a waiter who is the same age as my son who is an absolute native of Marrakesh. Why shouldn't he be? He finds me some cushions and I enjoy a solitary coffee, resting my feet, and munching on something I nicked from the breakfast table. When I come to pay the young guy at the till charges me thirty dirhams for my coffee because I was on the roof but then there is a problem with change with the whole crew searching their pockets for tatty notes and I end up paying twenty five.

Telling Le Gardien that I was impressed by the rose gardens around the Koutoubia Minaret he fulsomely praises the Menara Gardens which are the real deal. They date from the 12th century – ooh, a nice bit of history and are laid out in the Islamic style. As this is pronounced as gospel truth I take it upon myself to walk the long road, Avenue de la Menara, which terminates at the gardens. It is bordered on one side by extensive olive groves. What is it about this road? You walk and walk and never seem to get anywhere. Two girls advise me to take the bus but I can't see any buses or bus stops. I meet up with an elderly American couple and they are as exasperated as I am plus the fact that the lady has mobility problems. I leave them behind and sometime later I see that they have turned back. Cars and motorbikes whizz by. A youngster on his bike isn't going too fast and I flag him down. Are the Menara Gardens really at the end of this damned road? He assures me that they are and offers me a ride as you'd offer someone a Kleenex tissue if they were crying. He's so casual and relaxed about it that it seems absurd to refuse but I do. I walk in the midday sun (but this is November not July) and finally, somewhat footsore, I arrive at the oasis. On some scrubland next to the road are a herd of real live camels, including some babies. I wonder how they arrive at this spot and am told that they're there for the tourists. Outside the wide entrance to the gardens a guy is selling nut crackle bars which are tasty and will do for lunch. You can't allow yourself to starve. At the end of another long path there is a green tile-roofed pavilion overlooking a very large pool which is backed by stadium style tiered seats. You have to pay to go in and it's all a bit weird. Where are the gardens? I'm ready to have my mind blown on masses of purple bougainvillea. But I just encounter miles of olive groves, not a flower in sight. I even enter a no entry zone and it is the same thing plus an orange tractor. I sit on a stone and eat my lunch. I walk back to the pavilion and pay the four dirhams entrance fee, walk around the pool and sit in the sun. I decide to buy another nut bar to save my life. There's a little booth where you can buy fresh orange juice which is always nice although twice the price of what they charge in the square. I have no choice but to take a taxi back into town and it can't be denied that I give the poor guy a rough ride for his money. I insist on my price – proving that I'm in control of my life – and since he hasn't got change he follows me in his car as I go into one flipping hardware store after another on the Place Foucoult to change money. Only in the garage do I find a young mechanic who has a wad of notes in his pocket. The taxi driver accepts his wage grudgingly and off he goes. When you're miserable you're mean and I was a bit. Crossing the square I give a wide berth to the snake charmers and observe a bit of drama with the monkey man whose monkey, dressed in a long pale pink jumble sale style dress topped with a white frilly cap, has escaped and is bounding round the square being a real monkey and not a thing that earns money. Two British girls from the Midlands (how strange to hear the English language) express their distaste for all the primitive goings-on and, the night before, on their arrival, managed to find a bar in spite of the pouring rain. By now the owner has caught the creature and she, in her frilly cap, raises a terrified face to the man and their lips meet in a kiss. (How can you kiss a monkey – who knows what beastly germs she might carry?) She has been naughty, very bad, but has returned to her chains. A woman, laughing hysterically in fear and amusement, poses with the monkey on her arm. This will be a good picture to view back in Britain.

    Back in the hotel I think that I espy a slight staining of blood in my panties. Well, that's it, I have cancer of the uterus. I have to accept it. This once happened before and, to be on the safe side or whatever, I was sent for a medical scan at some damned hospital. As I lie passive and inert on the operating table I wonder what the woman is seeing as she scans her screen. Is she going to turn to me and say: 'there is a strange dark cloud on the horizon and we have to investigate further, under general anaesthetic.' I freeze in terror and want to scream: 'burn in hell you wicked witch, you've always longed for my destruction although I've done nothing to deserve it. It's not my fault that I am younger and prettier and far, far more sensitive than you. You really are the grim reaper.' Anyway I leave the aforesaid pink panties on the edge of the bathroom sink to be heavily scrubbed out later. Believe you me, innocent reader, in the Jewish Religion female blood is deemed to be bad. It's not the colour of blood when you prick your finger but the dark red of rust or chrysanthemums.

The owner of this pad, a Moslem woman in a headscarf, insists on booking me into Al Fassia for the following evening. The three women from Casablanca chat with her in Arabic. Maybe she's shown up on account of the leaking roof. Once again I've pulled open the thick oaken door and am out into the street. I decide to eat at a little restaurant/café on the edge of a little square at the top of my secluded street. It actually turns out to be pretty OK – brochettes, salad, bread and tea for about three quid. A European looking guy sits down at another table and eats ravenously. All well and good and I return to the hotel to read my book. I tell le gardien that I was pleased with the restaurant and he says that it's a good place and the guy who runs it is his mate. The hard-faced sister from Casablanca (originally Tunisian) has warmed to me, in her own sarcastic way, and suggests that I shouldn't sit around reading but should take more exercise. They want me to accompany them for an after dinner stroll. I have no reason to refuse and us four set out for Jemaa El Fna and the surrounding souqs into which I've yet to venture due to their claustrophobia. They express interest in all the things I ignore. There are still a few water sellers roaming around in their colourful costumes and tassel-fringed hats but no longer ringing their copper bells to announce their arrival. It's now about theatre. (Apparently the brass cups were meant exclusively for the Muslims while the white-metal cups were for the thirsty from all other religions.) The ladies, indicating the incense sellers, tell me that burning incense in the home when they had winter fires was a common practice but no more. 'Women go out to work' asserts the bony-faced sister. How small they are – certainly under five foot. The daughter isn't nice; sort of cold and empty and her aunt tells me she never eats that's why she's so lovely and slim.

We follow her into the souks. Ah, observing all the pointy-toed, brightly-coloured silly looking slippers hanging up I realise that we are in the Souk des Babouches. 'It's certainly warmer in here' I exclaim. We trail after what's her name who is looking at tea services which consist of brightly-coloured glasses arranged around a central pot. Apparently she already has one and anyone can see that they're all the same. I ask the sweet plump aunt if she drinks wine at home (she seems the wine drinking sort) and she replies: 'I am a Moslem we don't drink alcohol'. We go further into the souks and it's a good place for young men because they sell proper gear – jeans, hoodies and trainers. I don't think any of the local youth aspire to be snake charmers or water sellers unless they come from the desert. There are lots of people sitting at benches greedily devouring Harira (spicy soup) and snails. I expect I should have a go the following evening – see what I am missing. At a sedate pace we make our way back to the riad. On the corner of the road what looks like mince is being fried in a pan and packed into pockets of pitta bread. The plump aunt wonders how anyone can eat just bread and meat without vegetables. How dark it looks. On arriving at the massive oak door of our pad the daughter/niece produces a key, to my amazement. Apparently she has one because she is a friend of the proprietor.

That night everyone gets a decent night's sleep although the sweet aunt is afflicted by her back problems which have resulted in her having a huge stomach. After breakfast I tell the cook/housekeeper that I intend to visit the Medersa Ben Youssef, one of the city's most impressive buildings built by the Saadian sultan, Moulay Abdellah around 1565. He tells me how to get there. It seems that the road to hell is paved with good intentions. Reaching the point where my secluded pinky brown residential street meets with the poor busy road (whose name I never learnt) I see a guy on a motorbike whom I stop to check directions even though I know exactly where I'm going. 'Be gone coward under your burden of doubt!' He tells me that through the souq is the wrong way, the long way round and anyhow the Medersa is closed until 3pm and today is a great day to visit the Tannerie because all the Berbers are descending on it. His sister, married to a guy from Birmingham, lives in Wembley. He himself is from the Sahara Desert (really?) and if I hop on his bike he'll take me to the Tannerie, which will be enriched by the Berber presence. What to do? If the 16th century theological college is closed until 3pm I have nowhere to go, nothing to do. And I want to be like normal people who ski and play tennis and ride on the back of motor bikes. With some trepidation I get on and off we go, tearing through the crowded street (or rather people move aside to let us through) and with my arms around his waist he tells me that he felt cold this morning but now he feels warm (hang on mate that wasn't the point at all). On the open road, outside the city walls, he stops to put on his helmet ('it's the law') and I hang on nervously. I hear myself wanting to ask 'are we nearly there yet?' but I suppress this childish inquiry. 'You're beautiful', he says. This absurd utterance is followed by a heavy silence.

We have at last arrived at the Tannerie and I am relieved to be on firm ground. My driver (I forget his name) introduces me to the tannerie man who is going to show me how animal hides are turned into leather. Driver guy tells me that he'll wait for me whilst I am shown around. No sign of any colourful Berbers from the mountains. A clump of mint is thrust into my hand to protect me from the stink of the animal hides. He starts explaining all the processes and I realise where this is all leading. I'm more interested in the subconscious mind than in how the poor skin of camels and goats becomes a flashy leather handbag. Actually I'm thinking about the poor men who do this job day in and day out and live on the premises and how they must smell to their wives. At the end of the tour I am taken into the shop where the salesman 'spiel' is in full throttle and a mute lad lays out mats and carpets for me to inspect. I have to make it very clear that I'm not buying anything, that in fact I DON'T LIKE SHOPPING FOR BAGS. He gets the message and something rudely changes in his face and manner as if to say, 'well, get out then, I won't waste my breath any longer'. Well, fair enough to feel like that, as we all do, but one is supposed to behave in a more civilised manner, exercising some self-control.

I too feel a bit pissed-off; I'm fed up with people trying to squeeze me for money. (That morning after breakfast the gardien had presented me with my bill to give me time to make frequent trips to cash machines to withdraw the money. I wonder why they don't accept cards) I make my feelings clear to the driver. He realises that I am angry and says 'do you want to come back or do you want to walk?' Without a doubt I want to walk. Actually I don't think that Mohammed was bad – he just had the Marrakesh mindset whereby foreign tourists are swept off their feet and made to part with their money. I pass an old school and the boys are playing football in the playground (it is indeed a holiday) and one of them leads me through some alleyways in the direction of Place Jemaa El Fna. All the old city is an endless rabbit warren which is full of charm but nobody wants to live at the bottom of the pile. As my immigrant grandmother said, 'I wanted to raise myself in life'. I give the twelve year old boy (who is happy to practise his English) a tip but I think he expected more. Tough shit. I should probably trust more to my sense of direction and leave the poor locals alone. My daughter doesn't have this ridiculous soft, wet side to her brain. The truth is that Marrakesh is scrambling mine.

I decide to explore the souks to the north of 'La Place' although by my absence of reckoning it could be S.S. East or N.N. West like those horrible navigation problems that we had to do in Maths at school. ('Once again, you've got your knickers in a twist'). I'm following the Rue Bab Doukkala (I think) in order to find Dar Cherifa which is a beautifully renovated townhouse dating back to the 16th century. (The 16th century was obviously a boom time in Marrakech as it was in England after the crushing of the Armada and those damned aggressive Spaniards.) All along the way males of all ages are sitting by their shops, in close convivial connection with their neighbours. Lots of glasses of tea. It's amazing how these utter gems, open to the sky, are so difficult to find, buried in the maze of unlit alleyways. These homes, these hidden abodes, were cool oases for the rich. Better here than Caesar's Palace or any other place that advertises material wealth and its hollow emptiness. The truly rich have lots of passion and the discipline of work is a harness not a straitjacket.

So it's goodbye Dar Cherifa and a long futile search for Dar El Bacha, the former residence of Thami El Glaoui, the much-feared ruler of Marrakesh and southern Morocco during the first half of the 20th century. Quite normal then, especially amongst powerful men, to keep an extensive harem. No possibility of escape. Why do I want to go there then? I suddenly remember, with a great flush of embarrassment, that I'd left my stained pink panties on the edge of the sink for the poor cleaner to behold: oh, my God, the thought is awful, how disgusting am I, but there's nothing I can do about it. I walk this way and that and stumble on a riad called Palais Donab, down Dar El Bacha which proves to be a very long road with lots of jewellery and antique shops. Palais Donab draws me in and after using the loo I sit myself down at a table in the shade and soak up the peace and calm. A waiter passes me and I ask if it's OK to do what I'm doing – absolutely nothing and not taking up much space. It's a gorgeous spot; a central pool is surrounded by orange, grapefruit and lemon trees. A young man comes in, goes to the gents, emerges in his swimming trunks, takes a dip and prepares to sunbathe. I engage him in conversation and he tells me that Essaouira on the coast is a lovely place and he wishes that he and his girlfriend had stayed overnight. Their riad lacks a pool and that is why he's here. I think to myself that I should probably have gone to this significant sun-beaten port (I did see a shop advertising trips down the busy road that leads to the square but was in 'can't be bothered' mode due to length of time on the bus/coach and money involved.) today, my last, because, as the young man said, you can have too much of Marrakesh. He leaves and I stay. Actually I go up to the terrace where I too stretch myself out on a sunbed. I am in the midst of flowers and terracotta roofs and I tell myself that this is where I'd stay if I ever come here again. A riad worker comes over and l am full of praise; she replies, calmly and equitably, that you have to pay if you want to relax and I should make my way to the reception desk. I hasten to find my way out into the street. It hadn't occurred to me that that chap had probably paid to use the premises. I walk away as fast as I can. Dar al Bacha, surrounded by guards, looks like a prison and is closed to the general public.

Apparently the café Arabe in the Rue Mouassine is a must visit and I can see why. The roof terrace is typically Moroccan (there are even striped mattresses in alcoves on which you can lounge) as is the view across flat old terracotta Marrakesh. The spells of grilled lamb and aubergine are tantalising. It would be the place to come with your lover or family members although it is a bit too crowded with just such as these. It would be ridiculous on my lonesome ownsome to sit down and eat. And I must remember to ask Le gardien or the chef to cancel my dinner date for one at 'Al Fassia'. What's the point? I see a man with his wife who is also holding a copy of Top Ten Marrakech and I say 'snap!' He says that his is in Italian but agrees that it's a bloody good guide. It never lies.

For the life of me I can't find the Mouassine Fountain and the souks are closing in. I can't remember if I saw the Mouassine Mosque or not but the dirty dried-up fountain, which consists of four bays, three for animals and one for humans, is a sorry sight. This is the only black mark against the guidebook. And people must have thought me somewhat mad in my search for this neglected spot. An arched gateway next to the fountain leads to the Souk des Teinturiers. I am looking at scarves in a vague sort of way and suddenly I am collared and a young man is showing me what the dyes are made from – how dark muck can explode into cobalt blue and royal purple. I have absolutely no intention of buying a silk scarf but there is one that is rather nice in shades of pink and orange. It will match my lacy 'F&F' Tesco dress. I drive a hard bargain and when I come out with my usual wheeze of not being a shopper and rejecting technology he mentally dismisses what is so obviously an absurdity. He's impressed that I can do Maths in my head and we part company on equitable terms. Only those who have a real chip on their shoulder are dangerous enemies.

Back at the hotel I feel nervous about entering the bathroom but go in I must. The poor cleaner picked up my unwashed panties and put them, neatly folded, on the chair. What an angel – I hope she was wearing rubber gloves. I tell le gardien that I'll have to make another couple of trips to the cash machines which are at the far end of the square. Don't they trust cards? Apparently the machine is broken and I suppose there is no hurry to get it fixed on account of the shortage of guests. The Arab ladies have departed for Casablanca, never to be seen again. I make my usual trip to the square determined to eat snails. Three or four eateries are selling them and people are seated on benches, avidly picking the poor wet creatures out of their shells. I am invited to sit down and join the happy eaters but at the last moment I change my mind. On the way back to the hotel I buy two bananas from a stall and the grisly old man charges me about 80p. I'm getting fed up with this racket. On the corner of my road is a milkshake booth which is incredibly popular. I ask what the ingredients are or something of that nature and a young woman actually offers me her glass to try some. No fear about germs, what horrible disease she might catch from me – it's all perfectly natural and friendly. I drink. There is this generous open hospitable side to the people. Bread is the staff of life and is shared. I watch a young boy holding his baby brother and how responsive he is when the baby investigates his shirt buttons. Other youngsters are crowded round, all eating that pile of dark mince packed into a pocket of pitta bread. I inquire the price and it's only about five dirhams – 30p.

I buy and eat and it's tasty. I had cancelled my dinner at the fine restaurant in town.

Reading my book all evening I am aware of a very heavy head – something is not right. Before I go to bed I lie for ages in a hot bath – perhaps that will do the trick. During the night I am horribly sick – I just want to lie prostrate on the bathroom floor – and what is just as bad is the delirium – my mind is full of souks, souks, souks. When I relate all (nearly all) to my son back home he gets angry and asks me why I didn't call for help. 'Who would have heard?' I reply. In the morning I know that I have to traipse to the cash machines to withdraw the rest of the money. Le gardien and the chef are cross with me for eating at a disgusting meat stand and say that they warn all their guests never to eat in the square. (But the square is OK – all the foreigners are there). The chef says that at lunchtime he'll wheel my case to the taxi rank – near the droshkies. I wonder if he will; I doubt it – he'll probably have disappeared. The staff here keep very odd hours. I get them the money.

I lie on my bed all morning wishing away the hours. I talk a little to the cleaner – she probably thinks that I am lazy as hell. I was wondering about stealing the lovely lavender soap in the shower cubicle but decide not to in order not to smirch my reputation with her. These cleaners do a great job. I was once a cleaner – when my daughter was a baby – I had to clean a seven bedroomed house and an office every day and my boss checked the surfaces for dust … needless to say I wasn't much cop – too much other stuff on my mind – like coping with a drunken, abusive partner. The chef is as good as his word and wheels my case to the taxi rank and finds me a decent driver. Every hurdle surmounted brings me closer to the promised land. An end to fear and pain – I want to be home, home, home.

At the airport which isn't very far at all, just beyond the Menara Gardens, there is all the palaver over changing money (the Dirham is a closed currency) and filling out an exit form which has to be stamped at another desk. I am three hours early. Nothing to do but wait. On the plane I sit next to an English lad of twenty five who is travelling with his mate. He tells me that he never goes anywhere unless he has a contact in the place. We talk a lot about life – he studied philosophy at university (so did I – for a year – dropped out not because I failed my exams but because I was so shocked that I'd passed them) and was just about to quit his mundane boring job in a mobile phone outlet. He was fed up with being battered by people's complaints. How quickly the time goes when you can talk about books and the like. His friend's dad was picking them up at the airport. I asked about a taxi but the given price was eighty six quid. I waited for the train to Cambridge. 'I love England' I shouted inwardly. It's all about feeling safe. A taxi outside Cambridge station brought me back to Spring Lane, and home sweet home. I can't even bear to look at the stuff I bought in the spice emporium – everything connected to Marrakech makes me feel sick. My son says that I look pale and my daughter is angry with me for going it alone.

Nobody alive can understand why except me. I'm certainly not a poor lonely outcast searching for God knows what. But I need to prove to myself that I don't need anyone else and can endure superhuman feats of loneliness and isolation, sink to the bottom of the ocean, and then, by the grace of God, rise to the surface again. I'm not some frilly lightweight. But did I have fun in Marrakesh, do I take away warm memories, do I ache to return, did I make new friends? The answer is an unadulterated NO. The best thing was the gentle warm smile of le gardien as he handed me the dish of beans that he had prepared for me (hopefully he remained blissfully innocent of the out-of-control savagery I slandered him with) and the sight of the majestic storks atop the crumbling walls of the Badii Palace. And the abundant supply of fresh orange juice. Just another day in paradise.

Nuts in Naples

Well, I've done it again! I've made arrangements to go to a place where I don't know a soul and where anything untoward could happen-that is, if I don't keep myself to myself and not engage with all and sundry. But all and sundry are human and friendly. Surely I'd know if a bad apple crossed my path and I had to run for cover?

My flight to Naples is from Stansted (a Stansted that is now unrecognisable with its rabbit warren of shops; what happened to the noble spaciousness and glass dome that once was?) and I'm booked to stay at the Hotel Caravaggio in the historic city centre, behind the cathedral. The hotel is described as a 'restored medieval building exuding style.' Since I believe everything I read, am seduced by words, this is the hotel for me. Failing all else, the weather in mid-September is bound to be good. But who can predict anything anymore in our overheated war-torn unstable world?

Looking at my map it seems that the hotel won't be difficult to find (surely anyone in the street will be able to direct me to the Duomo?) and the city is only a short bus ride away from the airport. Unfortunately, my Italian has gone into hibernation and nothing much comes out when I try to locate the bus stop for the city centre. Finally, I get on the 'Alli' bus, and from my front seat observe that the driver is on his mobile as he negotiates the multitude of lanes leading out of the airport. He didn't open his doors for a guy who just missed departure by a hair's breadth and the angry man banged his fist on the glass panel. The bus driver retaliated with a rude gesture and a barrage of profanities. No one seemed shocked. But I wish he'd get off his phone.

I get off at the train station and henceforth no one knows anything. Not even at the information booth where the consultations drag on and nobody gives a damn. I can't believe that they don't know their own city. I poke my head down some of the narrow streets which are hellishly dark and sinister. No house painters, window cleaners or double glazers venture down these blind alleys and indeed the middle-aged men who are sitting together on the pavement, with their massive paunches, wear an expression of feral dissatisfaction. I won't ask *them* for directions. I ask everyone else, and the trouble is that there is such a maze of small streets to get lost in. Dragging my case behind me I traipse on and on, determined to find the damned address and hey, what a sense of satisfaction I feel when I finally locate Piazza Cardinale Sisto Riario Sforza, which is pretty well hidden away. Looking at the map in the quiet of my room I realise that I went the long way round town. But the Neapolitans, God bless 'em, have a habit of waving their arm in a general direction which I don't find very helpful. When you ask them to be more specific, they don't bother to repeat themselves. 'What, I have other fish to fry; I'm not going to waste any more energy over YOU'. Is this what they're thinking? I doubt it. I don't think they are thinking anything.

This piazza could be described as being in a poor state of repair which is not the same as 'shabby chic' but it does have some atmosphere – probably because the sky is blue and the sun is shining. The entrance to the hotel is an arched wooden door in a pale peach coloured wall – the surrounding walls are flaky and grey and the balconies of these apartments are flanked by washing. They are dismal indeed and a man in his vest, leaning over the iron railings of his balcony, espies me looking around critically and sends me an evil – but he's not quite sure if I deserve it or not because he can see that I am not cruelly closed and frowning but am smilingly admiring the wonderful obelisk and sainted statue in the centre of the tiny piazza and enjoying the sight of the buildings that passed me by on my arduous trek from the scary station area. From the architecture everywhere you get the sense that here were the Normans, the Bourbons, and the Spanish. History, which owes its fascination to the fact that it *isn't* about peace, love and understanding, and in my book I read about how the city suffered terribly during World War Two but there's no trace of devastation, nor any commemorative blue plaques. All the corpses have been cleared away and are now resurrected with our Lord and Saviour Jesus Christ. Maybe humans are all poised between God and the Devil, between the triumph of salvation and the abyss of earthly appetites. The lust to possess is bound up with the fear of loss, of not having. It's good to be above all that, to know who you are and where you're going.

I am greeted at reception by a nice young woman whom I later find out to be the same age as my daughter although she looks much younger. She is very smiley and friendly, and it seems as if her very lightsomeness is a willed response to something that is weighing her down. She shows me to my room and laughs off the problem with the door handle, overriding my slightly anxious bad-tempered irritation. Surprisingly, I soon get the knack of opening it. The room is quite bare and is at the back of the hotel (as always, I request a quiet room) looking out onto the general decay of the surrounding homes. I'm back down at reception because there is no soap in the shower area and no large bath towel. Ilenia, the receptionist, is apologetic as she hunts for the keys to housekeeping and when I comment on the Caravaggio painting in the foyer ('The Seven Acts of Mercy') enthuses that it is housed opposite in the 'Pio Monte della

Misericordia' which was a charitable institution founded in 1601. Just think – I am in the vicinity of a real live Caravaggio. Visiting the church – I pop out to take a look at it in the Via Duomo, and discover a gloomy place set back from the street by a five arch loggia – will be my first stop in the morning. The weather is balmy warm and I exchange my jacket for a light white cardigan. The lounge area of the hotel looked far nicer on the hotel's website; in reality it is medieval grim rather than chic, the red and yellow leather armchairs hardly mitigating the effect of the rough walls and the cave like effect. In the dark recess there is a bar and T.V. area and beyond that the breakfast room. I'm looking forward to the breakfast table; I hope there'll be delicious coffee and luscious continental croissants.

Well, it's time to venture out, equipped with my trusty guidebook, in order to find some supper. Years ago, a Neapolitan student, (boasting that Naples was the best place in the world – as they all do) prepared for me a list of eating establishments and top of the list was a pizza place called 'Sorbillo' beloved by students, on the Via dei Tribunali. I eventually find it (Via dei Tribunali is nearly as long as London's Oxford Street and cuts the city from east to west as the Via Toledo dissects it from north to south) and join the queue of hungry hopefuls, waiting for the place to open. Skinny old ladies with black headscarves, sitting on wooden kitchen chairs outside their family shops don't hiss at me or poke my eyes out when I politely ask if I'm going the right way but, on the contrary, are sweetly innocent and friendly, happy to encounter a new face on the block. I scan their lined old faces for a hint of malice but there is none. The old men are equally friendly. When I buy a single red pepper; old and wrinkled and deeply scarlet, from a fruit and veg man he doesn't rant and rave that all he's made off me is sixteen pence. But, in order to justify my minimal purchase, I feel obliged to tell him that it's a present for my daughter so she can see the difference between a real pepper and the thin watery supermarket variety. He laughs (having understood) and it's clear that laughter is his stock in trade.

Once in the restaurant I make my way upstairs, to avoid the crowd, and sit myself down at a table for four. I hear English, albeit American English, being spoken at the next table and make myself known to my neighbours. The woman asks me to join them and then reckons she better check with her husband to see if he doesn't mind. Very unlikely that he'd reply in the negative (even if he didn't like the look of me). They come from Alaska or somewhere and they tell me about their road trip down the length of Italy and show me photos of their lovely Air B&B accommodation in Naples. Hmm, perhaps I should have thought of that? The wife, who is probably in her early fifties, tells me about her strict running regime which is loosening up a bit after thirty years or so. She seems very strict about everything. She informs me that swimming in chlorinated water poisons the skin. She says that their three sons are 'a pain in the butt'. She doesn't like the way that the table is laid in the restaurant, having been raised in a place where things were 'done properly', but finds no fault with the pizza, which I find lamentable. It's one of those cheapo pizzas which are stretched thin, like grey old skin, and give people the illusion that they are getting a huge generous piece of Italian goodness. I order mine with artichokes and it comes with the dead outer leaves of the artichoke scattered across the scant tomato paste. It is altogether a thin and pasty experience and the crafty owners of the joint, preying on people's gullibility, must be raking it in. Nevertheless, I am surprised because much of the clientele is local. In my abode I can safely assert that I make pizzas to die for, crisp and golden and tasty with spinach, anchovies, olives and the rest. Perhaps my paternal grandmother's genius for making something out of nothing has passed into me! Obviously, I can't complain but I vow never to visit the place again. Following the couple downstairs (she was looking ahead to her early morning run) I notice how the tendons in her neck, arms and legs are stretched tight, like wire. She'd be difficult to chew through.

Anyhow, I thank them for their company and make my way back to the hotel, taking in anything of note on the sidewalk. There's a grocer that sells packets of multicoloured pasta shapes, but I know I couldn't fit them into my overnight case (packed to capacity in great anxiety). I pass a kind of recess in the street where all the drop-outs congregate. No doubt I'll pass that way again and observe the space. It's always sad when you see a young woman dressed like a dolly bird with clown make-up and her elder sister in black, who is the saddest of the sad, mumbling to herself.

Back at the hotel (you have to ring a buzzer which prompts the receptionist, if he or she is around, to activate the door) I can't help telling Ilenia how tired I am. Why is it that I am attacked by an insidious sense of dread the night before I go anywhere (and the days prior to departure are just as bad). It's the fear of the unknown. It's like an exam. I don't, of course, expose all this mind-blowing angst to Ilenia, who is worked off her feet for seven hours a day six days a week and receives a monthly pay cheque of five hundred euros. 'Ah London', she sighs, dreaming of the Promised Land where the streets are paved with gold and employees are held in high esteem. She does have a friend in London but can't really entertain the thought of leaving home, which is an apartment shared with her widowed mother and unemployed younger brother, because her mother needs someone to moan to – she has 'lots of problems' and although she loves her, she can't bear to be in the house with her and it's an escape to come to work. She announces soberly that she has no father (ah, I think to myself, just like my offspring) – but, when the statement is expanded on, the comparison collapses. Her father, an electrical engineer, was killed five years ago in a work-related accident. So she had a dad for nearly three decades. But I suppose one should resist the temptation to compete in the stakes of human misfortune and suffering.

Unsurprisingly, jobs are scarce in Italy and she is grateful to have landed this post which she shares with Valentino, a young man who probably works less hours than she does. (The following evening I sit with him in the TV area where he is simultaneously studying for his maths exam and watching the football. The latter is more exciting than all those mental squiggles. He creeps out to smoke a roll-up cigarette and I think he appreciates my presence, as I appreciate his, although we don't converse). As regards Ilenia, I can't get over how well-read she is. She loves English Literature and is familiar with all the greats. She especially loves the work of Virginia Woolf which is 'secret and mysterious'. She tells me that she finds the English spoken by the American guests in the hotel very hard to understand. The most important thing about her life is the fact that she feels that she has a guardian angel and that God is always looking out for her. This explains her lightness of being when things go wrong but it doesn't get her away from her moaning mother. Probably we all draw our daughters into the damp and dismal closets of our personal histories. How many have memories of going out with mum to fly a kite?

As with the Princess and the Pea something prevents me from sleeping the sleep of the just and the just but I don't remember what. Oh yes, it was an inconsiderate neighbour banging their door just as I was losing **consciousness,** letting go – a difficult thing for me. I know the old-fashioned handles are problematic but even so … Maybe I should find out who it was and have a gentle word with them; more like a gun in their neck! But hey ho it's a sunny day and my 'Top Ten Naples and the Amalfi coast' is at hand and I'm ready to go. Breakfast is a little disappointing because there is no colourful fruit to liven up the brown of bread and hard-boiled eggs. But actually the rolls are lovely – soft, warm and fresh. The waiter is from Sri Lanka as are many of Naples' workers. Later in the day Ilenia had asked me how breakfast was and looked disappointed when I turned critical. Where were the oranges?

The church of Pio Monte della Misericordia is only a stone throw's away, across the cobbled Via dei Tribunali, on the corner of which is a divine cafe where fruit decorated ice cream cakes, too beautiful to attack with knife and fork, are kept in a glass case under lock and key and the scent of vanilla and croissants is gloriously fragrant and warming and soul stirring … and maybe that smell is my overall impression of Naples. (Why did my mother always go for the plainest, dullest stuff from Grodzinski or the A.B.C? **Likewise**, she wore frumpy shoes and insisted on me being religiously scalped once a month by the barber next to Hendon Central Station. I was a source of amusement to all the men, not least the barber, Mr. Joe, with his grey clipped moustache, as I climbed onto a plank placed across the red leather chair.) Well, I'm now going to visit Caravaggio and it's wonderful because I am the only one there and can appreciate the full beauty of this charitable church which was inspired by Counter-Reformation precepts which gave weight to such good works as a way of ensuring salvation. You can see the handwritten letters from prelates and princes which led to the setting up of this institution and view the large art collection in the noble rooms.

Caravaggio's 'The Seven Acts of Mercy', an allegory of charitable deeds, can be espied through an upstairs alcove or down on the ground with the help of an audio which costs two euros. The thing doesn't work properly and by the time I've gone back to the desk and returned with the good-looking bald guy who tells me what button I didn't press the 'talk' has finished. Never mind, I say, (although I probably do mind) I'll read about it later on the Internet. The painting is pure Caravaggio and it's difficult to square such talent and potency with someone who went around with a knife. Having a doom-laden soul is a terrible thing.

My next stop, just up the Via Duomo, is the Duomo itself, Naples' oldest cathedral which dates from the fourth century A.D. It has the oldest baptistry in the western world and I join the throng of people who are suitably awed. Charles the first of Anjou did a lot of repairs in the thirteenth century (good on him) but killer earthquakes hit hard in the following centuries although there are no lasting scars. I run around, down into the Baptistry and then up again, looking for the remains of San Gennaro who was beheaded by the Emperor Diocletian in A.D 305 because he was an early Christian, the leader of an off-shoot Jewish sect, but can't spot his skull bones. The myth had it that, if you were a believer, his dried blood, kept in a vial, liquefied on demand.

You have to see the sights but I can't say that the Duomo is much of a turn-on. It's quite an amazing thing that the Catholic Church, headed by the Pope, still has so many adherents. He's just a learned man who eats pasta with parmesan like everyone else. Talking of food, on my way to the Archaeological Museum I pass a man who has a stall selling, wonder of wonders, fresh green figs. He has two boxes, one of which is filled with those that are ripe, split open, releasing their scarlet jammy interior and another filled with those that are cool, upright, superior! Like a fool I fail to live in the present and go for the ones I don't really want. I buy half a kilo of the stiff, correct variety and am knocked out by the way he wraps them in fig leaves and then puts the parcel into a cone of newspaper so that they will stay fresh. Now that's a man who knows his ass from his elbow.

There's no doubt that the Museo Archeologico is a bit overwhelming but what can you do? When in Rome … Well, I certainly have to push myself and every so often I sit down to check what I've seen with the guidebook recommendations but still manage to miss some of the most notable exhibits. I don't really find anything personally moving – I'm not so interested in the ancient world. 'Yea, the Gods have spoken' is the message that comes across as one gazes up at massive statues of Hercules, Zeus and the like. Actually, it's not about speech but action symbolised by their massive muscularity and wrinkly scrotums. Was Alexander the Great in the collection? These guys, in their conquering drive, were the equivalent of the force behind big business and the American skyscraper in the twentieth century. However, you can't not be impressed by the 'Farnese Bull' which is the largest sculptural group to have survived from antiquity. It recounts a story of crime and punishment and might be a copy of a 2nd-century Greek original since it is Hellenistic in its execution. Even if you really don't care you have to take these things a little seriously.

If you visit the museum, you don't really need to visit Pompeii because everything from Pompeii's Casadei Fauno (an aristocratic mansion of the 2nd-century BC) has been moved over here. I am bowled over by the friezes, frescoes and murals which are so sophisticated and give you a real sense of what society was like in those far-off days and it certainly wasn't nasty, brutish and short (well, not for the ruling class, as is always the case). They had a great time as is evidenced by the secret room which abounds in erect phalluses. They are the advertisement above bakeries and the entrances to other shops and enterprises – symbolising prosperity. Who can deny the potency of the male seed? They enter woman, the soft receptive vessel, from in front and behind. It's clear that physical pleasure and delight was seen as part of man's divine essence and it was only natural to enjoy sitting around, eating grapes and partaking in sexual, as well as verbal, intercourse. Only too true that guilt and shame, fear and repression result in perversion. There is the bronze called 'Dancing Faun' which is a joyous image of freedom and exuberant health. Who could ask for more? The way humans acquire material things is the equivalent of a dog filling a hole with bones. Run free, howl at the moon, find a nice bitch to receive your sperm and never get out of bed again.

Heavens, it's so tiring looking at all the stuff; entering the world of Pompeii and maybe even a little bit fruitless if it's not your area of study — you forget most of what you've seen. I am pleased to leave the long stretch of Greek and Roman busts which line the mezzanine gallery and the stone vessels which weigh a ton but can be used for sitting on in order to eat my figs.

My next stop is Capodimonte and at the bus stop (mercifully found) I chat to a woman from Sri Lanka who works as a carer in an old people's home, where she also lives. She tells me that women from Naples live to be very old; ('how old?' I enquire, thinking of my mother.) Most are in their nineties and some are sweet and others are difficult. (I say nothing, thinking of mother, whom I only occasionally visit). She, the woman from Sri Lanka, is not so keen on Naples. I wonder whether it's because the bus service is so bad. Are we supposed to wait until Kingdom Come? So many people are on scooters, speeding from A to B, many of whom are helmeted women and I wonder why I can't imagine myself entering the fray. I even see a baby or two, sandwiched between dad driving and mum sitting behind. There are no lanes but nobody is colliding; it's obviously the best way of getting around.

I was told that the ride is about ten minutes or so (too far to walk) but I'm not sure where to get off and don't want to miss the stop and end up in the middle of nowhere so, standing at the back of a packed bus, I ask out loud if anyone speaks English. How friendly everyone is – they don't laugh or mock: a Neapolitan guy (when I say Neapolitan I always think of Wall's brick ice cream which came in blocks of pink (strawberry) cream (vanilla) and pale green (pistachio?) who lives in Perth, Australia, comes to my rescue and sets me off at the right stop. I ask him about his life there and he's only too keen to tell me his story.

Capodimonte is a palace (also a museum and a porcelain factory) that was built in 1738 and, set in hilly gardens, it has a very French feel. It's where Italians take their kids on a Sunday afternoon; many are riding their bikes and playing with their dogs, allowed to run free. The art collection came and went according to the fortunes of the French in southern Italy but things stabilised with the unification of Italy in 1860. It was opened to the public in 1957. Under the arcades I espy an English couple who are staying at the hotel and whom I'd spotted the previous evening walking together down the Via dei Tribunali. Tall, pale, thin and thin she looks and sounds like an art critic. She makes the comment that I'm certainly getting around. Am I? Her companion is mute; she's the leader.

Prior to buying my ticket (a reduced rate after 3pm) I enjoyed a cappuccino at the cafe opposite the main gates, sitting in the garden under the lemon trees enjoying the sun, in the company of a white cat sunning herself on the wrought iron table and wondering whether to text my son to check on the weather back home.

There is a great a long walk through the arcade in order to get to the galleries and the man I am following (I later recognise him as a gallery attendant) lets out a massive fart. That would never happen in Cambridge! Saying that you are from Cambridge commands respect; I think the response would be different if you said you were from Luton, Bedford or Norwich. I am more at home looking at paintings rather than marble busts unless they've been brought into being by Rodin or Jacob Epstein- both of whom were touched with genius. It's wonderful to see so many Titians – his popes and his monarchs, namely Charles the fifth and Philip the third. They all have the unmistakable Titian touch! The art critic lady was right in that the paintings are badly labelled but that doesn't really bother me. I make my way through the empty galleries stopping in front of El Greco's 'Boy with a Candle' and of course the stars of the show are Caravaggio's 'Flagellation of Christ' which has an alcove to itself and Artemisia Gentileschi's 'Judith and Holofemes'. Proud woman conquers all and buggery bastard gets what he deserves. I discover a wonderful Anselm Kiefer – is it called 'Our Sea'. It is a sea that is thick and brown with detritus and seems to me to convey the sordid material world of the 21st-century. I am fixated by an anonymous thirteenth century wooden crucifix; I love it because it is simple and quiet and accepting, with its drooping head. It has complete trust in its creator who knows best. Death is painful indeed but it's not the final word. Loving arms will raise you aloft and you'll walk freely again. Maybe it's not so ridiculous to be a Catholic after all. Simone Martini's 1317 painting of St. Ludovic of Toulouse also has its private alcove and I'm not surprised because it's so beautiful and rewards close inspection.

There is a cafe under one of the arcades where I enjoy a thick slice of spinach, olive and mushroom pie. Anything you order they promptly heat up in the microwave. That's the thing about southern Italy and Sicily; the snacks are so fulsome and tasty; you can make a meal of arancini. Nowhere do you see a chip frying establishment or any fatty pasties although, in all honesty, bread spread with tomato paste isn't very inspiring. Fuelled up I walk around the grounds a little and then start my descent to Naples proper. Waiting at the bus stop necessitates a tent, or a three-legged stool. But I didn't realise how long a walk it was and I seem to be passing through wide deserted streets with wave after wave of depressing grey apartment blocks. I stop to ask an Arab youth if I'm going in the right direction. He's Moroccan/Algerian and pleased to practise his English; he tells me that it's not sensible to walk. After about five minutes a bus arrives and I get off outside the Archaeological Museum. I know my way from there. The Arab boy and his mates wave goodbye. Walking back to base down the Via Foria I notice that some older guy in brightly coloured clothes is tracking me. I quicken my step and lose him. Not difficult since it's broad daylight and there are people around.

I do admit that I am on a mission to find the most darling piazza in Naples. I consult my guidebook like mad and Piazza Bellina, at the end of the Via dei Tribunali, (not the train station end), fits the bill and although I visited it on my first evening, I didn't really take it in because it was dark. I could make out the statue of Bellini in the centre plus the archaeological excavation, revealing 5th-century BC Greek walls of large stone blocks. The mind boggles; Who could have erected these monstrous weights? How did they do it? How important it was to put your foot down and make a stake.

It sounds like the Piazza S Domenico Maggiore is the one to visit. It takes some finding through the dark back streets but the kindly old Neapolitan ladies wave me on in the right direction. I once again pass the 'drop-out' square where I again notice the red cheeked woman in black who talks to no one and looks extremely sad. She's in her forties. I wonder what happened to her. Did she lose a child? She looks as if she needs comforting; I am tempted to approach but my better judgement wins over. Most of these people are mad. There are also a group of quite lively hippies, complete with tattoos, piercings and electric green hair who congregate outside the church of Santa Maria Maggiore, which dates from the 10th-century. Perhaps someone is watching over them in their frenetically aimless existence. One young woman has a baby who is freely handed around. I wonder what the Italian system is as regards benefits.

I finally arrive at the square and it is indeed a very attractive place bounded by an old church and old established cafes which exude charm and presence. Having been a cake and chocolate addict in a former life and having nearly came a cropper through this compulsion I no longer indulge (or only rarely) and am content just to look. (My benighted mother thought that chocolate was the thing to eat – replacing fresh vegetables and constructed meals). 'Scaturchio' has been around a long time and sells exquisite chocolate cakes and patisserie. I order an iced coffee and sit outside in the square. The Gran Caffe Aagonese is perhaps a rival and dominates the square. Everywhere in this part of Naples the buildings are something to look at, a legacy of the Angevins, the Aragons, the hefty Spanish under Charles fifth (with the famous Hapsburg jaw) and the 18th-century Bourbons. It all comes together marvellously. If I remember **rightly**, I bought some arancini (rice balls with spinach and mince) for my dinner which was heated up pronto in the microwave. There is a lot of street food being sold in this area. I have to watch my step a bit because of my experience in Marrakesh. But Naples ain't Marrakesh and anyhow you don't die twice. What you worry about seldom occurs so let life be a miracle of the unexpected.

The foreign waiter is friendly (how hard they work – backwards and forwards on their feet all day delivering drinks to lazy people) and points out, as I get up to leave, my white cardigan on the back of my chair. I hadn't forgotten. Maybe he's wondering why such a nice lady is on her own, minus a husband or companion. I wander up the enticing Via Bella Croce and discover an ice-cream place which puts real live fruit into the mix. Do I dare to indulge and put on weight? I'll be **back at the** same time tomorrow.

I proceed to find my way back through the darkening streets, pleased to bypass 'Sorbillo' and already I am feeling very familiar with the Via dei Tribunali as if it's St. Andrews St. Cambridge, although there is no John Lewis, Marks and Spencer and Oxfam bookshop, but funnily enough my favourite cafe,

'Savinos', round the corner on Emmanuel St. is run by a family who come from a village in the area. I get the impression that they don't view Naples through rose-tinted spectacles. On the wall is a photo of the delectable Sophia Loren as she was in her thirties, looking down on us all as we sip our cappuccinos – a reminder that, no matter what, we all get cooked dry by time.

Back at the hotel I sit in the TV area with my book and watch Valentino's pleasure as he follows the football match, occasionally breaking off to glance down at the textbook on his lap. I suppose it's not really much of a fun evening but worse is to come. I get into bed at a suitably late hour (that way I'll hopefully avoid the door slammers) having anointed myself with my 'Fresh Look' skin creams from the Dead Sea (face, arms, hands and feet) but no sooner have I blocked my ears with ear plugs and closed my eyes than I am plagued with the noise coming from one of the flaky buildings in the courtyard beyond my window. Two old ladies are talking at the tops of their voices about God Knows What. Obviously, it's nothing to do with human rights, the right of an individual to get a sorely needed decent night's sleep. Their loud nattering continues until the early hours and finally I am driven to step out onto my narrow balcony and shout 'SILENCE!' I was going to shout, 'silencio!' but 'silence' came out. I no longer cared who I woke up; anyhow why aren't the other occupants of the hotel as disturbed as I am. How can they not hear it? Suddenly there is indeed silence but then the old biddies retreat into their living room/kitchen and carry on the conversation as before. It is now getting on for three and I am livid and distressed. I get dressed and go downstairs to find the night porter. It is the Sri Lankan waiter and he comes with me in the lift to my room to locate where the noise is coming from. He asks me how old I am (implying what?) which is a bit of a liberty. He comes into my room and tells me apologetically that he can't do anything – he can't tell them to shut up or bang their heads together. The two fat ladies finally go to bed but I am so tense that the rest of the night is a write-off and I'm worrying as to how I'm going to cope the next day. It better be sunny.

The boss is at reception; apparently, he makes a daily appearance, and he's quite attractive and stylishly dressed. I tell him about my bad, unhappy night and he raises his eyebrows, shakes his head and says 'Naples!' – what can you do? I ask him the way to the Castel Nuovo and the Palazzo Reale area and after scrutinising the map (doesn't he know his own city?) he tells me to take a bus from the Corso Umberto. This street turns out to be jam-packed busy and crowded so instead of remaining stationary and passive at the bus stop I decide to walk. It will do me good because I feel dreadful, as if a piece of iron is lodged in my brain, although I can still love the wafting aroma of fresh croissants which pervade the air. I finally make it to the Castel Nuovo and the whole area is a mess of roadworks. A monstrously huge Norwegian cruise liner is moored in the harbour. What kind of hell to be inside that? I reckon that the expression 'See Naples and die' is out of date.

I don't really have the mental energy to apply myself to this medieval fortress but there is no other option. I can't lie down prostrate on the pavement. I've read the guide book over and over and am taken by the fact that during the reign of Robert of Anjou the place became an important cultural centre, attracting the likes of Petrarch, Boccaccio and Giotto (when I was twenty odd I got deeply into reading Dante, Petrarch and Boccaccio – remember that story about the poor girl crying for her lover over a pot of basil) for productive sojourns. It must have been a lively place! It was the Spanish bullies who, in the 15th-century, turned it into a fortress. It has been said that Rome is the heart of Italy and Naples is its soul: but if that is the case take a look at the massive cylindrical towers and think again. However, the Triumphal Arch, (to celebrate King Alfonso the fifth) is, by way of contrast, quite pretty and delicate with its Roman inspired sculpted bas-reliefs. I grab a leaflet showing where everything is but due to my collapsed state I go to the wrong places and waste precious energy charging up the wrong staircases. I do manage to locate the 'Sala dei Baroni' where I sit on my own, imagining, to the background of 15th-century Renaissance music, the fate of the barons who were invited here to a ball and were then arrested and taken away for execution. Such is the fate of traitors! It's a very atmospheric hall. At the entrance to the museum are 15th-century bronze doors, depicting royal victories over the rebel barons. The excavations have revealed skeletons of monks but I can't find them nor for that matter the dungeons. I note that chairs are being set up for a concert that evening in the inner courtyard.

I'm not too disappointed to discover that the Palazzo Reale, (the Royal Palace) is closed to visitors and with its edifice of scaffolding plus the noisy roadworks I find it difficult to imagine that, in Naples' heyday, this was the home to one of the Mediterranean's most glittering royal courts. The Royal Family lived there until 1946 when they were exiled, punished for being supporters of Mussolini's Fascist regime. A glimpse, through the inner court, of a cedar tree in the gardens beckons but I can't be bothered.

Almost next door is the Teatro San Carlo which is the famous opera house, predating Rome's 'La Scala' by almost forty years. It opened its doors on 4 November 1737. I didn't know that opera was inspired by classical Greek drama. To see the interior you have to join a guided tour but I can't wait around for the next one. I sneak past some 'no entry' sign, make it to the gallery and through one of the doors catch a glimpse of a sumptuous red velvet stage curtain and a group of people in seats being spoken to. Emerging into the foyer some official asks me how I got up to the gallery and I reply, with a great sigh of fatigue, that I don't know.

There is a beautiful indoor cafe adjoining the opera house where you can sit on a small red sofa and enjoy screenings of famous operas that have been performed next door. I start to watch one of the 'greats' but am distracted by a group of artistic looking men who are drinking coffee, eating pastries and, no doubt discussing a forthcoming production. In the corridor outside are huge photos of women attending a first night, or whenever, in the 1950s. I'm struck, not so much by their beauty – although they are all good-looking – but by the fact of their wonderful grooming and the quality of their clothes, accessories, and jewels. And, accompanied by equally handsome men, they look so happy and serene as if the sky is always shining on them. Loved and cherished, they are doubtless surrounded by those they can love and cherish. I spend some time looking at these black and white photos and wishing that I had a smooth unfurrowed brow. My mother looked sparkly and glamourous in her ballgowns but the only thing she enjoyed was her own reflection in the glass. 'Mirror, mirror on the wall ...'

The time has come for me to get my own back on the old hags who kept me up all night and to this end I am determined to reach the Excelsior hotel on the Via Partenope, a luxury pad which has housed monarchs, presidents and movie stars who deserve the red carpet but that's about all. I ask the porter if there is a garden in the hotel – how I am longing to relax in a paradisical garden – but he replies that there is no garden at all only a beautiful terrace on the top floor. Without hesitation I make my way to the lift and the nice old man, nor anyone else for that matter, commands me to STOP; no uniformed guard comes to arrest me. The terrace is indeed a pretty place with white wicker chairs and glass-topped tables in little alcoves surrounded by pots of red geraniums and exquisite smelling jasmine, which I have in my garden at home. Scents are life's greatest turn-on. The smell of someone's skin tells you a lot about them.

I have to take photos of our dear friend Vesuvius and the wide-open bay. It's not quite as spectacularly curved as you might imagine and I don't like the sight of joggers on the pavements. Is it *fun* to pound the concrete and the clay? Anyway, this is a view to enjoy (in spite of the monstrous cruise vessel stuck in the harbour) especially since both sea and sky are warmly blue. I settle down to read my book in peace and quiet and feel myself recovering from the horrible night in the prison cell where I was driven to bang my head against the walls. Ouch, ouch and ouch again! I think the hotel must be empty because nobody is around other than a solitary cleaner. A young man and a woman, obviously engaged in a business meeting, are far enough away not to intrude on my reading. After an hour or so I have had enough and need to be on my way.

I put my head in at the Grand Hotel Vesuvio and the sight of a fat foreign man speaking into a 'no hands' mobile and being served a mid-morning alcoholic drink by a poor waiter is enough to send me running. It is true, as it says in my book, that the foyer of the Grand Hotel Santa Lucia has a tasteful Art Nouveau decor but these expensive luxury hotels can be disappointing because they feel so dead.

From the terrace I had seen a group of older people swimming off a jetty and I would have liked to join them. But on closer inspection I discover that they belong to a private club and the gate is padlocked and chained and is certainly NO ENTRY. I observe a couple of tacky weddings which are taking place and wend my way towards Piazza Plebiscito. This is the area of Royal Naples and the Caffe Gambrinus – a belle epoque institution which was popular with free-thinking intellectuals and writers and was thus closed down by the Fascists. It is certainly, as beautiful stylish and sumptuous pastries are on display but the staff are formally dressed and there's no sign of any intellectual or revolutionary activity! Tourism is the new idol. I pass into the insanely crowded Via Toledo where I hope to drop into The Galleria Umberto 1 but miss the turning by a long chalk. I turn back and finally enter into a light-filled space with elegant buildings, Neo-Renaissance facades and marble floors overarched by a roof of iron and glass. This place was built as part of the Urban Renewal Plan, following the cholera epidemic of 1884. Naples was renowned for its overcrowding and problems with the sewage system. This oasis became famous with the smart and artistic set and it does have an air of bygone charm. The old photos from the 19th-century reveal Manet type 'flaneurs' in their black suits, canes and top hats. It's difficult to imagine 'the bustling optimism' of 18th-century Naples. Nowadays it's all about crowds of people attached to their mobile phones. For my lunch I buy some tasty snacks in a bar and no doubt irritate the waiter guy with my mental vagaries.

I did have a real desire to visit the monastery on the hill- namely 'Certosa di San Martino', built in 1325 by Charles, Duke of Calabria. Monks tend to be a really good set of people, quiet gardeners in the main. Asking my way as usual from any likely source of information, I arrive at the Funicular which I survey nervously and ask my neighbour if it is safe. Well, it's tried and tested because they use it every day to get to and from work. Once inside I start chatting to the man next to me who works in the ticket office at the opera house. Somehow, we get onto the subject of the Beatles and he starts singing 'Michelle, ma belle, ce sont les mot qui vont tres bien ensemble' which impresses me. I sing along, encouragingly. He also loves 'Yesterday', which, I don't confess, I find a bit syrupy. We shake hands as he leaves the carriage. My stop is at the very top and from there it's quite a long way to the monastery. But this part of Naples has a nice atmosphere and I guess it's very expensive to have an apartment here. I'm very tired, mentally if not physically, but I have to push on. The inside of the church is very impressive, full on with the Baroque art of the 17th and 18th centuries. The Monks' Cemetery is more interesting for me, because it's outdoors and simpler. Passing through a corridor which leads to the gardens are two carriages which were used in the 19th-century by Napoletan V.I.P.s They are amazing specimens and it's difficult to imagine them rumbling down the street. There is no one round and I can't resist touching the door handles. Well, the Queen still has one but it looks smaller – perhaps because I have only seen it on TV. The garden isn't as stunning as I was led to expect but the views certainly are. You can see the whole of the Sorrento coastline and the island of Capri.

On my way back to the station I buy some apples from a greengrocer; you don't see many of them downtown but this is probably an elite area. I also can't resist walking round a supermarket just to see how they do it in southern Italy. As you'd expect all the fruit and vegetables are lush and the fish counter is an eye-opener, full of whole fish with their mouths wide open. It is normal for cheeses to be presented for tasting and, as you'd expect, I help myself. How I'd love to do my thrice weekly shop in such a place; 'shop and eat' is the equivalent of 'wash and go' but the English are a different breed – they like lots of packaging. I pick up a packet of mixed nuts, to eat whenever, but get fed up with the queue and retrace my Back on the funicular I notice that a lady in the carriage has the same sandals as me which is an amusing coincidence. I point this out and she is similarly amused. She's from Moscow and speaks English pretty well. She's travelling with her friend and are staying at a hotel by the train station which isn't so nice. She warns me against going to Pompeii because it's a chore; Herculaneum is more interesting and not so packed out with tourists. The thing is that nothing today is fun or romantic or free. It seems that in the 1920s and 30s and during the war women felt the earth move far more than they do today in our ever more constricted materialist world which has been taken over by machines.

Back on terra firma I walk up Via Toledo all the way to Piazza Dante. What a bleak space it is although some may disagree. There is, unsurprisingly, a statue of the great poet in the centre and in one corner a pop-up stall selling freshly squeezed fruit drinks. Lots of kiwi, pineapples and mangoes. I don't treat myself because there's nowhere to sit and I don't fancy the vista. I head back to my haunt from the day before and (the Via B. Croce leading off the Piazza S Domenico Maggiore) and get my supper from a little place selling 'frittura' – deep fried titbits of aubergine, rice or cheese which are very tasty. It all looks very clean and I seat myself on a stool at a high wooden bar-like table outside and watch the world go by which consists of other people wondering if they should follow my lead. Dessert is the real fruit ice- cream from down the road and its full-bodied creaminess is divine. On my way back to the hotel I drop into a cafe on the Via Tribunali which looked as if it had a bit of pizzaz but it was a waste of time. It starts to rain and I dash into the hotel and start chatting with a fellow guest running for cover; he's a young Australian who has just arrived from Perth. It's his first trip abroad and he took sleeping pills to cancel out the long flight. He asks me if I'm looking forward to the rugby. Elenia's mother has come to meet me and Ilenia brings us coffee (more coffee!) from the bar. Her mum seems OK, friendly (she's lost something in her bag which she can't find) and no monster like mine. But other people's parents cannot harm you and might seem half-way decent and acceptable. I probably spent the rest of the evening chatting to Ilenia who has great bags under her eyes and is suffering from headaches. She has a doctor's appointment and I hope she is OK. She manifests the gaiety of those who have a lot to put up with and choose to laugh rather than cry. She says that her good angel is always by her side.

Tuesday is my last day and it feels as if I've been here weeks. (Nights are always lonely but that's a cross I've had to bear since God made the world in seven days.) I want to visit Pompeii (it's something you gotta do because it's so famous and all that) but I decide to start with Herculaneum and see how I go. The boss is at reception again (he looks a bit young to be the boss; perhaps it's a family affair and his elder brother is in command) and tells me the best way to get to the train station. En route I see mums taking their kids to school, one of whom is so heavily made-up that I reckon she's in deep psychic trouble. The station area is a bit confusing and when I enquire of an elderly employee of the Naples Underground as to where the platform might be (I soon realise that no one knows what I'm talking about because I say Herculaneum rather Erculeo which sounds quite different) he locks his arm in mine and escorts me to a newsagent to buy a ticket. He then stands around and jokes with the proprietor and asks me for a euro or two so that he can get a coffee. 'Hey,' I say, hands on hips, 'that's out of order' and the shop owner thinks so too. Momentarily distracted I leave my book at the till area which is annoying. Luckily, it's my last day otherwise I would have been in trouble. I help a West African woman who is coming down the long flight of steps with a full-size pram in front of her. The pram contains, not a baby, but a great mass of clothes/material stuff to be sold. She speaks good English and is in good spirits. She meets a friend on the platform who has a similar pram. The train is incredibly late and apparently that's normal. I tell them how, at English stations, there is electronic information telling you if the train is on its way. It's not fair to say this, to make people jealous and long to be in another country that isn't their own. But you have better supermarkets! The couple opposite me are off to Sorrento for the day. 'Just to get away'. I didn't realise that it's only an hour on the train. An Australian dad is pissed off because he and his family took the wrong train from Rome (the expensive one). That art critic woman had told me to take care on the train, to sling my bag around my neck because gangs of kids enter the carriage and snatch your belongings. Hmm. The Australian guy explains in detail how his wallet was nicked or was that a special someone from Grimsby whom I met on site at fascinating Herculaneum?

The town itself is nothing much (all the stops on the train looked out onto dreary industrial vistas) and, once again, it's quite a long walk to the place where, nearly 2,000 years ago Vesuvius erupted and all the poor people were killed instantly from the intense heat and buried under a tide of lava and mud, not to be discovered until 1750. So, miracle of miracles, we can view the culture of a people who were doomed, who, as eternal night descended, were in no doubt that this was the end of the world. What a nightmare! I wonder if *we* will ever get wiped out in an instant? But is that just undue morbid speculation?

I enter the site, survey the walled squares and rectangles and realise that, on this occasion, a guide is called for. I no longer have my book!

Back in the foyer I join a group of about six or seven people who, with the local guide, are waiting for the wife of one of the guys who is apparently stuck in the toilet. We wait for an age and we are all, or rather especially me, darting evils at the poor husband. Finally, she emerges and we can set off on the tour. The guide, who keeps apologising for his inadequate English – his English is in fact excellent – is the best, full of enthusiasm for his subject, bringing each dwelling to life. In those days Herculaneum was a sea resort where people went for relaxation. The women had their own baths; there was underfloor heating with sea-themed mosaics on the floor and mythical paintings on the walls. The two-storey local wine shop still has its clay vessels and upstairs there are the remains of a bed where visitors, having drunk their fill, could enjoy the company of a prostitute. Heavens, what would we do without archaeologists and their painstaking labour resulting in a resurrection of the ancient past.

I chat a bit to the woman who got stuck in the toilet and she's actually 'nice and normal and tame' as is everyone in our modem age. With her and her husband we go and look at the skeletons in their subterranean cages – they ran here in order to escape the molten tide but no such luck – fate was against them. I don't really see the point of staring at a collection of skulls and old teeth. I bet mine would never last that long.

We make our way back up to the entrance area and the 21st-century (is it better to live a long boring life, sunk beneath lava and mud or one that is short but full of sparkle in which the self is known). I emerge from the loo to see Mr and Mrs X sitting at a cafe table and digging into ice-creams. It is a warm day, even warmer in the subterranean level of Herculaneum, and too warm to push on to Pompeii. Anyway, everyone says that Herculaneum is better preserved and more interesting. Actually, a lot of the art treasures from both sites can now be seen in the Archaeological Museum. Well, long may it last.

The rickety wooden train is crowded and indeed nobody looks happy when they are squeezed up against some stranger. It feels like a long way back to Naples. I attempt to locate the shop where I left my little book but can't find it; all the newsagents look the same and this is a maze of shops. I emerge from a different part of the station and can't find the street that I'd mentally made a note of in order to get back to the Via Duomo. People are helpful but I'm in a total mess. The worst thing is that due to the heat the heel strap on my sandals is rubbing and every foot fall is painful on my raw flesh. I do of course arrive back at the hotel.

The boss is around and he goes to fetch antiseptic and plasters for my heels (I did have my own but they kept on being rubbed off) which he tenderly anoints. The poor Syrian migrants, trudging through the Balkan lands, are all wearing trainers; believe you me, you couldn't walk with flesh gouged out of your heels. Latterly my daughter and I bought a host of toiletries for the guys in the 'jungle' at Calais and took them to an old Norman church, in Stratton, Cornwall where they are sending over warm clothes and blankets. Feeling clean is the best way to preserve your dignity.

The rest of the day is spent re-visiting my old haunts and sorrowing over the loss of my book – furious with myself that I allowed that crummy old man to take me from myself. For dinner I enjoy a wonderful slice of vegetable flan from a cafe on the Via Duomo (the Cathedral end) and the waiter gives me a biscuit. I decide on a taxi to get me to the airport first thing in the morning, which is the normal and sensible thing to do. Anyway the 'Alli' bus is, I'm told, very unreliable. On the plane I chat to a girl, one of a couple from Sheringham, who is frightened of flying (I stroke her arm when we experience some degree of turbulence) and who tells me that no amount of rational explanation or repeated trips removes the fear and the dread. She can't decide whether to retrain as a physiotherapist or a P.E. (she's a dental nurse at present) teacher and asks my advice. It seems that the P.E. course of action is her best bet. On the shuttle train I see a group of orthodox Jews who have just returned from Israel where they've been celebrating the Jewish New Year. I can't resist asking one of them what the weather was like. 'Hot', he replies, without suspicion but with total indifference, in his gaze. If you are chosen by God nothing can dent your self-belief.

It's always good to be home and to feel grateful for the pitfalls that were avoided. Not to act is to remain stuck in a rut with your hang-ups. You gotta take the bull by the horns. Ilenia continues to email me and I wonder whether I dare treat her to this story?

Bananas in Tenerife

I was lonely and miserable at home so I decided to fly out to the warmest place in Europe. This was the first time, unlike the robin redbreast, that I hadn't stayed put and endured the winter. There was also another motive. A close friend had recently returned from a week in Sardinia. She had rented an apartment in a costly complex, picked up a car at the airport and driven herself there. I was in awe of the second part of her endeavour – I don't drive long distances in the U.K. let alone abroad, on the other side of the road. I might forget myself and do something daft. But as regards the flat thing, I decided to copy her example. Grave folly!

I found a nice-looking apartment online and corresponded with the owner who sounded nice. I booked a flight with EasyJet from Gatwick Airport. Don't I know that EasyJet ain't so easy and Gatwick Airport is a vile place? A few weeks before the departure date my daughter Rose was at my place, she lives in Bude, Cornwall, on her way back from London and I gingerly broke the news that I was flying out to Tenerife to get some winter sun. She was a little envious and decided to come with – after all, the flat was big enough for two. But aren't I supposed to be totally independent and self-sufficient, always going it alone? But on the other hand, she is great company and needs a holiday and it would be nice to depend on somebody when the going gets rough. We booked her flight, seventeen quid cheaper than mine for some reason, and made triply sure it *was* the same flight. I informed the owner that I'd be coming with my daughter and she seemed relieved.

God only knows why I get into such an anxious state before I leap into the unknown. All the instructions concerning picking up the keys from the housekeeper at some strange address were doing my head in. Can't I just float in on my magic carpet? And then there was a lot of emailing to an ex-student friend who lives in Santa Cruz who was imploring me to teach English at the academy she attended. My son thought it a great idea since I get on so well with foreigners. But he obviously doesn't realise that I'm not a teacher in my twenties … Children don't say as much but they are affected by the fact that their lone parent is sitting at home night after night in front of the TV., even when they're watching good stuff like 'The Sopranos', Danish crime thrillers and art programmes presented by brilliant young critics.

Getting to Gatwick on a dismal Saturday morning wasn't great and it's a depressing thing to join a great herd of people queuing for EasyJet flights to every destination in Europe. A young man with a very loud voice was calling out the names of stragglers. Since I'd arrived early I joined the queue but was worried that my daughter wouldn't see me or that I'd have checked in before she arrived. So worried was I that I totally forgot her mobile number. A young mother of three, travelling for the first time without her husband, advised me to wait by the ropes so that my daughter wouldn't have to queue all over again, once I'd been done. This worked well because I was clearly visible and when her bright, open smiling self appeared I could breathe a sigh of relief and start laughing. The laughter soon ceased when the family in front of me, a trio of very fat individuals, were taking forever to check in. What was going on? Was the check-in guy turning the job into a social event? Rose always looks for a rational explanation and thought that maybe they were first time travellers and their accumulated bags were too heavy or not heavy enough. Anyway, she joined another queue. I asked the black guy behind me if he was about to blow his top and he said that he was. Later on I espied the offending trio on the plane and sent a dark glower in their direction. An elephant never forgets.

I'd forgotten how EasyJet packs their seats tightly together so that you feel like a canned sardine. I'd booked a window seat – 11F – and Rose was in the seat in front. The captain came out of his cabin and told us face to face that we'd have to wait on the tarmac for an hour because we'd missed our slot due to Europe's wet and windy weather. I gave him a bit of a clap (for taking the trouble to appear in person) and other people followed. The couple next to me were returning home after the Christmas break and had been trying to sell their pad, half-way up Mount Teide, for four years. The woman was complaining about her neighbours in Tenerife (and her grown-up children who drank all their booze) and told me stories about hysterical fliers who had to be removed from the plane kicking and screaming and how that Boyle singer woman had been on board with her minders and was a 'retard'. Rose, sitting in front of me, minds her own business, engrossed in her book about how the white American settlers annihilated the native Indians, which they certainly did. It's a subject close to her heart. Waiting for the loo (best to enter the rabbit hutch early, before the queue) I see a lady in the front row in sunglasses and it occurs to me that she looks like the writer and journalist Julie Burchill. Of course I say this to her and she whips off her glasses and reveals herself in all her naked glory. We have a bit of a chat and she offers me a drink and introduces me to her husband. She wonders where I got my top and I reply, 'Per Una' in a tone of divine authority, ('I am the Per

Una Lady') and she looks a bit taken aback and shy. I tell her that I heard her on Desert Island Discs which she says she enjoyed. (Who wouldn't enjoy being on Desert Island Discs?) She asks me if I write and I reply, 'not really', which is a lie. It occurs to me later that she's the one who loves the Hebrew Race with a vengeance – a people persecuted like no other – chosen by God but rejected by man. But with survival comes monstrous egotism and as a close relative once said to me: 'The Jews are a remarkable people but I can't bear to be near any of them.' He hates the fixed, cold gaze of the judging Pharisees and so do I.

My complaining, blank-faced seat mate continues to cough and I vow to murder her if she's given me her virus. At the airport our cases are first up on the bandwagon and appear side by side. (That's never happened to me before – I'm always inwardly huffing and puffing as everyone else pulls off their baggage and I'm left waiting and fearing the worst …) The airport bus is also ready and waiting (we didn't know how lucky we were because the next one is not due for an hour and a half) and we set off in the dark for the north of the island and our resort – 'Puerto de la Cruz'. The bus is also huffing and puffing and finally the driver pulls into a layby and phones for a replacement. The Austrians on board who have spent the whole day travelling because their plane couldn't fly over windy Switzerland burst out laughing. What else can you do? After about forty minutes the replacement bus turns up and there remains the unpleasant task of transferring the luggage. I espy a Boris Becker lookalike but obviously it can't be; perhaps he's one of his illegitimate offspring? After a bit he leans over and asks Rose if she is Spanish. A conversation between the three of us ensues and he tells us that he's from Watford, his father is a policeman, he studied P.E. at University and he's working in a school in Puerto de la Cruz as an assistant English teacher. I tell him about my maverick teaching methods i.e. taking my students around Cambridge, showing them the college gardens and ending up at 'Sicilia' my favourite café after 'Savinos'. Rose wonders at the sliver of moon up above which is upside down, like a smile. Mark writes down her number.

When we finally arrive in this unknown, brightly lit place I get out my little piece of paper with the directions to the housekeeper which I wrongly mistaken to be somewhere other than the block of flats where we're going to stay. I can't get through to her and Rose realises that you have to text 00 34 because although you're not abroad you're dialling from an English phone. If I'd been alone I don't think the penny would have dropped. Rose takes control and the housekeeper, Elena, arrives at the ugly Hotel Turquesa where we have taken shelter. She leads us to the apartment block and we pass through a massive marble high-roofed lobby which is like a mausoleum and as eerie as hell. Long green fronds like tentacles hang from the landings on each floor. Once inside the flat Elena conducts a brief tour and shows us how everything works. 'What what what?' I want to say 'you're going too fast' but Rose is obviously on the ball. We unpack and go to bed and I wonder what I would have done if I'd been on my own. Would I have survived the desolation and isolation? It's one thing going away on your own and staying in a hotel and quite another being parked in a bleak apartment in the dead of night. I'm obviously not like my 'drive yourself' friend and I should have realised that. I sleep really lightly, waking up continually. The slightest movement from Rose and I jump to attention, feeling that I have to answer to someone. What a poor baby I am!

However, morning comes after the long dark journey into night and I sweep aside the curtains and am amazed by the sight which greets me. There is an extensive palm tree plantation with the snow covered Mt. Teide in the distance. Beyond the plantation is the sea which is dangerously active with massive curling waves, topped with thick, brilliantly white foam. 'Wow!', gasps Rose. We go out and explore. It's about nine and still a little chilly, although getting warmer by the minute.

We make our way down the street that leads into the town and we could easily imagine ourselves in Mexico or Peru. Every dwelling is a different colour, bright blue, terracotta, banana yellow with carved wooden balconies and the winding road is cobbled and lined with old-fashioned street lamps. Orange lilies have been planted around the tall palm trees. There's nobody about, no cars. The street is now lined with bars and restaurants and we pass a charming square with benches and trees and two restaurants and a bar. The Plaza del Charco, which is meant to be the lively hub of the resort is rather dark and grotty – a place to avoid. How *could* that man on the plane, the husband of the complaining wife in her thick travel socks, have recommended it to me? What planet is *he* on? The 'Bar Central' reminds me of the 'The Regal', in Cambridge. We have our morning coffee in the beautiful old Hotel Marquesa, which is opposite the old church in the centre of the old town. The flower bed outside the church is full of red poinsettias and the sheer number of them renders the solitary Christmas plant-in-a-pot a bizarre object of veneration. Orangey yellow strelitzias are sold in the street and the odd wall is festooned with purple and pink bougainvillea. The sun is now fully out and shining down on us. We can't believe it is January 5th and Rose feels guilty because we are cheating winter and leaving others to suffer it. We order cappuccinos (I'd forgotten that in Spain one tends to order 'café con leche') and we get coffees topped with oodles of cream, which we remove. (We don't want fat tums thank you very much). God, how good it is to sit in the sun, facing the pretty flower bed and cobbled square outside the church. It is Sunday and people are going to church, dressed in their smartest clothes. Rose and I discuss whether it could be fun to be a nun. Neither of us despise the calling but we don't like the idea of obedience and a uniform.

By now all has changed and our blissful solitude has been swept away. It is 11.30 and the place has become zombie land as everyone hits the streets. It's turning into a really nice day and lots of naked men with huge stomachs are lying comatose on the sand (I used to be one of those – sunbathing for eight hours a day) and other men, sitting on the stone benches around the harbour, are looking on. It's so nice actually that people can just sit and stare on their own, you don't have to be in a couple or, worst of all, a group (with the invisible rope keeping people together). The sea is still very rough and this downtown beach, beyond the main walkway and the blocks of forbidding hotels, like upturned match boxes, is not as nice as ours at the other end of the town which is a 'playa jardin', a beach garden, with sandy paths and palm trees. Everyone seems to be German – apparently the 'Brits' prefer the south of the island, where it's hotter. There seem to be a lot of perfume shops and once in it's difficult to get out due to harassment from heavily made-up sales assistants. Sadly, the lingo is lying dormant at the back of my mind and what comes out is an apologetic mix of Spanish, Italian and English. Anyway the perfume is all far too expensive. As we walk around we come across human statues painted silver or gold. Rose detects a scam whereby people are manipulated into parting with their money and we see a silver painted man who has taken time out to have a fag. 'He's not meant to do that!' exclaims Rose. She spots the real life statue by the harbour of a girl carrying a basket of fish and a tray of fish on her head.

Lunch is a thick slice of potato tortilla which we eat on a wooden bench in the lovely square on the 'Mexican' road leading back to our apartment block. Rose takes photos of the blue and yellow and terracotta walls so that she can use them in her work. The café in this square reminds her of one in Berlin and indeed it is managed and owned by Germans. Due to my poor night's sleep my mood isn't as buoyant as hers and I sigh inwardly when she says that she could sit all day in this spot reading her book. I am ill-equipped for the beach – I don't have a sarong to wrap around my swimsuit – but nevertheless we make our way to the black volcanic sands where quite a few others are sunbathing. The sound of the breaking waves is music to my ears and the smell of fresh salt air is balm indeed. I love swimming in the sea more than anything. This is probably because the annual excursion to Bournemouth was like being released from prison and on the beach at Branksome Chimes my parents were more relaxed, blessed/humbled by the immensity of water. Here the sea is a curse, grabbing you by the ankles, determined to pull you into its devilish clutches. The lifeguard is coming down heavy on anyone who dares to be something other than a spectator. Rose observes human folly, the obliviousness to danger, as she looks up from her book. We return to our sunbathing and I'm lying on my front when Rose sits up straight and laughingly alerts me to the incoming tide, which is almost upon us.

How fast it is swirling around our ankles! Without a moment's thought I grab all my stuff and run for my life, laughing all the while, amazed at my own alacrity. Maybe I'm always poised for flight. Rose says that it's not such a big deal – in Cornwall she and her friend were actually drenched by waves when they were reclining on some rocks. Back in the flat I see similar scenes of coastal wreckage in the UK but back there all seems miserable and grey. Not that our flat here is an ideal home, I don't like the dull banana walls and the brown and beige duvet covers and the old-fashioned beige sofa for oldies. However it is comfortable and the kitchen is better equipped than my own at home. I wonder where the owner bought her lovely set of white crockery. Rose has brought her own coffee from the Queen's own coffee makers in London but we both forgot the Earl Grey tea bags.

Rose isn't tardy as regards going for a run. She changes into the right gear, (she implores me to exchange my 'ballerina' shoes for sensible trainers) and she even has an app. on her phone which tells her how far she has run and whether she is a leader. I love the way her pony-tail goes swish swish swish as she bobs up and down on the pavement. I can't imagine myself turning lobster red and dripping with sweat. But I expect that's the way forward. I've managed in her absence to mess up the shower appliance – there are two and I've tried to operate them together – but she manages to put things right with supreme sacrificial tolerance and good will to all men. I wear my red and green 'poinsettia' top with its lacy cowl to go out for dinner. Rose has chosen one of the two restaurants in the charming square which advertises its tapas selection. It's not bad and the waiter is friendly and obviously charmed by my daughter and her warm, reserved, and gracious manner. After dinner we join the other walkers around town and it is this civilised walkabout which is so good for everyone. A guitarist is playing in our square (<u>not</u> the Plaza del Charco which caters for tourists) and Rose (who, since birth has observed everything) points out a man and a woman who are spontaneously dancing together. Her big soft bag is in the way. They leave off as casually as they started and continue their walk. Nobody claps or criticises or throws stones. Later we see them coming up from the beach and Rose says that the man is in love, you can see it in his face.

That night I fall into a deep sleep and only wake up once or twice. Bad sleep has been the curse of my life and this ain't due to a fairy godmother sitting by my bed. God, I am guilty of the great sin of snoring all night and when I awake in the morning the bed next to me is empty, minus the mattress. Rose has had to sleep on the floor in the sitting-room. But she's just pleased that I slept, even if she didn't. After breakfast at some joint where the waitresses look at you as if to say, 'piss off – you're a nuisance', we take a taxi to the Hotel Botanico; the uphill walk would have taken forever. My companions on the plane had told me that taxis cost nothing and this guy tells us that he'll take us for a special offer of three euros. What he meant was that that was the starting price. I always like to search out the best hotel in town – a luxurious pad where you are bound to get some peace and quiet. This place is no exception. We express wonder at the oriental lake they have created with its black swan (lonely or what?) proudly sitting on the rocky nest they have made for it, flat-backed toads submerged in water and huge winged Monarch butterflies flying about. The massive orange fish are obviously content and well-fed. We enjoy a delicious café con leche which is served with four little biscuits. Rose reads her story about the wounded Indians and I read the poems of Rumi, which date from the twelfth century but could have been written yesterday.

We observe the other people, not many of them, who are sunbathing on their loungers. There are two women on their mobiles with discontented, bored-looking teenage daughters, one of whom goes to swing in a hammock. There is a man, deeply bronzed, with a huge dome of a stomach, lying prostrate on his recliner. Quite a sweet-looking woman with hair dyed to a lovely creamy blonde colour sits next to him, but apart. No conversation. I can see that she must have been pretty when she was young so I warm to her. I smile at her and she shyly smiles back. She then goes over to her man and whispers 'I love you' before going back to the room. He actually looks slightly pleased, as if he's been fed a tidbit, and starts to move his head from side to side, exercising his neck. Rose is more interested, if interested can be the word, in another, German man who is chain-smoking, drinking wine and beer and making numerous phone-calls. His thin blonde wife is sitting opposite him and he's berating her for something. An English couple have their sunbeds on the grass, away from the pool and the man, with some paperback novel open on his knees, is looking around, very pleased with himself. A very thin young woman is looking after a two year old. A couple pad around in their white towelling robes, no doubt en route for the spa vainly entertaining the illusion that they are doing something for themselves. Thank the good Lord that the sky is blue and the sun is shining.

Rose wants me to have a treat so suggests that we order lunch. She tells me that wall outside the ladies room is covered with certificates and awards confirming the Hotel as one of the best in the world. Rose doesn't dare say that the salad is disappointing but it is. You could easily do the same thing at home and you probably wouldn't mix fruits and vegetables Tenerife style, or pay the earth. We leave the hotel and visit the Botanical Gardens which is sub-tropical and full of weird and wonderful growing plants. It takes us an hour to walk down the hill, passing, en route, loads of bars and restaurants, full of German people drinking beer. Rose suggests that the 'retired' get up, go for lunch, have a nap and then go for dinner. There is always something to chat about if you're part of a social circle. She observed one couple in the 'German' bar, in the dear little square, who were sitting opposite each other, looking in opposite directions, and not of this world, not even knowing where to look. She made a witty comment about marital bliss. But life isn't easy for anybody. It's a fight. You either carry your cross or sink into dreams punctuated by rage.

She is irritated by the way I obsessively ask people for directions – just to check. Calm, rational thinking on her part finally lands us at the Tourist Information Office (and not the Police Station) where I pick up a load of leaflets advertising places of interest in the north. A few years ago my elder brother stayed in Garachico and esteemed it highly and I'm curious to know what turns him on. Maybe it's best not to copy those with whom one has nothing in common. We enjoy walking down the lovely 'Mexican' road that leads to the 'Playa Jardin' and the first stop out of the 'city centre' is a rough and ready café cum restaurant called 'Oregon' which is directly opposite a funfair, with its ferris wheel and gaudy lights of mauve, orange and green. A guy with a soft voice is standing outside advertising the place and its fresh fish specialities. Suddenly another young man appears at the doorway to the eaterie and points to the chalked menu on a board and tells us that there will be other specialities in the evening. Certainly a lovely smell of grilling fish is wafting our way. We promise to return. Everybody who goes there returns, not because of the fantastic food, (isn't it a bit odd to serve sea bream with shredded beetroot and carrot and a ring of tinned pineapple and half a tinned peach?) but because of the personality of this waiter, who is a law student in Madrid. Nothing suits me better than a friendly waiter (not the sort who asks you obsequiously if everything is OK) and a platter of grilled catch of the day washed down with a 'cana' (a long slim glass) of beer. This place is warm and cosy with a tiled terracotta floor and about seven tables covered with a green and white check plastic cloth. The wooden chairs are draped with green and white sun lounger mattresses which creates the cosy and slightly eccentric nature of the place. The door is always open as David the waiter sees people out and beckons them in. As Rose continually reiterates, 'he's extremely good at his job'. We wander over into the funfair and are greeted by a stall where a family is selling 'churros' and other sugary snacks. We buy and eat because the dad is so nice as are the son and the daughter, all heavenly smiles and good humour. A lovely family. Entering more deeply into this funfair abode we change our minds and head back home. En route we pass the waiter at the restaurant where we'd eaten the night before – he's leaning against the wall, having a fag. In couched terms he tells us that his boss is mean. He certainly is, charging unwitting customers a couple of euros for a bread roll. (That however seems to be the norm here in Puerto de la Cruz and David has reluctantly taken on board the fact that we're not swallowing it.) Just before our home stretch we pass the open-air municipal pool where brave souls are ploughing their furrow; it has a friendly feel with turquoise blue tiered seats for the observers and there is music playing. They're at it first thing in the morning too. Back in the flat I watch the news and lament the terrible floods back in the homeland. Rose says that whenever anyone tells me about anything I always go, 'that's terrible, TERRIBLE!!!' I suppose that's my way of expressing empathy with life's horrors.

A new day dawns and we decide to make breakfast in the flat to eat on the terrace, although it doesn't get the sun until the afternoon. Rose is disappointed about this but perks up at the prospect of facing the sun at tea-time. The view of the banana plantation, the sea and the snow-topped Mt. Teide is quite special. Rose reckons that if I spent a month in this resort I'd meet people by joining the swimming club and I expect she's right. We head into town, the keen swimmers are being taken through their exercises at the water's edge by an enthusiastic coach, and Rose sits on the steps outside the church whilst I explore the hotel opposite. I want to check out the swimming pool on the roof in case I decide to stay in a hotel next time I visit Puerto de la Cruz. When I emerge I espy Rose on the steps with a curious expression on her face, as if something curious and strange has entered her conscious domain. Ha! There's a man sitting on the same step, near the wall, who reminds her of 'dad'. Apparently it was the way that he sat himself down, meticulously placed his glasses on top of his book and set to work making trays out of old drinks cans. It was such a simple process that even I could have followed it. They were one euro each and we bought two. He was oblivious to the people at the tables in the hotel opposite staring at him and Rose was impressed by the discrepancy between someone using their hands to make something and sell it for next to nothing and the people staring across at him – none of whom looked particularly content, all of whom were smoking, drinking, or texting. A fair-haired middle aged couple got up and crossed the road and I asked them where they were from and what they thought of 'canman' as Rose subsequently nicknamed him. They were Danish, friendly and, surprise surprise, they had already purchased his wares. I approached canman personally in order to find out more. He was, by his own estimation, an 'old man' aged sixty nine, from somewhere in Holland or the Baltic Sea and he worked for an hour or two and then went to drink and smoke. He slept in a tent and hopped on a boat to Portugal or Spain when he fancied a change. (He was indeed disconcertingly like dad). Rose, an artist, registered his physical appearance exactly. He wore flip flops, slim coral jeans, a plaid flannel shirt and an Arab style headscarf. He had a long creamy beard and looked like the head on a pint of Guinness. Well that was that and we never saw him again. As we made our way downhill to the harbour we were pressed against the wall by the 'Day of Kings' procession. A toy train followed by a group of drummers (cor, whacking a drum must be a good outlet for anger and frustration) and led by a number of children dressed up as Bible people, was making its way through the main street. The outfits were beautifully made. Rose noticed that the seats were packed with presents for children in hospital and we vowed that that's what we'd do come Christmas day, doing away with the empty ritual that Christmas has become.

Eva, my ex English Language student, was our next port of call. I'd managed to phone her and we'd arranged to meet her outside the apartment block at midday. Rose had become very quiet obviously not knowing what this woman would be like. She was soon to find out. Eva too hadn't realised that you have to phone using the 00 44 code and had been driving around for half an hour unable to find the place. She was heavily made-up and wearing a flowery top with tights and high boots. She's about forty five years old, single, and her elderly parents from Madrid had come to live with her in Santa Cruz because she, as the female daughter, was called on to take care of them – a fact she resented. I befriended her in Cambridge because she didn't like the other teachers (they'd labelled her as 'difficult') and I supported her obsession with learning English, becoming English, driving her in the rain to extra classes. Over lunch she had told me about her disastrous marriage. But this was sometime ago and I realised how I no longer got sucked into the quicksand of other people's egos.

Rose was friendly but reserved. We finally found a parking place in town after Eva had gatecrashed a number of NO ENTRY signs and then spent ages in a perfumerie. Our patience exhausted Rose and I went to stand outside in the fresh air at the water's edge. The thing was that she was waiting to pick up her 'elderly' parents from the medical centre nearby – she'd killed two birds with one stone by coming to see us. When they were picked up it was lunchtime and there was nowhere to go other than the Plaza del Charco because her father couldn't walk and she reckoned that the Plaza del Charco was nice. Not *my* cup of tea. As the plastic menu was shoved into my hand I tried to say that Rose and I had other plans – we were going to have lunch at a restaurant overlooking the beach and the sea – on the Playa Jardin. Eva's parents looked lost and timid and Eva, in an air of authority, told them that I spoke no Spanish. The atmosphere was awful as my head dropped onto my chest and my heart sank into my boots. I spotted fresh grilled sardines on the menu and my mood improved. I started to dredge up some Spanish to the delight of her parents and the annoyance of Eva who wanted to practise her English. She said that she could understand Rose better than me. At the end of the meal, which was actually fine – they serve those 'papas arrugadas' (small baked potatoes which look like dark grey pebbles) with everything – she badgered Rose into having a dessert. I was impressed by my daughter's polite emphatic 'Nos.' Unsurprisingly Eva tucked into the biggest slice of gateau I have ever seen. Her mother badgered me into having an ice-cream and I succumbed, seduced by the fancy wafer. Her father got a chance to speak about himself and insisted on paying the bill. Her mum and dad were in tears when they hugged us and said goodbye. They hate provincial Tenerife and miss Madrid. Eva was on holiday and wanted to drive us to the south where we could sunbathe all day and enjoy the beautiful resorts. She couldn't understand why I didn't fancy the prospect. Rose backed me up. She said that she'd take us to a different place every day. Oh my God I'd got myself into something I couldn't get out of. Finally I promised to phone her in the evening. 'I will', I said and I realised that, as a matter of principle, I had to and I would. On the phone I explained that since Rose lives in Cornwall I don't see her that often and we just wanted to be together. (It was of course the truth but the full truth was that her company was not desired.) She couldn't really understand why I couldn't accept the gift of being driven round the island so I had to politely cut her off. Goodbye Eva. Dumped. As Rose said later, 'it's a good feeling when you shift a human burden. You have to.'

She'd gone to meet Ben, the Boris Becker lookalike, and I'd arranged to meet her at eight outside Oregon, our local fish place. I had nothing much to do in the mournful flat so I set off at about 7.30 pm, intending to walk slowly and look around. Rose had told me that she liked the look of one of the waiters in the German bar in the charming square and he'd expressed interest in her too. When Rose was born in Bastia, Corsica the paediatrician had said to me: 'You're going to have trouble with this one. When she's fifteen you're not going to be able to keep the boys away.' This prophesy came true but now that she's thirty two she's almost the only one who is single and not a mum but that's probably something to do with having a canman type as a dad. Anyway I decide to espy the attractive waiter and as I approach the bar I stumble on Ben and Rose having a drink outside. I don't think that Ben was too pleased. He politely suffered my zany conversation but I had the sense to depart sharpish when he was getting Rose another drink. I arrive at the restaurant at about ten to eight and David welcomes me in. I wait and wait and wait. If she doesn't arrive by 8.30 I'll give her a ring. At around 8.18 I see her outside, hugging Ben goodbye. As she comes in David says to her, 'you shouldn't keep your mum waiting', in a tone of gentle fatherly rebuke. This support feels proper and good. I think David likes me. The only support my father provided was financial. I know money makes the world go round but an arm around your shoulders keeps it at bay. Mother is the Golden Calf before whom we bow down, worship and obey.

Rose tells me about her date beginning with 'you're right ...' Ben is twenty four years old, younger than her own brother. She likes him but it's not on. Actually she's never forgotten Brendon, a Canadian musician whom she met in

Vancouver three years ago. His father was a community chief, a descendant of Red Indians, but absent as a real father to his own children. He's her soul mate, the one with whom she'd want to have children. He's with someone else now, a singer, but she knows that they're not really together. He's also got a steady job in Toronto which he didn't have before a fact which aligned him suspiciously with 'canman' dad. She sends him a text telling him how she feels and decides not to look at the reply until she gets back to Bude. On the menu is the catch of the day. David always treats us to honey rum liqueur after our meal which goes down a treat. Maybe that's because we give him a big tip, thinking of euros as pounds. He thinks his English is dreadful, a cause of some distress this, and wants to improve. He's a bit flabby and pale even though he has no vices. Rose can't get over how good he is at his job. He makes everyone feel that they are special and supremely welcome. I enjoy his bustling presence. After dinner we walk around, like everyone else, and find a nice shop near the church where I buy turquoise and gold butterfly earrings and a ring and Rose buys a fine floaty white dress, ideal for summers in Bude and marvellously reduced in the sale. I'm a bit tightfisted with money (though not where my children are concerned) but Rose is tolerant of this characteristic since she knows I've had everything stolen from me by the canman.

Rose would be quite content to read 'Bury my Heart at Wounded Knee', sunkissed in her favourite café but I insist on an outing. What do I expect to find? Certainly it's an uphill climb to the bus station and the bus is packed with chattering Germans and what looked like a twenty minute drive on the map is actually more than an hour's drive, along the twisty coastal road. In the seat opposite me, glued to the window is a young guy with a headscarf, baggy trousers, a dark grey thick woollen hoody style poncho and Addidas trainers. His musical instrument, which resembles a bow (as in bow and arrow) occupies the seat next to him, and when he removes it to allow a girl to sit down she makes it clear that she preserves the step. He shrugs and says something in English. I lean over and ask him if he's a Londoner. He tells us that he works as a healer and has learnt his mystical healing arts in Gabon, West Africa. 'Bwiti' and 'fang bwiti' is his mantra and it's all about getting in touch with his unconscious, the shadow side, with these powerful African drugs. As usual I trustingly believe everything that I hear and am always up for some lively discussion. Rose is the most intelligent and sensitive person in the universe and keeps her own counsel.

By the time the bus stops I'm up to my neck in the healing powers of fang bwiti and because Mark is a good-hearted guy he comes with us to the pretty square in Garachico where I buy him an orange juice. His main purpose in coming to Tenerife was to give up tobacco – he'd recently had a chest infection and still had a raw cough. He lives in a camper van in Glastonbury not far from his dud family although he believes that parents must be respected, however awful they've been. He's worried about his new girlfriend who likes her man to be hostile and indifferent. Rose somehow thought they'd been together for seven years (he is thirty one) but he met her in December 2013, in Tesco. She works for a radio station in London and wants him to perform his music on air. He expounds his knowledge and it's fascinating to learn how the lungs represent grief, the bowels fear, the hips sexuality, the hunched shoulders the burden of others. I ask him which organ is the seat of being unable to let go? 'The heart of course'. He tells us that the dragon is the freely expressive male whilst the macho man keeps a pale virgin tied to a post in his cave. That figures. He calls himself a shaman and what I do remember is his description of his Gabon attire – the black and white painted face, the patterned black and white cotton wrap around skirt (which is in his back-pack) and the dead cat which is tied around his waist, its head facing heaven.

By now we're friends and he's really pleased that he has found us, 'good souls' on this island where he's been for ten days and bored to death. He hates the pushy Germans. People are prejudiced by his appearance. We split up because he's going to find a hostel for the night. We go off to explore Garachico and find lunch. It's a pretty unspoilt place but not that great – nothing to write home about. The public loos are pretty rough. It used to be Tenerife's most important harbour, exporting lovely Malmsy wine and then there was a volcanic eruption in 1706 which destroyed everything. There are a lot of steep cobbled streets to climb, pleasing views and the sun is hot on face and arms. A man is planting geranium cuttings in window boxes. He clears up very carefully after himself. The pink and white roses in the main square are divinely fragrant. One could die for that scent. We have 'goatmeat' and French fries for lunch. The place is very very quiet. There is a monastery and I'm still wondering what my brother enjoyed so much – he was probably in a luxury hotel on the hilltop. Was it the peace and quiet, the absence of shouting and screaming? We think a lot about Mark and wonder what he's doing – maybe sitting in his hostel. It's not a good place to be on your own. We reckon that Mark is brave and good-hearted. He's trying hard to find his way. Rose is genuinely concerned about his welfare. The lady in the tourist information office tells us emphatically that the buses depart every half hour but she is emphatically wrong and we end up waiting half-an-hour for the bus back to 'Puerto', as it is commonly known. A couple of Canadian ramblers turn up and ask us what we've been doing. They don't expect to hear us say: 'meeting funny people'. I don't expect them to say what a miserable street this is, which it is. Luckily we get the last two seats on the busy 4.30 bus which was lucky because Rose almost let them get on before us. Rose is the sort of person who never pushes to the front of the queue but is securely first in everything – certainly in common sense and laughter. She isn't tainted with any of the deadly sins. She gives up her seat to an elderly English lady, a rambler from Reading, who says to me, after a long bus ride during which we've been chatting about things, 'say thank you again to your daughter.'

On the first stop out of town we espy Mark at the bus stop, looking tired and down in the dumps, and I nearly jump out of my seat in jubilation. He looks incredibly pleased to see us and moves to the back of the bus where he stands with Rose. Back in Puerto we purchase ice-creams and he drops two euros into my bag. Poor boy! I find out about single rooms in the Hotel Marquesa, that old hotel (built in 1712) opposite the church and emerge triumphantly since they have single rooms which are 40 euros a night. Rose hopes this is OK since his budget was 35 euros. She knows what it's like to live beyond your means, always in debt, outgoings permanently exceeding money coming in. Money doesn't make you happy but lack of it is a big worry. We check out the room with him on the ground floor, at the back of the hotel. It smells sourly of drains but is otherwise OK and he is pleased. We spend the next hour or so talking on a bench near the square. He tells us about his ten days in prison for not paying parking fines; being of no fixed address the penalties were sent to his mother who, he tells us, has gotten over her victim mentality since having breast cancer. She now jumps out of planes. He hates the way his uninspiring dad shows off about his ailments – it's a way of getting attention. It gets a bit cold and he gives me his ritual skirt to wrap around my shoulders. He's very thin and doesn't seem to eat which is worrying; my son is the other extreme which is also worrying ... I hope the latter's lack of Andy Murry type masculinity doesn't bring him down. It's not the right thing to do to ask him to join us for dinner – boundaries are boundaries – and our time together at Oregon is private – time to reflect on the day's events and enjoy a good laugh at the world's expense. I think however that we did arrange to meet him at 10pm, for a drink. It's my birthday in a few days and Rose, a deadpan expression on her face, suggests that we have a party at Oregon for all our new friends; there'd be Julie and her husband, Ben, Mark, Eva, David the waiter and the gay middle-aged German guy at the next table whose partner fell sick at the airport. The combination is so ludicrous that I'm convulsed with paroxysms of laughter. With Mark, after dinner, we go into a bar that Rose has spotted. Mark takes an olive off a stick from a plate that is about to be taken to a table and the manager is none too pleased. (As a side note, olives seem to be out of circulation in Tenerife). He says that he can't serve the plate since the guests have seen the interference. The thing is that Mark doesn't simply apologise for his thoughtlessness but gets shirty with the manager and we are forced to leave. He continues to justify his behaviour. It rains like hell later in the evening and Rose and I get soaked on the way back to the apartment block.

She reckons that I should get myself a pack-a-mac cagoule thing (not particularly stylish are they?) as well as a sarong and trainers. Maybe I should also follow her example and take up jogging ...

The next day we meet him for breakfast and he looks decidedly gloomy. He hates everyone and can't wait to 'get off the fucking island'. Rose is up to date on what pills he has and hasn't been taking but I just register what he says and how he looks. The fact that we got soaked in the rain doesn't register with him. He's back on his rant about the mindless herd and how everyone treats him suspiciously. (Rose told me that on the bus to Garachico she was quite embarrassed when this 'mindless herd of tourists' talk was going on because there was a mild English couple sitting behind us and what are we if not tourists?) The way she sees it is that we human beings are all in the same boat together. The way he spends his day literally killing time is a bit disconcerting. In spite of the high minded stuff about entering the unconscious and what affects his mood are the emails from Sophie his girlfriend. She was initially keen to get him on her show but isn't responding to him asking her how she is because she likes hostility. It's an overcast rainy day and we take our leave, planning to buy all our stuff for lunch from the family run grocery on the Mexican street. Rose comments to me that he doesn't explore, doesn't look at anything as he's too busy counting his pills. The evening before she had asked him what his hair was like. It was such a simple direct question such as a child might ask. He pulled off his headscarf to reveal total baldness; 'my dad's legacy', he laughed.

It's so nice to shop locally. There's a young man about in a white coat about my son's age who is busy outside, with the boxes heaped with bananas, avocados, oranges and satsumas. The dad makes deliveries down the road, carrying huge cartons of water in the basket of his three-wheeled bicycle. The daughters inside are on the till. Everyone is open and interactive, living in the moment. The dad helps me with my Spanish when I say that I want a large ripe ('matura') papaya and the handsome son is aware that I'm looking at him admiringly. The loaves of bread are forty cents each and we buy four avocados for about 40p. A tin of sardines is also 40p – in fact everything is. The cheese however looks processed and the white cheese in Rose's salad at the Hotel Botanico was bland and unpleasant. The best thing are the short fat bananas which are yellow and sticky and remind me of the banana lollies I had as a child. (My mother, in the summer, was always filling the ice-making compartment with chocolate, raspberry and banana lollies and strawberry 'mivvies' which were a luxury (due to the vanilla ice-cream filling) at sixpence each. You dived in as soon as you got back from school – our brilliantly rough primary school called 'Algernon Road'. Everyone went there – from future Nobel Prize winners and Simon Schamas to those who were barely literate but could run like the wind).

Supermarket bananas are long, pale, dry and tasteless in comparison. One hardly dares to imagine the scale on which they are produced.

Back in the flat Rose gets cracking on preparing lunch. She loves cooking for people and entertaining. The table is prettily laid on the terrace, with folded kitchen roll serving as serviettes. How we enjoy our modest wholesome meal until the rain comes and forces us inside. Hence my mood gradually begins to change as the blue sky becomes grey. Rose explains her new app. which was shown her by her friend Tamsin who has had cancer and is doing a Ph.D. on taxation. (This has prompted Rose to question her own ideas on the subject and how stupid it is to be blindly obedient to authority. Mark's knowledge of civil law has enabled him to outwit the police force.) The app in question enables you to control your finances through typing in your budget and expenditure for each particular item i.e. petrol, food, going out etc. and then it tells you how much you've got left for the month. Talk about Big Brother! All these clever apps unnerve me. What starts as one of our delightful philosophical conversations goes on for too long and becomes a bit heavy and intense and I find myself talking, as usual, about my son and his insecurities and what I see as his passive aggression. I think she's had enough of this airless hothouse stuff and rain or no goes out for a run. I put on my winter clothes. Apparently I told Mark that we'd pick him up at seven (I tell myself that he wouldn't mind if we just didn't turn up but she thinks otherwise) but seeing that this isn't possible due to Rose's nap (this is true) and late run I have to trek into town to tell him that it's not to be and we'll meet him at nine. When I go to reception desk in the hotel and ask if they'd telephone Mark for me, a guy emerges from a magisterial office and asks me if I'm a policewoman. 'Do I look like one?' I reply humorously, insulted to be identified with some uniformed nonentity in the Force. (Rose said that I should have said, 'Yes, and I'm here to arrest YOU!') Mark, meanwhile, appears on the scene and I give him a hug. Perhaps he is a long lost relation, muses the manager. Actually, to be honest I wouldn't want anyone to think that he is my own darling son – who has dark soulful eyes, a marvellous sense of humour and doesn't wear a dead cat around his waist. I feel a bit odd being with Mark on my own. He asks me if I want to go for a drink but I decline. Talking about Sophie he tells me that women really like him and he doesn't need to waste his time with someone who is so unresponsive. I feel bound to tell him how great Rose is and he reckons that she understands him really well. He says he'll come to Cambridge so that I can help him write his life story. He walks with me all the way out of the town and then stops abruptly when we reach the beautiful 'Mexican' street. He *is* grateful that I came to tell him we couldn't make the agreed time.

It's Thursday and Oregon is closed so we eat in the bustling Italian restaurant in our favourite square and Rose tells me later that I appeared sunk into myself and that I was looking at all the waiters and anyone who went past as if I wanted them to give them something. I was just aware of how everyone looked so smiley. Anyhow, it's nice to eat pasta for a change. Mark joins us later for a drink and we hear more of his story – a complex tale of growing cannabis in two different houses, outwitting/befriending the police and drawing in £1000 a week. He has two dealers who are his mates. Is it really possible that one ounce of the weed (a minuscule amount) sells for £200? There are other stories of how his cousin, as a child, took some pills that were left on the table and was a demented retard for the rest of his life; and how his uncle abused his stepdaughter, 'such a nice guy you never would have thought it …' It's been a grey day and it's getting colder. I mention Toby. He says, 'Tony … is he your man? Rose mutters under her breath something to the effect of, 'he might as well be'. 'What's your dad like?' asks Mark out of common human interest. 'He's sort of in his own world' replies Rose, as if he has a mild character flaw. Mark would like to know how he managed to get our house in Corsica blown up. It's a big topic and there's no point getting started on it and Rose isn't the sort to reveal all to a relative stranger – or anyone for that matter. Sort of passively, without huge conviction I say, 'we ought to go now', because I want to get back. Rose hasn't quite finished her wine and Mark his beer so I decide to give it another ten minutes. As we get up to go Mark puts his arms around me and hugs me but I don't respond because I wasn't expecting it and am too sunk in despondency. Whenever I feel the urge to cry I instinctively SWALLOW it and put humour into gear. As we hit the road the heavens open and once again we get soaked. I am definitely angry, angry at myself because I didn't say, 'WE'RE GOING NOW' – no choice in the matter. Rose tries to make light of the matter: 'it's only a bit of rain – haven't you been in the rain before' but I allow myself to be angry with her. I feel acutely angry. I don't fancy my black shoes being wet on the inside. We finally make it back with water running down our faces and necks. As we enter the flat I burst out with, 'what the fuck have I had in life?!' and I really mean it. Poor Rose appears, like a good fairy, with two balls of kitchen paper which she attempts to stuff into my shoes – 'which aren't wet at all!' she joyously declares. I am touched by the little girl who can't bear mummy to be upset and tries to make everything alright. We talk about my inability to cry and Rose says that I've got to let myself go – how can I ever be in a relationship if I can't be natural. What I marvel about and give thanks to God is the way that it is possible to snap out of moods, rise up from the bottom of the ocean. I feel guilty that I didn't respond to Mark's hug and vow not to forget to explain myself to him. When I do, he says: 'spirit told me to give you a hug'. Rose says that he reminds her very much of the dope-smoking crowd she used to go around with when she was fifteen.

In the morning I get into bed with Rose (she doesn't complain about being on the living room floor) and apologise for my misery. Outside it promises to be bright and sunny. Due to yesterday's bad weather Mt. Teide is covered in snow and looks spectacular. People are walking their dogs – a common occupation in Puerto de la Cruz. I always toy with the idea of getting a lovely dog. But I know that I'm the dog and as Rose says humorously, 'in need of an owner.' We decide to buy stuff from the grocers and then go down to the beach. It's nice when you are recognised in the local shop; I buy a can of octopus and sardines to take back to Cambridge. We sample the plain biscuits which are piled up on the counter. Short stocky women, jabbering away in Tenerifian Spanish (Rose noticed from the start that they say 'graci' for thank you rather than 'gracias') buy potatoes, carrots and massive leeks 'for my husband'. It's normal here, as in all Mediterranean countries, to eat a load of fruit and vegetables. But where are the olives?

I'm quite disappointed at not being able to swim in the sea but what can you do? Much of the beach is covered with volcanic rocks that have been thrown up by the violent tides and people have stacked them into piles. Still, it's something to paddle at the water's edge and to dare to venture further, experiencing the thrill of a breaking wave around ones knees. We then sample the swimming pool belonging to our block of flats which is set in an area of grass, dotted with comforting palm trees, with their thick scaly trunks and shady fronds. The water is ice cold and even after swimming for twenty minutes it feels sharp on the skin. Time for lunch when it's around two o'clock. After lunch Rose goes out to get my birthday present. She knows I'm going to like it! When we arrive at Oregon I'm very amused to see a 'reserved' sign on our table. David seems to welcome us with more exuberance than ever. 'Everything is special tonight' he says as be brings a jug of very cloudy looking sangria to the table. He certainly seems on top of the world. We are served a dish of langoustines followed by small green peppers, roasted and served in rough salt. They're bloody tasty. Then comes the paella with its watery tasteless rice and no chicken. It's the worst paella I've ever had; this Canarian chef should stick to what he knows. But it's all good fun. I chat to the German guy behind me who is on his own because his partner got struck down at the airport. We invite him to share our paella. He declines because he doesn't eat chicken (but there's no chicken in it) and tells me that Rose is far too beautiful to be left on her own. Suddenly the lights go and we all catch our breath but out of the corner of my little eye I have espied the chef cheerily bringing a chocolate cake to the table. He kisses me fondly on both cheeks and David leads the singing but gets no further than 'cumpleanos … I expect to be more embarrassed than I am. Rose is delighted and everyone is clapping. I blow out the single candle at the third attempt. We offer a piece of cake to everyone.

A couple smile but don't seem to understand. The man comes over and shakes my hand. The gay German guy joins us at our table and I can see that he's forcing himself to eat the cheap horrible cake. But it's all fun. A lone Swedish/American film producer is at another table and he's soon part of our crowd and inviting us to go to a rave Irish nightclub called 'Molly Malone'. I said that I would if it wasn't our last night. Rose isn't so sure: 'You complain about stuff and when you get the chance of having a good time you turn it down.' Every time I look her way she is having a 'last' photo with the other cook, who is much younger and is wearing a white headscarf. He's Italian but has worked everywhere, including Colwyn Bay in Wales where it always rains – although the people are nice. He also teaches paragliding and the American/Swedish man has tried it with him. A local 'learning disabilities' guy has appeared and is getting very excited, gesturing, gesticulating, running around the shop but not communicating anything. The cook knows that we know that he is harmless and he's sure that people will understand and his presence won't affect business. This is a real birthday party, with red balloons 'in spirit' which is all you need. David brings a bottle of martini to the table and regales everybody. The Italian cook is still sidling up to Rose. The German guy has a proper camera and takes a photo of me and Rose together. He expresses a lot of interest in her work as a bespoke shoe maker. David comes with the bill on a little silver saucer which he presents to Rose. She looks a bit nervous and uncertain as she passes it to me. 'I came along earlier and asked them if they could do something special for your birthday'. 'How sweet' I think to myself, 'I would have thought Rose was too shy to ask such a thing'. I forget that she is a professional woman of the world, always fighting her corner. My red balloon explodes somewhat when I see what they've charged for everything. How could that rubbish cake have cost thirteen quid is my first thought and if they like us so much why wasn't it on the house! Rose is amazed at my unbusiness-like attitude. I pay up. I do concede that we had a good time and that was the main thing. David says that he is on Facebook and gives me his email address. Maybe I should have gone to Molly Malone but we had to be up before 8 a.m. and Elena was coming round to pick up the keys.

I never sleep well when a deadline looms. Rose knows no Spanish but she understands Elena's instructions and directions better than I do because she's practical as well as being the child who is born on the Sabbath Day 'bonny and blithe and good and gay'. We've arranged to meet Mark at the bus station at 9a.m. He's terrified of not finding it although it's not far from his hotel. His EasyJet flight to Bristol Airport isn't till 7a.m the following morning. He'd already decided to spend the night before the flight at the airport but now, in order to be shot of Puerto de la Cruz which he fucking hates, he's decided to kill the day on the south coast. When we arrive at the airport he checks with Rose that he is at the airport in the south, not the north. Kindly she reassures him that he's in the right place (albeit at the wrong time) and she uses the same tone with me when I'm in the grip of some crazy anxiety. He seems very reluctant to leave us but it has to be. We find the EasyJet zone and looking behind us we see a bundle of grey poncho standing in the centre of the departure hall, totally isolated. It's no joke. Will he get a bus to Los Christianos or somewhere and spend the day on the beach. It is 10.15 am so he has all day and evening to kill before he can bed down on an airport sofa. I look back again and there's no sign of him. The first thing he'd said to me that morning was: I expect you guys were as fucking bored as I was yesterday – man this fucking place is the worst place on earth.' 'But no', I replied, 'we were on the beach and then at the pool'. No doubt he got through the day, the night, and caught his flight back to the UK.

Our plane is actually early which means that it isn't late. I espy Julie B. in the same seat as before and initiate conversation although I can see that she's not interested and probably wanted to shout: 'get out of my face – you're invading my space.' Rose mimics my 'hellowing' and turns away in disgust. The thing was that I wanted to tell Julie that I *did* write (although I told her I didn't) and everyone knows that it's contacts which get you on in the world. She's made it with her writing style of cheery malevolence. I do feel a little embarrassed too by my lack of restraint. (Actually all my faults, according to Toby, are Jewish ones). Rose thought that her husband looked very nice. To punish me she takes my window seat and I endure the presence of a Spanish man next to me who, God bless him, stinks to high heaven. I find bad smells very upsetting. Rose has finished her book and really needs something to read. I give her the choice of Rumi or Nigel Nicolson's 'Portrait of a Marriage' (Harold Nicolson and Vita Sackville-West.) Rose declines my offer of the latter, saying tactfully 'you have to be into that period' and buys today's newspaper, 'The Times'. Actually one does realise how unbelievably ghastly the English Aristocracy were, a century ago, with their pretensions, hypocrisy, and coldness. My mother used to fantasize that she was the Queen and my brother and I were Charles and Anne respectively.

Rose is fascinated by the cargo ships in the Thames – there are so many of them. It always feels good to be back in England's green and pleasant land – although unfortunately a lot of it is waterlogged. Poor farmers! I bet they're not reaching for the champagne. Our baggage is first out and side by side (what a miracle!) and we head for the same train. Her plan was to stay with Tamsin, her clever friend, overnight and drive back to Cornwall the following morning. However, she's up for doing the gruelling five hour drive this very evening so that she can have Sunday free, back in Bude. But Tamsin is going to the ballet at six, and Rose doesn't have a key in order to pick up her overnight bag which she'd left there before the outward bound journey. This isn't the first time that a friend has left her out in the cold. I can't believe that Rose didn't tell her when her flight was or that Tamsin didn't ask. With any luck Rose might just catch her before she goes out. We don't part the best of the friends; I am furious and aggrieved and she's been 'harangued for half-an-hour,' all the way from Gatwick South to London Bridge. There are lots of East Europeans on the train and a young lad checks that the train is en route to St. Pancras. I can't imagine my son trying his luck in a new land. Too many things to worry about.

On the way home I pop into Tesco to buy food and because I'm going too fast in the dark my full trolley collides with a step in the car park and I fall flat on my face, still hanging on to the trolley. What goes through my head is, 'I've done it now, I've injured myself well and proper' but I get up and there is no harm done other than a slightly sore elbow. Thank goodness nobody observed this indignity. Home sweet home and I wonder if Toby has remembered my birthday. He emerges from his room with a bouquet of pink and white roses, pinks, dahlias and lilies and a beautiful card to match. Absence makes the heart grow fonder. Rose has sent a text saying that she's picked up her bag and she's on her way to Cambridge. I open her exquisitely wrapped present which is a bottle of honey rum liqueur. Us three enjoy a meal, a lot of laughter and I try and force on Toby a genuine real life Tenerifian banana which he declines.

Angst in L'Ile Rousse

Many people in the U.K haven't heard of Corsica, that small island in the Mediterranean where Napoleon was born. But everyone has heard of *him*. With my ex-partner, who fancied himself as a painter, I went there to live thirty four years ago. We bought a house in the Balagne region at the foot of a pretty mountain village, and, eighteen months later, it was blown up by the locals who had had enough of 'the Englishman who drinks too much' and God knows what else.

My daughter, who spent her first fourteen months at the house named 'Dom 'Alto' had for some years expressed a desire to revisit the scene of the crime. I never wanted to return to a place where I had had such a hard time and sometimes it is indeed better to let sleeping dogs lie. Also Corsica itself had an air of neglect and abandonment (my God the local bread was awful – white aerated holey stuff) which didn't appeal to me when I was thirty. I bought one of those marvellous TOP IO guides (I was surprised they even did one about Corsica) and was flabbergasted to find, under the 'Things to Avoid' page a section entitled 'Falling Out with Locals'. The reader is informed that 'Corsicans are notoriously quick to take offence and tend to react to any perceived insult with disproportionate force'. However, the insane tend not to heed written warnings.

How nice it is to ditch the no frills budget airlines and travel with a company where you are welcomed at the airport and receive a glass of champagne on the plane. My daughter and I, her name is Rose, kept on stretching out our legs, revelling in the space. Stansted used to be a spacious airport which had a leisurely feel but now it's like a cage. Arriving at Calvi Airport was a bit of a hairy experience since the approach through the mountains is not straightforward and the plane seemed to tilt precariously to one side but we survived (the pilot is God and so you must let go and trust him completely) and were greeted on the tarmac by a blast of warm air and a canopy of blue sky, not to mention massive mountains. That morning at Stansted we had been engulfed by the cold grey drizzle of north west Europe.

A taxi awaited us to take us to the Hotel Splendide in L'ILe Rousse. Heavens, what a relief to be treated like a V.I.P, taken care of, and not have to hunt around for bus stops and stand in queues, feeling lost and uncertain. Of course I'm the seasoned hand, having been thrown in at the deep end on the island, and keep up a wearisome commentary on this, that and the other as we make our way to L'Ile Rousse. The driver has a smoker's cough – poor man. Actually I don't speak *that* much – I'm taking in the wonder of returning to a place where so much happened off the tourist track – so much bad stuff against a background of beautiful wild nature. We pass Lumio – a picturesque village with its Romanesque Pisan chapel founded in the eleventh century and Algajola – now a holiday destination in its own right but in 1981 it was a spot by the sea where we set up our tent on a camping site and I first noticed a change in my figure, amazed that a living creature was growing inside me. Wasn't it also the place where Roger went into the sea for a late-night dip and didn't return till lunch time the next day? He'd walked to Calvi to collect his trousers from the dry cleaners. And then what? He loved walking at night. He blamed me for not having learnt to cope with my anxiety. If I start relaying the past to Rose I see her eyelids gently lower and the sides of her mouth imperceptibly droop ... what torture are you now inflicting on me?

The 'Hotel Splendide' appears as THE SPLENDID HOTEL which looks and sounds altogether wrong and it is situated down a side street smelling sweetly of pink oleanders; (unfortunately Latins seem to be more casual about their dogs defecating on the sidewalks). We're not brilliantly impressed by the 'Splendide' with its puddle of a swimming pool (it's the lie that gets you – how do they make it look so much bigger in the photo but anyhow I suspected as much) and its grey breeze block staircases. (I wanted to see diamond and crystal chandeliers and cascading bougainvillea). Everything seemed so dull and plain. The lounge/bar area with the big flat screen TV suspended from one wall was a venue for pensioner social events just like the British Legion in my Cambridgeshire village. But all this was French and everything about the place grew on us – I loved the old-fashioned wood panelled restaurant dating from a hundred years ago and the general feel of provincial France (not that I have ever visited provincial France). The fresh croissants were served on napkins in baskets and the coffee was good enough. God knows why they present a buffet which includes strips of ghastly packeted ham and cheese. Look away now! I thought the French liked quality.

But the first thing we do on arrival is to scout the town to see if I remember anything. Where is 'Codec', the supermarket where we used to do the shopping once a week, catching the blue bus driven by Benoit, which went through all the villages picking up the excited inhabitants on their weekly trip to the big city. I used to worry because Roger would always buy fresh 'Roquefort' – bursting or rather ignoring the budget – as was his way. I remember the big fat woman with her rosy cheeks and hefty white forearms who served the cheese. All is gone, replaced by a faceless hypermarket which sells everything from birdseed to lawnmowers. There is a great new crop of foreign owned villas on the hills above the small town. I drag Rose round the dull streets (I always remembered L'Ile Rousse as a very dull place) until I see a plaque outside a tall house with a solid brown wooden door which is where I saw the lovely Dr. Emmanuelli (everyone had the surname Emmanuelli or Columbani) with the husky voice, during my pregnancy. Another doctor is there now. Finally, after a couple of wrong entrances, we find the Hotel Napoleon where my parents stayed in the autumn of 1982 in order to visit us at our mountain outpost. I think that my father was more worried than he let on, especially since the jewellery which my grandmother had left me in her will have been sold in order to perpetuate this Corsican adventure. What happened to the English lessons Roger was going to give (he did acquire one student but that didn't last long) and the bed and breakfast business that never got off the ground? Any money, always, that he earned, he spent on himself – his Taoism project (he'd order books from abroad), child support x two to his ex-wife and bars, bars, bars. As my father rightly said about him – 'what is mine is mine and what is yours is mine'.

Poor Rose having had a father like that. Wonderful, gay, talented, witty Rose wasn't her usual up-beat self because a relationship she'd been very hopeful about, 'I thought we could be happy together' had ended because the guy had a lot on his plate due to his divorce (two years previously) and was the principal carer of a six year old daughter to whom he was devoted. That is really going to hurt when your own inner little girl was abandoned by dad at the same age (not that he'd ever been a positive supportive influence) – so you've been ditched in the same way all over again. And when you give your all your womanly generosity takes a beating. A lesser person would have resented coming second in his affections but Rose isn't the envious type or rather she'd deal with her own sorrow rather than act on it, abominably, as is the way with all the little egos straddling the world stage. We're here in Corsica because it's important for her to actualise her roots – to turn the myth into reality. What she didn't bank on was me snoring the night away, causing her grief. Every time my snoring reached a crescendo she'd gently nudge me and it would stop briefly. But then it would start up again ...

Our first day was spent exploring L'Ile Rousse and getting our bearings. We discovered the market place in a Roman type forum where some pale-faced Corsican guy (whom Rose didn't like – and later confided to me that she was unable to look any guy in the eye) was going overboard spouting the merits of local honey and encouraging us to taste – from the sweetest and most soothing to the roughest, the sharpest on the throat, and, where there used to be an old family grocery – I remember the scraggly thin older ladies dressed in black –

surrounded by sacks of beans – there is now some anonymous fast food outlet. Rose comes to life looking at the daguerreotype postcards showing the old Corsicans, men and women, young and old, from the last century. It must have been a hard life, living on the land. There does exist a certain narrow-eyed Corsican look, which bears no resemblance to the French or the Italian, with their big eyes and smiling mouths. I didn't know that the Corsican resistance, or Maquis, had fought the Nazis in the second World War with great spirit, forcing them to retreat. And what fool would invade mountainous Corsica in the first place? We see the older men playing 'boules' in the Place Paoli which is dominated by the statue of the patriot Pascal Paoli who founded L'Ile Rousse in 1765 but failed to keep Corsica from the French, and overlooking the square is the old church with its broken steps and palm trees. The 'Cafe des Platanes', dating from the nineteenth century, shaded by ancient plane trees and providing a delightful overhead canopy is oh so typically French and we enjoy a Corsican beer, (a 'pietra biondo') at one of the outside tables; you can sit for ever in the round cane chairs. We feel that we're in the land of Pagnol's 'Jean de Florette' and 'Manon des Sources', which we are. Geologically, Corsica and Provence belong to the same family. Talking of families it was tragic how the Yves Montand character unwittingly, due to his peasant greed, destroyed his own son.

We discover the French bakery where a 'banette' (pointed at each end) costs one euro and you can either sit inside or on the pavement with your coffee. The vanillary smell emanating from breads, buns and pastries, wafts over you like a caress. It must be nice seeing the same people every morning at the local bakery. Rose notices the shelf labelled, 'Reserved'. Nobody wants to miss out on their daily bread. As a Frenchman once said, 'A day without bread is a day without sunshine'. With the eye of an artist Rose notices the detail that is most commonly missed – she was born with a sober observant expression on her face. I like Modigliani's dictum that 'happiness is an angel with a grave face'. With nothing else to do we walk up and down the promenade behind the beach reached by crossing the railway line which takes trains from Calvi to Bastia. There is a string of restaurants which all seem rather pricey and we settle down on a bit of beach at the far end of town where there are some vacant sunbeds. I don't remember nothing from the last century other than a bit of sandy beach. I suppose I had my mind on other things – like buying fresh liver from the butchers. (He'd reassuringly inform me that the animal had been slaughtered that very morning). We marvel at the white sand and the glorious turquoise sea which is like liquid silk. Rose tells me that she has had an 'abnormal' smear test, the second one in three years and to my barrage of questions simply says that she didn't want to tell me because she knew I'd worry. Her best friend in Bude has had the same thing – misfortune shared is always a comfort. All the alarm bells start ringing

... just as they did in darkest December when a 'significant' measure of microscopic blood was found in my urine. You should only have good things growing inside you. I've been depressed for so long I don't know what to do about it. Only the aroma and taste of coffee cheers me up – my wonderful stimulant! Walking around the old town – heavens we want to close our eyes to save them from the eyesore of all the tourist junk – God only knows what this place can be like in July and August – we decide to have our evening meal at the 'Cafe Rouge' which turns out to be a bulls-eye choice, except for the stray hair in my raw squid. I think that the waiter was surprised that we left such a large tip but the tasty food (in spite of the hair) deserved it. Rose gets very unhappy because she is shy and can't speak French and is envious of me because I can. It's not the fact that my French is good – it probably isn't but I seem to have the common touch, the knack, and can communicate my meaning. She wants to tell the waitress who is serving the desserts that we'll have the strawberry tart and the lemon cake because they complement one another. I tell her that she wouldn't get the meaning in English let alone French. Rose is more like a Japanese person – neat and shy – but I don't know why this upsets her. I'd love to have her intelligence and skills. I didn't realise how different we are or rather I'm realising that she's finding me difficult to bear. I don't think that thirty three year old daughters should go away with their mothers after a failed love affair. The rejection is rubbed in. But Rose is still Rose, always willing to do her best to help anyone with anything, and she promises to set up this wordpress.com site so that I can write my stuff. Maybe she is still a bit shut-down, having been hurt by 'a lot on his plate' forty four year old Matthew' whom I never met. My son said that he looks and sounds like a prick.

    Wendy our rep, has promised to take us to Speloncato to see the house since it's not far from where she herself lives and has lived for the past thirty years. Needless to say she's ecstatic about the island with its forests, gorges and crumbling villages. When she arrives on Tuesday morning, a few minutes after nine o'clock, she apologises for being late but she got caught in a traffic jam due to a 'family murder'. She doesn't seem particularly shocked by this aspect of Corsican culture – telling us how kind the locals were to her when she was living alone – putting heavy stones on the roof to keep the tiles in place and helping her water the land. That's indeed it – they hold onto their land with an iron fist and are fiercely possessive. This brings to mind the beautiful old convent in L'Ile Rousse which is adjacent to the Hotel Napoleon, barring some fast food outlets which make it impossible to walk on the pavement, is totally derelict because no one can work out who it belongs to. Maybe it's morbid but I like the sight of the holey cream lace curtains caught in the windows. Rose too loves the building. When she was a baby our hippy friend Michelle gave us a huge bagful of beautiful French clothes from the convent – and how grateful I was for their charity. I have to interrupt Wendy's apologies for her three minute lateness with my declaration that Rose is feeling unwell and so we won't be able to go to Speloncato. I offer to pay her for her time but she won't hear of it. Relaying her symptoms I am beginning to feel them myself as I write. She had had a similar funny turn in London about three weeks earlier after we'd been to William Morris's 'The Red House' – a place she'd always wanted to visit. On the underground she felt totally weak and faint and we had to take a taxi to the house near Green Lanes where she was renting a room from friends whilst doing freelance shoe design work in London. Frequent trips from Bude to London are gruelling. However, the rough Corsican wine might have upset her and she'd been sick after taking a Nurofen – oh dear, these young people with their pain killers. Maybe a contributory factor to her 'weakness' was being back with me all day (and night!) and my 'splish splash' approach to life, which probably overwhelmed her as a child. Actually for such as us dependence is problematic since it involves tears and tears are seen as weakness and defeat. Good Wendy immediately made an appointment with the doctor in L'Ile Rousse for that afternoon but when I went up to see her in THE ROOM she felt even worse and we decided that the A&E at Calvi was the best bet. En route Rose spoke about the pains in her side she'd had in London which she'd just lived with for a few days. Her work is responsible and demanding. She also runs moccasin making workshops both in Cornwall and London. Wendy had herself suffered appendicitis (the pain was so bad she thought she was going to die) and gall stones and she was also diabetic so we speculated on all the possibilities. Rose had developed an aversion to black olives and pancetta which suggested gallbladder problems – or an ulcer? Wendy was the right person to be with in a crisis – sympathetic, caring and practical. She waited in the waiting-room whilst I stayed with Rose, on and off, in the hospital room. I was expecting her to complain about the long wait but never a word. Back in the 'medical room' the nurses had difficulty finding a vein in her arm to get a blood sample and taking it from a vein in the back of her hand really hurt. She too never complained. After a long wait the blood test came back normal and Rose cried because she felt she'd wasted everyone's time. Since she is fundamentally rational, a self-effacing silence, rather than shouting and screaming, would be her operative mode in a crisis. However, the site of the pain was indeed her gall bladder and the doctor advised that she get a scan in the U.K. In the car there'd been a spot of fretting over the absence of the E11 card and passport and medical insurance but in the event nothing was required at all. Reciprocal health care as part of the EU deal. Wendy drove us back to the hotel and amidst hugs and kisses told us to phone her even at 2am if needed. Her phone was playing up, her car was playing up (maybe I should learn to drive on the 'wrong' side of the road; my suspicion that we might not see the island if we didn't have wheels had been confirmed) but it was all human and endearing in the best British bulldog spirit. I'm well aware that this prose is dull as ditch water on account of the dark cloud hanging over us but patience, dear reader, the clouds will clear leaving a sky the radiant blueness of which bespeaks a blessing of abundant life, not the curse of ill-health and death.

The rest of the day was spent on the beach, renting sunbeds off the Tamarind Restaurant, at the entrance of which was a Tamarind tree in flower. These sunbeds don't come cheap and at thirteen euros a day each we got a good deal – some of the restaurants were charging twice as much for the privilege of stretching out on their bit of beach. The Tamaris Bar and Restaurant sported gay blue and white sun umbrellas and sunbeds, which hit the right note exactly. This has turned out to be my most favourite beach ever with a view of the old town, a jumble of old houses, in one direction and mountains in the other. I get the sense that L'Ile Rousse is becoming the new Cannes/St. Tropez/Juan les Pins as these lovely spots have been screwed up by rank commercialism. Long, long ago are the days on the beach at Riccione, Italy, when me and my best friend Philippa nymphed about in our Cote d'Azur bikinis partaking of the nectar of the gods, namely toffee grapes on sticks, brought to us by God knows who. How hard life must have been for those poor men in their white rolled up shorts traipsing across the hot sands; there was one who came with beautiful linen lace-bordered tablecloths in pale blue, pale mint green and pale pink and sat patiently folding and unfolding them on his knees at my mother's feet, who, as usual, couldn't make up her mind. Which one for her sister, her mother-in-law etc ? ... none of whom could have cared a damn. These days poor African immigrants come round with their gear. Philippa and I weren't simply friends, we were peas in a pod (as her mother put it) so alike in our fun-loving feminine sensuality and straightjacketed by the hand of patriarchy. As I'm looking around me, observing 'the older French woman in her bikini' and noting how slim and stylish they appear Rose is immersing herself in a biography of Fleetwood Mac, written by Lindsay Buckingham's ex-girlfriend. She makes it all sound fascinating but I am profoundly disinterested and indifferent to their goings-on and have never even heard their music. I'm surprised that Rose is so reluctant to get into the sea (admittedly the water is more than a trifle cold) and swim for her life. Advanced yoga is the thing that keeps her afloat. As a youngster she was into gymnastics and diving. I get the feeling that she is slightly envious of my swimming and the way I stick to it religiously. I think that she finds my total animal immersion somewhat ridiculous. I am the hokey cokey fool who puts 'their whole self in' ... she prefers to think before she speaks. She is logical. When I talk enthusiastically about something or other she points out, with some displeasure, that I have food in my teeth. (And my kitchen is far from clean enough and my garden overgrown) Not that she isn't enthusiastic and full of laughter. She is and we always have a great time together. It's just that her mojo is temporarily dampened. And the underlying truth is that being in life's deep end, where the waves are rough, is dangerous. She's tired of being in the deep end. But today the sea is absolutely gorgeous to swim in – you're never really in a place until you've swum and put your face under water – and Wendy told us that the Corsicans are very conscientious about keeping the sea clean. Rose tells her how different it is in Cornwall where there is now a protest group called 'Surfers against sewage'; perhaps murdering family members is preferable to polluting the sea.

When you're away in a foreign place nothing is more important than what you eat. In Puerto de la Cruz, Tenerife we found a fish restaurant where the dishes weren't that great but the welcome and the atmosphere was. We debate the benefits of returning to the Cafe Rouge or having a closer look at the buffet at the Hotel Napoleon which we'd caught a glimpse of on our first day. This hotel is now owned by the Langley Group and everyone, including the staff, are Swedish or Danish, with a young Polish chef and a Latvian receptionist thrown in for good measure. I've developed a real penchant for anything Scandinavian, especially Danish, having fallen in love with their drama. Rose tells me that they have a very strong set of values – she's been to Copenhagen a few times in connection with 'Pointer' the company she used to design trainers for, before she went freelance. (Indeed she spotted a man at the Cafe des Platanes wearing her shoes but wouldn't approach him in case he wasn't totally satisfied with them). The Danes certainly looked out for their Jews during the war, unlike the French and the Hungarians. Anyway, the food is just our cup of tea, full of variety and wholesomeness and we reckon that twenty one euros for a four course meal is good value. (The butter is home-made, creamily silky and smooth, and a real treat to eat). In Cambridge you pay eight quid for a little bowl of mushroom risotto. No colour, no generosity, no joie de vivre. We have a laugh with the meat chef although it still is the case that Rose is keeping her distance from the rough sex. A Swedish waiter, clearing our plates away, happens to get distracted by Rose's beautiful face and lets a knife clang onto the table. Embarrassed, he mutters, 'sneaky bastard' as if such a phrase is normal, everyday English. The young waiters and waitresses talk to you naturally so there is no need to go round the tables asking if everything is alright and instructing customers to 'enjoy'. Grrr! I look around and take in the scene in one greedy mouthful but Rose focuses on details. She's delighted by a certain Swedish lady, well into her nineties, who is wearing a beautiful blouse and fine jewellery; she looks a treat and obviously respects herself. She and her husband are both tall, thin and white-haired and how elegantly they deport themselves. Every evening from then on Rose notes what she is wearing and on the last day we get to speak to them on the promenade by the beach, where they are sitting in the shade on what was also our favourite bench, under a gnarled old tree, with ferny leaves. Is it a maidenhair tree? The husband tells us that they are newly-weds. We think he is having a laugh but the wife proudly shows us her ring. We loved to observe their slow, careful pace and the way they supported each other as they went into the sea. He'd been to the Cotswolds. Like other Swedes in the hotel they were from Gothenburg and heading back, reluctantly, to a temperature of thirteen degrees.

Supper over we head down to the promenade and walk from one end to the other, checking out the dinky little station so old, so quaint, from which we'd planned to take the train to Bastia, a long three and a half journey, on Wendy's advice. This is where we were stationed a week before Rose's birth and where the consultant obstetrician harshly told me that I was too old to have a baby. We reckoned it was an interesting place to visit if you had nothing else to do but the weather was hotting up and we decided that relaxation was key, especially for Rose, and we'd prefer to take a boat trip to the Scandola National Park with the Scandis from the hotel. The promenade is the place where people walk their cute dogs but now that the sun was going down there weren't many people around and we walked to the end and sat on a bench and listened to the lap of the waves gently breaking on the beach. We couldn't help but burst into laughter as we contemplated our lonesome state and the fact that this is what lay in store for the rest of the week. There ain't much going on in L'Ile Rousse. It's beautiful to see the sunset and the lights from the boats reflected in the water but is that enough, night after night? We stroll back to the 'Splendide' passing the L'Ile Rousse Bridge Club with its small barred windows.

Talking of nights it was a matter of some import that I move into another room. There was one remaining room in the hotel – a single room on the fourth floor which was 'very small'. As the key turned in the lock I was expecting one of those maid's garret rooms which I was given in Paris when I was an au-pair. Rose and I were given such a room in 2002 in Bellagio, Lake Como, which was crucifyingly hot and disgusting. This was your lot if you were a servant. I was pleasantly surprised to encounter a room that was a great deal bigger than a broom cupboard but certainly only suitable for one person. It had a large oval mirror over the sink and to the left was a shower and to the right the toilet cubicle – behind a door that didn't close properly. Just enough room to sit down. There was a view of houses on the hillside. I really liked this room because it was compact (Rose's word), and simple without spotlighting or other modern fads. It was the room you'd expect in an old-fashioned seaside hotel. I slept well for the next two nights and so did Rose. Unfortunately it was booked for the last two nights of our stay and I decided for the next night to enquire about a room elsewhere. The Hotel Napoleon showed me a 19th-century room with a high ceiling which smelled dank. They told me to return the next day to see if anything else was available. They weren't sure what was going on because the computer was playing up.

We realised that it really does take a few days to settle into a place. We were pleased that we'd found a good venue for our dinner and went to morning market to buy fruit and cheese. We bought a big jar of honey for Wendy and the honey man was very pleased with me because I also bought the mead vinegar. We couldn't believe that fresh black figs and cherries were selling for fourteen euros eighty cents a kilo – a preposterous amount. When I was pregnant with Rose I used to eat my fill, picking them off the trees. The vendor didn't seem to know why the price was so high – except the cost of living was generally soaring. Corsica has sold out to tourism. Chatting to him or rather asking unanswerable questions I realised that Rose was no longer by my side and I couldn't see her anywhere. I communicated this to the fig vendor who shouted out in full voice: "Ou est Rose, ou est Rose?" She turned up eventually – she was looking for presents for her close friends – her band of sisters – and thank goodness she hadn't heard the fig and cherry guy belting out her name. I never want to shake Rose off (although maybe she does me) because she, like me, has her own space and, unlike me, has an excellent sense of direction. The market is pretty crowded with people sampling randy sheep's cheese and strong-tasting salami which is the devil's meat, Rose tells me in a whisper, since it can give you bowel cancer. Things are hotting up. Wendy told us that first thing in the morning the traffic into L'Ile Rousse is horrendous. She reckoned that things will be OK if the building stops now. But why should it?

You're apparently a bit backward if you don't get bored with a 'beach holiday' but I can't get enough of the views from this beach and how wonderful the sea is, although there are no waves. I'm reading a late Jean Rhys book 'Leaving Mr. Mackenzie' which, on account of its droopy-eyed, sophisticated melancholy is right up my street. Loneliness is a planet I know well. Maybe some of us never get what we want or need. Still, a trip to the local pharmacy is still fun because it's French and all the contents are ordered according to 'things for the eyes', 'things for the feet' etc. which is a very direct and purposeful way of doing things. Rose is after a ladies razor for her legs; she is repulsed by the stray hairs she can see on mine. In the main square, opposite the French pharmacy, is the pick-up stop for the choo choo train which goes round the town and a bit further and it is full of pensioners who seem too stout for the seats. You can't really wave at them. We enjoy a beer at the Cafe des Platanes along with all the other Frenchies. The men seem very gay and flirtatious. I'm thinking about Rose most of the time, wondering if she's OK. Maybe such a 'rara avis' (rare plant) as she is, so talented, gets struck down at an early age? The thought is unbearable and makes me go all giddy. Why do I think such things? She shouldn't have things going wrong with her body at her age. I see the way she observes young married couples with their offspring on the beach, living together harmoniously. and I pray this will also be her future. Love makes the world go round.

Back at the Napoleon and booking a packed lunch for the boat trip I espy a great leather bound book at the reception entitled 'Liste des hotes de l'hotel Napoleon Bonaparte a L'Ile Rousse' which is a record of all the people who stayed at the hotel in the year beginning 1931. It was built in the nineteenth century presumably to house Napoleon's family – with its turrets at either side it has the look of a fortress – but was then bought by an Italian a hundred years later who turned it into a hotel. In 1931 what is now the town car-park and the string of fast-food outlets between the hotel and the convent was all garden. Just imagine it – gardens which led all the way to the sea. The very first guests were from New York and then they arrive mainly from Paris – a few from S. Kensington, London. Were these the aristocratic refugees from the fading Cote d'Azur? What a long journey it must have been for them ... The name, addresses and dates of their stay are written in a fine, curly ornamental hand in purple ink and in 1933 the script is written by someone else but just as beautifully. There is a great gap of sixty or so years and then some names are entered in 1993 – a lady psychoanalyst from Zurich and a French couple from one of the smart boulevards off Napoleon's Arc de Triumphe. The handwriting is a rough scrawl which contrasts so markedly with the graceful romantic hand from the 1930s. But why use your hand if a machine can do things more efficiently? I was unaware that L'Ile Rousse was a destination of choice in the 1930s when Germany was busy armouring itself for war. What could have been further from their dreamy graceful existence?

I'm quite aware that we're not getting to see much of the island; I had it in mind to visit the wild coastal wilderness of Le Sartenais with its sublime beaches and prehistoric standing stones, Corte with its mildewing 18th-century buildings and spectacular modern setting (actually I'd been there when I was camping with Roger and tasted the sweetest spring water ever) and St. Florent and the Nebbio in the north – the "Land of Mists". But that's where it was all going to stay since I wasn't prepared to drive and anyway, we'd settled for the beach, the sea, the boat trip to Girolata through the Scandi Nature Reserve (it is mentioned in my book under boat trips) and the highlight of the trip, the purpose of the visit, which is Wendy driving us up to Speloncato to see Dom'Alto or what is left of it.

We arrive at the 'Napoleon' (apparently the great general hated the island of his birth) at eight sharp and pick up our hefty lunch box – they know how to feed you those Swedes and I wonder where everyone is. They are already all seated in the bus which is waiting at the side of the hotel. A lady in a lovely lemon yellow lacy shift tells us that we will be accompanied from coach to boat ... as if this infantilising control is quite normal. Rose and I are split up and I'm pleased that she has someone new to speak to – a young single female. I'm next to a young Dane whose parents are seated in front. I love hearing the Danish language and the fact that I don't know what they're saying. I'd imagined that the boat would depart from L'Ile Rousse but we have to drive to Calvi – which is good in that Rose will get a chance to see a new place. It is now a posh resort, with flash restaurants and bars along the quay Landry, which I don't remember in 1981 although I do remember rows of boring yachts in the harbour. You can't forget the impregnable Genoese citadel presiding over the bay and all seemed grey as Roger disappeared into bars and spent too much money. He picked up a dog on the beach and seemed envious of the French Legionnaire – hard men, big and strong. They're still around. I'm pleased to see a couple from Gothenburg to whom I'd told the story of Roger the painter and the house being blown up. The previous evening we'd discovered the bar at the Napoleon and exciting cocktails and the idea of not going straight back to our rooms after watching the sunset. I like this Swedish woman and know that we could be friends. As we are guided en masse to the boat I notice, by the side of the war memorial to the fallen in both world wars (the Corsicans fought very bravely and suffered terrible losses – apparently the economy of the interior, after World War I, lapsed into a decline from which it has never recovered) a hibiscus plant covered in red flowers which I point out to the Gothenburg lady, telling her that I have one in my living-room. She enjoys telling me that I must have 'green fingers.'

I'd imagined that we'd be on an open boat in the blue Mediterranean Sea as in 'The Talented Mr. Ripley' and perhaps diving off the side. Rose had wondered why I was fretting about whether to wear my swimming costume under my top ... Did I think that we'd be on a gleaming white yacht costing thousands of euros to hire for the day? In fact we were on your standard boat trip vessel with seating downstairs under cover and a crowd of pretty common Frenchies on a day trip. I was expecting some special magical atmosphere. I didn't realise that the Scandola National Park was not a wild forest through which you trekked but a stretch of soaring red volcanic cliffs which we meandered past on the boat. They were certainly something to see but the frenetic frenzy of people with their cameras was something else. When they get home are they really going to look at their fifty shots of red volcanic rock and show them to their friends? Standing on deck a French woman shoved me out of the way to get a prime shot and I was surprised to hear Rose say, 'that's VERY rude!' She understood and backed off. I enjoyed seeing the Genoese watch towers perched high on the mountain tops. On the return journey Rose mischievously pointed at the same crowd who were either asleep or chatting to one another – totally oblivious of the scenic rocks which they couldn't get enough of on the way out. It was too funny and ridiculous for words. On one of the rocks the authorities had nailed a pretentious sign reading 'Scandola National Park', which was totally at odds with the splendour of the place and the wild birds calling to one another as they built their nests. Rose was appalled and suggested that 'Private Property – FUCK OFF' would have been more apt.

We arrive at the pretty village of Girolata in the heat of the midday sun to the sight of cows at rest on the pebbly beach. Lauma, the youngster Rose was sitting next to on the coach, is our new friend. She's working on reception at the Hotel Napoleon for the whole of the summer (she was a little bit displeased when I mistakenly took her to be a waitress since she's obviously a very bright girl) – a Latvian whose family emigrated to Sweden. We hear her back story – how her parents have acquired a dog to love because they miss their children so badly – and how the Russian presence is being felt in Riga and it don't feel like bright sunshine. Rose later tells me that she wishes that she'd worked abroad for the summer – all the employees working and living in a hotel together ... It is indeed hard when you have to go it alone, carrying the weight of the world on your shoulders. We climb into the hills, admiring the views and taking some photos and put off eating our packed lunch until Lauma has found a snack. I point out to Lauma how the Corsicans construct walls – they just put the stones together, all shapes and sizes, and somehow they just 'stick' together. I couldn't resist leaving my mark on a wall by tampering with a stone. Lauma expects the edifice to collapse but it remains as strong and stable as ever. We search around for a shady place to sit. There is a group of young teenagers, boys and girls, who have come to stay for a few days and are frolicking like mad in the water. The girls in their bikinis are all thin but curvy and the boys are just beginning to look like men. It's all intensely playful and sexual and us three singletons look on silently, pretending not to notice but obviously thinking our own thoughts. Life is love and freedom. Lauma is fascinated by Rose's career in shoe-making and likes her a lot. She wants to read Shakespeare and asks me to recommend a play for starters. I tell her about 'Othello' and the theme of jealousy. Rose looks a trifle uncomfortable as I descend into darkness although she's also proud that I can speak so articulately about what interests me.

All this business about the sun and how it can kill you – I mean attack your skin and make you prematurely old. Of course it's scientifically proven – I can't ignore the sight of the shrivelled skin on the back of my hands which is the result,

I'm sure, of lying in the sun for hours at a time during my teens and my twenties. It's what you did if you wanted to metamorphose from a pale sad insect under a stone into a brave, bold beautiful being, the colour of burnished gold. But you can get quite neurotic worrying about your feet and the backs of your legs because, believe me, if you venture out into the Mediterranean sun there's a bit of you that's going to get burnt. To escape damage you'd have to cover up from head to toe, like a Saudi lady. And I reckon that all those sun protective creams are a multi-million dollar money-spinning con. Needless to say my feet and my ankles became a little too pink for comfort. And I didn't rub the cream over Rose's back as thoroughly as I might have done.

In spite of the Napoleon's sophisticated technology there is a bit of confusion as to vacant rooms and a receptionist who apologises for being out of uniform (as if I'd noticed or cared) shows me a room in the new wing which is actually a massive suite, pristine, perfect and hard-edged as it's possible to be and tells me that she'll only charge me eighty euros for the night because that's what I'd been quoted for the musty high-ceilinged pad from 1930. Rose is amused when I tell her this – the suite could probably be let for hundreds of euros – and secretly oh so relieved that she'll have another night with a room to herself – although she's far too polite to say this. But they don't think they'll have another room for the night after and anyway it's our last night so I reckon a decent night's sleep doesn't matter so much – Rose can sleep on the plane. And anyway, being a tight Jew, I don't want to spend any more money if I can avoid it. Rose is too unselfish to protest. But I note the almost undetectable change in her facial expression when I say I'll be back – me and my humungous snoring, for the last night of our stay.

Actually I'm feeling a little nervous about my overnight stay at the Napoleon; I relocate in order to shower before dinner – finding the Swedish 'wet room' a bit daunting. I see Lauma at reception and am a bit curt with her, telling her I'll speak to her later. She asks me where Rose is. Dinner, as usual, is entirely to our taste and it's nice to acknowledge nice-looking people. I tell Rose about the couple who, for the first time, are chatting and laughing together. She replies that they probably had sex last night – the first time in years. Lucky bastards! – but it's nice to see them so playful and happy. Something is wrong when I prepare for bed in my show bedroom. I feel as if I'm bedding down in a coffin. The bed and the pillow are marshmallow soft and this feels totally wrong in a Mediterranean climate. *Everything* is remote-controlled. I sleep fitfully in this barren bed, barren room, barren suite. I hate it. I lie awake in the middle of the night and the silence is overpowering (anybody I know would wince when they hear ME complain about SILENCE because I loathe loud voices at night and banging doors) because it's the silence of outer space or the morgue. I expect that everyone else on the floor, all the Swedes, are fast asleep, as is normal and natural, and the only person who is wide-awake is poor, unloved me. At around 5.30 a.m. the rubbish men (?) enter the back car-park making the noise that their carts make and I realise that that's probably it for the night – I won't get back to sleep. At around eight when I make my way to the lift (en route to the 'Splendide' for breakfast) a little girl appears in the corridor and says 'he he' to me affectionately (the Swedish for 'hi') and I respond in like manner. Rose can tell from my face that I didn't sleep well. 'But I thought you liked soft beds' she says, a little perplexed. I'm pleased that she's feeling so much better and she's absolutely delighted with her new bra which was purchased in a French lingerie/swimwear shop. French fashion in the 21st-century consists of tarted-up rags.

What is foremost in her mind is the desire to pull down one of the posters, which have appeared everywhere, of a very attractive, sexy Corsican singer and guitarist from the mountains who is performing in the church the evening of the day that we leave. She really would do this but I restrain her on account of the Corsican Mafia who are always waiting and watching. Instead she takes a picture of him with her camera (to share with her friends) although acknowledging the fact that he might not be what he seems. She's come to the knowledge that if you're too fussy and critical you might end up with no one. There's a guy in Bude who is a definite possibility – he told her that he'd still be around if things didn't work out with Matthew (the guy who let her down and was jealous of her freedom) – in spite of the fact that she doesn't like the way he dresses and his house is a bare bachelor pad. I tell her that a man without a woman is sterile and a woman without a man is boundless energy going nowhere. We always have long, funny, enlightening talks. There is a group of polyphonic Corsican singers who are singing in a church th*e very next evening* and this sounds a good second choice. I remember Roger joining the Corsican locals in song around the fire at the Christmas party in Speloncato where every child, including baby Rose, was bought a present by the local municipality and all the lovely cakes were made with the Corsican staple, chestnut flour. Rose also wants to hear the singers but minus the delighted thrill, the licking flame, which the long-haired guitarist evoked in her.

Back on the lovely sand (it's certainly better to be raised up on a sunbed because sand can be a blasted nuisance) Rose looks longingly at the statuesque yachts moored within swimming distance of the beach and muses on what it must be like to own one. You can certainly keep your distance from people. I look at the elderly couple who are so in life, not looking over their shoulder at the grim reaper. The lady reads her book with the help of a giant magnifying glass. Out of the corner of my eye I watch them changing from beachwear into swimwear and how they accomplish this task, preserving both energy and modesty. At the water's edge *she* nearly falls over but he steadies her. They both lie on their backs in the water. Why not? You do what you can. *He* sits on the wet sand and can't get up again but finally, in his own time, he manages this feat. They are not ashamed or embarrassed by their age; her elegance is expressed through her clothes and not lurid face paint. I can't help thinking of my mother in her early forties, sitting on the Italian beach in her snot green swimsuit, the very picture of bad temper and dissatisfaction – resembling Rouault's 'Prostitute at her Mirror' – a very sad female figure. (My father, like a desperate dog, lays expensive gifts at her feet). God knows what happened to her as a child – too many chores at an early age and too much negative criticism. The lovely aged couple enjoy a slow lunch at the Tamaris, not without wine of course. Before we leave I'm determined to make contact. How I wish that both Rose and I had someone to share our lives with. This is why our being solely together is past its sell by date. We need some fresh blood in the place.

She can't stand me as we're waiting to go into the church to hear the Corsican singers because I suddenly panic, thinking that I've run out of euros (I'd put the remaining notes in a separate compartment in my wallet) and asking her bluntly how much money she has left and maybe insinuating that she didn't pay me for the bra. This is all horrible stuff of which I'm deeply ashamed, reminiscent of my own upbringing. It's the fact that I'm *still* thinking about money when the finances have been squared up. Rose tells me, with some distaste, that I'm mad. In the church there are some consoling statues – St. Peter graciously holding out his hands – but also one of Christ buried alive in a transparent coffin. Rose grimaces. The singing is so wonderful, full of passion and soul, and they concentrate on listening to one another. Rose, who was the star of the guitar when she was at school – she gave it up because it interfered with her social life as the belle of the ball – comments on the twelve string (?) instruments and I comment on the cute youngster of the quintet. The others, pale and pink, like the honey man in the market, don't look Corsican. At the end of the performance they receive a standing ovation and cries for an 'encore'. The following evening Rose and I, friends again, are walking along the promenade when Rose spots the black-haired, cute looking youngster of the group who is out walking his cute black-haired little dog and listening to tunes on his iPod. We have to approach him. We tell him how much we enjoyed the singing and Rose is curious to know how they learn so many songs. He tells us, choosing to speak English, that there's a network of friends all over the island singing together over the years. The problem is getting together in order to practise. Because I liked the last song so much (did I ,or was I just flirting with him?) he says that I can listen to different arrangements of it on 'YouTube' and writes the name 'L'anniversaruu di minetta' in my little notebook. I am very nosy about people. (My son has also made this observation). Rose is tickled by the way the little curly-haired dog was frightened and was hiding behind him. I said that I wanted to stroke his curly black head (as he bent down to write in my little book). Rose thought that I was referring to the little dog. Anyway, we were both tickled that we'd spoken to him. Oh what it is to have real roots in a place, to love the country of your forebears.

Saturday is our last day and Wendy is going to drive us to the infamous Speloncato. She arrives punctually at 9 am and tells us how suntanned we look. She's pleased to hear that Rose hasn't had a relapse. This is of course the moment of truth, the reason why we're here. I didn't realise that it's a forty minute drive from L'Ile Rousse to Speloncato nor did I realise how mountainous the region was and how high up in the mountains we were. These days there are numerous coach tours to the 'pretty villages of the Balagne'. En route Wendy points out a famous bandit dwelling from the last century built so deep into the mountainside that this outlaw could put a finger up to his enemies. For the life of me I can't follow her directions. I feel a bit of a fool when Wendy expresses her bewilderment not as to why the blowing up of the house was never investigated but as to what the situation was as regards ownership; I was the owner – albeit of a ruin. What monies were exchanged in the transaction in 1984? All I knew was that I received a lump sum in insurance for which the waiting time was about eighteen months, when we lived in B&B accommodation in Cambridge. So that I didn't sound too dependent on my father (who handled the insurance claim through his French lawyers) I said that I was back in the UK 'doing other things'. Wendy could understand that. I felt compelled to add that the other thing was working as a cleaner in a seven bedroomed house in Old Palace Lane, Richmond, Surrey. Wendy said nothing and seemed confused. I was the thirty two year old cleaner with a baby of eighteen months. I remember their late evening return from a historic Wimbledon semi-final/final and how I felt like Cinderella. All the teenage children went to Bedales – lucky beggars. Roger was always drinking in the small pub over the road and meeting famous actors and the like. Maybe I should go back and visit that place too.

Wendy keeps on asking me if I remember the villages we pass through and I have to reply that I only remember the names; I knew the names so well because they were on Roger's walking itinerary – often at night. She wonders that I didn't get lonely in my mountain stronghold ... and looks at me as if I might not be human. Rose enters the conversation, saying that I'd never known anything different. I don't mind her saying this because it's true. We reach Speloncato, the village and Wendy goes to the cafe/bar, leaving Rose and I to explore for however long we want. There are a cluster of men in the square and I expect one of them to turn to me and say 'weren't you the concubine of the Englishman who was such a nuisance to us all?' but not a word in my direction. We stand outside a church and an elderly lady and her sister/friend lean over and shout out that it's open and we can go in. I bet *they'd* remember something. We pass dwellings adorned by pots of geraniums, petunias, roses and fuchsias, as pink as pink can be but not a sound emanates from within. Noone in the narrow streets. All the old people have gone and their children live and work on the French mainland and return in high summer to take over their inherited homes. It's no longer a living village. We pass a house the gate of which is festooned with flowering jasmine and the scent is heavenly. Actually that is what I do remember about the Balagne – the sweetly scented super fresh air.

Back in Wendy's car and driving down to Dom 'Alto (a faint awareness that if Roger knew we were here now he would, in spite of his mental illness i.e. that of being totally in his own little world, like a hamster on a wheel, he'd be eating his socks off in envy since he loved Corsica so much) I feel a bit nervous, as before an exam, (although it doesn't take much for that nasty feeling to creep up on me). On the right we pass the big house where the French lady lived with her two sons at whom she was constantly shouting and then we've arrived at Dom 'Alto – the place where I lived on the edge for about eighteen months. The first thing I do is show Rose the view beyond the stone wall (where Roger used to lay out the dead rats that used to make a helluva row in the loft under the roof) which is all of the Balagne plain, and in the far distance you can see the sea and the southern coast of France. Perhaps you could swim to Nice! But let it be said that this is an awesome space, dense with trees and maquis. The house itself is exactly the same although it has been spruced up quite a bit. No sign of Pistach, the donkey or Gypsy, the chained-up dog, surrounded by piles of excrement. (He belonged to Gacon the honey maker who had his factory on the ground floor). The front door is open and there are sounds of voices within. I want to go inside. Rose thinks that I shouldn't and Wendy says nothing. I noticed that she didn't do her best to take a nice photo of me and Rose outside the house. Quite the opposite in fact. Also in the car she told me that the Dr. Emmanuelli that she was acquainted with wasn't the same one I'd known and seemed irritated by my confidence that he would have remembered me. Indeed he would have – all the argy bargy about me wanting to have the baby at home (!!!) and my intolerance of the blood pressure pill ('catapressan') that I had to take daily and his wonderful husky-voiced attractiveness and his constant avowal that 'ce bebe va tres bien dedans', (this baby is very happy in the womb). Anway, I get to go into the house, followed by Rose (I notice that there is a proper gate at the side entrance – something we never had) and the present proprietor (since 1984) of this 'gite' is happy to show me around. The bedroom looks so much smaller –

probably because it's been nicely decorated and I point out to Rose where her cot was, near the window. The guy thinks that I'm telling her where she was born and we laughingly correct him. The bathroom too had been totally revamped and modernised. The kitchen and small living room (with the fireplace where Roger made the most amazing fires from logs he'd chopped himself with the sad irony that he was never around to enjoy the bright warmth) have been knocked into one and this is the point at which I have to say something about the house being blown up. The weird thing is that there's no sign of any drastic re-building – I'd always imagined Dom 'Alto to be a heap of rubble or a flashy hotel ... He confirms that there *was* an explosion and indeed it *was* the kitchen area and he purchased the house off a monsieur in an estate agents in L'Ile Rousse. 'I was the owner' I assert and perhaps he thinks I'm coming back to reclaim my property ... and this is how wars start ... It's certainly been his for a long time and now that my father isn't around I'll never know what really happened and what monies changed hands. I can't really be bothered to walk around the terraces but I note that nature is far better tended and cultivated than it was in our time. The peach tree, from which we made umpteen jars of peach compote, is still there and so is the arbour where I placed Rose's play-pen and where she swallowed bits of twig. She wasn't very pleased to hear that. I didn't believe in toys. What a foolish extremist I was. What bad things we do when we're unfree; we take appalling liberties – desperately trying to get something for ourselves. The drama, indeed the terror, of the past has gone and nature remains the same, goes on as ever. The present owner has made a very neat herb garden outside the kitchen door where the bomb was placed.

Rose and I walk to Ville di Paraso, following the road I took when she was a baby in her push-chair. The road seems smoother, newer, whiter. And you can no longer climb over a low rocky wall to pick the jam- like ripe figs off the trees – in fact I can't even see any fig trees – the whole area seems less like a wilderness. The old grocery is no longer there but the bar is – although obviously I never frequented the bars. They've also made a very attractive cafe with stupendous views over the Balagne. The purple and pink petunias in pots nod their heads merrily. Rose follows me into the bar and I literally proclaim to all and sundry that I was here thirty four years ago and someone must remember something! I give my little spiel of a story and the plump dark-haired lady drying glasses behind the bar comes onto the stage, so to speak, and says that Madeleine Columbani (yes, that was the first name – the woman who was always so pleased to see Rose as she sat quietly in her pushchair and when things deteriorated asked me pointedly where my mother was) had passed on but her sister still lives over the road in the big house. A nice-looking man of about my age tells us that he was born in Speloncato and has always lived there. My story is vaguely familiar;

I expect that my appearance has livened up his Saturday morning as he reads the newspaper over his pietro biondo beer or whatever. Wendy said that she'd meet us at the church which is at the far end of the village (she has errands to do – dropping off parcels and the like) so Rose and I slowly walk past the beautiful lemon and orange orchards, marvelling at the beauty of nature and her adorable scents. As we're waiting under a shady old tree opposite the church a car draws up and the nice-looking man in the bar asks us if we need a lift somewhere. Unfortunately we don't. At that moment Wendy draws up in her car and seems a little disturbed and annoyed to see us talking to a local. She drives us away pronto. Rose also thought that he seemed nice – a missed adventure/opportunity for a bit of 'parley-vous francais'. I remember that in the hospital Wendy had told me that as a mother one always thinks that one is right and I should let Rose decide what she wants to do as regards having a scan here or waiting till we get back to England. She thought maybe that I was the dominant mother and Rose had never separated from me. The opposite is true in fact but I don't want to go too deeply into psychological stuff which is always complex. We're all a mixture of Eros and Thanatos. Maybe only Jesus Christ was completely free, completely open.

It's our last afternoon on the beach and the temperature is hotting up. The thermometer outside the pharmacy reads thirty three degrees and indeed the sand is too hot to walk on. Apparently it's never so hot in the first week of June and I certainly don't remember it being so all those decades ago. It can also get extremely windy. These details count and send the native Corsicans rushing to place stones on their roofs. Rose goes off for a bit by herself and I sit and read my Christopher Isherwood book, 'A Single Man' in the Cafe/Restaurant Tamarind with its blue and white striped awnings – so pretty and French in the sunshine. Some time later she returns for a swim and we tell each other that we only want the other to be happy. To this end Rose thinks that I should move to Bude, Cornwall where I would have far more fun. I could join the jiving club, play table tennis to my heart's content and we could walk our cute little (imaginary) dogs together. I could get so much more for my money and be by the sea and be near her for when she meets someone nice and starts a family. As she talks I am thoroughly sold on the idea; when I get home I realise that I'd only move down there if she did indeed start a family. My son tells me that Rose could talk me into anything. 'And who will I have?' he adds. Sitting at the Cafe des Platanes, under the leafy plane trees, with all the others who are finding it too hot in the sun we espy the Swedish couple from Gothenburg who are waiting for their pick-up to the airport. The man is longing/looking for 'un tarte tatin' and we direct them to the bakery. Rose is surprised that they've been here a week and didn't even know that there was one. There's a big wedding on at the church and everyone is arriving in their best clothes and standing around chatting outside, awaiting the arrival of the bride and groom. All the handsome young women are heavily made-up, wearing sleek dresses and high-heeled shoes. Rose seems to feel a little uncomfortable. Who are we to stand there staring. And she herself isn't 'dressed to kill' and dresses, not to catch a man, but to express herself. Rose had got a bit pissed off with me in town because in a small supermarket (how I love the super clean scrubbed fresh smell of these supermarkets) she bought some 'cheese bread' (we thought the bread was filled, from what the cashier/owner said, with brocciu cheese but in fact it was just cheese flavoured) and I had asked the man for a bag. As if she couldn't speak for herself.

En route to the airport the next day we want to talk about something but the driver wants to practise his English. He wins. The airport is very small. In the check-in queue a couple are lamenting the parking problems they had in both L'Ile Rousse and Calvi and the best angle at which to exit the latter. Simultaneously both Rose and myself move to the outside of each side of the queue because we don't want to be drawn into the conversation. We can see a storm brewing in the sky and everyone wants to be airborne before the heavens open and the rain comes crashing down. Taking off from Calvi airport is obviously far easier than landing on it.

Back at Stansted the weather is pleasantly warm and Rose has decided to come back to Bottisham because if she went back to London on the Stansted Express she'd be alone in her friend's house – who had texted to say that she'd be out for the evening. About thirty minutes later another text follows informing her that they're all meeting round her sister's house for a late supper and Rose regrets her decision to stay at mine. These friends are the 'Mary Poppins girls' as Toby calls them, because they are set up for life on account of their grandmother's legacy. I think that Rose has a certain dread of the loneliness/isolation which has always been the main feature of *my* life. There is a fear of the evil one getting in. There is also fear of the little sack of poison within ourselves. 'To be or not to be' is still the question.

Traipsing through Copenhagen

What is the best way to get bruised toenails? Don a pair of slip on black leather shoes, albeit worn with thick socks, and tread the streets of a European capital city.

I was dreading this trip, as I dread everything I have to do, and would have preferred to have stayed at home with a collection of Hans Christian Anderson stories but hey you have to be brave and adventurous in this world otherwise you become one of the aimless crowd following the leader, never stepping off the beaten track, never encountering danger and split-second decision making. However, as much as I attempt to give myself a good talking to for a week or so prior to the expedition I can't dispel the 'fear of the unknown' which just won't go away.

Indeed the worry that assaults me before I go is too severe to be communicable and anyway who wants to be privy to someone else's catalogue of fear. Things weren't helped – in fact the darkness within was greatly accentuated by unseasonable end of April weather – bitterly cold biting winds, sleet and hail. Why doesn't God love me is the arctic scream. But according to the BBC weather forecast something approaching normality was meant to occur on the very day I was to travel, ushering in a period of nice, decent weather. Could I trust this prediction? It would be unwise to leave myself exposed so into the smallest of cabin cases went a black umbrella, a beautiful black fur-trimmed hat such as the Jews wore in Krakow or Warsaw, a thick black and white jumper and a fluffy pair of slippers to relax my feet, in my lonely bedroom, after a hard day's walking. As Freud said 'there is never the wrong weather, only the wrong clothes'.

Before the trip I do my homework, studiously consulting my trusty companion 'Top 10 Copenhagen'. It's not a bad idea to find out where my hotel is more or less situated (the rough map of the city that the book provides suits me fine) and to locate the art galleries, castles and palaces. It's going to be a lot to do, a lot to take in. And of course there is the ordeal of going by coach to Luton Airport and the dismal airport experience crowned by the waiting in line to go through 'Security' where you become impersonal grey matter, blending with all the other bodies around. I never fail to set off the alarm, in spite of removing metal objects, necessitating a body search. This time round they lose my slip-on black leather shoes which end up in a grey tray on the assembly line; I deliberately choose to direct foul angry looks at the attendants. How dare they lose my shoes! Chatting to a fellow passenger speeds things up a bit; the guy I chat to is en route to Ankara, Turkey for a golfing jaunt with his mates. Chat to a man, any old man, and they never fail, some way into the innocent human discourse, to bring in 'my wife' with just a hint of emphasis – just so you know, just to maintain a necessary boundary. It's all right by me mate – I wasn't trying to get off with you!

Waiting in a horrible little room prior to boarding the plane (there aren't even any loos as there are at Stansted; Luton really is a shit-hole) I spot a man who looks pure Danish and not mongrel English. I tell him as much and enquire as to the distance between the airport and the city. We get chatting and he tells me that this journey is his weekly commute since he works for a Danish finance company situated in Covent Garden. I think that was it; the facts seem to lag behind my sympathetic absorption in the person. I sigh deeply when he tells me how he missed his plane just last week because of some absurd security scare on the train. He had to spend the night in a hotel. 'Oh hell, all in all that must have cost you' I exclaim. He brushes off my exclamation with a dismissive admission that the firm pays. He's a nice soft-voiced Dane (working in finance – not so sure about that) and offers to give me a lift to my hotel. We agree to meet up in passport control.

I didn't realise that, by plane, Denmark is a stone's throw away from merry England. Sitting in my window seat I look down at my wrist and realise that my Faberge inspired bracelet has gone. All that's left is my bare wrist. It's as if I've lost my soul, my eternal treasure. It must have happened when I was taking off my watch and my belt in preparation for inspection and some rough thug behind me told me to get a move on. It must have just got knocked off and I curse the stress that comes upon me during 'security'. Nothing to be done; all objects can be lost. This is a lesson in non-attachment. But I can't help feeling it because the bracelet belonged with a pair of earrings which will be forlorn without them … I can't help telling the man in the seat next to me (he is travelling with his little boy who has Down's Syndrome) and he asks me if it is insured. It's comforting just to hear another voice. I don't badger him because even I can see that he's under the pressure of travelling with a child who needs a lot of attention. However, he does tell me that he has four daughters (but he looks so young?) and a house in Sweden. It transpires that I'm stuck in my seat until man and boy are ready and so I miss the Danish finance gentleman in the long dismal queue at passport control. He might have got through quickly since his seat was at the front of the plane. However, it's probably not a good idea to get into a car with a stranger, however normal and nice he may seem, and actually I have no problem buying a train ticket and getting on the right train. I speak to a female software engineer who has recently arrived from Miami, Florida and is getting off at the central station – where I too am heading – in order to visit the famous and fabulous Tivoli Gardens. As I'm checking my change from the purchase of the rail ticket – becoming familiar with the coinage – she or we bemoan how expensive Copenhagen is likely to be.

My hotel, the Guldsmeden Carlton, seems more than a ten minute walk from the central station. I can't pronounce 'Vesterbrogade', the road it's on, although I'd probably get the hang of it in time. The Danish people seem very calm, open and friendly; they are a quiet, thoughtful people and I like them a lot. They are obviously law-abiding and orderly; they don't cross the road before the little green man goes. Even though I've heard that ignoring this rule can land you in trouble I can't resist the temptation to zip across if no cars are coming. I have trouble finding the hotel because it's set back from the street, reached through an archway. What is scrawled artistically on the wall is 'Organic is the new black' and 'love drives out hate as light drives out darkness' and something about the futility of ever more speed in our world.

In the book the hotel is described as sophisticated but relaxed and so it is. I must say that I am of total accord with the opinions expressed in these 'Eye Witness' travel companions. I really like my room with its dark wood furniture, white walls and a four poster single bed with pretty white tied-back cotton curtains and white sheet and duvet cover. There is a narrow balcony and the view is of typical, low-key Copenhagen dwellings; neither fancy nor run-down; just plain, modest and functional. I open my suitcase and really can't believe my eyes when I see my lovely bracelet sparkling up at me. Is this a miracle or what? Is God looking after me? I must have actually taken it off and put it in the case in the course of the authoritarian search. (When I go downstairs I can't help telling the story to the lovely young blonde receptionist who loves California and speaks English with a marked American accent.) The bathroom (oh, life is so much easier if there is a bath to lie in and there isn't one) is all organic in accordance with the hotel ethos. Upside down lotions and liquid soaps in orangey red plastic dispensers hang from the wall and you can swap your conventional tube of toothpaste for chewy tablets. Hmm. The towels are rough and a sort of pale pinky brown – yes, there is definitely a sweetness in the Danish people. There's a bible in Danish in the desk drawer – it's amazing how quickly you begin to recognise words. (The underfloor heating in the bathroom is a godsend since I accidentally flood the russet tiles with my misdirected angling of the shower head. I also soak my poor slippers …)

Well, I can't sit in my room for the rest of my life so I venture out into Vesterbrogade, in the direction of the central station and the Tivoli Gardens. Above my head I can see people whizzing around on all sorts of crazy rides. I'm surprised at how much it costs to get in – after all, it's just a walk round a crowded garden. But the Tivoli Gardens were founded in 1843 and you can't help but be impressed by the landscaping of gardens and lakes and exotic buildings. I'm surprised that there aren't peacocks strutting around but the place is too densely packed with people for that. It's obviously a good place for a family outing. There are open air concert stands and I take my seat to listen to youngsters performing, conducted by their bejeaned, bespectacled teacher who looks so nice and organic. I clap heartily and think to myself what a good thing it is for children to be musically involved from an early age. They're all so relaxed and happy. At another stand some pop singing is going on and what is so lovely is that a lady in her seventies is jiving with a younger woman who is twice her size. All eyes are on the older woman with her long white hair – and her too big sandals which are falling off her feet – on account of her rhythm and sheer joie de vivre. She is certainly stepping it out in her own unique style. You'd never see such a thing in any of the London parks; maybe the Brits are too uptight – take themselves too seriously. There's no hint here that the men in white coats are coming to take her away ...

God knows where I would have gone to eat if my guide book hadn't suggested 'Wagamama', which is a bit difficult to find as it's in a tunnel surrounded by candy floss stalls, shooting galleries and other funfair delights. There's an old shop selling wonderful striped sugary confections which must have been known to that delicious man Hans Christian Anderson. I can only eat half my dinner and I ask if I can take the remainder away. They're obviously used to such requests because I get a special takeaway box or perhaps they simply do 'takeaways'. It's so busy that the staff are almost literally rushed off their feet and you can watch the cooks, most of whom look Malaysian, hard at work in the kitchen, continually glancing up at the orders which are placed above the open window. I'm far too hot in my winter outfit but that's the way it is – what can you do – better than the other way round and the next day, Sunday, I'll probably dispense with my thermal vest. Meal over, I walk around the gardens and resist going into the 'amazing' aquarium because you have to pay all over again. I'll have to forgo the rays and the eels and the five hundred varieties of fish ... I sit on the verandah of the old Tivoli Palace which is now the seat of a very refined and expensive restaurant. A waiter asks if he can be of service and I tell him that I am just enjoying the late sunshine – proceeding to recount the horrors that I have left behind. He is pleased to recount the horror of the preceding days in Copenhagen with its snow and no going out to the Tivoli Gardens. I am left alone to admire the view whilst the posh diners on the other side of the glass tuck into stuff that probably doesn't measure up to the magical sounding menu. The sun is still shining as I leave the Tivoli never to return since it's not free. It's certainly an exciting place for children and young adults and apparently the place was a great inspiration for Walt Disney when he visited in 1950. Michael Jackson wanted to buy it. Maybe it spoke to him of the childhood he never had.

    I'm so tired after the day's travelling that I go to bed early and sleep well in my lovely 'white' bed in spite of being rudely woken up sometime before midnight by someone who is unaware of hotel etiquette as regards turning keys and shutting doors quietly. I always look forward to the surprise element in hotel breakfasts and the fact that you can help yourself and even take away a few choice extras to get you through the day. The organic breakfast that awaits me is indeed special and of course the price has just gone up to about £17 which is probably, as the sky is high, more than you'd expect to pay. The muesli is home-made and slices of kiwi and pink grapefruit are everywhere to the fore. Pink grapefruit juice is delicious. To your yogurt you can add mulberries and almonds layered in honey plus other nuts, berries and raw grated chocolate. The Danish rustic and chewy black breads are just my cup of tea and there's lots of dark tahini and nut spreads and palm tree sugar. Long cat's tongues of organic chocolate, milk and plain, are laid out for the taking. There are also plates spread with small slices of different cheeses and dried meats. Foregrounding the plates of food are wide ceramic pots of mint, basil and thyme which match the mugs on the opposite table The pinky brown serviettes – the same colour as the bathroom towels – are printed with the hotel slogan: 'Love Food – Hate Waste' and advice about not piling up your plate. I'm not used to eating a proper breakfast – at home my fare is a handful of seeds so I ask if I can make up a roll (or two) and take it with me. They don't mind at all (they can't really object when the price is so steep) and offer to wrap it up for me in cling film. The only criticism is the coffee which is somehow insipid; I don't know why that is. Coffee is meant to feel like a jump lead to your head. In this joint you can help yourself to coffee, and herbal teas (though there is Earl Grey) at any time of day, which is certainly useful when you come in at 5pm after a hard day's traipsing.

    I am the first one in for breakfast and set out for my round of sightseeing at about 8am. It's lovely and quiet down Vesterbrogade because it's Sunday. The early bird catches the worm. It doesn't seem to me to be a very characterful street although it does have an interesting looking Lutheran church. I love these narrow churches with their tall spires, built so tightly with narrow bricks; no sprawling laziness, or wasteful extravagance therein. Protestantism is about wilfulness and control; it is not absurdly idealistic and embroiled in fantasy because Daddy Pope likes it that way.

Maybe this bird is just a bit too early because there's no one around to ask for directions. I'm en route for 'Slotsholmen', the site of the old palace, and of course the present parliament where the Danish drama 'Borgen' was filmed. I'm one helluva fan of Danish crime drama because it is so undramatic – the devil's horns are certainly not on show – and hate is the other face that we all share. I don't recognise anyone from the show or any of the buildings which all look so closed and forbidding. Apparently the small fishing village of Copenhagen was founded on this site way back in the 11th-century. Kings and bishops have to have their castles – a manifestation of their authority. I still don't know which king sits on the great green horse outside the palace; I don't think it was the lovely Christian the fourth – the one who built the ornate stock exchange to the right of the palace. I see a young Dane about to get on his bicycle and I ask him, with minor embarrassment, if he knows where the Danish Jewish Museum is, because, for the life of me, I can't find it. I remember Daniel Libeskind, its architect, being interviewed about its deliberately claustrophobic and skewed interior. The friendly young Dane had been out partying the night before, eve of Labour Day and tells me that it's not a museum he knows. He points me in the direction of the old Latin quarter which is my next port of call.

I don't mind a long trek so long as I am going in the right direction. I accost a North African- looking cleaner guy wheeling his cleaning machine who's not too well acquainted with the old university. He tells me that he comes from Lisbon and has been in Copenhagen for thirty years. 'You pay a lot of tax but that's ok because you get well looked after by the state. The tourists eat and shop and leave a mess in their wake. But what can you do?' On I go and hey-ho, I think I'm passing the old Jewish synagogue – built in 1833. I like old roads where the buildings are all different and you can imagine a time when you could still hear the birds and the gentle throb of human discourse. Not that human nature changes – the inner organs are always the same. There are two security guards outside the synagogue one of whom is very chatty in his impeccable English. He is dismayed that there's nobody around to let me in and have a look round although I know what a synagogue looks like. Apparently this is the only one that wasn't burned down by our good friends the Nazis. The Danish guy does this job with conviction 'because we can never allow something like that to happen again'. There isn't a trace of anti-semitism in his voice. As we all know the Danes rescued its Jews from the Nazis. Perhaps this is because the Danes remained free of the teachings of the Catholic Church? They obviously didn't feel threatened by commercially successful and energetic Israelites.

I like talking to locals because you get a real sense of what it's like to live in a place and these Danes have such a lovely manner. Round the corner from the synagogue is the city's oldest church, Sankt Petri Kirke, which dates back to the

15th-century. Not so old really! It survived the great fire of 1728. It's closed of course (and anyway I'm not so hot on church furniture) but from the outside it has a quiet intimate feel with a small courtyard running round it. Maybe I should sit somewhere and abide by myself but I have to push on because there's so much in Copenhagen to explore and I want to reserve the next day for a trip to the Louisiana Museum 'with its lovely seaside location'.

I arrive at what must be the original university, founded by Christian the first in 1479. The buildings are very grey with busts of eminent scholars all over the place and I keep on stumbling over the cobbles in my black slip-on shoes. I sit on the steps and can't help overhearing a loud conversation (it is first thing Sunday morning so the participants can let themselves go a bit) between some sort of recovering deviant and his counsellor. I am waiting for some gem of insight or self-understanding but it's all the usual stuff about getting the right support in order to turn over a new leaf. I thought that tete a tetes were meant to be enlightening and revealing although the guy does say that he's no longer ashamed of his past and his woman chasing. As I walk by I say 'good luck' (and mean it) but my tidings are unacknowledged. Looking at my guide book I seem to have missed the important squares and equestrian statues of founding fathers; I think I am put off by the Danish names of things. I realise that Kirke means church and it becomes clear that 'have' is place and 'slot' castle. You have to admire immigrants who take on a new language like a new set of clothes and it's not just nouns they have to acquire but the use of verbs in all their bewildering tenses.

Obviously I need to visit Nyhaven which is the pretty picture of Copenhagen which we all harbour in our mind and which probably inspired Danny Kay's wonderful song about 'wonderful, wonderful Copenhagen.' I wonder where it was that my father bought for me a treasured yellow enamel and silver bracelet (with matching brooch) which I compared and contrasted with the heavy gold and black Spanish bracelet with its corresponding fan-shaped brooch. The main draw for me here is the fact that Hans Christian Anderson lived, at different times, in three of the brightly painted merchant's houses, writing 'The Tinder Box' (that strange tale of guard dogs with ever huger eyes) at No. 20 in 1835. I am irritated that I can't find the other numbers but a guy who is tying up ropes puts me right by pointing to the odd numbers on the other side. I am pleased that I'm here early before the tourists descend on the expensive cafes which line the harbour. My god, it's the same everywhere. People like to gaze at expensive yachts or what have you – although this is a modest, yacht-free place, than goodness. People are crowded around an iron anchor which commemorates all the Danish sailors who were lost at sea during the last world war. The thing about war is that it doesn't have to be. I actually locate the two streets 'Store

Strandstraede' and 'Lille Strandstraede' which used to be a buzz with sailors and prostitutes, brothels and pubs. It's nice to get a taste of the past although there's nothing here now to suggest any wild, racy activity. But what is on show, at the harbour's edge, is an exhibition of vintage cars, shiny and new in colours of bright red, black and champagne. They are a real magnet for English men in late middle age, accompanied by wives who conceal their boredom. Inside the leather upholstery is plump and pristine and there's something wonderfully cosy in the way the two front seats are so intimately connected, as if they're engaged in a private hug. I can't help sighing as I imagine trips in bygone days through France and Italy, when women wore headscarves and the world was pink and blue, grey and green and full of loving kindness and laughter and not grim and mean, dominated by the machine. These handsome vehicles are a testimony to something more personal. In some cars the gear stick is on the steering wheel.

As I'm strolling round the other side of the harbour trying to locate the Hotel d'Angleterre, Copenhagen's oldest hotel, built in 1775, I stumble upon a landing stage offering harbour tours for only 40 kroner. The ticket lady tells me that the next one is setting off in two minutes so I jump onto the boat. (This turns out to be a waste of a jump since two minutes becomes ten minutes). It's a nice trip around the clean waters of the canals, listening to the accompanying commentary and learning about the smartness of the Danes when it comes to renewable energy. The lady keeps on apologising for the Danish tardiness as regards the completion of building projects. The opera house and the theatre and, above all, the 'black diamond' Library are attention grabbers and indeed the library is so called because on rare occasions, such as this, the sunshine reflecting on the water bounces back onto the glass front creating a dancing sparkling wall of light. Heavens, this sounds like the afterlife. At one point during the tour she has to stop speaking because politicians, in their smart pricey flats, have objected to the sound of her voice. Of course we pass 'The Little Mermaid' (I decided on the cruise because walking to it would have taken twenty five minutes) which is surprisingly small and surrounded by coach loads of Japanese tourists. I probably would have liked to have seen her from the front. The guide tells us to take a trip to the tower of Christiansborg Slot, 'the only thing in Copenhagen which is free' and also recommends climbing to the top of 'Our Saviours Church' where, 'on a brilliant clear day like today you can see over to Sweden'. Well, that sounds exciting and a must do. I keep on forgetting the name of the Church and keep on asking her to repeat it. There is a group of Israelis on board who are filming everything and enjoying being in a foursome. As I alight from the boat (should I have left a tip as the Israeli man did?) I vow to do what I'm told and climb the aforesaid towers, if I find them. It was nice to see the gaily painted worker's houses which were the only ones not destroyed by the massive fire in 1728 which wiped out 1,600 houses, almost all of northern Copenhagen. Things couldn't have felt so wonderful then.

First and foremost though I have to check out whether the writers of the guide book are leading me a merry dance when they say that if you go into the Magasin du Nord, originally the Hotel du Nord, and now Copenhagen's oldest department store you can find the room which housed Hans Christian Anderson in 1838. He wanted to be near the Royal Theatre. The trouble today is the presence of massive building works in the centre of this square – is it Kongens Nytorv? – on account of a new metro system or whatever. It certainly spoils the atmosphere. The department store is much like any other although I am curious about the basement food store which might be like that of Fortnum and Mason in Piccadilly where there are tasty morsels on offer. No such luck – I thought I might pick up a free sliver of smoked herring – there are just a load of smorgasbord style café/restaurants which are for dull shoppers rather than hungry romantics. The glass lift is a cool circular design and on the second floor I do feel a bit of an idiot asking to see the room where H.C.A. lived. The shop assistant promptly leaves the till and takes me to it, along a long corridor. It's a room like no other because it is as bleak and comfortless as basic gets. 'Is that his original pillow, mattress and cover?' I ask in some trepidation and doubt. It's rough and dirty and I lie down on his bed. 'He could just as well have slept on the floor' I tell the young girl. Well, he obviously wasn't in this life to feather his own nest and feast on quails. In one corner there's a small wood-burning stove and on the wooden desk in front of the window (a view of the roofs of Copenhagen wherein all families were living happily together – ugly duckling and all) is his candle holder. But hey, I notice his black silk top hat on a high shelf above the bed. I can't help but touch it. I tell the retail sales assistant what my son said about a 21st-century man and his 'softness' and she says that she agrees with him, in a tone of 'he's someone I'd like to meet'. Her observation is that 'All people do is eat and buy things'. I ask her if many people come to visit this room. She replies, in her cool measured way, that they do 'but none get as excited as you'. Ha!

Well, I thank her for her time and leave the department store to climb the tower. The tower is the tallest in the city and is part of the reinforced concrete and granite construction which is Christiansborg Slot. No sign of the High Court or the elected parliament. I join the short queue to go up and it's a long wait. Inevitably I get chatting to other waitees, namely an Australian couple who are off a cruise ship carrying thousands of people. She has a wretched cough. They are pleasant and normal and limited – proudly recounting their assorted stops in Europe and elsewhere. Two youths from Hong Kong who work in finance in respectively New York and London join in the increasingly banal conversation as we wait to go through a security system equal to those at airports. The Hong

Kong guy attends all the major tennis championships and his excitement grows. I feel depression like a heavy fog falling on me and I want to get away from these people and the gloomy enclosed space we're in. The high-up view of the city is what you'd expect and I wonder about the blue-green colour of some of the roofs and domes of old buildings. The Australian dude tells me that this is what happens to copper when it erodes. I thank him for that – facts do indeed come in useful – and decide to discreetly remove myself from this crowd and make for the lift. Even exiting this place isn't straightforward and easy.

Outside in the clear light of day – the weather is so mild that I'm overdone in my snuggly jacket – I attempt to find the Church of the Sacred Heart, or whatever it's called, so that I can get a bird's eye view of Sweden. I stumble on a canal area that could be Maida Vale in London, or Amsterdam. It's such a nice day that locals are out and about. I peer into a bakery selling patisserie and it's clear that fancy concoctions of custard and cream, French style, is not their forte. Not that I see any sticky 'Danish pastries'. The cheapest bun costs about twenty kroner. When I get to the church I am staggered by the cost of the ascent and the guy tells me that the viewing point is, anyhow, packed to capacity. I'm on the border of Christianshavn, the old hippy commune from 1970 but I can't be bothered to explore it because my mental energy is flagging and I'm weighed down my bobbly wool jacket and jumper with its massive roll neck, which is becoming very droopy.

I decide to visit the Ny Carlsberg Glyptotek in order to see some post-impressionist paintings; apparently it's free entry on Sundays. Oh dear I am 'following the money' like the protagonists in 'Follow the Money' who came to a sticky end. Better to put people first. It really is a long 'shlap' back to the Tivoli Gardens area but I finally make it only to be told by the front of house guard that it's only free entry on a Tuesday. My guide book is out of date – as regards the small print that is. Sometimes there's no point arguing with the world although one wants to. The kindly Danish lady suggests that I go to Denmark's National Gallery – the 'Statens Museum for Kunst' – and take the 26 bus which is left out of the museum and then first right. Oh God how I hate the complication of directions and I can see that she's not absolutely sure of what she's telling me. At the bus stop an elderly Danish man tells me in very formal English that I'd be better off taking the 6A which is across the square, behind the roadworks etc. etc. I argue with him politely (I don't trust that I'll find it) but finally accept his advice. Apparently the 26 doesn't stop exactly where I need to be. At the 5A, 6A bus stop there are a lot of people and the buses are slow because it's a Sunday afternoon. I get chatting to a group of teenage girls, one of whom is very blonde and sparky, who are off for a Labour Day picnic. They tell me that the worst thing about Denmark is that it is far more crowded than it used to be. I wonder what I am doing here, waiting in a queue in a noisy anonymous urban space for a bus that isn't coming. Finally the 6A arrives and the driver promises to tell me when to get off. My fellow travellers on the bus are the citizens of Copenhagen who are less able and attractive. Some of the men are pale, mute, podgy and sad. The bus gets so packed with youngsters that it's an uncomfortable squeeze, for all parties, to get past them.

I am desperate for a cup of tea and enter 'Kongens Have' where you can find 'Rosenborg Slot', the wonderful Renaissance castle built by Christian the fourth (1588 – 1648). It has a fairy-tale demeanour and was originally built as a summer house. I can't remember if it was closed, or nearly closed and so will the museum be if I don't get in there quickly, after my cup of tea. Nobody knows where you can get a cup of tea in these lovely old gardens with paths that pass through the rose beds. I feel a real pang of loathing for a blonde tarty looking female who tells me that there are lots of places on the road. I finally get my cup of Early Grey in a café behind the castle, next to the shop, and put my feet up.

Over the road, in the public park known as the 'Ostre Anlaeg', awaits the Statens Museum for Kunst. It is indeed free to the public, excluding exhibitions, on a Sunday. On the second floor, greeting the faithful, is a prominently placed 'Portrait of Madame Matisse' by Matisse. It is so stunning and bold because it uses colour to depict light and shade. There are two rooms given over to the 'Fauves' and you can sit comfortably with earphones and listen to the commentary. I hardly take in what I'm hearing, like someone who is chewing gum, but I'm impressed by the Fauve paintings of Derain and Vlaminck. I like the way they believed in colour as an absolute force, not so much brash as wholly expressive. There is a Rouault – my oh my, his women are degraded creatures – and paintings by Dufy which seem to lack his usual vibrancy. The best ones are in the south of France. I like a mauvy Matisse painting which I have never seen: 'Still Life with Nutcracker'. The gallery attendant comes over to tell me that food is forbidden in this sacred space. On my way out I tell him that I was just having a bit of chocolate that was in my bag (I don't tell him that it was taken from the breakfast table). He calmly replies, with a tolerant smile, that chocolate can only be eaten outside.

Once outside I'm not sure how to get back to 'Vesterbrogade'. I'm sure not having anything to do with the buses any more. An elderly woman asks me if I need any help and if I want to walk with her and her friend. I certainly don't. A bad smell emanates from her clothes and she has a horrible crusty sore in the corner of her mouth. She's a witch. Anyway I've worked out the direction and luckily for me I stumble on the Botanical Gardens and it's free to get in – well, if not this is a very conspicuous gap in the vegetation. But it is indeed free entry for all. There's a lovely lake and a steep path bordered by pine trees and suddenly a squirrel – a red squirrel appears in front of me – and I can hardly believe my eyes since I haven't seen one like this for fifty years. It's as if the robin redbreast had died and been resurrected. I'm surprised it isn't clutching a hobnut in its little paws. I express my amazement and a Danish guy tells me that the grey rat-like variety never invaded Denmark and they see the red ones all the time. It's almost closing time and I promise to pay another visit when I can also visit the imposing looking palm houses.

I've made the mistake of taking the outer road instead of cutting through town and it isn't a very pleasant walk along Norrevoldgade and then Hammerichsgade. The roads are very wide and the din of the traffic is monotonously intense, so that a hammering starts up in my brain. Anxious humans are buggering up this planet. Where the hell am I and why am I here? I get a bit lost before I recognise Vesterbrogade; I'm coming into it from the other direction. I can't wait to get to my room and finish off the Wagamama meal which has been in the drinks cabinet in my room. I hope I'm not going to give myself food poisoning as I did in Marrakesh in November 2014. I'm the sort who has to get badly burnt twice before they avoid the flame. After my dinner I go down to the sitting room breakfast area and make myself a cup of tea. I get to talking to an American couple, having initiated them into how to use the organic paper tea bags. They're very grateful for my help but I've got nothing else to do and enjoy playing the part of confident initiator. I wish someone had done the same for me.

What is it about these Americans (and Australians too) and their stories of daring do? This guy had been a fighter pilot in the Vietnam War and served with the Israeli air force in one of their wars. He and his wife have been all over the world. Needless to say they are on a cruise and she has some sort of cough and cold like her Australian counterpart. I realise this over the tea and coffee urns when I am exposed to the full brunt of her germs. I'll kill her if I get ill. And it would be my own flippin' fault for not sufficiently keeping my distance. The husband seems in awe of me for some reason; it's actually making him nervous. You can see that she caters to all his needs. They met at college and as he reminisces (not too much please!) he covers her hand with his. Well, it's obviously an ok marriage and the proof of the pudding is in the eating because they have a multitude of grandchildren whom they take away with them, two at a time.

At reception my little blonde friend, who was privy to the bracelet story, asks me what I'm going to do on the morrow and with emphatic certainty I tell her that my destination is Louisiana Museum, an art museum by the seaside. She lets fall the bombshell that it's closed on a Monday. Oh well I'll go to Roskilde instead – since I fancy getting out of Copenhagen. She tells me that she went there on a school trip as a child and it's of doubtful interest; indeed, according to my book there's 'a wonderful Viking Ship museum' which at this present moment in time is too much for my burdened mind. I suggest other venues which she checks online and they are also closed. This buggers up my itinerary since Monday had been put aside for museums rather than streetwalking. I tell her that no such rule exists in the UK (except in Cambridge where the Fitzwilliam Museum is also closed on a Monday) and she hardly believes me. We are both getting a bit angry and defensive about how our respective countries operate, me more so since I am so exasperated. Exasperated with myself and trusting my guidebook which was published in 2007. As in all things it's wise not to ignore the small print. 'The devil is in the detail' as my father used to say. In the visitor's book I leave a message about my comfortable bed and the helpful staff as if to make up for my aggression at the water's edge. The next day I also apologise to Heidi (as a child I adored the 'Heidi books' which were about a lovely girl in the Swiss Alps, looking after her herd of sheep and goats with their tinkling bells) but she wasn't at all aware of me being angry and calls me by my first name, which is nice. She tells me about how she'd been stuck in the train for two hours that morning on account of the failure of overhead power lines or was it because something had smashed a window; she shows me the photo of the shattered glass.

    She tells me to visit the beautiful 'Marble Church' – her favourite place in Copenhagen. However, other people's favourite places are not mine and when I follow their lead, as yesterday and the trips to the tops of towers, it turned out to be a mistake, a wild goose's chase. I would have been better off visiting the 'Dansk Jodisk' Museum for an emotional feed as to how people survive under extreme pressure. Tourist attractions aren't my cup of tea. I watched a programme on TV about Denmark's art in which Andrew Graham-Dixon visited all the places I would love to have seen, including the childhood home of Hans Christian Anderson and Frederiksborg Slot – the lovely lakeside castle with the beautiful chapel built in 1560 by that lovely King, Christian the fourth. But I bet it would have been closed. How did I manage to miss the Thorvaldsens Museum – home to the works of the Danish sculptor Bertel Thorvaldsen? How did I bypass it, in the Slotsholmen area, with its orange walls? Am I such a stupid creature? I'm going too fast, that's for sure.

    Well, I better do the pages in my book that I've missed out – namely Amalienborg which is the complex of palaces inhabited by the Royal Family and Christiania, the inspirational new society, the hippy enclave, set up in the 1970s. Two places couldn't be more different in their aims and objectives. On the way to Christiania I foolishly take a right rather than a left in the vicinity of the Ny Carlsberg Glyptotek (which I use as a landmark) but I think the reason for this is that my inspiration is on the wane. I end up trudging across a long bridge alongside a multitude of cyclists (in their wide cycle lane) who obviously know where they're going. It's Monday morning so they're off to work or maybe to visit a beloved close relation. Indeed, it is better to have a cat or a dog rather than no one. I can't even see anyone to ask, although it is quite nice walking along the deserted canal after the hurly-burly of the traffic. I see a mum pushing a pram and she seems pleased to speak to someone. I am actually near a famous church from my book but it's closed of course because it's too early. I so much like these unobtrusive, inward-looking churches. One thing that has really struck me in Copenhagen is that you're far more likely to see a young guy pushing a pram than a woman. They're all at it.

A Pakistani fellow leads me into Christiania – he's jabbering on about the drug laws and I don't think I quite get it – which is a sort of little village affair done up in bold primary colours – red, blue, green and yellow. There is a little booth on Pusher St, which from the smell of it, is still doing business. Apparently Christiania has changed from the old days in that the inhabitants now pay tax, like the rest of society. There are cafes and a concert area. I wander around – which is ok since it's nice weather. I ask a guy to take a photo of me as 'drug pusher of the day'. He takes two nice photos on my camera and tells me about his drug history. The whole area is a bit of a maze and I have to ask the rubbish collectors, the 'dustmen' for the exit. It's right past the blue tractor, in the far distance. I see a guy with conspicuous 'man boobs' who is, unselfconsciously, trying to train a flock of thrushes, to the amusement of his friends, who are sitting smoking and chatting outside their dwelling place.

Hopefully I won't have too much trouble getting to the royal palaces. Maybe I am beginning to come to my senses and find my way around. Actually the Royal Palace area is the other side of Nyhaven, where all the boats are. A young Danish guy directs me up Bredgade and I am relieved that I haven't run into difficulty. I ask him if the Danes like their royal family and he shrugs his shoulders as if to say 'why shouldn't we?' We talk a bit about Danish history. He tells me that the Danes only protected the Jews in World War Two because they, the Danes, couldn't fight the Germans. Unlike England, which has always had a class system, Denmark is a genuinely socialist country. Danes are happy. It certainly feels that way as you see cyclists and pedestrians occupying the octagonal square of the palace precinct. There's a splendid fountain in the centre. The palace guards, in their Hans Christian Anderson blue and white uniforms, with little square pocket bags attached to their waists, march up and down outside the palaces, guarding the monarch in residence and the crown Prince Frederick and the Crown Princess Mary. I say to the clockwork soldier ' I know you're probably not allowed to speak but can you tell me if the Queen lives in this palace which I see before me'. With a sharp jut of his chin he confirms that they do and gets back to marching. I really can't get to grips with who lives where and who lived there before. They were obviously a very close family. It's nice that you can sit in the gardens which are designed in a compact geometric style.

This is an aristocratic area inhabited by people you never see. The 'Marmorkirken' (the Marble Church) does have an impressive dome, (apparently it's one of the largest in Europe) and you can sit in the church and gaze up at the paintings of the twelve apostles. Obviously a lot of building work took place in Copenhagen in the 18th-century. The sound of pealing bells draws me to the Russian Orthodox Church around the corner with its golden onion domes. Apparently it was a gift from the future Tsar Alexander the third to mark his marriage to the Danish Princess Marie Dagmar in St. Petersburg in 1866. What a different world these people inhabited; it was one that didn't countenance change or produce anything other than feeble dependency. I race up the carpeted stairs and enter the intimate space of the 'cathedral' where a Russian orthodox priest is chatting in Russian to his congregants. The atmosphere is quite relaxed and informal and I ask two elderly Danes, who are seated in simple black chairs by the wall, if they are frequent visitors to the church. Well, I asked them something anyway – something which leads into a discussion about Simon Sebag Montefiore's latest 'bloodthirsty' book about the Romanovs. Why does he have to tell me his wife's opinion of it? They always emphasize the word 'wife' as if to relieve themselves of any guilt they might feel as regards speaking to a strange woman. I am surprised to learn that he visits Moscow, 'a lovely place', once a year. He tells me that there is a bust of Marie Dagmar in the courtyard and so there is. Lucky for her that she escaped the punishment meted out to her descendants.

Well, it's coffee time and I'm determined to find the café in Kongensgade which I've plotted on my map. A guy from Newcastle who has settled in Copenhagen and speaks fluent Danish (married to a Dane of course) confirms that I'm on the right track and tells me that Danish pronunciation is very difficult. I find the 'Ida Davidson' place but I made the mistake of thinking it was a café rather than a restaurant. Yet another incidence of coming unstuck because I haven't read things accurately. (I wouldn't trust me with someone's medication – just take the whole lot – you'll be ok!) Everyone is having lunch and I ask for a coffee. I admire the exciting variety of smorgasbord on display but shudder at the cost; I can't pay that much for lunch and anyhow it's not much fun eating delicious food on your own. I feast my eyes as is my wont. My coffee comes in a small cup and is one of the worst cappuccinos I have ever had and certainly the most expensive. I come away aggrieved; it would have been better to have paid another fiver and had lunch.

I'm not so far from Kongens Have which is a lovely area; I can have a nice relaxed walk around. Why didn't I go back this way the day before rather than walking round the outside of the city? Right on the corner of this back entrance to the tranquil park is a café/restaurant which I never saw the other day (actually it was only yesterday). It's called the Orangeriet and for some reason I like it enormously. I put my feet up and ask the very young waiter for a glass of water. I tell him about my experience of having to drink the worst coffee in the world and we talk about how bad the weather has been and how wonderful it is now. Everyone speaks perfect English because it is a compulsory subject from an early age at school. As someone said to me 'we are only a little country and have no choice … without English we'd be sunk'. I am allowed to sit as long as I want with my glass of water – I watch other people come and go. The Danish women who pass by, with their dogs, are stylishly dressed which is nice to see. Maybe it's the openness of this place with its vistas of white cherry blossom which is so relaxing. In the restaurant itself all the diners are tucking into their food. I ask to look at the menu and decide that this would be a good venue if I ever came to Copenhagen again – although you'd have to stay clear of Mondays. Standing in front of the statue of Hans Christian Anderson, an American guy tells me that such statues make him feel guilty. I struggle to understand why. A conversation about American politics ensues and you can tell that, deep down, he doesn't trust black people; he thinks they have violence in their blood.

In the Botanical Gardens, where people are sunbathing on the terrace outside the huge domed palm houses, loneliness, being on my own, hits me with a vengeance. I should have brought a book with me or the current issue of 'The Spectator' magazine, although I only really like Lloyd Evan's theatre reviews with their acerbic wit and penetration. It's boring to sit and look at other people; there are certainly a lot of dads with prams. People are queuing for drinks from a mobile van and I note that they sell 'Illy' coffee. Damn, I missed my opportunity and it's too late for another one. I wander through the glasshouses and the tropical one is so hot and humid that you could faint on the spot if you were so inclined.

I return to base via Kongens Nytorv where rich Americans stay at the Hotel d'Angleterre behind the obstructive building works. I see a very young couple emerge from its swishness and get into a taxi, emanating smugness and arrogance. However, I really wish that, like them, I'd brought my sunglasses. But I just couldn't conceive of such a benevolent change in the weather. That's lack of faith for you.

The waitress at McDonald's tells me which turning to take to return to the area of the central station. I'm doubtful but she seems certain. What ensues is a great long walk down some major shopping street packed with pedestrians. I hate it but they don't. On and on I have to go checking my map; is this place called 'Stroget' or something. It feels like hell. I admire the street vendors with their offerings of almonds roasted in dark sugar like the ones you see outside the Tate Modern. I wonder if these cheerful street vendors, frying pancakes or whatever, manage to make a living. Eventually and that's a big 'eventually' I arrive at a square which looks delightfully old. A young guy with a horse-drawn taxi is selling his wares. Apparently he's from Poland, like many others, and is doing his best to get on in the world. I walk and walk and walk and breathe a sigh of relief when I espy Tivoli. There are always people up in the air, dangling their legs and screaming to high heaven with the thrill of the ride.

That evening I decide to have my dinner in a sushi hang-out near the hotel. It seems popular and reasonably priced. Prior to dinner I make myself comfortable in the breakfast area where, I notice, some of the wooden tables are round, with leather upholstered gold studded chairs to match, bedecked with animal skins. There's also a small verandah with a cosy hammock affair also covered with skins. They've lit the small wood burning stove indoors although it's not really necessary. The wood is stacked in an alcove. In the background jazzy love songs, strictly non-saccharine, are playing on a loop and they seem in keeping with the relaxed sophisticated ambience of the place. People come and go and conversation is muted. I really feel fine here (what sort of person doesn't mind where they sit?) and have to drag myself away to go to the Japanese eating-house with tables on the street. I made another mistake with the price because it's the starters, not the mains which are about 99kroner and counting. The young Thai waitress advises me that a starter won't be enough to eat but loses the argument. Where I'm sitting, in the bar area by the window looking out onto the street my line of vision is straight onto some girl's fat pink lips as she talks, laughs and shovels food into her mouth. A quick snack for me and time to leave. Back in the hotel, afraid of going to bed hungry/starving to death (although I did bring with me a reserve of 'Naked' bars and I have an apple or two left over from my breakfast stash) I espy a jar of chocolate powder, along with the teas, and I make myself a filling mug of hot chocolate. That should do the trick; I'm a bit *cunning* but that's how it is in the circumstances!

It's my last day and I'll be sorry to leave the breakfast table. The two middle-aged gay men, both absorbed on their phones, are still around, as is the attractive young man with one empty shirt sleeve who is on speaking terms with his girlfriend. I tell the breakfast provider that I need to take two rolls with me because I don't want to buy food at the airport. It's gonna be a long day. My plan is to get to the Glyptotek place when it opens at ten (it *must* open at ten – no need to check online) and take advantage of the free Tuesday entry. It doesn't exactly take me very long to pack which in any case is always the way when you're leaving a place. I plant myself on the steps leading up to the museum and – guess what – it doesn't open till eleven. I get chatting to an intelligent young woman from Bulgaria who works in a 'notary's office' and I find out a lot about that country, how corrupt it is. We're sitting facing 'Hans Christian Anderson Avenue' and the traffic is speeding by. She tells me that she visited the beautiful quiet Frederiksborg Slot outside Copenhagen the day before and it was open! My wrong decision-making is very disheartening. Just before 11a.m, and the surge forward of the other sad cheapskates who have discovered a freebie she re-applies her bright orange lipstick.

Conveniently, in the basement, where the ticket desk is situated, you can store your belongings in a locker, free of charge. There is no complicated technology to deal with. In order to get to the galleries – I intend to make a bee-line for the post-impressionist third floor, ignoring all the dead statues ('glyptotek' actually means 'a collection of statues'). Can that really be Rodin's 'The Kiss' in front of me? Surely it must be a copy. But actually, I am informed, it is one of the three originals … To get to the galleries you pass through the winter garden which is a glass-domed garden with statues, white pebbles and trees. It is typically Danish in its bright, light, fluid coolness and elegance. The wide glass staircases are a dream and I want to go up and down again and again just for the spacial fun of it. On the top floor you step out onto a charming roof garden area where the view is much better, much more intimate, than the advertised views from the top of towers. There are some nice white Danish chairs to sit on.

As regards the paintings I think Copenhagen must have picked the short straw; there is obviously a lot of artist's early work which no other major gallery wanted but curious in its own right because it shows you how art develops from wishy-washy uncertain beginnings. Is that really a Renoir or a Monet? There's a lovely Degas of ballet dancers in poppy red dresses. The paintings are crowded very closely together and labelled atrociously, on slips of paper near the floor. However, there are many paintings by Vuillard and Bonnard which I have never seen before.

Helter skelter down the wide stepped glass staircase I descend to the basement in order to purchase a ticket for the Gauguin exhibition which is currently showing. There's no way you can get in free. I have to wait ages in the queue because a small group of people are taking forever to buy their damned ticket. 'What in heaven's name can they be discussing?' I express my exasperation to the two lovely Danish ladies behind me and they smilingly agree that some people are like that. Are they sorting out last year's back payments or what? Damn them – I have a plane to catch!

Thank goodness the gallery space isn't packed out and what I like about the Danish visitors, as compared to their British counterparts, is that they read about and look at paintings in thoughtful, subdued silence; you don't have to overhear anyone's silly opinions. This exhibition is on a modest scale but clearly brings out the struggle Gauguin went through to realise himself through his art. This is something far deeper and more difficult than deciding which supermarket to shop at. Although it is true that there *is* something beautiful about a freshly baked golden loaf of bread. There are many of his wood carvings on display – so distinctive and expressive.

It's always a bit of a relief when you emerge from an exhibition because there's so much to take in. It must be quite a small museum because I've bumped into my Bulgarian friend two or three times. I try to eat my hotel roll in the winter garden but food is not allowed in the holy of holies and I think they're quite right to impose this rule. Outside in the garden I observe a statue of the Devil. I don't know who made it but it's the best devil I've ever seen. He has huge muscular calves and a face that is monstrous in its grimace. He exudes fierce energy. One sinewed leg is placed in front of the other and his back is bent. Maybe the message is that the more we are utterly aware of our utter sinfulness the better we are.

The trek back to the UK awaits me and it doesn't pass without incident. I lost my bookmark on the plane and was worrying that I'd miss the coach back to Cambridge and would be forced to wait for another two houses in the airport in one of their shiny red plastic anonymous lounges. I arrive home at exactly 7.45pm, as I said I would, and my son is standing by the open window smiling his lovely smile all over his face because I'm back; safe and sound – for the time being.

Door Slamming in Dublin

Going away on your own isn't such a tough ordeal; what is truly tough is the night before when you sleep so badly because you are afflicted by a sense of emotional abandonment – which is terror – that you wouldn't wish on anyone. As a ten year old I was sternly reprimanded by my friend's mum because I said that my mother was dead. Children know stuff.

But the morning always comes and you have to get out the front door and be on your way otherwise you'll end up as a stone at the bottom of the ocean. Stansted wasn't too crowded and I discovered a quite nice café where I had a chat with a very politically aware woman (her husband was deaf) who was en route to Lanzarote. She was very proud of her sons. She's with EasyJet and I'm with Ryanair. On the plane I got a shit seat by a board – the worst seat on the plane as regards looking out the window but the guy from Essex next to me is ok and offers to buy me a drink in a very polite, genuine, understated kind of way. I decline and then change my mind. He tells me that I might meet a nice Irish man.

Why Dublin? Well, you can't go through this life without setting foot in Ireland and trekking through its wonderful countryside. But hey, I'm not going to see the wildness of Connemara or W.B. Yeats country in Donegal; I'm just going to stay put in Dublin and hopefully experience something of the spirit of this city, home to James Joyce and birthplace of Oscar Wilde, where so much powerful protest took place followed by grim reprisals. I am re-reading Joyce's 'The Dubliners' which I read with so much delight when I was sixteen years of age. What impresses is the sheer quality of the writing; maybe it's the depth of feeling, of response combined with sheer detachment and objectivity. The prose has wings, like an angel. It rests lightly in the mind. The beast invades. Its religion is revenge.

The woman I met as we queued to get on the plane I meet again on the 41 bus which goes to Dublin proper. She makes the journey once a month to visit her aged mother in her care home; she, the mother, is very fussy about what she eats. The daughter works as a receptionist in a medical practice in Enfield. Like me she's braced for bad weather and is wearing a thick jumper and winter jacket although it's the last week in April. She gets off the bus at the care home. She advises me to visit a pub called O'Donoghue's for a good old-fashioned shindig and writes down the name for me on my tatty boarding card.

The bus driver is English and doesn't like Dublin for some reason. I alight from his bus, he's obviously unaware of its blue and yellow gayness, in O'Connell St which is a wide busy street with lots of statues of famous Irishmen, including that of Daniel O'Connell and 'The Spire'. My knowledge of Irish history is confused; I don't know who's who; who is hated as a traitor, revered as a martyr/saviour of the people? Maybe the time is nigh for some applied reading on the subject. One thing we know for sure is that in the 12th-century the chieftains Dermot MackMurrough and Rory O'Connor (do you remember them?) decided to look to the Anglo-Normans for help in trying to conquer Leinster. 'Strongbow' answered the call and arrived in Ireland in 1169 with his knights. He routed Leinster and conquered Dublin and then affirmed his loyalty to Henry the second. This began centuries of English hold over Irish land. Oh dear, oh dear, oh dear.

I manage to find my guest house lodging 'The All Day Inn' in Talbot St, a bit of a rough street north of the River Liffey and having been shown my room, which is clean and functional, I am out onto the streets, armed with my precious book, in a hurry to start finding places. It's sharply cold but, God be with us, the sun is bright and the sky is blue which keeps my tiredness at bay. I make my way to the National Gallery of Ireland (I don't know why but looking at paintings makes me feel gay – lifting my spirits) passing, en route, Trinity College, founded in the late 16th-century by Elizabeth Tudor and attended by all the greats: Jonathan Swift, Oliver Goldsmith, Oscar Wilde, Bram Stoker and Samuel Beckett of 'Waiting for Godot' fame. Unfortunately there are noisy obtrusive roadworks everywhere since they are improving the tramlines, or something. With roadworks no one knows exactly what is going on.

I love the sight of trams because they are romantically European and also the electronic countdown for crossing the road – the beep beep beep of how many seconds you have left before the lights change. But everyone crosses way before the little green man appears. The cars have stopped and no one is angry. What's going on? Is something not working properly?

The café at the National Gallery with its pale mauve, turquoise and jade green chairs and lofty skylight is a pretty picture in itself. It's obviously a place where people like to congregate. There are women of a certain age chatting excitedly and other women on their own, looking around and enjoying their tea. I make my way to the late 19th- century gallery which is on the ground floor.

The first picture I see is 'Stella in a Flowered Hat' by Kees van Dongen. How exciting is that? And then a passionately expressive work by Emil Nolde lights the fire in my eye. Bonnard is there in abundance and terrific stuff by Jack B.

Yeats, the brother of W.B. Yeats, the famous Irish poet. What a family they must have been. As in any exhibition you have to breathe deeply and brace yourself for an intake of biographical information which is a big ask when you are tired. Deep down I just want to dream. It's nice to see Chaim Soutine's twisted countryside path; I like all his stuff precisely because it's so tormented, so thick. Graham Norton's huge portrait is on the left hand wall as you come in and I reckon that it looked better on television when I actually gasped on account of the total likeness. But in real life it lacks something and the hands are far too big – two massive mitts – as is the head in relation to the body. The gallery attendant isn't afraid to voice his criticisms and prefers to sing the praises of Ryanair's big boss. How did we get onto that subject? Finally he says to me 'And what might you be doing this evening?' 'Oh my God,' I think to myself, 'what can I say?' He chuckles, saying 'You thought I was asking you out on a date; I nearly was but I just wanted to tell you to go to St Patrick's Cathedral which is going to be lit up tonight.' He is very friendly but I've heard enough about the Ryanair man and have to complete my tour of the gallery.

I make it to Merrion Square and see the house where Oscar Wilde was born and raised. I try to imagine how his brilliance was fostered therein. There is a statue of him stretched out on a rock inside the park and in the late cold afternoon I take a photo, bowing to convention. I walk round the square and don't find it quite as knock-out smart as I was led to believe. Still, I love all the elegant Georgian architecture as much as I hate Victorian buildings with those ugly wide sash windows which make me think of the parlour games that went on behind them. Or maybe we're just sitting therein, waiting for death.

I make my way back to the guest house via Nassau Street and over the O'Connell Bridge. There are certainly a mass of people around and lots of language schools and cafes. The city has a dynamic feel. I have to find somewhere to have my evening meal and the cheapest place, according to my book, is the Epicurean Food Hall in Middle Abbey St. I am damned if I can find it. The young policeman outside the General Post Office (a most impressive building – I went back to see the actual bullet holes in the pillars that were fired on that fateful Good Friday day in 1916) isn't much help in a very friendly and nice kind of way. These Irish people don't beat themselves up if they don't know something. They are as fresh and fluid as a burbling stream. I don't think they're suited to giving commands and orders. They're all about feeling. On Abbey St Middle I accost a guy about the whereabouts of the 'Epicurean Food Hall' and he tells me that it no longer exists but he and his girlfriend have just dined in a Chinese restaurant that is down Abbey Street Upper and is really good. And so it is. The proud chef takes a photo of his creation before it is brought to me and for once I'm given a bowl that is satisfyingly full and flavoursome. I feel impelled to fit in as much as possible and am at pains, after my dinner, to find the Custom House which dominates the north side river bank. I finally make it but seem to miss the fourteen heads decorating the building which represent Ireland's rivers. I don't want to be out when it's dark and racing back to my hotel I pass the statue of James Joyce, in ambulatory mode, on the corner of Earl Street. O'Connell St reminds me of a wide, wide street in Lisbon, also full of statues of worthy men.

I trek back to my hotel room which faces the noisy street. I can't really sit in it for the rest of the evening so I make my way to the lounge area which adjoins the breakfast room. It is a bit chilly and the black leather sofa is off-putting. The best thing are the old daguerreotype photos of amazing Irish personalities such as Brendon Beehan and courageous women I'd never heard of, all long dead. Lots of brawny sportsmen too. A crowd of lads, maybe in their mid twenties, seat themselves around a square glass table and get going with their cards, music and alcohol. They're aware of me, sitting some distance away with my book, but have sussed out that I am tolerant and won't cause them any trouble. I probably remind them of their loving, long-suffering mums. Actually it's quite amusing to observe how they change as the alcohol flows through their veins. Hey, everyone wants to loosen up and have a good time. There are many discreet departures to the loo. There is a rowdy ringleader. I wonder where they've come from and on which floor they're sleeping, all ten of them. They are all dressed in tight-fitting jeans and fitted shirts, not tucked-in.

And so to bed. All the rooms are packed closely together and when people come in after midnight it doesn't occur to them to whisper to one another or gently close the heavy, fire-resistant doors, using the handle, rather than letting them slam shut, with a huge resounding 'thwack' which is guaranteed to wake a baby up. That baby is me but luckily I manage to get back to sleep without the sense of my brain being tortured which is what occurs the following night and is, I might add, a deeply unpleasant experience. Rape of the brain I'd call it.

In the morning I release my woe, politely and humorously, onto the Lithuanian receptionist but he is phlegmatic and unruffled. 'Good for you,' he says, 'that you're not here Friday and Saturday when people go out on the town in a much bigger way.' I tell him about my Lithuanian forebears but no sense of solidarity is established; that was all so long ago and it's not as if I speak his language. The restaurant staff are all Polish as are the employees of the Tesco opposite the hotel. I have to experience breakfast in this joint but it's not much cop. All packaged and bland. Dinky pats of margarine and jam. The overcooked scrambled eggs are floating in water and obviously salt is left to the taste of the customer. The couples at neighbouring tables are scruffy Italians or stalwart Germans.

I have to hit the road and although it's very cold the sky is blue and the sun is gold. God knows where I'm going to go or what I'd do without my trusty guide. I'm still not very familiar with the streets and I have to plan things so as to avoid the crowds. I make my way to Trinity College and explore what I can – discovering the buttery where, it seems, you can get good coffee for two (or was it three?) euros thirty. I'll come back later when the library opens in order to see the Book of Kells. I love the layout of this college, its 18th and 19th century buildings, the maple trees on the lawns, and the hallowed calm. Think of all the luminaries who walked where I am walking. I read Beckett's 'Waiting for Godot' at the age of twenty, sitting on a rough stone in Jerusalem, and felt its anxiety like an iron brace. Nature says 'live' but reason says 'die' because what is man-made has bound you so tightly, weighs on you so heavily that you may as well cut your own throat, put a gun to your head or jump off the nearest cliff. Let's face it you'll never defeat the forces of death.

I walk down Grafton St to St. Stephen's Green which is really beautiful with all the flowerbeds and the central lake with its ducks and ducklings ambling along in the sunshine. It's the case that a lot of history happened here what with British troops stationed in the Merrion Hotel firing on the locals in the summerhouse. How can mankind ever love its neighbour as itself when it wants to be the winner? I remember my father being very keen on Dublin in the 80's, flying over every week to oversee the erection of a new shopping centre, his beloved project. I wonder if the beautiful glass greenhouse style white and green shopping centre on the edge of the green could be the place to which he was so devoted. Nobody seems to know when it was built. I take the lift to the second floor where you can have a coffee and look down into the central area. This is the panoptical layout which is used in many prisons and is ironically very open. I speak to the doorman and he tells me that it was built in the mid-eighties. His mate turns up and they jokingly refer to St. Stephen's Green as their very own Central Park. They thank me for my company and one of them tells me that I seem to be a nice person, with a nice face.

I check out the luxury Shelbourne Hotel on St. Stephen's Green as I'd checked out The Merrion the day before. I'm curious as to who is staying there and I enjoy the beauty of Georgian architecture and general grace and charm of the interior. A cut about the 'All Day Inn' whose narrow doorway you can easily miss as it's part of a commercial terrace. The Merrion, however, was disappointing; a lot of smug-looking silly people sitting around chatting and having tea served by over over-solicitous polish waitresses. In the Shelbourne suavely attired Indians are doing business under heavy glass chandeliers and you get the same atmosphere I want to escape. I find a small room which has photos of the famous people who have stayed there in the past and heavy books which record all the guests ever and the servants. One girl was paid pennies in her role as polisher of silver spoons. I'm sure, in her white cap and apron she was a willing, cheerful lass. The books are too heavy to move, too entrenched in their positions and a young American offers to help me. He grew up in New York City and his mum studied in Cambridge for a year. He now lives in Texas with his girlfriend. He doesn't respond when I tell him that I hate the 21st-century. Oh God, how nice this place would be if it weren't so crowded. As I leave I wish for my son to have a girlfriend; someone to keep him afloat. Isn't that how it works?

I don't know what I'm letting myself in for as I make my way back to Trinity College Library. The exhibition introducing the Book of Kells and other manuscripts is called 'Turning Darkness into Light'. Unfortunately the groups of noisy Italian tourists have got there first. It's an effort to see and to read; I remember the upright stone which displayed Ogham inscriptions, (consisting of a variety of notches) the earliest written Irish based on the Latin alphabet. Up against the crowd I search for my pen in order to write down the words of an Irish monk at St. Gallen, Switzerland, from the 9th-century. 'I get wisdom day and night/turning darkness into light/'Gainst the wall of knowledge I/All my little wisdom try'.

I catch a glimpse of the precious book itself although I'm elbowed aside by some ugly old Italian man with hair growing out of all his orifices. The attendant tells me that the tourists come in waves and droves and sometimes, if you're lucky, the table is clear. Worse is to follow in the Old Library, built between 1712 and 1732. Its main feature is the magnificent long room with its tiers of antiquated oak bookcases holding more than 200,000 books. Needless to say the desire for knowledge is our God-given heritage. The place is swarming with Italian teenagers who are pointing their phones here there and everywhere. Are they going to look at these pictures when they return to Italy; are they going to share them with 'friends and family'? How I'd like to look them straight in the eye and ask 'Why'?

I buy myself a lovely tuna mayo sandwich in the college refectory. Everything seems to taste much better in euros. I then walk back down Grafton Street in order to join a guided tour at the Little Museum of Dublin, situated in a grand old Georgian House. En route are the flower stalls run by Polish women; what a gay turnout of tulips and lilies. Once in the house I am worried by the presence of a French group of teens; June, the tour guide, with a shamrock in her black trilby, sympathises but assures me that it will be alright. As it turns out her enthusiasm for her subject kept them all shtum. There are so many photographs, so many artefacts, so much history in this city. I remember the photographs of children from the slums and the music stand which John F Kennedy, Irish emigrant golden boy, used to prop up his speech when he visited Dublin in June

'63, four months before he was murdered. Irish politicians don't use stands; they clutch their papers and speak. The 60s passed Ireland by (what a shame!) because Ireland was a place where the Church had the first and final say. There was a packet of tea, plain digestive biscuits and a pot of Bovril behind a glass fronted cabinet. We learnt about Ireland's experience of boom and bust, the latter symbolised by 'monster munch' sweets wrapped in fake and flashy gold paper. June concludes the tour by telling us that Ireland is no longer cursed by the Catholic Church. 'What do you know, it's legal for gay people to get married.' I can't restrain myself from asking what the current position is on abortion? I'm so embarrassed by my audacity that I hardly comprehend the answer, which wasn't straightforward. We are invited to go to the top floor room which is devoted to U2, Ireland's globally successful band and the life and works of Bono. I vow to listen to their greatest hits but I know I never will. Once you're back within your own four walls the impulse is killed since it's removed from its source. What I remember most of all is the story of the doctor who continued to treat children after he'd lost his sight.

It's nice to buy a stamp in the famous GPO building, a sentiment I share with the post office lady. It's a matter of some merriment that she's too busy looking down to look up at the ceiling and fully appreciate her environment. I have so little time and so much to see; I'm not going to miss Kilmainham Gaol and Parnell Square with its homage to writers and artists. I attempt to search out the pub 'O'Donoghue's', which is back in the direction of Merrion Square; it is where 'The Dubliners' used to perform in the early days. I don't like it. It is so dark that I nearly go into the loos rather than the courtyard out the back and a group of drinkers laugh at my mistake. I ask the landlord about the history of the place and he directs me to a notice on the wall. Some man shouts out (to him): 'you should have got paid for that'. I'm out of there fast, wiping the dust from my heels. Maybe a lot of old Irish pubs are old and dark. I try to find No. 29 – the old Georgian House but nobody can understand where the arrow is pointing exactly and since the rest of the address isn't supplied … It seems that the Irish like to laugh rather than judge and a nice lady rests a fairy-like hand on my shoulder as she warns me about city directions. A business man spares the time of the day to attempt to locate No.29 on his app. I finally find it on the corner of Merrion Square and Fitzwilliam Street Lower (where the trendy business man got out his phone) but it is closed for renovations(?). I wonder where my energetic father stayed on his frequent trips to the capital?

I decide to trek back to the National Gallery of Art (thank goodness the sun is bright although there has been the odd drizzle) to take a look at some paintings by Goya, Velasquez and Murillo but damn it the rooms are closed. Like goddamned roadworks these are the things that you never find out beforehand. I sit in the lovely café and disturb the couple at the next table who are composing a business letter. They can't think of another word for conversation/talk and I suggest 'dialogue.' It wasn't right in the context but what the hell. They laugh, I laugh and the woman next to me, who is on her own, starts to speak telling me to eat at the 'The Winding Stair' and 'The Woolen Mill' on Batchelor's Walk; names which I scribble on my Ryanair boarding pass. She advises me to sit in the lounge of the Wynn Hotel on Abbey Street Lower which turns out to be not to my taste. (It smelt of fish 'n' chips; how could I have listened to her?) She points out the prime minister – Enda Kenny – who is at the next table but one with his wife and another woman. She tells me that they are trying to get rid of him and the wife is the power behind the throne. As he leaves I wave eagerly and it's clear that he's pleased to be recognised which is different, of course, from being mobbed.

On my way out I bump into the gallery attendant who nearly asked me out. He spontaneously shakes my hand and I shake his. I think he thinks that I have come back specifically to see him which isn't the case. I ask him for the quickest way back to College Green and the Bank of Ireland (which used to be the Parliament Building). He points me in the wrong direction so I end up walking all the way up Pearse Street which is a very boring trek indeed.

Back at the hotel I decide not to go out again that day. Too much trekking. I buy Falafel balls, cereal bars, a packet of fruit and nuts and a smoothie from the Tesco opposite and retire to my room. I'm not going to die from starvation. The cold walls force me to apply myself more seriously to 'The Dubliners' although I can't resist turning on the TV to hear the news and, more importantly, the weather forecast. I observe the endless drift of people passing by in the street beneath my window, walking fast because it's cold. There are people on phones, people with backpacks, people on mobility scooters. There are people in fluorescent green jackets, parents with babies, women trudging home with their bags of food. A bed and breakfast sign stares at me from the building opposite and on the third floor of the Irish Sufi Foundation a row of industrially sized washing machines are in progress. There is the swoop and cry of seagulls and plants are growing out of chimneys. Some of them are blocked in and I wonder if the reason for that is to keep the seagulls out.

That night I am sinking into sweet slumber when a whopping great slam of a door brings me brutally back into the world of the living. I tell myself that it doesn't matter, that I can easily go back to sleep, but I am left with a pain in my brain as if it's been injected with lead. I hate this life, I hate other people, I scream inwardly. I try not to be angry but I am and the repression of natural responses is painful. At breakfast, which is horrible, I look around and wonder who is responsible. They all look blandly innocent.

Fatigue is now the enemy but heigh ho the sun is still shining and I'm going to keep going and never give in to the insensitive bastards, never admit defeat. Not that it's easy; I can't take on the mental stress of too much reading.

My first port of call is Kilmainham Gaol, a not-to-be missed adventure. I find the tramstop in Abbey St Middle and someone, finally, knows where I have to get off. From there it's a helluva walk but I get there just in time for a guided tour at 9.45am. (People now book their tours in advance.) The west wing is unbelievably horrible and depressing – damp stone and no protection from the cold winds – but during the Great Famine prisoners were better off here – mercilessly unprotected – than in the outside world where there wasn't even a crust of bread. The guide is a lovely Irish student – he's so intelligent and engaging – just the kind of guy one would like to marry. We see the spot where the leaders of the 1916 rising were brutally executed. How can anyone kill another human being in cold blood? It is a cowardly and despicable assertion of superiority.

My next stop is the Kilmainham Hospital which is now the Irish Museum of Modern Art. A long tree-lined avenue links the fine surroundings and beautiful gardens with its bleaker neighbour. The gardens were designed by Edward Pearce between 1710 and 1720 to represent the crosses of St. Andrew and St. George and if it had been warmer I would have sat on a bench and proudly surveyed my all but it's bitingly cold and I'm going to the Lucien Freud exhibition in the new Freud centre. It's a real treat not to have to share it with anyone – although the attendant, I can see, is just a little embarrassed to be on his own with me and the fleshy bits of a naked Lucien Freud model – just as I am – even though we both know that it's ok to bite into the apple. There is a drawing of his London garden and I'm surprised that every stone and every leaf is drawn with meticulous care. I enjoy his portraits of his Irish businessman friend and his nineteen year old son. Lucien paints his mother – he was only interested in her when she left him alone – but no sign of his architect father.

I'm a bit concerned that I won't find the return tram stop but have no fear common sense wins out and soon I am back in Abbey Street Middle. I have to go back to the Trinity College Buttery for a much needed coffee and the coffee guy/barista knows that I want a proper cup rather than a polystyrene takeaway affair. And it's bloody good stuff. How I enjoy sitting at a clean pine table with two geezers to my right who are chatting themselves up over sausages and mash. I know it is incumbent on me to visit Parnell Square – north of the Liffey – and such wonderful places as the Dublin Writers' Museum, the Hugh Lane Gallery and the James Joyce Cultural Centre. I trek past the Gresham Hotel on O'Connell St. – mentioned by Joyce in his story 'The Dead' and scouting about inside I find it elegant but overly crowded; what do these elderly people find to chat about over their tea and cake? I expect they have umpteen grandchildren and have just returned from a Caribbean cruise, although I think the fashion today is to visit S.E. Asia. The Hugh Lane Gallery is full of wonderful paintings –guaranteed to keep me buoyed up and present in this beautiful universe. I used to adore my father's colourful stamps from Trinidad and Tobago, Kenya, Uganda and Nyasaland.

I love the magic of snow paintings – snow with its overtones of pastel blue, pink and mauve. Here we have Monet's 'Lavacourt under Snow' which is new to me. Pissarro was wonderful with snow but what greets my eye is his 'View of Louveciennes'. He seemed like such a reasonable man and liked to paint Norwood in N. London. Next to him stands a work, a naturalistic country scene, by Eugene Boudin. Manet loved to paint Eva Gonzales and Berthe Morisot, his sister-in-law, was also part of the Impressionist club; on display here is 'Jour d'Ete.' How well it was that they painted companionship and intimacy rather than the hellish destruction of war. Edouard Vuillard's 'The Mantlepiece', as with nearly all his other works, show us the detailed and delicate patterning of an introvert. Apparently his mamma was creative with fabrics and he had no problem living at home, rubbing shoulders with the ladies in her workshop. I wish I'd known all these 19th-century men; they must have been wonderful company. I'm not so sure about the Irishman Francis Bacon. I sit back and have a rest as I listen to him, in his studio, being interviewed by Melvyn Bragg. His work is highly memorable and impressive but the theme of sado-masochism screams out at you. It's good that he can exorcise his demons through his art. Unexorcised demons can eat you up. Later on I find Baggot Street where Bacon was born. No sign of a plaque anywhere along its once elegant terraces so I give up. Was it a pity that his father beat him so much? Adversity can give us the chance to shine. Oh I nearly forgot there was a very expressionistic depiction of 'The Ball Alley' by Jack B. Yeats – long may he be remembered.

I attempt to drag myself to the Dublin Writer's Museum – starting with the Book of Kells, the Bible Edmund Spenser and Jonathan Swift and ending with Brendan Beehan – no trace of Seamus Heaney – no doubt because he died relatively recently. There is so much stress in my head that I only manage to read snippets about each writer as I move through the centuries. What a soft spot I have for Irish Literature – I read Sean O'Casey's plays and Edna O'Brien's 'Girl with the Green Eyes'. I have the same soft spot for Andre Gide and George Duhamel, Balzac and Maupassant as I have for Dostoyevsky and Turgenev, Chekhov and Gogol. My brother sat on the beach in Riccione, Italy, a copy of Gogol's 'Dead Souls' at his side. He never read a word of it; his tortured expression said it all as he was powerless before the sadistic male.

Enough is enough and I decide to visit the James Joyce Cultural Centre on the morrow. I locate it though on Great St. George St and the receptionist is one of those hoity-toity young ladies with a very white complexion and very bright red lipstick. I've missed the Tuesday walk which visits places Joyce mentions in 'The Dubliners' or was it 'Ulysses'? and later on I regret not having made it to Henrietta St which went from being Georgian palatial elegant to the Queen of slums.

I've complained to the manager about my door slamming neighbours and he's transferred me to a back facing room (with a hideous view of iron and steel) on the same floor. A gay German couple are newly arrived and I knock on their door and explain my predicament; they promise to be good. Have another drinking party taken over my old room? I can hear some male shouting the odds. I dare to knock on his door and he answers with a bath towel tied around his middle. The truth is that I left my 'special' soap in the shower when I changed rooms and I wonder if he could get it for me – if the chambermaid hasn't disposed of it. He's quite willing and it's still there. Phew! I tell him why I've moved but I can't go so far as to threaten him with murder if he slams his door in the early hours.

I promised the Chinese guy in the restaurant 'TaKaRa' that I'd be back and I can't not keep a promise and the fare was indeed plentiful and tasty. However he is off duty and there's a girl to replace him. The chef makes an appearance and I can't help accosting him in order to say 'I'm back because I liked your cooking so much' and he remembers me. I have something different but I only remember the guy at the next table who has a cold and is slurping his soup.

After dinner I cross one of the bridges and walk along the quais intending to find the Clarence Hotel – a 19th-century building that apparently has been spectacularly renovated by U2. It's located in 'the buzzing Temple Bar area' but I fail to find it and since it's getting damp and chilly I can't be bothered to continue my traipsing over the cobblestones. Maybe it was under my nose.

Back in Lower Abbey Street I am determined to find the Abbey and Peacock Theatre. I don't ask people waiting at bus stops for directions because they look so dejected. But there it is, an unpretentious building on the corner of the road. Seated in the foyer I hear the final call for the evening's performance and it's only when they've all gone up and Samuel Beckett's 'Waiting for Godot' is relayed on a small screen for about five minutes (until the technology breaks down) that I realise what an idiot I was not to have brought a ticket. It would have been really something to have seen this play in the holy of holies so to speak, a theatre of real cultural and historical significance. The play indeed is the play of plays since it's about the weak, abandoned, vulnerable people who try and keep their spirits up while they wait for some greater power to come to their rescue. Damn me!

It's nice to know that on the morrow I fly back home but since I don't have to be at the airport until 2.30pm I have quite a lot of time for left over sightseeing. St Patrick's Cathedral, Christ Church Cathedral and Dublin Castle can wait to the end; surely all 'great' buildings are about power, control and institutionalism – all that kills the soul. I go to bed with bated breath but the door banging has abated; or sometimes it's the case that you are too tired to care.

I've decided to skip the hotel breakfast with its dusty muesli, watery eggs and cold coffee although the Irish soda bread was pleasant enough, unlike one of the waitresses. I buy a croissant and a 'pain aux raisins', still warm from the Tesco bakery, and make my way to The Trinity College Buttery where I purchase a cup of 'Illy coffee' from the guy who knows I like it in a cup. Is my cup runneth over? I don't think so. God I'm pleased that I've escaped formal breakfast at the hotel.

I make my way through College Green and along Dame Street in order to get to Christ Church Cathedral which was Dublin's first church, made of wood and founded on this spot in 1028 by Sitric Silkenbeard, the first Christian king of the Dublin Norsemen. In 1172 our old friend Strongbow got in on the act and changed things. Let's have hard stone; away with flimsy wood! Why pay to go in? Interesting stuff, like the original foundations and the 12th-century Romanesque Doorway are outside. I also have to admit that cathedrals don't have the same effect on me as poetry or wild life. It's difficult to imagine the patient toil of a hundred years shared amongst many. In the old days people knew their place.

Dublin Castle is just up the road and just as I am debating whether or not to go and trudge around looking at stuffy rooms decorated in the old style a group of noisy French teenagers descend on the place which helps me make up my mind. The main thing to remember is that this place was built by King John in the 13th-century and was a controversial symbol of British rule for 700 years, until it was handed over to Michael Collins and the Irish Free State in 1922. I note the Figure of Justice which faces the Inner Yard and the fact that it's facing the Upper Yard, turning its back on the city, has been judged by the Dubliners to be an apt symbol of British justice. In the yard I ask a guard if there's a garden I can get to and he directs me to the 'Dubh Linn Gardens', which are located on the side of the 'Black Pool' harbour from which the city gets its name. This round garden is charming and there's a tiny space between flower bed and wall with an instruction to shut your eyes and listen to the birdsong and inhale the scents. Up the steps is situated a nice café with a terrace, belonging to the castle, but I'm interested in the Chester Beatty library and gallery which is nearby, alongside the garden. What can one say about this great American collector who loved Ireland and contributed so generously to its galleries and cultural institutions? I so wish I could be bothered to go round and study the exhibits – his collection of Oriental Art and fine illuminated manuscripts from China and Iran. There is also Paul's letter to the Romans (AD 180 -200.) I reckon that I'd come back to Dublin just to make a morning of it as well as having a coffee in the quiet wood panelled cafe. There is a display of books and I spot 'God with Us' by Rowan Williams. I like the Jesus painting on the cover and since Sister Wendy Beckett says it's life changing it must be. I'll get it through Amazon even though it is said that they treat their employees like slaves. I'm not proud of being mean and penny-pinching like a dog that digs its hole and fills it with bones. 'Hey, what about me – who gave to me freely and lovingly?' The truth is that I need to really grasp the truth about life after death and do myself a favour. I see that the group of French teenagers are about to enter the museum with a guide so maybe it's just as well that I'm leaving.

The next stop is the unmissable St Patrick's Cathedral. It stands on an early Christian site where St Patrick is said to have baptised converts in a well in AD 450. It went from wood to stone as it became a cathedral but Cromwell, in 1649, didn't hesitate to use it as a stables. Huguenot refugees sought solace therein. I have a problem locating the north and south transepts and when I hear the announcement of an impending tour I join in. The Irish Lady who takes us round really knows her stuff and delivers it in charming Irish fashion, as if she's hopping around on one foot. I want to know about Jonathan Swift who was born in Dublin in 1667 and in 1694 took holy orders. In 1713 he was appointed Dean of St. Patrick's. Everything about his life is interesting and, in the Cathedral, he was buried standing up so that he wouldn't be swept away by unstable waters. His lectures went on for hours and he woke people up if they weren't listening to him. On his death in 1745 he left a legacy of £8,000 to build St. Patrick's Hospital for the Insane. The worst people care not for what others think and feel.

Once outside I reckon that I should plod back to the James Joyce Cultural Centre. The house, built in 1784 in North Great St. George's Street conforms to a pattern and I reckon that since I've yet to embark on 'Ulysses' proper (I hope that getting past page 195 is going to be a case of 'third time lucky') there's no point in seeing a display of the biographical details of its characters. Maybe I should have gone to the Old Jameson Distillery but I prefer looking at things than finding out how they are made. I also intended to visit Dublin's Jewish Museum, located in the neighbourhood once known as 'Little Jerusalem', a centre of Jewish life around the South Circular Road. 'The converted terrace house is within walking distance of the streets so evocative of Leopold Bloom's Dublin.' Next time I'll appreciate the city on a deeper level.

The flight back involves no delays but the guy next to me on the plane smells. I try to rise above it as I speak to him. The young guy in the aisle seat is a cabin steward for Ryanair but he's on a break and relocating to Spain because he can't stand the English weather and the high cost of renting. I catch the train I would have missed if there'd been passport control but coming from Dublin you're in the clear. I get talking to an 'artist' from Toft who lives in Amsterdam and was barred from getting his flight on account of the blurred nature of his passport photo. I found him on his website; he does installations showing people falling off their bikes in hard hats which break as soon as they hit the ground.

It's so nice to get home and see the real smile of a real person who loves you deeply without saying so.

Oysters in Antwerp

For years I've been thinking of visiting Antwerp – partly because it's been through the wars – and also because it was the stomping ground of the great Flemish painter Peter Paul Rubens but every time I nervously attempted to make a booking something would come up in the form of a 'terrorist attack'. Who isn't fed up with this outworn expression which is basically about crazy frustration and oppression?

After a helluva time of uncertainty and indecision I dive in and make the booking but cresting the wave of my 'strike whilst the iron's hot' activism I got the train times muddled up and booked them in the wrong order. The trouble was that I didn't know how to put things right; technology may prolong active life but it also stops you in your tracks. My heart began to pump overtime and I slept badly that night. The next day I managed to speak to a human and put things right – at some cost to both body and soul.

The day of travel dawned grey and cold and it was probably windy and wet as well. I arrived at London St. Pancras three hours before schedule, having taken the jam-packed 7.15 train from Cambridge to Kings Cross, and as I shuffled along in the dismal queue (why are those mums and daughters looking so buoyant and excited – don't they know that the golden age of travel ended decades ago and Paris has about as much charm as a dirty old glove and they'd do better to keep an eye open for guys with knives) it occurred to me to lean over the barricade and ask a grey shirted official if I was maybe too early for my train. I was indeed – the Brussels train wasn't up on the screen – so I had to go.

I went and sat in the attractive lounge of the St Pancras Renaissance Hotel which is obviously a popular venue for business meetings.

Having rejoined a much sparser 10.30 queue I proceed towards the waiting train and find my seat in a cramped compartment. I'm in an aisle seat and I'm not facing the direction of travel. I revise my wonderful Top Ten Guide to the cities of Brussels, Bruges, Antwerp and Ghent. I intend to visit Ghent the following day whilst my energy is still high. Arriving at Brussels Midi I locate my train to Antwerp without too much difficulty. As is the way when you're out and about I'm not thinking about men in black and their potential for harm but am surprised when a young cleaner perched on the steps of a carriage speaks to me naturally in French, as if I were a mate (in response to the eternal question, 'is this the right train?') and I'm too stressed to understand him. But it takes time to get your mojo back.

It's not too far to Antwerp – but it would be nicer if they announced the approach to the station since I don't want to end up in Amsterdam – and alighting from the train I approach an information desk and request a map of the city since my next job is to find the hotel. The lovely smell of waffles is wafting across the airwaves and this, I feel, is a good omen. I tell the information lady that I'm impressed by the station and she tells me that I haven't seen nothing yet, 'walk into the ticket hall and you'll get a real sense of its splendour'. How true this is. It's flippin' well like a Gothic cathedral. How is it that no one knows about this neoclassical art nouveau station built in 1905 by an architect called Louis Delacenserie?

Stepping out into the street I join the stream of people who, in spite of scarves and boots, look as if they are feeling the cold. I wish I'd brought along my blanket scarf after all. Is this wicked winter never going to end? Thank goodness the trusty BBC weather forecast has predicted some nice weather for Antwerp, if not for the UK. I obsessively check that I'm walking in the right direction, even though I know that I am. But local women tell me differently from the lady at the information desk, in spite of her tourist map, and I eventually arrive at the wonderful old 'Grote Markt' – one of the great gilded arenas of Belgium. It's so amazing because the buildings aren't hard and square and featureless, representing the hard God of mammon, but fanciful and feminine, with upward curving roof corners and old stone that seems modelled on lace. But then, more so than now, the executioner's axe came down hard if you didn't toe the line. These pretty open squares were no strangers to public beheadings. I am directed to 'Oude Beurs' (the old stock exchange) where my hotel is situated. I pass a lovely cafe called 'Cafe du Monde' where quiet intelligent people, male and female, are drinking real coffee. They grind and sell the coffee in a shop next door. Ah, this is a spot that I mustn't let slip by me. A few buildings along is a tearoom (Koffiehuis) called 'D'aa Toert' and its narrow wood panelled exterior seems to me to bespeak warmth, security and intimate relations. How foolish can you be – expecting love to emanate from a building. Having located my room in this smallish attractive hotel (the guide book describes it as romantic) I go downstairs and chat to the young Flemish receptionist.

I want to know if 'Zum', the fun cafe/restaurant recommended in my book, is any good. Apparently it no longer exists. She doesn't seem very au fait with the local eateries. I ask if I can help myself to a glass of sweet malmsey wine from the bottle on the desk – ah, it's lovely – just what the doctor ordered. Flemish hospitality also extends to a big glass jar full of mini Easter eggs in pale blue, pink and mauve foil wrappers. One is tempted to think of a Monet painting of waterlilies in his pond at Giverney. Surely you must know of somewhere local where I can go for my dinner I nearly say to her. She seems pretty sure about 'De Bomma' (Grandma's Restaurant) which, on Suikerrui, is only a stone's throw away from the Hotel Rubens.

For the love of God I can't find it. Nobody has heard of the place. Some poor guy, who has just descended from his motorbike, gets very frustrated when he can't locate it on his phone. I tell him not to bother – I'll stumble on it eventually. I walk up and down streets and espy a plethora of chocolate shops – no doubt popular with the many tourists. I like the way a local woman enters such a shop, exchanges kisses with its female proprietor, and proceeds to chat in a lighthearted fashion. There is no forced excitement or spilling of mutual guts over a cup of disgusting Costa coffee. 'De Bomma' was actually right in front of the spot where I accosted motorbike man but obscured by the scaffolding from the next building.

Once seated in the family style restaurant – the member of staff at the door is always slightly taken aback when I request a table for one – and after initial confusion they lead me to a table for two. I have to ask for an extra cushion since I can hardly reach the table. I feel that I'll be in safe hands if I ask the young Arab waiter to suggest a dish and he's over the moon about the star dish of the day which, when it arrives, is deeply disappointing. A bed of pale soggy leeks is covered by a thick cheese and ham sauce, served in a tureen. Only the tureen is ok and I wonder what planet this chap is on if this is his idea of a great dish. Still, all around me groups of friends seem to be heartily enjoying themselves. I leave a tip because I want to leave a good impression of the British; these things have their effect.

On my way back to the hotel I pass through the Grote Markt and gaze up at the Italian-influenced Stadhuis, built in the 1560s, which dominates the square. In its middle is a great fountain with its statue of Brabo, a legendary Roman soldier who freed the port of Antwerp by defeating the giant Antigoon and throwing his severed hand into the river. My attention is probably more on the book than the living statue. I see a souvenir shop that is blasting its wares onto the square and l buy some postcards and stamps. The Bangladeshi proprietor tells me that many people baulk at the price of the stamps and so the cards are put back on the stand. However, he agrees that his shop is in a very good position for the tourist trade. All around the square a mass of tables are filled with a mass of people eating pizza and drinking beer.

Back in my hotel room I manage to locate BBC1 and watch Finals Week of 'Masterchef'. I wonder what the response of the judges would be if they served up something in the nature of the soggy mush I'd just eaten. A cheese sauce isn't the equivalence of a 'jus' or a red wine reduction. And it's also pretty bad for your cholesterol levels. And so to bed and I'm woken through the night, not by my own crazy angst, but the din from the street below. Some say it's the drunk Dutch and others the students letting off steam. But at least I have breakfast in the sunny breakfast room to look forward to.

What a nice room it is, overlooking a courtyard. There is a tempting array of breads and continental patisserie as well as salad stuff, processed meats and cheeses. The coffee is passable but the cups are too small as is the way in this part of the world. Grapefruit juice is always good. But I'm all set on day 1 to visit Ghent, a city like Bruges which has a rich legacy of medieval buildings and art treasures inherited from its days as a semi-autonomous and prosperous trading centre. I'm also harbouring the illusion that it's a very tranquil place on account of being a university city. En route to the station, walking down 'Meir' (the Oxford Street of Antwerp and much more stylish) I pass the Boerentoren which, in 1932, was the highest building in Europe. It looks kind of art deco and is as cool as the fancy railway station. It has the letters KBC inscribed on its crest. It suits Antwerp just as the Post Office Tower suited London in the 1960s and the Shard suits it now. On the station platform I make eye contact with a lovely old couple who might be waiting for the same train as I am. I've never seen a train with an upper storey and mounting the steps to the first floor I bang my head on the glass door which I took to be empty space. I laugh it off and hope that I didn't look too stupid but, as is the way, people are too preoccupied with their own affairs to notice the stupidity of a foreigner.

The day bodes fair – thank the Lord – (how scared I am of the beast from the east – that bitter, spitefully cold wind that takes no hostages) and I am seated with two women friends who are taking their brood to the seaside for the day. At my side is a big black woman with a little black boy who is being cradled by the white woman opposite who has two girls, both of whom are seated with the black woman's other children further down the carriage. They are talking in French and their destination is Ostend, not far from Knokke which used to be a popular holiday place for Jewish families from the UK. I still have the photo of Annie, the daughter of the hotel where we stayed, with her long plaits and her lovely dog, and a vague memory of her taking me into the warm kitchen to sit with all her family. I was about four years old and my mother said that she adored me, as did Bruna our Italian maid and the married dentists from Leeds who didn't have any children but, of course, I was already taken – safe in the monster's grip.

Finally I have to spill the beans and tell these ladies that I am English because I can see that they are wondering just a little as to my nationality. Or maybe not. We speak about life in England, life in Belgium and I try not to get too heavy and depressing. The white woman flies frequently between London (where there are more cinemas and theatres) and Antwerp and would never take the train. I can't help commenting, out of friendliness, that the black woman's other son has exactly the same face as his younger brother and am surprised to learn that they are in fact twins but the smaller one had trouble feeding as a baby and he's obviously still the weaker one. Of course she is concerned about him. She thinks a day at the seaside will pep him up but it's still only early April and mildly warm. I'm worried that I'll miss the stop for Ghent because there are two and I nearly follow the lead of the white bossy business woman opposite who is totally pleased with her life and career and why shouldn't she be? I fail to say goodbye to them in the kerfuffle of their getting five kids off the train. I hope they had a nice day.

It's clear, standing outside Ghent station, that I have to take a tram to the city centre. There is something I like about trams – maybe because they are closer to the ground and don't run in straight lines – like hard old buses. A pair of Flemish lovebirds from another city haven't a clue as to which tram goes to the city centre and don't seem to think to ask anyone. Finally, a woman approaches and tells us which tram to take, where to stand and she even gets my ticket for me. She is clear as daylight and you feel properly helped and guided.

Sint-Nicklaaskerk was the merchant's church – built in the 13th – 15th centuries – and is Belgium's best example of the austere style called Scheldt Gothic. It does look a bit grim and, standing alone, marooned in a windy spot, I am lost. But not for long. My trusty guide book never lets me down. And I have learnt to say Dank u (thank you) in Flemish which isn't exactly very difficult. The locals look at you as if to say it's so easy it's not worth the bother you might as well speak English. Soon I have paid my euros to see the famous 'Adoration of the Mystic Lamb' housed in St. Bavo's Cathedral. It wouldn't mean much to a 21st century person without the assistance of an audio guide. A group of noisy Italians are spoiling the vibe and annoying all the sardines who are trying to listen and concentrate. I have to keep on returning to the desk because I have trouble with the gadget. You can understand why this giant undertaking by the brothers Hubrecht and Jan van Eyck is one of the greatest cultural treasures of northern Europe. And it was nearly destroyed by Protestant vandals in 1566 which proves that human nature doesn't change. In those far off days not to have Christian faith was to be swirling in the torments of hell, physical and mental. The age of atheistical materialism is upon us and people, lacking a secure place, are swirling in the hell of the here and now.

That said, I want to find a nice spot serving good coffee. Such a spot doesn't materialise so I set off for the 'Klein Begijnhof' some distance from the cathedral. I am assisted by the sisters of mercy or rather two nice ladies who point me to my destination. Thank goodness it's warming up and I'm looking forward to finding these 'Beguinages'. A feature of the Low Countries these communities were founded in the 13th century as sanctuaries for the many women (beguines) left single or widowed by the Crusades. Although deeply pious the beguinage was not a convent and women were free to leave and marry. This place breathes peace and quiet and how charming are the step-gabled, whitewashed houses set around a little park and Baroque church. I sit down on a bench and eat my banana, taken from the breakfast table, along with a roughly made cheese and tomato sandwich. (A Flemish guy at the next table had seen me stuff it into my bag and had politely looked the other way. My argument is that I don't really eat breakfast so I might as well take it with me for later). I enjoy walking around this site that was founded in 1235 although most of the present houses date from the 17th-century. 'Is anyone at home?' I wonder.

Back in the street I arrive at a crossroads and am trying to remember the road back to the cathedral when a woman crosses my path and asks me how I enjoyed the Beguinage. She's the one who pointed out the way. 'I must be your guardian angel,' she exclaims, in all honesty. She bemoans the fact that property is so expensive in Antwerp and from what I can gather the semi-sacred nature of this site is gradually being eroded. They are no longer used for social housing – for women, single mums – who were experiencing real difficulty. There would be no trouble in the world if selflessness and virtue had more power than violence and killing. And the trouble is that sin and crime is liable to be perpetuated through the generations, as it says in the Bible.

But heigh ho it's turning out to be a lovely, warm day and I'm off to find the wonderful Wizard of Oz or rather the more down to earth Groot Vleeshuis which is a centre for East Flemish food – part restaurant, part delicatessen – located in a medieval butcher's hall. There is so much life and activity in such a small area. Middle-eastern youths (what is one to call them – Arabs, Muslims?) are shouting their wares – waffles, sweets and chocolates – from a stall and people are queuing outside tiny bread shops with their appetising offerings of apple strudel. Is it the sunshine which is bringing everyone out of their shell or do the Flemish folk have richer blood than their British counterparts? It seems like I've entered a Breughel painting in which everyone is up to something in a physical world.

You can imagine the Vleehuis in its glory days when whole carcasses of cows, a la Rembrandt, were hanging on a rail and nowadays there is a variety of honeys for the visitor to sample on a tiny plastic spoon. I sit outside and watch the world pass through what was the old market. I order soup which comes with a load of tasty bread in a basket. I would dearly love to be partaking of a great big Flemish sausage, as are the women at the next table but this isn't something you order on your own.

After my meal I see three men at the pub next door sitting outside and drinking their beer. They are in late middle age but they have red cheeks and twinkling blue eyes and I would have loved to have joined them. But this isn't what you do unless you are a demon.

Grasiei and Koreniei are the nearby quais and are lined with the most adorable step-gabled guildhouses of merchants and tradesmen that date back to the 12th-century. Tremendous activity must have taken place as the great trunks of merchandise were unloaded and stored on different floors. The quai at Copenhagen is brought to mind and the noble terrace of picturesque houses, one of which was inhabited by Hans Christian Anderson for a short time. However, the street next door was where the prostitutes lived. I do the same thing as I did in Copenhagen – I take a boat trip. It's lovely to cruise through the canals seeing old churches and buildings but I feel my spirits start to sink as I listen to the guide's informative commentary. His jokes indicate a hatred of those who are rich. He's probably sick to death of this job which he's been doing for years and with no real share in the business. I think that I have lost my lovely gold watch bought in a charity shop but find it on the floor. I can't help looking at a Flemish family sitting near me. There's a mum with her two daughters, aged about twelve and fourteen and a very quiet son. They all had the same short Flemish nose and the younger girl was oh so pretty. The mum scolded her daughters when they obviously weren't listening to the commentary but she couldn't stop the younger one reaching up and running her hand along each low stone bridge as we passed under it. But she looked as warm and human as they and protective as a mother hen.

As I climbed out of the boat, lining the guide's hand with silver, my spirits were rock bottom and for the life of me I can't remember where I got off the tram and whether to go left or right or round in circles. There are so many people around and I feel lost and nowhere. So what? At least I'll know where I am when I arrive back at Antwerp Station. On the train I re-read the 'Ghent' chapter in my book and see that I missed visiting SMAK, the museum Voor Schone Kunsten and seeing works by Hieronymus Bosch and Magritte but that would have meant getting a tram to another part of the city and there's only so much that a poor girl can take on.

Back at the hotel I chat to the student receptionist who wants to practise her English. For dinner I make my way to the warm-looking 'tea-house' opposite but they tell me, regretfully, that they only do omelette lunches and close at six o'clock. There is another place further down the road which is recommended from a list in the bedroom (guests are provided with a black pack which tells them where to go, what to do etc) so I try my luck. I sample their risotto but I thought that the golden rule about scallops was that they had to be initially browned in the pan so that they weren't served up as white insipid blobs. However, the risotto was delicately flavoured and they served bits of bread with tasty fish pates. I wolfed down the lot. I observed that the locals eat out as an enjoyable treat; maybe, as the business woman on the train lamented, Antwerp lacks theatres and cinemas but it doesn't lack an identity. The couple seated near me are fondly aligned, a man and a woman who are enjoying one another's company. Leaving an acceptable tip I slip out into the street.

That night I can't sleep and it isn't the fault of the students beneath my window. I've got into the habit of jerking myself back into consciousness the moment I feel myself drifting off, sinking into peaceful slumber. I am punishing myself, putting a gun to my head, turning sleep into the enemy rather than the beloved friend that it is. From then on, I am metaphorically banging my head against the wall, willing myself to relax and not be so wilful and stupid. The hours pass, the world almost shuts down completely and I worry about how I will cope the next day. I tell myself that rough sleepers in their dirty sleeping bags and inmates in a death camp are probably more relaxed than I am although fear is their master. For me this sleep ordeal started when I was about ten years old; I needed to hold onto myself, my living soul, in the face of a mother who was all ego and no caring.

Hearing the twittering of the birds as they awake from their repose calms me down somewhat at around 4am and I wake three and a half hours later feeling more alive than dead. A nice breakfast in a bright room will revive my spirits, I hope. As I exit my room I see the chambermaid with her trolley. What a hard tedious job that must be, making beds and clearing up after people.

We begin to talk and I learn that she's from Tibet and she's doing this job because her Flemish isn't good enough for her to work as a nurse. She's a single mum with one son who is eight and another who is eighteen and lives with his girlfriend. She tells me that I have 'a bright, open face' not like the other guests who are 'self-centred'. 'How much do you pay for this room?' she inquires with some disdain and I really can't remember since I booked it so long ago. She really wants me to return to Antwerp and stay with her and her son in her beautiful flat near the station. She's so pleased to have met me. Indeed, I'm in a cold impersonal hotel room and there's always the risk of noisy, inconsiderate neighbours although last night the trouble was within.

A workman on the Grote Markt directs me into town via a shorter route – people always tell you to follow the direction of the tram – and I find myself walking down a narrow cobbled pavement down a long dark street – trying not to twist my ankle on the uneven cobbles. There is no one about. I finally arrive at 'Wapper' where the Rubenshuis is situated. My guide book has advised me to get there early to avoid the queues but I'm too early by far and so have to meander around a bit and when I do approach the ticket office in the tourist shop in the middle of the wide, wide street a British guy is in front of me and, dammit, he's in charge of a group and has to buy umpteen tickets, fill in an insurance form and, irritatingly for him as well, see that their bags are stored in lockers. I am standing behind him pulling out my hair but he turns round and apologises to me with good grace. When this palaver is over I see the crowd, mainly Scottish, in the entrance hall and I mutter something about not liking groups in response to something someone has said. A Scottish lady pipes out, 'but we're very nice!' In the first room to be viewed a few of them are discussing their flight details whilst others are chatting aimlessly. It's all very off putting, spoiling the atmosphere of this special place.

Is this the reason that I'm not warming to this 17th-century patrician house? It's not like Rembrandt's house in Amsterdam which has a cosier feel with all his tropical shells and curios laid out and you can even see his easel and his paints but this place is supremely formal. I wonder where his young lady love laid her beautiful auburn head but she was obviously very happy with Rubens who was thirty seven years her senior. Following the visit I peruse the book and don't recall seeing 'The Kitchen', 'The Large Bedroom', 'The Parlour Room' and wonder whether part of the house had been closed for restoration. But I do remember witnessing one of the group ladies interrogating an innocent gallery attendant about the inadequate numbering of paintings and showing off her knowledge of art. 'Escape, escape!' was the noise ringing in my head. I found the lovely formal garden where I sat on a bench and ate my banana and tried to ignore the scaffolding. In Rembrandt's house I was struck by the short box bed in the downstairs room where he received important guests he wanted to impress. Rubens too slept in such a bed. These 17th-century box beds represent the thinking of the time in which you slept half sitting-up to promote good digestion. Being prostrate was a prelude to death. I also remember the marble-lined room on the ground floor which was used by Rubens to exhibit his collection of sculptures. There were antique busts of various notable Romans such as Seneca. Oh I wish I'd seen some more paintings! But maybe I do vaguely remember 'A Lady at the Fish Market in Antwerp' and 'Interior of the Jesuit church in Antwerp'. Apparently Rubens painted thirty nine ceiling paintings for the church's aisles in 1616-1618. He knew what he was good at and got on with it.

'Hopland', where the market is situated, is a huge space at the end of 'Wapper'. Once again it is a lovely day and because it's Saturday everyone is out doing their shopping. I find the old wooden cafe which is spoken about in my book but it is already packed to capacity and the poor waiters seem harassed and rushed off their feet so I give it a miss. To the left of the market square I espy a clothes shop by the name of 'Sedona'. The model in the window is wearing exactly the kind of stuff I can see myself in. I go in and try on the fabulous Michael Portillo style jackets with a hint of sparkle and the pretty blue and white check cotton tops. The name is 'Forte dei Marmi' and, strangely enough, this is a beautiful holiday resort on the Mediterranean coast of Italy where I stayed with my family in the 'Hotel Augustus' in the summer of 1962. Family? Nobody spoke to me for two weeks. I remember my single room with the green tiled floor smelling of insect repellent, the bowls of black olives at the tiny bar and the beautiful comtessa, in Schiaparelli pink, being courted by a handsome youth. Well, I have to leave 'Sedona' empty-handed because I reckon that ninety nine euros is too much to pay for a shirt. What on earth is the world coming to?

Plates of olives welcome us into the market proper and in the noonday sunshine I notice an orthodox Jewish man smilingly – and a little guiltily – help himself to one or two or even a few. I expect the Passover, with its special food, must be over or else he'd be in trouble. I can't believe how different this market is from the one in Cambridge city centre. The stall holders are all set for battle – anticipating a day of rich takings – and the people are all ready to fill their bags with fat Flemish sausages and strong cheeses which you're allowed to sample. It's difficult to resist the warm earthy tang even though we know that cheese harms your arteries. The red strawberries glisten in their punnets and are a glorious sight in their multitudes. The pots of coriander, basil and parsley sing verdantly in the spring sunshine and one can't help but be enthralled by the spears of white asparagus, perfect little cauliflowers, fresh new potatoes and huge bulbs of garlic. Needless to say there are stalls selling dried figs, dates and apricots and all the nuts in the world. The pink azaleas in their pots and the rows of tulips couldn't be brighter or more radiant. People are buying up trays of yellow and black pansies which seem to be smiling in the sunshine. I alight upon a stand where people are eating oysters and drinking white wine at little white tables. A young lad is super busy chucking them open with a sharp knife. They cost nine euros for six. I hover around debating whether to have the oysters for my lunch or a soggy sandwich from my bag. There are a group of young men grouped closely around a table downing their oysters and their wine and having a fine old time, full of laughter. Do I really want to stand alone at a table, like a lemon, no doubt enjoying the oysters but presenting myself as an odd and lonely spectacle? Some things are made for sharing. I walk away.

I return to Rubenshuis and sit on a bench in the middle of the square eating my sandwich and observing two elderly ladies who seem to know each other well and are enjoying one another's company. My next stop is 'Rockoxhuis' which is another example of an elegant 17th-century style house. Round the corner from Wapper, on Meir, is the palace that Napoleon Bonaparte took over and renovated to his taste. The cafe at the entrance to the premises is full of people but further back there is an empty garden where I take my ease on a wrought iron bench draped with a sheepskin. A Spanish group with a guide listen to the story of before and after the little man from Corsica came, saw and conquered. All the information is actually posted up on a pillar in all the major European languages.

En route to Rockoxhuis (Nicholas Rockox (1560-1640) was a philanthropist and a friend and patron of Rubens) I pass a shop from which the dulcet tone of Paul McCartney singing 'I'll Follow the Sun' from the 1964 album 'Beatles for Sale' is filling the airwaves. If there was anyone who was passionate about the Beatles and especially 'Paul' it was I. Obviously I can't resist taking a look around this fantastic vinyl shop which has every LP under the sun and record players to boot. The owner is an easy-going, laid-back sort of guy and is surprised to hear that there is nothing like his shop in Cambridge. Not that he really cares.

The truth is that I'm too tired to absorb much of the art in this fine house and I didn't expect to have to view the paintings on a tablet. You locate the painting on your tablet and then you listen to the commentary and it's heavy to carry. I return it to the desk since I don't want to carry it around nor do I want to look at two paintings at the same time – the original and the photograph. In one of the rooms I get into some sort of political discussion with the young gallery attendant; it's good for him but I've heard it all before. I recognise the painting of 'Atlanta and Meleager' by Jacob Jordaens because Sister Wendy has written about it. It's good to look at it in the flesh as it were. There is also a portrait of the Rockox himself by the great Van Dyck who did all those flattering portraits of the weedy Charles the first – the one who lost his head. What a boon it is to enter the garden and I walk round a few times inhaling the scents of centuries' old plants. The balmy air seems like a real blessing after endless months of winter. I could sit in the sun forever.

Tramping back to the hotel I stumble on Sint-Jacobskerk just as it's about to close. It's the church where Rubens is buried and I try to imagine what it must have been like to walk down this street in the 17th-century. Rubens loved his country and was so much happier than his 20th-century counterparts; no grisly end for him! I whizz round the church and see paintings by all the leading lights of the day – Rubens himself, Jordaens and Van Dyck. I can't wait to see Rubens' 'Descent from the Cross' in the cathedral. At the entrance a big American guy is trying to force his way in although it's 5pm and closing time.

I now have to think about dinner which is a bit of a problem. Yesterday evening, following the pale risotto, I prowled round the Onze-Lieve-Vrouwekathedraal, with its wedding-cake spire rising up to heaven, where most of the eateries are situated, with tables spilling onto the pavement. I come across a buffet style place where you are charged according to the weight of food on your plate. This is a Swedish idea apparently. I made a booking for this evening and now I can't find the place, having lost their card. Finally it comes into view, it's tucked away behind a canopy, and I help myself to the buffet. Dear oh dear, one mousse after the other tastes soapy. When I pay the proprietress asks me if everything was all right and I tactfully reply that the hot aubergine dish was the best. I leave a nice tip. On one side of the cathedral is a huge square dominated by a statue of Rubens in painterly mode, holding his brush and palette and filled with what seems like thousands of people standing around, or eating and drinking. I return to the hotel to watch 'Masterchef' and the amazing dishes that the talented finalists have cooked up. If you are truly tired the body takes over and you sleep.

The next day, my last, dawns bright and sunny. I espy the Tibetan mum in the lobby and we find a place on the stairs where she gives me her details and tells me that when I come to stay she'll take the time off work. 'Of course,' she says, 'I don't know what's in your mind'. She is right or rather I am thinking that I'm not sure if I will come to Antwerp again. However, I tell her that I'll keep in touch. She found it difficult adapting to this hotel work but apparently it's ok now.

I'm off to the museum Mayer Van Den Bergh and this is a place I remember – probably because I'm not so dog tired as I was the day before. Fritz Mayer van den Bergh (1858-91) died very young and his poor mum created a museum to display his collections. It's a thrill to see famous paintings for real and especially so when they're displayed in the intimate setting of a house. But it was a pity not to see Pieter Bruegel the Elder's 'Dulle Griet'; a blank space because it had gone away for cleaning. Sister Wendy described this painting as possessing an unforgettable presence and a sinister vitality. It is hell, she concluded, a place where there is no love or sharing.

Well, I know hell well. Her beloved piece was a wooden sculpture 'St John Resting on the Bosom of Christ' by Master Heinrich of Constance. In contrast to 'Dulle Griet' it is about prayer and surrender to God and, she tells us, a devout nun like herself takes a great gamble in that 'without the normal fulfilment of a partner and perhaps children, she will still become a complete woman.' She truly believes that resting on God will mean human fulfilment, as is depicted in this sculpture. What a wonderful person she is, full of grace, and the sculpture is indeed moving. I chat to the gallery attendant who tells me what he knows about the only other Bruegel painting that hasn't gone for cleaning.

Outside, I stumble across the Botanical Gardens and there is a massive magnolia almost totally in flower. All the plants are so lovely in the warm sunshine. I share a bench with a woman who makes some comment about her energetic little boy who is running round the lake. I didn't connect them since she is very white and he is black. But I'm very surprised when, as I'm leaving the park, he runs up to me and asks me for five euros. I say no and turn away. What game is this, I wonder.

I am quite near the theatre and this is obviously a nice area. In a shop window I am struck by a tan leather coat with a turquoise fake fur collar. You'd think it would be vulgar and tacky but it's right on the money. I have to consult my map in order to pay a visit to the Jewish quarter. I'm not interested in Diamondland so I don't really know what the point is: is it to confirm my hunch that Jews will only feel really safe when they are dead; we have insecurity in our DNA. I mischievously accost a bearded gentleman in his sober black garb and ask him the way to the Jewish quarter. He has big baby blue eyes and looks at me as if to say. 'What do you expect to see?' We work and we pray. A more jovial character who is standing outside his shop smiles a blessing and a welcoming 'shalom'.

But it's a long walk past the length of the train station and, at the traffic lights indicated, I turn right into a long street of closed front apartment houses where everyone is tucked away inside. The window of a delicatessen is full of fried fish, chopped herring, potato salad and other such things that are the staples of the Jewish ghetto. A woman on an upper floor calls down to her bearded long-coated man as he walks along the road. He returns her call with a 'what's your problem, woman?' in a 'leave me alone' kind of voice and gets further away from the house. On the other side of the road is a synagogue and the wall next to the locked door (they don't want people like me bursting in) is a plaque which simply states that this was the deportation point for Jewish residents in 1942 or thereabouts.) It must have been a grey day but highly expected. At a corner co-op a pale young girl in woollen tights is, no doubt, homeward bound. A woman, slightly built, but with big breasts, pushes a pram with a trail of young children behind her. It's a fact – there's nothing much to see. I recall my time in the old age people's home called Romney Court, in Belsize Park, in 1974. Of course nobody in their early twenties is in an old age people's home but it felt like that because I never saw anybody except one very elderly couple emerge from their flat opposite mine. The deal was that my father would pay the rent in return for me studying at the Lancaster Gate Law School. When I should have been poring over the thick textbooks I was consuming a whole tin of 'Quality Street' sweets and making myself sick. Who invented those glossy purple and gold wrappers? I had some very attractive, intelligent male visitors but was too depressed, at death's door, to take any interest in them. Sexy is as sexy does and I did nothing except moan.

I head back towards the station and decide to take a look in at the zoo – to see if there's more going on. Families are streaming through the gate and there is some strange performance taking place on a massive stage. Men and women, in 19th-century clothes, are walking together and dancing, all in slow motion. As soon as the skit is finished it starts all over again. On another stage, almost blocked from view, someone in a long-nosed animal costume is lording it over some other animals and, once again, the tableau is in slow motion and endlessly repeated. I reckon that the twenty five euros entry fee to the zoo proper is too steep – and I can't hear the roar of lions or the trumpeting of elephants. There are however a flock of pretty salmon pink flamingos on the banks of a lake adjoining a cafe. No way can one get through its iron gate without an entry ticket to the zoo. I walk to another gate to try my luck and notice that the two security guards are eyeing me up. I bet they've been told to look out for people on their own. I smile at them as I walk by and can hear them thinking that a woman in her sixties in a wine coloured washed wool Per Una coat and an F&F blanket scarf from Tesco can't possibly pose a threat to society.

It is now approximately tea-time and I head back to the cathedral. What seemed such a difficult route a couple of days ago now appears as a straight road – albeit with extensive roadworks. Outside the cathedral's main entrance a musical trio, two violinists and a cellist, are playing a classical repertoire for the delectation of us, the public. I remembered seeing them the day before, outside Napoleon's palace, on Meir. One of the violinists looks oh so nice, just my cup of tea. Whatever they were playing, lovely Mozart melodies, the setting was just right, the perfect backdrop to the music. I gathered together my small change and walked over to the red velvet lined empty cello case lying on the pavement. Everyone seemed moved to do the same.

I enter the largest Gothic church in the Low Countries. Apparently the cathedral was still a work in progress after 170 years. It was the church of the wealthy guilds, richly adorned with their shrines, reliquaries and altar pieces. Van Gogh, during his sojourn in Antwerp drew it. He was certainly no shirker.

I've come to see Rubens' 'Descent from the Cross' and the 'Raising of the Cross' on the other side of the nave. It is true that his paintings exhibit a wonderful mixture of Italian grandeur and Flemish lucidity and he wrote confidently of himself, 'I consider the whole world to be my native land.' He was an energetic, optimistic, spiritual man with no hint of any neurosis. The dead Christ is taken down from the cross by those who form a river of love and care. Similarly, in Michelangelo's 'Pieta' the eternally feminine Mary carries the weight of her dead son. Rubens painted these works specifically for the cathedral and all around there are other great works by Flemish artists. Some of these are cordoned off because a Roman Catholic service is in progress. Everyone seems extremely devout. One can still get up close to 'The Madonna of Antwerp' – literally a doll in her pew. She has been a focus of devotion since the 16th-century and has a changing wardrobe of robes and crowns. She is a doll for eternity, with her head held high and her straight back. Frustrated that I can't see the pulpit or the Burgundian Window (do I really care or do I just want to extract the most from my book?) I speak to an attendant who kindly tells me that if I come back in the morning she'll show me around personally. But there is a Flemish artist with a difficult name who isn't out of bounds and she advises me to take a look. I had in fact already taken a look – a weird depiction of the dead Christ which was coveted by Queen Elizabeth the First whose reign was as uncomfortable and challenging as any monarch's could be.

Heavens, it's now as warm as toast and I have to while away the late afternoon and the evening. Unfortunately the time has never been right to enjoy a cappuccino in the 'Cafe de Mundi'. I could really have returned home a day earlier – the visit to the Jewish quarter in search of local colour had been a non-event (I would have been better off visiting a diamond making shop/factory) likewise the excursion into the zoo area.

According to my book the Vleeshuis (Meathouse) is 'one of the most beautiful buildings in Antwerp.' Built in 1501-4 as the guild house of the butchers and the meat market it is now used as a museum of music. It is all turrets and towers and Gothic detail. I am content to simply view it from the outside since I can't be bothered to look at harpsichords or read about the history of the city through its many forms of musical expression. In the street outside a band is playing and I sit on a wall and listen appreciatively although the antics of some groupie who climbs to the top of a wall and lies down on the ground, fully outstretched, in order to get a good photo is supremely annoying. Maybe she too has been a victim of female repression whereby there can be no celebration of femaleness and fertility because she belongs not to herself and her maker, but to a man.

Down by the River Scheldt (I take note of my downward path so that I don't get lost when returning in the dark) is a dark castle which is the oldest construction in Antwerp and started out as a prison. It is devoid of beauty, wholly forbidding. Its coat of arms over the gate displayed a penis which the Catholic Church removed. The river on which it stands is so wide that you can hardly see to the other side and apparently this easy access to the North Sea made Antwerp Europe's second largest port. It also played its part in defeating the Nazis. It's the case that those who are hard and cruel are scared of being soft and weak, like a woman. They need to wake up and smell the coffee, see the wide open sky.

On the pier overlooking the river people are taking the air and even sunbathing. I'm pleased that I packed a cotton top and thank the Lord that I've been blessed with going-out weather. I walk along the pier, its upper and lower deck, so to speak and find a seat on a bench where I take off my socks and allow my feet to be sunkiss'd, like the N.African (or Spanish) oranges. I can't help looking at a group of girls who are sitting on the lower pier, their legs dangling over the edge, their machine blaring out some sort of rap for all the world to hear. One of the girls resembles a living version of the Antwerp doll in the cathedral. She's of mixed race origin, has long straight dyed blonde hair – which contrasts wonderfully with her brown skin – and her occasional arm movements in time with the music are so talented, so in the groove, that I am mesmerised. They finally leave their perch and she is tall and slim and carries herself like an Egyptian queen. I'd like to tell her this. She might be flattered and pleased or reckon that I was a stalking freak.

I'm fed up with the Antwerp restaurants. I should have taken the advice of the guidebook and the business woman on the train to Ghent, both of whom advised me to eat in the 'Huis de Colvenier', one of the most respected restaurants in town. It's at 8 Sint-Antoniusstraat – to the south of the city – on the way to the Koninklijk museum voor Schone Kunsten (KMSKA). This is the fine arts museum, second only to Brussels, which has been closed for years on account of getting a new roof. Maybe next time I visit (if there is a next time) it will be open and I can also dine in style at the above mentioned restaurant. In the meantime I wonder whether I can keep going on my breakfast sandwich and a cereal bar and Pink Lady apple that I bought from home. I doubt if I'll wake in the night gripped by the deadly pangs of hunger. Naughty children used to be sent to bed without supper in order to punish them for their bad behaviour. This was always about too much laughter and play, disrespecting adults with their ferocious rules.

In the morning I leave the hotel in good time to catch the train which involves descending onto a subterranean platform where there is a lovely little stall selling delicious loaves of fresh bread and I am tempted to buy one and stuff it into my already stuffed small suitcase. Once again I merely feast my eyes and walk on by. Waiting on the platform I find myself getting increasingly nervous as two storey trains arrive and depart and what if I miss 'Brussels Midi' because nothing is announced and end up in gay Paree? When my train is almost due a word comes up which I suspect translates as 'delayed'. I accost a black station guard who confirms my fears and makes the mistake of telling me that the train would be fifty minutes late, not five. I'm angry with him (although I don't show it) for being so slack and casual. (My father's one criticism of other humans wasn't that they were lazy, dishonest, duplicitous or whatever but CASUAL.) I stand shoulder to shoulder with a young Dutch guy who is also perturbed because his first train from Leiden, in Holland was delayed by a long chalk and he's already late for his business meeting in Paris. But I can see that he's calmer and nicer than I am.

On the train we are packed together like sardines and nobody speaks. Towards the end of the journey (anticipating that I might miss the bold sign of 'Brussels Midi' I speak to a lovely couple from Bruges who are on the last leg of their return journey from Singapore. I tell them that I think that the Flemish are livelier than the English, they enjoy their food more. They are impelled to put in a good word for Liverpool, which they really enjoyed. I wonder whether I should make a return visit to North Mossley Hill Road where I lived in a University Hall of Residence in 1972-3. How seriously I took my studies and the Nazi escapee Jewish Italian professor from Trieste told me that I looked as if I was terrified of being consumed alive when it was my time to do the exercises. But at least I had my angel of a boyfriend in bed with me every night. I am aware of the lively Belgian couple being warmly met by their friends at Brussels Midi but I'm pleased to finally see the sign for the entrance to Eurostar. The departure lounge is much nicer than its (non-existent) St. Pancras counterpart but, foolishly, I attribute its spacious absence of people to its design rather than to the fact that a train has just departed.

On the train my travelling companion is a twenty something girl from Bath who has dropped out of Leiden University. She couldn't take the strictness and formality. It was like school in that they took a register before lectures. She was on her way to stay with her parents, leaving her football mad boyfriend behind in Holland. He phoned during our long discourse and she shooed him off, assuring him that she was perfectly all right. She showed me photos of her self-portraits and I told her, encouragingly, that she should apply to the 'Portrait Artist of the Year' competition, televised by sky. During our talk she managed to decide that she wouldn't be happy at 'posh' Bristol University but would apply to somewhere less exclusive. She wasn't at all sold on white, conservative Bath. We stopped at Lille which looked pretty bleak and the weather worsened considerably as we approached Calais. All we could see was barbed wire wreathed in mist.

It's always a relief when the wheels stop turning and you can stretch your legs. I attempt to exit the station and cross the road to dear old Kings Cross. But heigh ho what do you know you can't step out the door but have to walk for ever and take a down escalator. In my impatience at being stuck behind a crowd of people pulling their wheelies I veer one way whilst my wheelie veers the other and I feel something twist in my side. Damn and blast – I'll kill the whole world!

On the train from Kings Cross to Cambridge I am seated opposite a couple of lovebirds from Kings Lynn and the woman falls asleep with her head on her partner's shoulder. They seem very well suited, very happy together. Before they drifted off the world of nod they'd been talking, along with myself, to a Belgian man married to an Englishwoman who despairs of his directness. She worries that he'll upset people.

Finally I arrive home and come in the back way, down the garden path, because I want to see if the parsley and coriander has come up in my absence. My son opens the door, beaming a beautiful warm smile of welcome. He's somewhat wary of me travelling abroad because I 'talk to strangers' and he knows that Belgium isn't safe from some disaffected individual who will mount his vehicle on the pavement, mowing down pedestrians, or use his knife on unsuspecting tourists. Maybe there's something to be said for a more backward unsophisticated age – a time before the invention of 'Spinning Jenny' when man's savagery and hatred was more naked. Who can cope with the increasing unreality and madness of life on earth?

My Day Out

It's not such a good idea to never go out – to stay at home wringing one's hands, crying over spilt milk and lamenting the past – that is to say wallowing in regrets and huge, horrendous mistakes.

Sitting on a sofa in Kettle's Yard I was busy, as usual, lamenting the soullessness of the 21st century (who could deny its neurotic nature?) when an American guy, taken aback by my vehement assertion, suggested that I visit Monk's House in the village of Rodmell, East Sussex, the former home, of course, of Virginia and Leonard Woolf. I bore this suggestion in mind, to be acted on at a later date.

The date was far later by half since Bottisham to Rodmell is quite a long way to go for a day trip and because for nearly three months I have been caring for my son who is afflicted by the abnormal mental condition which goes by the name of OCD. Believe me when I tell you that OCD is not just a matter of checking that the door is locked before you go to bed or looking in your bag, just one more time, to see that your passport, ticket and wallet are where they should be or not walking under a ladder on Friday 13th. It's about having to undergo crazy rituals, all the time, to create a barrier between oneself and a monster who invades and hates and wants to smash your knees with a crowbar and throw you sky high in the air. Parents who firmly institute rules and boundaries along with lashings of personal love and acceptance 'for you who you are wholly' will provide a root and enable them to fly. Self-esteem will be sky-high.

God only knows I do my best to help him but I am not literally chained to this abode and I fancy a trip into England's green and pleasant land, hopefully taking in some of the beautiful Sussex countryside. God only knows how much time I have spent looking up the times of trains and buses and driving myself mental. There is a little internal voice which tells me not to bother – who wants to be cooped up for hours in a crowded train? But the other face is telling me that I might be losing my independent spirit. Unfortunately, it all goes wrong the night before I've planned to go – I wanted to catch a lovely warm day in mid September before the weather suddenly turns vile – when my beloved son, exceedingly nervous about setting up a business account with his mate (he can't do anything that is important to him if anything untoward crosses his path beforehand) wants me to see him out of the house to make sure that he doesn't touch anything. The cherry tree at the end of the path is the enemy, not to mention the presence of snails crawling up the wall. If he but knew it, he himself is the precious trepidatious snail, minutely attuned to detail. I have to help him, offer all the reassurance I can – it's a matter of doing one's best to keep calm and swallowing my own upset and fear. But we still LAUGH together at his compulsion to have 'hands in pockets' as he walks through the door. Humour is the antidote to grief. Humour defuses the bomb, makes breathing easy so to speak.

    He's so sorry that I've had to forfeit my day out and promises to take me to a National Trust property of my choosing. I so love these stately homes with their wonderful gardens and minimal incursion of people. This may or may not happen (never trust the contrite enthusiasm of the moment) but I venture to suggest that it will be ok for me to do 'Monk's House' trip on the following Saturday. According to the BBC 10 day weather forecast we are promised even more lovely September weather. I know that if I don't go I'll hate myself forever. The other week when his mental associations and fear of contaminations were so extreme I felt like tearing my hair out or banging my head against the wall. My father actually did this; he rammed the door of my brother's bedroom with his head and I would point out the deep imprint of his skull to my mates. I laughed – it was an amazing dent – but my friends didn't care to join in the mirth. This was VIOLENCE – no joke.

    Mid-week I am informed that the last part of the business set-up will take place on Saturday morning – the date of my trip and so there will be a repeat performance of the 'hands in pockets' scenario. I make it calmly clear that in that case he'll have to leave when I do – I have a train to catch and can't hang around until 10am. He accepts my order and decree. Neither of us sleep well on the eve of battle but morning comes, as it always does, and I hope to God that things go well even though I am always braced for failure. I sort of breathe a sigh of relief as we set off in our separate cars – me to the station, him to the bank – but to my astonishment as I'm driving up the long road that leads out of the village I see him passing me, homeward bound. I only realise it's him when I catch sight of his number plate and then fleetingly see his worried face – like a frightened child. My heart sinks. What can I do? There's nothing I can do. It's a lovely sunny day and it's my day out and I'm going to try and make the best of it. I won't get another chance. Obviously he had to return to retrace his steps, to wash his hands one more time, or whatever, but there is the horrible nagging fear that he has been overpowered by fear, and, like a coward, he has retreated into his corner, withdrawn into his shell never to re-emerge. At worst, in practical terms, I'll have to spend another agonising week awaiting his bank interview and the anxiety will be all the greater for having been postponed. Can I take it? I have no choice. But I know he isn't a coward; he's brave and resilient and upright. But demons are hard to fight.

At the station an assistant who sits behind a glass panel (are there glass panels or is there a free and open space between us?) suggests that I could take the Brighton train and change for Lewes at Haywards Heath. But sir, I protest, I've spent weeks writing down train times for the other route. Was that all a total waste of time? He prints out a wonderfully easy to understand schedule and suggests I come back the way I know. (What a friendly soul he is). I reckon that the Brighton train is the simplest option and as I am damned early for the Kings Cross train I might as well run for the other train which leaves in about ten minutes.

On the train I search for a window seat by a table so that I can read the damned 'Spectator' magazine in peace and quiet. I call it 'damned' because it contains articles by intelligent, educated individuals who are often pretentious and more often than not barking up the wrong tree, twisting events to fit their fancy. What do they really know? The train soon fills up and the mother of a little boy – he must have been three or four – is encouraging him to show off his counting skills. We're up to thirty one and it seems that his target is one hundred. The guy sitting next to me murmurs something and I reply that if he carries on ad infinitum, I might bang my head against the window. The grandfatherly-looking guy sitting opposite smiles indulgently. The little boy is quite noisy – they leave the train at Croydon East (what could they possibly be going there for?) but the younger child, really only a baby, smiles at me very sweetly from a gap between the seats and I smile back. I could have smiled at him forever – he was so sweet – but I turn away deliberately to call it a day. The dad looked pleased. Opposite me is a girl with a blank face who is brushing her amazing mane of long dark hair. I'd be overjoyed and shouting from the rooftops if that was me.

It's a bit of a rough ride through the dark wasteland of the city of London – I'm not turned on by the glassy 'Shard' or the hexagonal 'Gherkin' although the distant sight of St. Paul's Cathedral is something lovely to behold, pulling at the patriotic heart strings – and I'm wondering when we're going to be finally rumbling through England's green and pleasant land. Not for a long time it seems. At Haywards Heath, on the platform, I ask a guy about the connecting train to Lewes. He turns out to be the driver and is amused that I haven't pronounced it 'Lewis'. 'You're the only person I've heard who has called it 'Loos'. I make it clear that the fault is mine. He proceeds to tell me about various family members who live in East Anglia and the cost of their houses. He's bemused by my story of wanting to have a trip out before the bad weather sets in. He's very keen to direct me to the right coach. There are some lovely dogs around who don't seem to be interested in biting me.

I love the brick nature of old English stations and next door to this one – Lewes – is a lovely florist lightly perfumed with the scent of so many cut flowers. How lovely to buy a handmade bouquet for someone you're visiting. I climb the steep road which leads to the High Street (so I'm told by a young dad with a kid on a trike) and stumble on what looks like my kind of cafe – I forget the name. The coffee is great – a pity about the never stream of traffic which passes the window. I ask the foreign waitress about 'Anne of Cleves's House' and although she hasn't a clue she's pleased to learn something new. Everyone around looks cool; men in their sixties with long hair, beard, and no sign of a paunch. A big woman comes over to my table and tells me how to get to the aforementioned house and tells me about the beautiful walled garden which shouldn't be missed. Southover Grange Gardens was once the private garden of the Grange and was built in 1542 and was briefly the home of John Evelyn the diarist. The Tudors knew a thing or two about garden design and it's a joy to see all the flowers rejoicing in the September sunshine. It's indeed true that this garden 'is a little piece of heaven on earth in the centre of Lewes town'. Accosting innocent passers by I finally arrive at the house in question – although I could have found it without bothering so many people – and wonder whether I should bother to buy a ticket to go in. The man behind the counter tells me that Anne of Cleves never actually lived there and it's now a museum. Anne of Cleves was the wife whom Henry didn't fancy – to say the least. She was sent packing but he left her some property. The priory was over the road. He told me some stuff about how the house was affected by Henry's reckless dissolution of the monasteries but I forget what.

My next stop is the castle. A must see. Built to last in the 11th century. I make my way back to the High Street (it's good that I found that stylish cafe since there are no others around) and pop into an old hotel to use the ladies and step onto the terrace to admire the view of the South Downs. This is a lovely part of the country and I say that because in the late 60's all the dishiest guys went to Sussex University. Not so me. I got a job as a library assistant at the L.S.E. in Houghton St. Sitting like a doll on my perch on the 'ins' and 'outs' all the boys asked me out. But that is all ancient history.

I pass charity shops that look as if they sell decent cast-offs but I'm not a frequenter. It's quite a smart High Street really and the area with its steep side streets reminds me a bit of Hampstead in north London. I enter a corner book shop which has a bell ring and is totally crammed with books. Where do they all come from? How is extra space created? There is very little walking space around a central table piled with children's books – Enid Blyton featuring heavily. I read that the creator of the 'Family from One End Street' – Eve Garnett – spent her final years in a care home in Lewes. I loved that loving family who never had any money ...

The book seller doesn't tell me to turn right, on leaving the shop, to get to the castle so I walk on until the end of the High Street. I can't really blame her though because she didn't know which way I was coming from. No sign of any castle so I ask a man who is going the other way. He tells me I've passed it and I'll see it, clear as day, if I cross the road and go up the side street he is indicating. Before he enters a pub en route I learn that he's originally a Londoner and that he and his wife live two miles outside of Lewes. He seems to be in a hurry to get to the pub. It's good to see the looming castle – they didn't mess around when it came to defence. Defence was everything.

I decide that it's time to make my way to the 123 bus stop on the road outside the station. I sit on the bench and wait. A lady, hunched with age, approaches the bench. I ask her something – I forget what and we begin to talk. A constant refrain is the passing away of her friends. She paints and she also writes poetry. She has lived in different parts of the country and it seems that she still wants to get around. It seems that I never fail, in most conversations, to voice my loathing of the 'Tate Modern'. All that cold impersonal space. She hates it too. She tells me that I should visit Charleston – the country retreat of Vanessa Bell and her husband Duncan Grant and much frequented by the Bloomsbury Group – with its beautiful garden. I hear about her children – one of whom has a mobile home and is presently in Italy with his family picking olives. I tell her about my son with OCD – it's the truth after all – and she comments, innocent lady that she is, that 'one wonders where these things come from'. I don't say that it might be the consequence of growing up without any structure/discipline/authority or of me receiving blows to the head during pregnancy. 'Keep your poor ugly sores to yourself madam!'/ 'You're not the class of person I want to talk to!' She lives in a terrace of cottages not far from Rodmell and has 'gay' musician friends in Cambridge. As we get on the bus I ask the jovial looking driver if he can 'call out' when we get to the 'Abergavenny Arms' which is my stop. I also ask him about return times and he gives me the bus timetable booklet. As I go to sit in the place I always take on buses, a quiet looking lady asks me if I'm going to 'Monk's House' where she herself is heading. I am indeed and tell her that she can follow me. A married couple are also on a Virginia Woolf pilgrimage and as they get off they ask the driver about the last bus and it's clear that they've done no homework whatsoever and deserve to get stranded.

My new friend is from Prague – studying English in Brighton – and has read work by Vita Sackville West (Virginia's lover). The road down to 'Monk's House' is a broad lane and utterly quiet and peaceful, a far cry from the comings and goings in Lewes. This young woman also has a non-intrusive quietness about her and is intelligent into the bargain. We split up at the wooden gate entry into the cottage discovered by Leonard Woolf a hundred years ago. He wasn't a ghetto or an orthodox Jew – far more like an eminent Victorian but his wife Virginia looked down upon his Jewish family. Snobbery is not an attractive quality. But I have no qualms about being a cultural snob and feel that a friendship is jeopardised if the friend watches stuff on TV which is sensationalist, dreary and childish. People don't like uncomfortable home truths – that's for sure.

The thing about the Woolf's living-room which most impressed me was Leonard's desk. Was it really on this small modest surface that he wrote so much, conducted so much correspondence. It is the opposite of grand or showy. I remember the spool of brown thread and the yellowing time marked envelopes relating to the Hogarth Press. These National Trust volunteer people are all the same; you ask them one question – in my case 'who painted that?' and you get told a ton of stuff you know already and don't want to hear. Better not to ask. I felt tempted to say that Trekki, Leonard's later love, wasn't much good as a painter but I held my tongue. It was the same in Virginia's bedroom. I didn't ask for a ton of information from the masculine looking woman in charge – I just wanted to be there and absorb the atmosphere and not engage in conversation. I wanted to look at the bed with its white bedspread and imagine her terrible nights and Leonard's devoted care. The mattress felt like straw. I admired the 'curvy' chest of drawers and was told that they'd bought it in France. I wonder to what extent Virginia appreciated the lovely garden with its miniature lakes and abundant fruit trees and interesting lay-out. I imagined her walking from the house to her writing 'shed' in the garden. An austere looking lady. I imagined Leonard in the narrow greenhouse and wondered if the absolutely glorious 'Morning Glory' – it was a radiant hue of purple – was there when he was. He had to put up with a lot and did a lot. The thing is that these illustrious inhabitants are dead and gone and you can't resurrect their spirit, their daily life, by walking around. What you see are tables and chairs, beds and bookcases and no one there.

In the wide expanse of garden facing the Downs a man is performing from 'Mrs Dalloway'. I don't want to join the crowd and explore the back part of the garden where the allotment is. There are tomato plants loaded with ripe tomatoes that are a beautiful red and I reach out and pick one. This is a bit more fun than sitting in the stalls but the quality is a little disappointing – too woolly under the skin. Other people are wandering around – taking photos – as always and I sit on a bench opposite the rectangular pond, out of the sun, in order to eat my sandwich. Later on I bump into my Czech friend who is just about to explore the house and is worried because she has lost her ticket. I vouch for her entry.

Well, I for one have had enough and I need to catch the 15.05 bus which departs from the bus shelter opposite the pub. I love the wide village road through which no traffic passes. A man (with his wife) asks me the way to the house and addresses me as a lady who looks as if she knows ... I am grateful for the compliment and always like to help people. I am early for the bus and observe the people drinking outside in the pub opposite. The sun is so bright that I have to take shelter. At exactly three o'clock my Czech friend – her name is Gabriela – saunters over to the bus stop. Apparently she didn't know the time of the bus and I tell her that she's lucky that she came when she did, otherwise she'd have had to wait close on an hour and a half for the next one. She seemed nonplussed. She tells me that her visit was 'very satisfying'. I ask her about her Prague and stuff since I'm always interested in foreign places. I tell her about Sue Perkins' Japan and the robots she encountered. We shudder in distaste. We also agree that we wouldn't want to walk across a zebra crossing that is 'the longest in the world'. We get onto literature since I tell her that I used to read Kafka. (She's probably getting the message that BLACK is my colour). As we talk the countryside is more or less ignored. I am definitely impressed that she's read all of Shakespeare's plays and I guess correctly that 'Macbeth' is her favourite. I say that Shakespeare knew everything – more than any 20th-century psychologist. I can't help myself telling her about how Macbeth is terrifyingly propelled into action by his wife's brutal threat – the bit about how she'd smash her baby's brains out – even as it was smiling in her face, contentedly attached to her nipple through its boneless gums – if she'd known he wasn't going to go ahead with their plan. She tenses her shoulders in excited horror. We part company outside the station – she's off to see the castle and I write down her email address and she writes down the name of a great Czech writer. A Japanese woman once waxed enthusiastically about a Japanese nobel prize winning writer and I couldn't for the life of me connect with his work – in translation of course. Same difficulty with a Turkish writer whose work meant so much to my lovely Turkish student. I wonder why Russian literature translates so well.

Waiting on the platform at Haywards Heath a woman with smart shoes and a rucksack on her back sits down next to me. She tells me that she's en route to Nice. I tell her where I've been and, with a sigh, looking into the far distance, she tells me what a dreadful family Virginia Woolf came from. I learn about the big house she shares with her husband, from whom she's divorced/separated and the set-up doesn't work in spite of maximum living space. They were married for forty nine years and she knew from day one that it was a mistake. I ask her if he was abusive and indeed he was. However, she loved being a mum and her four children are all in relationships although 'they don't know who to trust'. She had had quite a heated argument with her son-in-law the day before because she didn't approve of him letting his child skip school in order to protest against climate change since 'the law is the law'. I don't resist the temptation to talk about my son because I think that it might ease my mind and, you never know, someone just might shed a ray of light, say something new. I also get to voice my resentment of those who don't appreciate how having no father affects a male. She categorically states that a boy needs a father. When I tell her about my background she replies that I'm still punishing myself but as a daughter of Abraham I have a very strong root. I hear about a woman she met who has just been diagnosed with Alzheimer's Disease and is very upset. People seem to gain comfort from talking of those who are worse off than themselves. I wonder what she'll do in Nice until the end of November in her rented flat. She leaves the train at Gatwick Airport and blows me a kiss. I wish her well.

    The train finally arrives at Cambridge and, luckily, it is less crowded than on the outward journey. I couldn't text Toby to tell him when I'd be back because the sad little mobile phone which I only use to ask him if everything is OK has finally given up the ghost. He's probably a bit worried because it's 7pm and starting to get dark. I could have shouted 'hip hip hoorah' when, at around lunchtime, he replied to my 'everything OK?' text with a triumphant yes. All went well and the business is set up. I stop off at the M&S shop in the station in order to look for something nice. But he can't eat pasta or anything 'sticky' because, if he but knew it, such foods underline a deep connection to mother. Pumpkin seeds are also off the menu and lentils because they rhyme with mental. I bet he's relieved when he hears the door rattle open as I am, always, when he returns home. Do I dare say that he's in the kitchen looking for maggots (we had a minor infestation months ago during a spell of extremely hot weather) by the light of his phone. With humour and charm he says 'I think I'm going mad – the stress of the day has been ocean deep, mountain high – and he proceeds to tell me how things nearly didn't go according to plan but he relaxes in the telling and humour gains the upper hand.

    I look round this room and notice that the windows need cleaning. Cleanliness is next to godliness after all. It's true too that only God knows what we go through. And only we know who we really are. Oscar Wilde said that 'we should sympathise with the joy, the colour, the beauty of life. The less said about life's sores the better; it's too ugly, too horrible, too distressing'. The 'whoosh whoosh whoosh' sound of Toby anointing his head with water god knows how many times a day lets me forget that life is a blessing and that all is well and that we have to do our best to root out ignorance and hate in order to rise to the surface. But can I heal another's wound? Do I have a magic wand? The answer is No.

Lifting the Stone

How happy I felt in my blue and white spotted sunsuit in Alassio, a little seaside resort on the Italian Ligurian coast, in June 1956. The world was a simpler, slower, more relaxed place in those far-off days; there were no crowds, no laptops, no pesky walkie talkies. The obsession with speed had yet to take hold. The sky was blue, the sun was yellow and a gentle breeze came off the sea. But maybe the real reason that I felt so happy was because I hadn't yet been dumped by mummy. My baby brother was born the following April, when I was six years old. I already had a brother, only eighteen months older than me, with whom I shared a room and whom I adored. But back to mother; her gaze alighted on me, so cute in my sunsuit, and she felt immensely gratified that I looked so good. I suppose I was the apple of her eye – her pet mascot. I can't remember our hotel but she came to my room and kissed me goodnight before she set out, with my father, to the local casino. There are photos of me with her on the beach, me standing on a pedalo, my arms devotedly encircling her neck. Her glass eyes stare fixedly ahead. I can't believe she was only thirty three years old.

Without any religious feeling whatsoever she was nevertheless deeply attached to her racial origins and we had to attend Hebrew classes three times a week from a very early age and I remember struggling with the Hebrew characters and trying very hard to get things right. The method of teaching was rote learning – memorising chunks of the Old Testament stories. God was always speaking to his earthly representatives and getting furiously angry with his Chosen People because they weren't obeying his commandments. Our local rabbi was also forever thundering from the pulpit – raining fire and brimstone on our enemies – the gentiles. My father banged on the wall when my brother and I were having great fun pretending to be Adam and Eve (I used the mattress as a slide – a great invention I thought) and when our laughter would begin again after a short stunned silence he'd make a fearful appearance in his pyjamas and dressing gown. Was his fly partially open – could I detect something large, dark and mysterious? He was certainly grim-faced and murderously angry.

I certainly enjoyed getting new clothes for the Jewish New Year in September and the Passover Festival in April. I have no memory of taking the bus to Golders Green Road so my mother was already driving and she had a grey

Morris Thousand which was the love of her life. She reckoned she was the best driver in the world. She'd shake her head dismissively and with pity at those who couldn't pass their test the first time. She once threw me out and left me at a bus stop near Selfridges in Marble Arch because my taste in dresses differed from hers. I was about eleven. I recall the surprised faces of the other people standing patiently in the queue as she drove round to pick me up, reinstate me in the passenger seat. Driving up to the west-end she'd vent what felt like a tsunami of bad temper – spitting curses on the outside world.

But as we walked up the path into 'Betties' which was under the bridge in Golders Green Road we were both scouring the windows to see if there was anything we fancied and filled with anticipation at the prospect of seeing what Madame Betty kept in her magic cupboards, always packed tight with smart dresses for affluent little girls. What was going through the head of the humble assistant as she 'swiped' one dress after the other until I nodded my head: 'yes, I'll try that one'. My mother was secretly impressed by my decisiveness – as regards buying for herself she couldn't make up her mind about anything and ended up with frumpy 'round the house' clothes or expensive satin ball gowns. My parents' regular dinner haunt was 'Antoines', a lovely fish restaurant in Charlotte St., in the West End, on the edge of Soho. It was either there or at 'The Etoile' (down the road) that the manageress told her that her mink coat was far superior to Princess Margaret's. Both had been secretly tried on. This was obviously very pleasing to my mother as she loved to boast. Anyway, I loved my fluffy winter berets and summer straw boaters. I had little navy blue suits, black or red patent 'Birthday' shoes and white cotton gloves. Madame Betty said, with restrained relish, that she could put me in the window of her shop. When we got home ladened with parcels, which were spread across my bed, my elder brother wore a face of 'what about me, what do I get?' as he went into his bedroom. But he was a boy and was expected to work hard, do well, and swell the family name. For his bar mitzvah suit my mother insisted on the royal tailor and to this end we visited a shop in Mayfair where there was a lonely wooden rocking-horse in the window. There were quarrels at home as to which suit material was the most suitable. 'Mohair' suits for boys were the 'in' thing but my father might have disapproved. In our living-room – called the 'lounge' – aggressive confrontation and losing one's temper was all the rage.

As a very young child my brother and I would attend the synagogue with my father on a Saturday morning, dressed in our 'Sunday best'. I was probably wearing my little navy blue suit with the pleated skirt. He held our hands and his grip was such that you'd only escape with some crushing of bones. He was young, slim and fit. He never spoke about himself but we knew that he'd fought Oswald Moseley's brownshirts in the 1930s and come home with a bloody nose.

He liked to fight. Like a bullet propelled from a gun he set off for a funeral. He grew up in the Soho pub which his parents owned 'The Blue Posts' and attended 'The City of London' School where he did well and was very happy until war broke out. His father died of stomach cancer when he was eleven and his mother, when being consoled by a kindly relative, said, in the presence of her sons: 'Your husband is everything and your children nothing'. His extended family were a secular crew so he never went to the synagogue or kept the commandments but his wife loved 'Yiddishkeit' absorbed from her father and he willingly took on this mantle. Walking through Hendon Central on a Saturday morning we'd cut a swathe through local people doing their shopping – entering 'Welshes' the greengrocer, 'Walton Hassel and Port', where they'd buy their cheddar cheese, ham and digestive biscuits and the ABC which sold sugar coated buns, jam tarts and doughnuts, as well as the ubiquitous sliced white loaf. (My mother raided the ABC and 'Jacks' the local confectioners on a daily basis. This led to my increased girth and her resulting fury when the zips on the dresses in Betties got stuck at the waist) These Saturday shoppers in their homespun clothes were very aware of us because we looked so strikingly handsome and well-made but they looked thoughtfully critical as well probably due to our stubborn pride. The truth is that the Jews rejected Jesus Christ, the saviour of mankind.

Seated downstairs in the synagogue with the men I whiled away the time knotting the silken fringe of his 'tallus' (prayer shawl). I know he wasn't thinking about his soul – wasn't thinking about anything really – just doing his duty. At the Saturday lunch table, eaten formally in the dining room, my mother required him to say the blessing for bread and wine. We'd all be standing up and he'd be stumbling over the Hebrew. Jonathan and I couldn't stifle our giggles. That was our downfall. We were taken out into the hall and ordered to bend over to receive 'six of the best'. I don't so much remember the whacks as the feeling of total humiliation at being told to bend over. It is still there whenever I have to bend over in order to do the most menial chore. But one can't ignore the cause of his brutal behaviour. He was a boy when his father died and he was called on, as the eldest son, to intone the prayer for the dead. Hardly able to read Hebrew and grieved at not being allowed to attend the funeral he was outraged and humiliated by this responsibility. And here he was again, a child being laughed at by his children. On occasion, when his efforts to please mother totally failed, I was punched in the head. I refused to cry because this would be a sign that the enemy had won. I punched him back instinctively. My brother cried and got beaten up more because he was so soft, a 'boobie'. I felt my head with some pride: 'I must have a very hard skull' I said to myself 'because it is still in one piece. Extraordinary!' Crying is a weakness and, with me, tears are NOT ALLOWED to surface; in a split second they are turned into words and the need to maintain control, to suffer and endure. But being bounced on his shoulders (a rare occurrence) was bliss as was being chased. Boisterous games! He loved being blindfolded and playing 'Blind Man's Bluff' and chanting or rather shouting the end bit of 'Oranges and Lemons', in the climax of: 'Here comes a candle to light you to bed; here comes a chopper to chop off your head ...' Having progressed to the 'Ladies Gallery' my father would nod his head in acknowledgement when I entered in all my finery with my two mates – one of whom was the daughter of a dress shop owner in Queensway and had more access to new clothes than I did and the other was the daughter of a garage owner who got all her tacky clothes from C&A. I berated her for wearing red patent stiletto heels and a hooped skirt and for being so scruffy. She never fought back although I deserved a whack. We spent the service chatting and playing noughts and crosses on her C&A suede coat. Ever so often the 'chamester' (or whatever she was called) – a mole-like woman who was hired to give out books and keep order – would approach us shaking her fist ... She was a grey/brown image, a human woodlouse and we'd stop instantly. For a bit. She always wore the same turban and a long wool cream coloured coat, never removed.

My favourite summer dress was a grey and gold shirtwaister which had a seahorse in every big square. I also had a primrose yellow shirtwaister with a very pale stripe in some sort of silky material. My friend over the road had the same dress in pale pink. I admired her greatly because she had long blonde hair, big blue eyes and was thin. Her father was a German Jewish jewellery merchant and her mother wasn't. Their house was very clean and there was always a cake, of the 'continental' variety on display in the kitchen. (We had a plain 'pound' cake, topped with icing sugar from 'Grodzinski', the Polish/Jewish Bakery at the top of the road. Mr. Ilsen obviously really dug his gentile wife – he had such a happy look on his face when he went off to work in the morning and she told my mother how satisfied she was in bed. My mother said that Mrs Ilsen, although a German, was ok because she was pretty. She told my mother that I too was pretty and I was surprised to hear this since I was aggrieved by my small eyes. You were only noticed if you had big eyes – like a cow – or dark hair with the scintillating contrast of green or blue eyes. My father told me that my eyes were like 'black beads' – uttered with some spite – as he charged off to play squash on a Saturday afternoon. The squash court and the Golfing Green were where he liked to be – as well as the RAC Club in Pall Mall – and, come to think of it, he was probably thinking about his golfing handicap during those long hours in the windowless House of Prayer. He was always on about improving his handicap – was it 7 or 9? – and practising his swing in the lounge. He was at home at the Golf Club. No women allowed.

Back to my dress with the divine sea-horses. It was August 1962 and we were en route to 'Forte dei Marmi' an Italian resort on the Mediterranean coast. I'd really loved the drive down south six years earlier passing by fields of red poppies in Provence and staying in a friendly 'pensione' where the lady of the house gave me a cheese grater as a present and trusting my father to take the narrow mountain bends with care but now it was all about flying B.E.A. which was also exciting. We stayed at the 'Hotel Augustus' – a beautiful villa surrounded by pine trees. My father always found, not the flashiest hotel, but the one with real class. I remember how my heart sank when I was shown to my room (why couldn't I share with my brother? – I was still only eleven although at home I'd been turfed into a single room, years earlier, when my little brother was born) which had green tiles, white walls and the smell of mosquito repellent. We were in this divine spot for two weeks but not a single word passed between myself and any other family member. But I do remember the small bar with its bowls of tangy black olives and the presence of an Italian countess, holidaying alone, who was always dressed in pink. She wore a pink swimsuit and a swimming hat made of pink (rubber) petals. She had an Italian admirer – a handsome young man who knelt at her feet. There was a similar beautiful dark-haired lady in the synagogue whom I would literally look up to when I sat in the downstairs stalls with my father. She too was immensely calm and composed. My father had a cine camera and spent much of the time on holiday taking home-movies. He had total control over his machine and it wouldn't have occurred to him to let anyone else have a go – except my mother – when he needed to be in the shot. He'd be standing there, arms crossed and looking exasperated. The film was sent away to be developed and it was a moment of great excitement when the yellow and black package returned. The screen would be set up in the lounge and we couldn't wait to see ourselves on film. Is this who we really are? I am sitting on my sunbed in my pretty 'shocking pink' swimsuit. I smile for the camera – a big genuine smile – but suddenly it is as if a black cloud passes over my face and I collapse backwards onto the sunbed. I'm surprised I didn't hurt myself – I allowed myself to land with such a thump. In the next shot I am lying on my side, looking resigned and thoughtful, as if accepting the fact that no one smiles back at me. The Mediterranean Sea was gorgeous, blue and clear and I loved to take out my dark red linen lilo and ride the waves. It was bliss to be tossed around and I was struck by how the crowd on the beach became ever smaller midgets as I ventured out and grew back in size as I swam back to the shore and strode through the lacy puddles. There they all were, same as ever.

Humans certainly loomed very large on the return walk from the synagogue. Not very often my mother would make an appearance, in her grey tailored suit, at the end of the service. She was too busy with household chores and preparing

Saturday lunch (although the cold fried fish had been cooked the day before) to arrive any earlier. In the forecourt of the House of Prayer families would group together, knowing where they belonged and holding the hard book of the Old Testament under their arm. In our group there was no easy-going chat. Here comes mother in her grey suit and short hair. We'd begin to walk and I'd feel a whack on my back and an order from 'the grey suit' to 'walk straight'. My brother would echo this with a 'back up!' command and a mime of what constitutes correct posture. My father would grimly concur in the assault. My response was to stoop as low as I could as I trudged along in my lovely pale pink boucle wool spring coat from Wallis. A lovely garden fronting a massive house imprinted itself on my mind and I wondered why one never saw the inhabitants. The dwellings on the other side of the road were poor and mean. My younger brother, on another occasion, says to his friend, as they pass the Gaumont cinema where 'The Hunchback of Notre Dame' is showing: 'My sister should be in that'. This order of 'back up' is a constant refrain and when they are all standing around me with their pokes and admonitions I am like a curly coated white dog who is being kicked by its owner. I love my pink coat with its soft round collar and double breasted buttons. Needless to say I fail to be awarded the 'deportment badge' at school; the awarding body has obviously noticed how my shoulders are permanently hunched. Some quality time is spent sitting with my mother on the sofa as she makes a list of what she has spent on me in the last season. She never forgets the 'Sox' which come at the bottom of the list as the least expensive item. But it must be said that she teaches me to knit – although I never proceed from plain to 'pearl' – and when I ask her if she can help me to put steel grips on my hair to make 'kiss curls' she lets her pretty hands lead the way. Normally it's as if an iron rod is governing her body, not allowing it to be soft, spontaneous, yielding.

At the end of March 1961 we flew to the Holy Land with 'El Al'. Our cousins, who were seen as the poor relations although Uncle Monty, a lovely Welshman, was manager of an M&S store – having secured the job because his wife, my mother's sister, had been the girlfriend of someone in the Sieff family – came to see us off. I was wearing my blue and grey jersey suit and black patent 'Birthday' shoes. My girl cousins didn't want to be there – indeed they hated the infrequent Sunday afternoon tea-time visits whereby they were made to feel inferior on account of their clothes although their capable mother was able to run up things for them on her sewing-machine. We were up in the air for ten minutes when we had to descend because one of the engines had failed. Then followed a six hour wait in the terminal for things to be put right again. After every hour a cheery voice apologised and predicted only another hour's wait. We waited. We didn't complain.

We had an extra suitcase because my mother had bought a mass of summer clothes for her brother (whom she despised because, like Monty, he was soft and enjoyed his food) and his poor children. In our hotel bedroom – 'The Dolphin House' just outside Haifa – she sat on the bed with the case and doled out clothes as if she was Father Christmas. The poor relatives seemed quite indifferent in spite of their polite thank yous. Nobody paid me any attention at all – although my aunt did ask me if I brushed my hair a lot because it was so shiny. I didn't know what to reply because I wasn't used to benevolent personal questions. My mother mocked this good woman because she lacked film star looks ... hardly a Sophia Loren or Elizabeth Taylor (mauve eyes) look alike! ... But being ignored was a matter of small moment; I was in the land of Israel and the boring Bible had come to life – stones could talk after all. It was the end of March and the weather was beautiful and there were camels on the road and in the hotel garden I had the climbing frame all to myself – didn't have to share it with the seething mass of thin kids at Algernon Road Primary School ... There was nowhere we didn't visit – my father was especially interested in the Crusader fort at Acre and dragged us in his wake, too shouty and vehement to properly share his enthusiasm. I was fascinated by the swarm of thin Arab girls who swarmed round our black 'Hertz' car with their unkempt black hair and their slip-on strapless shoes (I had to be strapped into mine because I had 'poor Jewish flat feet'). At the foot of the blue green mauve Galilean hills I picked up a rock as a keepsake because it came from this ancient land. I was aware that Jesus had preached in this area and taught people about sharing, an aspect of letting go, actually. Walking alongside my mother by the Sea of Galilee, lobster red with sunburn, I gazed at all the dead fish floating alongside the wall and could only look down, back bent and head bowed. We stayed for a couple of days at the King David Hotel in Jerusalem – where a whole wing of the hotel was blown up during the conflict between the British Mandate and the 'Irgun' terrorists prior to the establishment of the new state of Israel. As my parents talked or argued amongst themselves in the next room I looked out wonderingly at the separating wall between east and west Jerusalem. I'd reckoned that Nazareth and Bethlehem were dumps and in the northern town of Safed my mother noted that the women were still wearing jumpers although, by our standards, it was pretty hot. She had no interest in History or anything beyond blood ties although, as a Jewish woman, she had a deep, unconscious sense that her blood was bad, polluted.

Prior to this trip new clothes had been bought from Marks and Spencers – specifically turquoise and navy blue cotton slacks. M&S were excellent for sensible clothing. From Betties I got two lovely silky tops – one was sky blue and the other in pale primrose yellow. I stood in front of the mirror in my hotel bedroom and gazed at myself in the yellow top which was full of creases, like ugly scars, and felt woeful, to say the least. Later on in the day the doctor had to be called in because I had a bad attack of asthma and bronchitis – something I was used to. My mother, in mirth, used to call me 'wheezy Anna'. Any illness, difficulty or disorder was frowned upon, forbidden. You were obviously a weakling who would be better off dead, if not down the well. If you were ill in bed she'd storm out of the house, slamming the door behind her. She did cook you, however, a nice dover sole with (lumpy) mashed potato. My father would rent a television set for the bedroom and once, he sat down on my bed and read me Edward Lear's 'The Table and the Chair'. He felt for the table and the chair who could not feel. I loved being in bed, all warm, snuggled up and cosy and it didn't bother me that I was off school. Strangely, as the sober Israeli doctor entered the room they showed him the nude calendar photos of Marilyn Monroe in the central pages of her latest biography. He didn't know what … he was a doctor and wanted to see his patient. And who could deny that she was the most feminine creature ever created. 'Nature had given her everything' as it was said. Awaiting him was me with my 'short back and sides' haircut.

My father was seriously delighted at this time, grinning from ear to ear, because his shares were rising beyond his wildest dreams. All the relatives came over to the hotel and my father paid for all the women to have their hair done. There is movie footage of everyone having a good time – my mother's young sister, Esther, (beloved of a teenage Arnold Wesker whom my mother nicknamed 'Wizzie') is playing table tennis with my brother and my eight year old cousin – Yehudit – is wearing her new M&S dress and sitting on my mother's lap. I am wearing the badly creased primrose yellow top and sitting away from the group on the ground – pulling up the grass. No one notices other than the camera. This newly opened hotel – I think we are the only guests – is almost on the beach and I look longingly over to the clear sea, blue as blue with foaming white waves. I am in love with the sea. Back at home, I gaze at myself in the gilt-edged hall mirror before I set off for the synagogue in order to see my friends. My cotton summer dress is of the sweetest, palest sky blue overlaid with pale pink blossom. I feel as if I'm touched with grace. Mother has emerged from the kitchen, eternally in the act of drying her hands, and says, with a look of pleasure on her face, 'let's have a look at you'. Being anywhere near her brother fills her with the dread of being poor, not having 'gelt'.

I am always calling on people and I like to visit the Wolfson household, where my friend Berenice lives. In the bedrooms there are piles of clothes on the carpet and I wonder how they can live in such a mess. I tell her, in a bullying way, that she is a 'schloch' (an unkempt woman). The parents have a TV in their bedroom and a bar downstairs. Kay, the mum, is plump and voluptuous and when she helps at 'Kosher Dinners' (prison fare could be no worse) she always manages to get us seconds and thirds of the super sweet jam tart dessert. She also leaves out smoked salmon and cream cheese beigels for us to eat when we have our Sunday afternoon meetings at her house where I, the sole mover of our magazine 'The Weekly Blab' see how everyone is getting on with their tasks. Berenice teaches me how to jive in the large hall where the bar is and a record is playing which immediately strikes me as 'different.' It is called 'Love me Do', by a new group called 'The Beatles'. It is 1962. Berenice's elder sister hangs out at the 'El Toro' club in Finchley Road and is hardly sweet and quiet. She hates me because I know she has a false front tooth. I take vicarious satisfaction in the fact that the family always goes to the cinema together on a Thursday night. I am about eleven and I get into trouble with their mother because she hears me telling Berenice that my mother is dead. I really believe what I'm saying. Kay knows that my mother isn't dead – she's probably seen her around the shops in Hendon Central – and tells me that I must never ever say such a thing. Her own mother is probably still alive – a lovely, warm, kind Jewish lady.

Back at home I am sitting in my room when my mother enters and thrusts some paperback artbooks at me. They consist of Vermeer, Van Gogh (the painting of the 'The Sidewalk Cafe at Night' is on the front cover) and Goya with his portrait of his ladylove the 'Countess of Alba' in all her black finery. She IS this lady in her cold haughtiness. The books are almost thrown at me and indeed my mother's favourite word is 'chuck' as in 'chuck it out!'. On the bookshelf above my bed there is a dull sandy yellow biography of Van Gogh entitled 'Lust for Life'. I note the titles of books. My father has one in his bookcase by someone called Zoe Oldenburg called 'This World is not Enough'. I do read Anne Frank's diary and lament the fact that I am not clever enough, as she was, to write. I'm not clever enough; period.

It is August, 1965 and we are on the beach at Riccione, a resort on the Adriatic Coast. In those days the sea wasn't a repository for people's rubbish. Consumerism too was kept at bay. You got fat because you only ate potatoes, lockshen, pasta or cakes. We are here because I insisted; Riccione was the venue for the Jewish youth of north-west London. One of my friends, or rather a 'leading member' of a group of flashy fourteen year olds who made war on me because I said that the boys they liked were 'common', was staying with her mother (her father was always working, managing his string of ladieswear shops) at the old-fashioned Hotel Mediterranean down the road. We were staying at the 'Atlantic', a small, attractively modern family-run hotel. The Italian family had their sunbeds in key position at the front of the beach and they were burnished to a deep shade of mahogany. This is what we all aspired to. 'I am suntanned so I am someone, after all. People will look on me and wonder!' I have a pale almond blossom pink cotton dress that I bought in the sale from 'Wallis' in

Marble Arch and I am sitting on my own on one of the leather sofas in the lounge. The proprietor appears and beams at me affectionately, appreciatively. Usually he looks very serious. I am so embarrassed that I don't know where to look and blush, as the saying goes, to the roots of my straightened hair. It is 1965 and it is a crime not to have dead straight hair.

On the beach, in my black and white bikini, I like to take a walk along the water's edge where it's breezy but most of all I love the way all the young men sit up, literally, because they are knocked out by my beautiful curvy figure. I relish the attention and the sea breeze, walking free. Suddenly my father, with his hooked nose and thin lips, is standing next to me. He tells me, grimly, that I am like a predatory hawk, picking up men. It's that beady eye again. I am taken aback because I harbour no mean or calculated intention. I feel entirely innocent. And I am very vaguely aware that if I was getting some wholesome male attention at home I wouldn't be driven to 'parade'. My brother and I used to be friends but now we fight viciously and my father sees me as a scratching cat, a vicious female.

My parents jet off, on their own ('free of children') to Monte Carlo, staying at the 'Hotel de Paris' which is situated opposite the famous casino. My mother brings me back beautiful bikinis. The summer '66 model was a beautiful pale turquoise blue cotton affair and I try it on in my bedroom. My parents and my nine year old brother peep in to look at me. Out of the blue my brother mischievously undoes the bikini bottom tie and I let out a great yell, clutching at the sides. They could have seen my black pubic hair! The three of them bid a hasty retreat and I lock myself in. My summer 1965 model resembled a Monet painting of his water lilies – all pale greens, blues and mauves. The bra top had a scalloped edge but I don't do it justice. Why has everybody else got breasts like melons with that thing called a cleavage? At school I am always glancing down at my flat chest, trying somehow to force some growth. And what would we do if we couldn't go abroad for two weeks in August? Being burnt alive, being as tanned as teak furniture is an important achievement. I have a white cotton double breasted trouser suit with big black buttons which I wear with a black sleeveless 'skinny'. (I dyed it from white to black, with my friend, in my mother's zinc bucket on the kitchen stove and she actually had a fit). I have arrived. That summer we had travelled down to Naples, after the two week stay in Riccione, to see my mother's sister and family. Her husband, who worked for 'Zim' the Israeli shipping firm, was stationed there. There was a cine film of all of us traipsing around Pompei (or was it the Vatican in Rome?) in the heat. My brother suffered from terrible rhinitis and he is wiping his nose non-stop with an outsize handkerchief. My father is striding out, intent on seeing the ruins. My head is bent, like some poor flower, as my mother scolds me. At one point the camera turns on me and, with furrowed brow, I am mouthing the words: 'I'm so thirsty'. My mother and her sister enter some dark room and observe an erect phallus. Some silent inside knowledge has taken place between the adults; the women are smirking in amusement and the men are unsure as to how they're supposed to react.

The same August finds us in Florence although I don't remember how we got there. There is a cine film of my brother and I standing on the charming old 'Ponte Vecchio' looking lost and nowhere. We're neither looking at one another or looking into the River Arno. It is a very hot afternoon in mid-August. We are waiting for my mother who is trawling up and down the bridge, in and out of small jewellery shops whose windows are bright with gold, looking for a bracelet. She is accompanied by my father who never expresses irritation at her indecision – he has the resigned patience of a dumb slave. What does she finally gain? A ball and chain. A chunky gold chain with a ball attached to it which is meant to be the world or the planet earth? Needless to say we don't see any works by Michelangelo although my father is enthusiastic about visiting Carrara, the old quarry from whence his marble came. The famous marble was infused with anarchic power and life.

The Saturday morning trip to the synagogue is a thing of the past. Years earlier, on the way back we'd pass the local Gaumont cinema and me and my mates would eagerly look at the trailer photos outside to see what was worth seeing. In the holidays we'd go to the cinema two or three times a week. My mother would tell me to take 3/6d out of her black bag which was always on a green armchair in her bedroom. Fancy sleeping with your black bag and purse within easy reach. I didn't like taking the money. A pity that my father would repeatedly forget to give me my pocket money and it was humiliating to remind him. Outside in Hendon Central we'd see who was about. Children weren't allowed into an 'X' certificate (because of bare breasts and executions and the like) but you could get into an 'A' if you were accompanied by a parent. My trick was to approach some neutral man who was going into the cinema on his own and ask him if he'd 'take us in'. No one ever refused or asked any questions.

In October '65 Michael Kelsey spotted me standing at Golders Green Station in my new autumn trouser suit. He then ran off somewhere telling his mate 'to keep her warm until I get back'. When he returned he took me to see 'The Spy Who Came in from the Cold' with Richard Burton. I remember this film so well precisely because I didn't see any of it. We were magnetically attracted as it were and couldn't stop snogging. It was sheer bliss. I'd fancied him for ages. Coming back from school on the bus I added up the numbers on the ticket and if they were 11 or 13 – corresponding to K and M in the alphabet they'd be kept. I still remember his telephone number: 'FIN 3010'. His father was a doctor and he was set to follow in his footsteps, studying medicine at 'Barts.' He also resembled my father physically and emotionally. My friends couldn't understand how I could be attracted to someone who seemed so detached and cold. They were looking for their own dads – friendly, chubby out-going guys. Still, if he hadn't been around I wouldn't have been able to endure the 'SS Nevassa' School Cruise in November '65 – the psychiatrist I saw asked me if I had anyone to come back to and told me I had sensual lips and then laughed when I blushed. If you were nervous and scared of anything (leaving the person – HER – on whom you were so dependent) she'd say harshly; 'Do you want to see someone'? Talking at home wasn't on the cards. My doctor lover was around again some years later when I was eighteen and a half and my psychiatrist friend told me that I had to 'get out of that house'. I needed male support. I found a flat to rent in Swiss Cottage and advertised in the Jewish Chronicle for other girls to share it with. I was a tyrannical landlord – shame on me.

But on a Saturday morning I sat on the boiler in the kitchen whilst they were all at the Raleigh Close Synagogue. I had orders to do the housework – dusting and hoovering and brushing the stairs. There was an au-pair and a cleaning lady – Mrs Smith – but my mother was always complaining about all the work. There was nothing my father wouldn't buy her to ease her woes, not caring to see that the woe was her neurosis about touching things, getting her hands dirty. (As a child she didn't skip through the daisies or lie on her back gazing at the stars). Jobs done – you didn't dare refuse because Father would turn white with rage and we all knew how he could whack a ball or a human head – his aim at the coconut shy at Bertram Mills Circus was ferocious – l sat on the boiler and read 'Lord of the Flies'. This was a GCSE English Literature set text but the teacher's choice had been George Eliot's 'Silas Marner'. I didn't want to read this book because I thought that it was probably about suffering and misery – Christian style. With some hostility she said to me: 'Well, alright then, you do 'Lord of the Flies' on your own. (I'd always loved the book since my brother bought it for me 'on the occasion of my 13th Chanukah') For this English teacher I was the bright girl who had fallen down the well, a source of grave and angry disappointment. She threw my exam paper at me, declaring that I had 'a good brain, but a weak, careless and sloppy mind'. In those days lack of success was attributed to laziness and not pulling your socks up. Anyway, I was more than content to study on my own. I felt an enormous sympathy for Piggy and the horrible way he met his demise. His cracked and broken glasses were a symbol of his humanity and sensitivity, his saying to Ralph; 'I wonder why Jack hates me so much'? And the answer was, of course, because he was fat and weak.

When I'm sitting on the boiler my attire couldn't have been more different from my Saturday night black velvet sophistication or my Mary Quant casual wear for Sunday afternoon attendance at the Golders Green Road Kenco Coffee house. When I'm 'round the house' my mother tells me that I look like Princess Anne. 'How can that be?' I say to myself disconsolately. (Indeed she, my mother, likes to model us on Charles and Anne and she herself wears headscarves like the queen. However, the queen looks like a nice lady who is into country pursuits of dogs and horses whilst my mother looks like a wolf in waiting). She also tells me that I remind her of the actress Sarah Miles. I wonder what that implies.

At least I now have a bosom buddy – a girl who was a former foe on account of my habitual exclamation of 'honestly!' when they mocked me for expressing the view that everyone they liked – mods on their bikes en route to Margate or Jewish 'wide boys' with their E type canary yellow jaguars – were common. We'd been brought together because we sensed the other's anxiety concerning the forthcoming cruise where you'd have to rough it in a dormitory (no rosy wallpaper or satin eiderdown) and we must have been alike because we often ended up with the same lovely clothes from 'Wallis' in Marble Arch. It was our Aladdin's Cave of exciting delights. But, sitting on the boiler, I am wearing a beige lambswool cardigan from M&S; grey 'pure new wool' (who hasn't seen that label?) trousers and black nylon fluffy slippers. My fringe is swept to the side – a la Adolf Hitler and held diagonally in place by a row of steel grips. No make-up. I'd NEVER go out without the full works; no boy could see me looking so plain. I keep a diary: every entry begins 'Dear God' and it is all about the other girls and desperately trying to get a boyfriend.

Autumn '63 was a good time. Surely everyone on the planet fell in love with 'The Beatles'? How could you not – unless you were a corpse or someone so devoid of natural rhythm that you might as well have been fashioned out of wood, if not iron and steel. (Gone was the memory of my father beating time in the dining-room, with his iron rod, as I practised my piano pieces. I stopped practising, much to the disappointment of my teacher, and all I could see was the steel bar of the music case weighing me down and wiping the smile from my face). I loved the cover of the L.P 'With the Beatles' with its shiny black background. Some years later I was similarly taken with the image of Leonard Cohen, alone on the record sleeve. At the age of twelve and three quarters I jauntily set off for the local youth club 'Danescroft' which was situated in the hall of a 'reform' synagogue at the other side of Hendon. I probably wouldn't have gone if I hadn't wanted to follow in my beloved brother's footsteps and all his clever friends – although some of them were far from handsome. I wore my brushed wool dress with red and black horizontal stripes and a white pointed collar. It was from Betties, the child's shop in Golders Green Road. A friend calls it my 'bee dress' – on account of the stripes I guess. But my lovely turquoise sleeveless wool dress with the big pussy cat taffeta bow under the collar was from 'Polly Peck' in Bond Street. I had taken the 113 bus to the West End and, in high excitement, gloriously alone, searched for clothes. In the future this became a normal Saturday morning activity – armed with a blank cheque from my mother and an attached letter saying ' this cheque must not exceed £50'. On one occasion, as I was walking to the bus stop, I saw the sober faced rabbi en route for the synagogue and it was as if God had seen me, caught me in the act of desecrating the sabbath. My black shoes with the kitten heels were from Lilley and Skinner and the next autumn/winter I'd have a pair of black suede shoes with cross- over straps and a chunky heel which went a treat with lacy tights and my cinnamon coloured smock dress with the lace bodice. At the ill-named 'Country Club' in Belsize Park the boys queued up to dance with me and I turned all of them away because they weren't the messianic prince I had in mind. But this early Beatle world was the bright sunshine in our lives and I knew every song by heart. At the end of Saturday evening at Danescroft they always seemed to play 'Twist and Shout' and I'd pray to heaven that Jeremy Gee would ask me to dance. He rarely did. My friend Tina Kartoon said that he looked like a duck. I just wanted to be close to him – as close as close can be. Another boy, who travelled by train from Willesden, would ask me to dance instead. His name was Jonathan Wilson and was the quiet type. In those days 'quiet' equalled 'blank' rather than thoughtful. About ten years later, when I was under house arrest in a block of flats called 'Romney Court' in Haverstock Hill, Belsize Park, NW3 we became intimately involved for a very short time. He emigrated to the States and became a lecturer in English and a novelist.

When girls come home from school mums are meant to greet them affectionately and ask about their day. Since the age of about ten my mother hadn't been around – she was shopping most days in the West End – Selfridges was her happy hunting ground. I'd sit on the boiler and consume a whole packet of 'Penguins'; I loved the shiny wrapping paper – royal blue, green and red. Or else I'd consume biscuit after biscuit – all the well-known brands. Most mornings over her morning tea she'd peruse the paper – to find out 'what they were wearing?' Once in a while I'd return from school in leafy Mill Hill (God knows what I was doing there wearing that horrible uniform) and she'd literally whisk me off in her car to South Kensington and Mary Quant's newly opened boutique shop called 'Bazaar'. Her clothes were made for me. A mustard and beige tweedy pinafore dress with a very low neck which I wore with a frilly white blouse was so 'made for me' that, on doing up the zip in my pink bedroom, I experienced what can only be described as psychic agony. It was as if my being had been zapped with a chemical weapon, a constraint that was attacking me at my very source. It was a weird and horrible feeling – torture I guess. My 'tin soldier' dress, (so named by my friend and she commonly, affectionately, calls me 'muckfuck') a sort of tunic in her trademark dusty soft pink wool didn't attack me in the same way and, complete with the cream lacy tights and black suede shoes I went (with a friend) to the Mod Ball in March 1964. My father always managed to get tickets for things. Billy J. Kramer was performing with a very tanned face. Brian Epstein, the Beatles' manager, forbade him from appearing on Juke Box Jury because he couldn't speak proper. What a time this was – so pulsatingly exciting what with the songs, the boys and the clothes and yet so anguished because of the competitive females with their sharp claws. I didn't understand why my peers were so keen on smoking and wearing 'Miners' white lipstick and pale blue eye-shadow. I did the same and my father told me to take it off yelling, in some distress, 'that I looked like a tart in Piccadilly Circus.' With some scorn he also said that I resembled a clown. He ordered the magazine 'Knowledge' which arrived every week and it lay in the wooden rack – unopened. The Jewish girls could be divided into three groups; the orthodox sect, the clever/artistic sect and the daughters of shopkeepers who embraced promiscuity and seemed to want to debase themselves and boast about it. I pursued this last group.

What could one do? As a teenager you have to go out. In the summer of '65 the '71 Club in West End Lane was the place to go. The music blaring out was Bob Dylan's 'Like a Rolling Stone'. Everyone was saying that it was the first four-minute-single ever recorded. I didn't take much notice of the lyrics but his nasal passionate drawl was unmistakable. And he was Robert Zimmerman, I later discovered, a damned Jew like us. I wore a blue and white striped skinny with cut-away sleeves and a polo neck along with a slim fit beige cotton skirt with a hessian straw belt. Beautiful raffia looking pinky beige shoes from Elliots in Bond Street. A boy, Neil Lindsay, asked me to dance and told me that I reminded him of Gina Lollobrigida. I didn't know what she looked like but knew that she was a famous Italian film-star. I foolishly told one of the gang who relayed the information to all and sundry. I was henceforth called 'Gina' accompanied by mocking laughter. Who could have enjoyed hanging around in those clubs waiting to be asked to dance or to sit in some midget's lap? I remember two boys – David Morrison and Paul Bloomberg – less than five feet tall and always with a cigarette hanging out of their mouths – even when strutting their stuff. They were vile as hell. They made up a song about me – it was short and sweet; '21, 21, never been done – Queen of all the virgins'. Neil Lindsay, who had been nice to me on account of his attraction, was in with the boys and in on the joke. Persecution is fun. Humans enjoy the sense of being on top and crushing the poor loser beneath their feet, as if wiping away the muck, the perishable flesh and blood with all its anger, lust and desire for reconciliation.

In Israel, earlier that year, I sat alone at a little round table on one of the delightful terraces at the 'Accadia Hotel' in a place called Herzliya, a resort outside Tel Aviv. As usual, in the spring, the weather was beautiful and I'd return to school with a suntan, to the envy of all my friends. 'Some of us have to help in the shop – we can't go jet-setting to the Holy Land'. Relatives be damned – it's such a bore seeing them – although I love my little boy cousins; the elder is thin and peevish and the younger is chubby and cute. My brother and I literally can't keep our hands off him. I have my lemon coloured linen Mary Quant dress which zips up at the front. It is pure acid. It occurs to me that I'll be a laughing stock if I return home and have nothing to report as regards hooking a boy. I set my sights on a Jewish lad, similarly on holiday, sprawled out on a sunbed. I am impressed by how relaxed he is. The record I am listening to, over and over again, is the one that begins 'Please don't wear red tonight, this is what I said tonight/ because red is the colour that my baby wore/ and what's more it's true/yes it is. Yes, it was called 'Yes it is' and sung, simply and truly, by John Lennon. What would I have done without the Beatles and their sweet melodies? (On the plane coming over I was wearing a lovely pastel-coloured soft tweedy suit with a brown suede belt and, coming in to land, my father said to me: 'You're looking a bit green'. End of conversation. Indeed I felt queasy. Travelling around in the hire car we would always stop for hitch-hiking Israeli soldiers. Handsome, strong and purposeful they never really responded to my mother's flirtatious interactions. My father, without any interest in Zionism/the Jewish State, seemed proud of them, reassured by their tough male presence.

It is August '66 and we're back in Riccione. My best mate has come along with me, my parents and my two brothers. In the dining-room me, my elder brother Jonathan and my mate Philippa sit at one table whilst my parents and my young brother sit at another. We seem to eat a lot of melon; my friend is 'Philippa Aqua' and I am 'Judy Melone'. Her mother remembers us as 'peas in a pod'; we each sensed the other's dread of leaving our comfy beds to go on the SS. Nevassa Mediterranean (School) Cruise and in the small living room of the big house opposite the orthodox synagogue (Jewish people often bar entry to the main living room where nothing must be soiled or disturbed), we dance like mad things, collapsing with laughter, and, above all, we wear the same clothes. Her flowery smock from the summer of '64 has a pale pink background whilst mine is pale blue. In the spring of '65 her frilly jumper is black whilst mine is pink. Before I set off for the Kenco coffee house on a Sunday afternoon I jive with the lounge door handle and my father, in his chair, reading a book about Napoleon or the Second World War, tries to ignore my frilly twirls and whirls.

But Philippa gets the guys. We go to hear some Italian group at the Hotel Mediterranean and I'm surprised that she is wearing a lovely silk green dress with a 'Monet' design from two years earlier. I had the same dress – from Wallis in Marble Arch – but with a different neckline. Her dress has a keyhole whilst mine has a scalloped collar. However, I wouldn't dream of wearing the same dress the next year, let alone two years later; how depressing is that? I am wearing a cotton dress with a 'V' neck and a belt at the back. Its blue and white vertical stripes are reminiscent of the concentration camp uniform. The lead singer of the group comes over to our table and sings 'Il Mondo' straight into her eyes. There is no doubt that she is exceptionally attractive (she looks like Botticelli's feminine goddess in 'The Birth of Venus') but what I envy is her calm, her smooth aplomb. How does she manage that, I wonder? Everyone knows that her father worships the ground she walks on – she has a gold watch with a solid gold bracelet strap and a fox-coloured handmade suede suit. This suit puts her on a pedestal. We are all silently aware that her mum is prepared to take a back seat, like a peahen. Her hair is thinning but she frequents the salon of Vidal Sassoon in Bond Street, as does her daughter. In our family it's MOTHER who gets all the slavish attention, the jewels and the animal skins.

There are photos of us together on the beach. We are both wearing our 'Cote d'Azur' bikinis – but hers is a bit prettier than mine. But all trouble and stress dissolves as we lay on our sunbeds soaking up the sun in no small measure. We think we are doing ourselves a favour, giving ourselves something great when in fact we are storing up trouble for a much later date. Yet all is well as we listen to the Beatles' beautiful song 'Here, There and Everywhere' over ad infinitum on the tape-recorder. We'd bought the newly released 'Revolver' LP that morning (from Michael Summers music shop in Hendon Central) and hastily recorded it and the chunky tape recorder was taken on the plane as hand luggage later that day. (In those days there were no crowds or queues or security measures. What is this madness with security?) Every day a deeply tanned and lined Italian man, in white rolled-up trousers and white T-shirt trudges through the sand calling out 'gelati, gelati' as all the foreigners and the natives crowd round him and the great refrigerated boxes he carries on his back. This is a far cry from 'Mr Whippy' in his singsong van. But best of all is the man who comes with 'toffee grapes' on sticks which are divinely delicious. There is cine film, taken by my father, of Philippa and I dancing around with our sticks of honeyed grapes, translucent green and purply black. My mother sits in a chair, legs apart, wearing a swimming costume that is the colour of a sick frog. She is scowling. All is murk. Nothing pleases her and she never catches the sun. My father takes cine film of a mother and her daughters sitting nearer the sea and licking their ice-creams. Their hair is windswept and delightfully messy. They smile cheekily at the camera.

Not so Mother. She feels like an ever-present background threat. A very funny extrovert solicitor friend of theirs tells me, in no uncertain terms, that she is 'a fate worse than death'. As a little girl I categorically and emphatically told her that she should be locked up. 'You spoil everything and cause trouble,' I said. God is grace and she was obviously someone who had slipped from his embrace. As a young teenager I watched as she went into the garden and cut, with a pair of secateurs, a beautiful fragrant deep red rose and placed it in her dark dead red vase in the gloomy hall. All mine! Maybe such people can't let go and simply celebrate because they never played with anyone, never had any fun, and their sense of self was gradually eroded through external force and discipline. It's a crying shame and MAN, in his darkness, is to blame. Us three teenagers go to the go-kart track one evening and observe my brother, unlike the others, driving round in a circle. His car has to be repeatedly dragged back by the groundsmen. Philippa and l nearly die laughing. We get back in the early hours and the next day we receive nothing from our parents other than grim stares. They are furious. There is a great chasm between us and them. Philippa says: 'It's like Yom Kippur!'

She and I have our hair done at a local hairdresser in Riccione. There is no chat – the young lady hairdressers are committed to making our hair look as sleek as sleek can be and they also paint our nails a lovely pink – applying the varnish in a central panel and not covering the whole nail as is the way in the U.K. We walk back to the Atlantic Hotel like hierarchic Egyptian princesses not daring to move our hands or our heads and we are wearing identical pink strappy sandals which we bought in some truly bijou local shoe shop where all the boxes are round the front rather than stacked away in some secret back room. There are groups of Italians youths crowded around their motorbikes and as we pass by they call out somewhat indifferently, 'bellissima' followed by a more emphatic 'beLISSima', unable to believe their eyes. We regard them as inferior foreign boys with nothing to offer. Philippa's boyfriend back home is an up and coming stockbroker with a nasty streak; I will soon be courted by a Baker Street hairdresser who treats me like a goddess and who gets practically nothing in return. We go for a walk on Hampstead Heath; I am wearing my pea green coat with its revers, epaulettes and double breasted gold buttons and I'm so straight-jacketed that I can't even run, let alone have any fun. So the curse of mother has come to pass; the threatened 'iron brace' to make me walk straight has become a psychic reality.

Normally when he picks me up on a Saturday evening in his green and white Triumph Herald I am dressed to kill. We might be going to a West-End restaurant (he invites my scorn because he mispronounces 'sole bonne femme') or cinema or the 'Sands' coffee-bar in Bond Street, haunt of pop stars. I love my black velvet dress from Wallis with its diamante clasp on the belt, its high Victorian neckline and leg-of-mutton sleeves. My eyes are severely outlined in black and my lipstick is Mary Quant's 'Sex Pot'. I am no sex bomb but a glamorous doll which meets with my mother's approval. My parents and my young brother are silent as I descend the stairs in my black attire. They like Warren (he wears a pea- green corduroy coat) and my mother castigates her brother-in-law who has presumably said that he'd never let his daughters go out with a hairdresser. I reckon that my folks are also unconsciously relieved that there is someone around to take me out so that I'm not sobbing my heart out in my bedroom as I did, at the age of ten/eleven when they were always out in the west-end – theatres, cinemas, restaurants. I am following in their footsteps.

As a young child I longed for a rose pink twinset and sheepskin lined Moorland boots and slippers. I longed for these things as a boy (or a girl) might long for a pair of boxing gloves or a racing car. I got what I desired. I loved the footwear that came my way before the stay at the Normandie Hotel in Bournemouth with its green tiled roof and promise of blessings. East Cliff Road was lined with pine trees and as soon as we entered Bournemouth and could smell the sea it seemed as if we'd been delivered into the Promised Land, out of the House of Bondage. The atmosphere in this hotel was easy-going; punishment and 'do it now!' weren't on the cards. I had beige and white pumps with jewelled elasticated thread, in which to run around. My favourite haunt was a Scots Pine in which I made my home; I was a tree nymph on an uppermost branch and in the photos (taken by the hotel photographer) I look rapturously happy. I didn't know or care as to the whereabouts of my folks; for all I knew they could have disappeared into the ether … In the morning I enjoyed having breakfast on my own and would invariably order kippers. Lunch at the family table lasted an age on account of rowing and my father being called to the phone. Mother poked and decried the 'iced swan' with its glorious choux pastry and I felt as if I were sinking. But prior to these holidays she enjoyed spreading new holiday clothes on my bed and shared my delight when I came home from primary school and saw these invitations to the sun and fun. If I couldn't get to sleep at night she'd tell me to think of something nice. I thought of the 'Normandie' and my swimsuit with bows, my three-piece sunsuit and my magic slippers.

However, it was a different story when I was fifteen or sixteen and failing at school. I couldn't invent stories and hated cold science subjects. I loved the Latin poetry of Horace and Catullus and Robert Frost's 'Stopping by Woods on a Snowy Evening'. Standing in the lounge I hear my mother saying, in harsh and resentful tones: 'You like clothes so you should leave school and work in a shop'. (This is the nature of the 'discussion' about what I should do when 'O' levels are done with). My father is standing by and concurs with Mother, as he unfailingly does. Over Sunday lunch I call him 'an impotent bastard' before tearing upstairs and barricading myself in my room. On more than one occasion he chases me up the stairs, yelling 'I could murder you' and I get to safety and lock myself in in the nick of time. I lock my room every night with a proper key, albeit brown and rusty, such as were used in 'The Tower of London'. On Jonathan's bedroom door there is a great dent which bears the shape of my father's bullet head charge. I feel that my head is permanently enclosed in a mental steel helmet.

As regards my future Jonathan was there in the lounge and I remember him saying – supportively -, 'Most parents want the best for their children'. She's probably right – I belong in a shop. In December of 1964 my father had got me a job working in 'Neatawear' in Marble Arch. I really enjoyed helping the nice young women who came in the shop. They were all after a lovely flared boucle wool skirt which came in black and plum. They didn't react furiously if the size wasn't available. Payment was in cash which was put in some sort of metal container and then whizzed down a chute. It returned with the right change. At lunchtime I walked through Mayfair to my father's office in Upper Brook St. where a solitary lunch of smoked salmon and brown bread was laid out for me in the boardroom. Lonely and distressed? Not a bit of it. I loved the smoked salmon and the view of the gardens. Distress comes at night when there's nothing to eat, no one to talk to – let alone provide a hug.

In those days the bar-mitzvah was an affair for the boys. Thank God for that – I would have hated all the attention, the presents, the speeches, the performance. My father presented me with two new exquisite charms for my gold bracelet; one was a pair of engraved ballet pumps topped with a pearl and the other was an enamelled Toby jug with a lid that opened and closed. He thought that these gifts would counteract any envy I might feel at my brother getting so many presents (briefcases mainly) but envy was the last thing in my head since I wholeheartedly loved my brother. (He, father, was quite upset when, a decade later, I sold the bracelet to some shop in Shepherd's Market. Who throws away their heirlooms?) My envy was directed towards girls who had long hair and more dresses. I broke the pink and white hair bands which my best friend's aunt sent over from America. I simply snapped them in half. I expected some retribution, which never came, from Phyllis's mother. (Phyllis and I also competed as to who could produce the worst ulcer on their inside lip by biting away at the fulsome flesh). Of course my dress for the bar-mitzvah had to be right and this entailed numerous trips to Betties where I couldn't choose between the pinky-red chiffon with the red velvet bows and the long-waisted chiffon with its print of pastel blues, green and mauves. Finally I go for the former and it is the wrong choice! It even accentuates my fat waist. I choose mother's blood over the cool outside world … And shoes are a nightmare because I have poor Jewish feet and because my mother can't stand the stress of shopping with me – nothing is right, everything is a failure – my poor grandmother is roped in to traipse around the shoe shops of the West End, searching for fancy pink shoes to match my ball dress. Searching for magic slippers is a feminine world which is totally alien to her. She has no bust, wears long black 'bloomers' (to my great distress) and in the 1930s played golf and drove a car. She never recovered from the death of her husband, Jack – a Jewish father who instilled terror in his son, threatening 'to cut him off without a penny' if he didn't toe the line. (She taught him about 'business'). Primitive cutting of organic human tissue is anathema to the enlightened people of the western hemisphere). Anyhow, the right shoes, and very pretty they were, were eventually found, although the slog to find them took the pleasure out of the found treasure. I had a pale gold clutch handbag. On the morning of the 'do' in the 'orchid suite' (my mother's handmade satin dress, beautifully decorated with pearls and diamonds, matches the pinky mauve walls and this choice of colour was deliberate) at the Dorchester Hotel I am taken to the hairdresser 'Carol London' in Hendon Way to have a 'shampoo and set' to match the occasion. When I emerge from the salon I am upset that 'I look like an old woman'. My mother ignores my distress. Every Saturday afternoon she goes to the hairdresser for a 'shampoo and set' and then sits disconsolately over a cup of tea. She blames Martin the hairdresser for not doing it right.

 The bar-mitzvah of my best friend's younger brother, four years later, was a different matter altogether. Roaming through Brent for some reason or other, I spotted a dress in the window of the shop opposite the Odeon cinema; a flared new-born-chick-feather yellow nylon/chiffon affair with splodges of purple, green, and turquoise. It cost eight guineas. I loved it. Tina Kartoon, the friend who named my dresses called it my 'Batman' dress, for some reason. We were all expecting Philippa's dress to be something out of this world since it was a hand-made affair – requiring her to attend numerous fittings. We were all mightily surprised when she appeared in a long pale yellow satin dress with a beaded top that was so tight that she literally couldn't walk – she could only hobble over to meet us, albeit with a smile on her face. I was a bit amazed and felt sorry for her. However, the pale blue patent shoes which I found in Kurt Geiger in Bond Street were responsible for my twisted toes. At my brother's bar-mitzvah, the saxophonist Michael Summers and his band was the entertainment; at Philippa's brother's bar-mitzvah they hired the dancer, Lionel Blair, and we all did the 'conga', him in the lead. A dress manufacturer fondled the hem of my dress as I sailed by and asked me where I got my 'bit of schmutter'.

 This vibrant yellow was nothing compared to the daffodil yellow midi-length linen coat which I saw in the window of 'Wallis, Marble Arch' in the spring of 1970 – a copy of a Chanel original with wide revers and a loose tie belt. I was wearing it when I met my Israeli ship captain boyfriend at the East India Docks and he told me that he was dazzled. But, unfortunately, I cast a giant shadow and there is no way you can have a boyfriend/mate/ husband if you feel a deep affinity with Michelangelo's 'The Captives' – those poor souls struggling to emerge from the imprisoning rock. You're on your own, in a cold, hard place. The spiked helmet is drilled into your brain.

My 'bee' dress, my 'Tin Soldier' dress, my 'Batman' dress come and go. I had enough Mary Quant clothes to furnish an exhibition but all this gear is sent to my 'poor' relation in Israel. Not exactly suitable gear for life on a kibbutz. She holds onto the 'Batman' dress for all eternity although it's mine, undisputedly. In May 1966 they visited Rome for a few days and returned with a bag full of gifts. There were never any hugs or kisses and there were no experiences to talk about. Contemplating my presents was depressing. I surveyed the little pumps in turquoise blue two tone soft kid leather with a mink pom-pom on the end of each tie. Not to be worn ever. There was also a silky knitted turquoise top with a round neck and short sleeves. The material is lovely but the style is so dull and plain. It's not 'what they're wearing' in liberated, swinging London. On a previous trip to Rome she'd brought back soft kid cream gloves embroidered with little pink rosebuds (which got ruined in the washing machine) and black leather ones with gold trimmings which I tried to like because of the quality of the leather and because you're supposed to like the things you've been given. 'Thank you very much' was my ritual response. My mother obviously enjoyed walking down the Via Veneto in Rome and purchasing luxury goods. The trips to Paris would yield her a store of perfumes packed in beige suede boxes. A full-length mirror on the inside of her wardrobe door was continually in use revealing the boxes of 'Madame Rochas' perfumes stored on a shelf. My boyfriend, Warren the hairdresser, bought me Carven's 'Ma Griffe' which I loved. Scents are deliriously uplifting. Me and my friends were absolutely crazy about a Helena Rubenstein scent in an opaque blue container. It was powerfully thick and sweet. During my friendless period prior to the dreaded cruise I wore my new fox brown suede watch strap to school. In truth, it's a thick wrist band, the hallmark of a slave since time immemorial. (Sometimes the ball and chain are invisible). Of course it is admired – as were my Parisien putty-coloured key-hole leather gloves which offered no warmth whatsoever. Standing in the classroom I was like a Giacometti sculpture, totally cut off from the surrounding noise and bustle generated by a class of thirty five schoolgirls preparing to go to morning assembly; Christians knelt in the hall whilst Jewish girls, delegated to a classroom, recited the 'Shema' parrot fashion and then sung clap-happy kibbutznik/pioneer songs. I can't help being struck by the harmonious singing of the hymns compared to our singing voices, which sound like talking. At

Christmas time I receive the odd Christmas card from a 'pitying' girl. Others reckon that I am a 'nonentity' but, in reality, I am doing my best to block myself out, just as I blacked out my face (the face of a lovely ballet dancer in her flaming red and orange tutu) when I drew a picture for the child psychiatrist, Dr Newton. In the corner, I drew a witch, her mouth an ugly squiggle, her face covered in attacking black lines. I espy Miss Pickard, form mistress and maths teacher, glancing at me with concern written on her face. Maths is cold and anonymous and I wonder why she isn't.

'O' level results were better than predicted and would have been better if I had compared Sweden with Switzerland as the question stated rather than comparing Sweden with Norway, as was always the case. I was so disappointed after the exam because I'd worked so hard, memorising umpteen facts. (They were all names on a map with no reality whatsoever). As regards language I seemed to be a million times better at feeling it than putting it together correctly. I loved Horace and Catullus but the little hard-back book of 'Caesar's Gallic Wars' caused my heart to sink – who knows why? Others didn't mind so much or maybe they were more prepared to do what they were told. So doing, they got on in life, made it to the next grade. Hard facts are what count, after all.

My 'A' levels started on a high because a nineteen year old Israeli paratrooper had fallen in love with me in the aftermath of the 'Six Day War' which broke out on June 5th 1967. He was also a sergeant which added to the romance. When he came to pick me up at the Dan Carmel Hotel I noticed that his trousers were a bit short (maybe he had grown out of them?) and this was not something I could tell the girls back home. However, he was as handsome as a Greek god and built like one, and a totally un-neurotic action man. He was an Israeli hero, as were all her soldiers. For him I was probably the fruit of peace in my earrings that resembled a cluster of pink grapes and my blue and white polka dot sundress. And I came from a place where people didn't bother to murder one another. We sat together on a bench overlooking the city and the night was as balmy and sweet as it's meant to be in hot countries. I was wondering when he was going to kiss me and thought to myself: 'why do I always have to get the shy, sensitive ones?' He finally overcame his nervousness and late that night he wrote 'I Love You' in Hebrew on a bus ticket and taught me how to say those three magic words. I was smitten or rather raised to heaven. The next day he came to the hotel and as we went off to play table tennis, me wearing my pale green crepon shirt (crinkly crepe shirts were all the rage and I had another in tangerine) and very short denim shorts my father called out, 'She likes to win!'. Whatever was he talking about? Over the next three or four days he'd pick me up from the hotel and in my fancy clothes and decorative eye make-up I must have seemed like an exotic dessert.

On arriving back in the UK his love letters were so simple and sincere that I was floating on air, carried along by a fresh breeze, a buoyant wave. My mother was also sweetly thrilled by the arrival of his letters and placed them under my pillow. She showed off about him to everyone, as I did. She reckoned that he was the man of every girl's dream. She was indifferent to my father's feelings and told me, when I was about eighteen and in her bedroom, forever helping her make her bed with its heavily embroidered satin fitted cover, a dull mauve, that he was 'useless' between the sheets. I felt very sorry for the poor man as I watched him from her bedroom window get into his car, en route to work. For a split second he looked up, looking truly sad. He also told me, grimly, when I came out of my room, ecstatically turned on by D.H. Lawrence's 'The Rainbow' that 'that wasn't what life was all about'. And he meant it. He thrust a copy of Marx's communist diatribe into my hand; I never opened this little red book. He was obviously recalling the passion of his teenage years. But the present reality was that the sun had come out, I had come to life, and my first year in the sixth form was one of great enthusiasm. Here were writers who spoke to me and History was about analysis rather than copying stuff about 'Pitt the Younger' off the board. I wrote an essay in History, all writing was a very painful exercise as if I was trying to get through an iron wall and Miss Walters didn't believe it was all my own work although it absolutely was. I loved French literature and told my English teacher, the blonde blue-eyed fiancée of a priest, that I wanted to BE Carmen (Prosper Merimee's original creation). She bought me a book by Cyril Connolly – 'The Unquiet Grave'. I received my love letters, 'May the girl in my heart be the girl in my arms/ then I'll hold her tight/and never let her go/ and tell her how much I love her,' and this didn't prevent me from being taken out by Warren on a Saturday evening, wearing my short black corduroy skirt and cape to match. (A religious friend of mine, a lovely, lively jewess told me that it was wrong to use people. Unlike me she wears a freshly laundered shirt to school every day). Philippa and I went to a fancy dress party at his house – she was the perfect Indian squaw and in his bedroom we espied a photo of me by his bed. I am a bit naked and exposed – or rather you can see my bare shoulders and upper neck. After the July trip to Israel my mother had sent me to a photographer she knew in West Hampstead. A mass of photos of me in the most ridiculous and artificial poses. I have one hand behind my neck and another on my head. The photographer circled one – the only one in which I looked natural and human. I hated it. And what was Warren playing at with a photo of me near his pillow. My friend and I found everything a source of cataclysmic humour. Her father slapped her round the face when she temporarily ditched the stockbroker boyfriend and his maroon mini. But all is well on New Year's Eve when we all attend some function in town. Everyone is dolled up to the nines but I have found myself the plainest long grey silk dress with black lace trimming and a flat collar and short sleeves. It is something out of Jane Austen or the Oliver Cromwell museum. My fringe doesn't fall loosely over my forehead but is combed to the side (clamped down every night with steel grips) to resemble the hairstyle of Adolf Hitler. All my rage must be turning inwards. I know that I don't want to be like my mother with her loose tongue and silly jokes. I am deadly plain and serious. Warren makes no comment about my unspectacular attire because I'm not in rags or a filthy old overall, streaked with grease or bodily fluids. We go to see the drag artist 'Danny la Rue' and I am not amused. Nor am I turned on by 'The Sound of Music' and all those happy children singing in the mountains although my best friend loves it and is always going back for more. I subsequently go in for plays about mental illness at The Hampstead Theatre Club. Angela Pleasance, daughter of actor dad Donald, is a fine actress.

If you are studying for French 'A' level you are supposed to be able to speak French and I can't. My father arranges for me to visit Henriette Cantor, a French violinist who was married to some distant relation of his. She lives in Green Lanes, north London and I get hopelessly lost finding her place. I don't like driving at night. She has a sore bruised patch under her chin from all the practising. Sans malice she wishes suffering on her ex-husband on account of all the suffering he caused her. She speaks to me in French but somehow we don't get very far. Was it because I kept on getting lost on the nightly expeditions? My father arranges for me to travel to Paris in the Easter holidays in order to stay with 'the French cousins'. Apparently they sew their shekels into the lining of their coats so that they feel safe when they go out. I arrive at the flat of an old lady and she takes me to her bedroom full of dolls, just like my bedroom at home, yet somehow more ancient. She seems ok if not somewhat impersonal. I ask her where I am going to sleep and she replies: 'With me, in my bed'. Did I hear right? How can I sleep in the same bed as an old lady? I telephone my father and he tells me, not to grin and bear it, but to leave immediately and get a room in a hotel in the Avenue de l'Opera which couldn't have been very far away. He tells me that he'll be there in the morning. I leave without further ado. Walking up the Avenue in my spring suit with its large red and biscuit-coloured checks and big red buttons and Mary Quant red beret, and 'Sex Pot' lipstick in its granite grey cylinder (the handbag is biscuit patent in the style of a box and the shoes are round-toed biscuit coloured sling-backs) I pass two elderly men obviously enjoying each other's company. One of them sees me and comes out with: 'Comme elle est mignon!' (isn't she cute?) unaware that I am a loose end, rootless, but with a stony head. I spend the night in a dreary hotel room and my father arrives in the morning. He takes me out to lunch and I am happy because the restaurant is swell and daddy is a different man to the one he is when he's with mummy. It's just me and him together. He enjoys the way I enjoy everything and relishes my company. (He's good-looking, strong and in control – a survivor like James Bond). At school the French teacher asks about my intended two week visit to Paris in order to learn French and when I relate the tale of my overnight stay the whole class burst out laughing. The teacher struggles to contain her mirth and she's thinking that I am a pampered child. They don't know, of course, that after my father's father's death he was expected, aged eleven, to take his place in his mother's bed and so presumably he wanted to save me from such a perversion.

The following summer I returned to Israel to see my beau. A very successful year you could say since three top universities offered me places with low grades. There was no question that I'd study anything other than LAW. In the interview room at Bristol, (I'd made my way there on my own and developed on the train an obsession about not being able to turn the door handle – this simple action might prove very difficult and complicated) one of the men in the room – a young one – asked me if I liked to read thrillers. I replied: 'No'. He said 'why not'? – doubtless expecting a supersubtle explanation. 'Because they don't thrill me!' was the answer they got. Young and old burst out laughing. (The only thrillers I'd ever read were Enid Blyton's 'Valley of Adventure' and 'Mountain of Adventure' and they thrilled me loads).

But things were about to take a terrible turn into a black hole. I went to Israel with my friend Carole and we stayed at the Green Beach Hotel just outside Netanya, a ghastly place but it was all her parents could afford. The hotel had overbooked and there was a problem with the room. We had to share it with two French girls. I remember sitting on the edge of a bed, like one of the desolate ladies in an Edward Hopper painting and wondering, in despair, where I was going to sleep. In fact, the hotel was full of French Jewish teenagers and a couple of girls we recognised from N.W. London – one of whom was the daughter of Warren's Baker St. boss. Her and her cousin's hair was naturally blonde and someone was teaching them how to dive – and they were doing it! Carole had got herself a sweet Parisien boyfriend called William and they all had fun in the pool. Two guys hired a car in order to visit Jerusalem. I cried a lot, bereft and abandoned, waiting for David Zion to show up. But the army came first – they needed him. I remember a Jewish lad from London being totally upset and appalled by the Russian invasion of Czechoslovakia; he really cared. One hot afternoon I walked down to the swimming-pool area wearing a black crepe dress with pearl buttons and a little Marilyn Monroe type Peter Pan collar. A French guy admired me and didn't take notice of the fact that I looked utterly ridiculous – a fish out of water if ever there was one. I participated in nothing; I was waiting. One evening we were having horrible food in the horrible canteen when my distress went overboard; had I lost my love altogether? Carole responded and ran from table to table, asking adult guests if they were, by any chance, going to Haifa (where David was stationed) and whether they could take me. She REALLY cared. Nobody was and that was expected. I was left in my black pit of despair. He did finally show up. I espied his masculine he-man silhouette in the bedroom talking face to face with Carole and he told me that he'd told her that he couldn't understand why I was such a baby, a real cry baby. Why wasn't I swimming and having fun like everyone else? On the night before I was due to fly back to London we lay all night side by side and wide awake, not touching one another, but struck by passion. There was something between us, something heavenly and glorious, that we didn't want to disturb through gross bodily connection. For him I was the 'fairy of peace.' Deep down did he want to keep on fighting wars and killing Arabs and feeling the weight of it all on his strong back? Love of life and earthly delight is in our blood and bones and the good earth supports us all. We have to have the courage to heal our wounds and make ourselves whole and thus eliminate the threat and danger which comes from our own untreated sewage, so to speak. War stinks.

Back home in Hendon I am no longer going out with Warren. After all, I never really fancied him. He had presented me with an antique silver powder compact on which he'd had my name engraved. I accepted it very ungraciously because I thought it was dead and old-fashioned. He's hardly dead on the tracks; he finds beautiful new girl-friends. Stella is the daughter of the owner of 'Pan Books'; she is beautiful and loving and he gets her in the family way. Denise Garvin, an earlier or later attachment, is a natural blonde and attends the Aida Foster Drama School. My mother says that that is where she would have liked my brother and I to have gone but my father wouldn't hear of it. In fact he believes in single sex schools; 'girls should be with girls and boys with boys' and he also pronounces that one should study Latin not German.

The thing is that my passion for study has altogether gone to the dogs. My essays are turgid and repetitive and confused – they've fallen flat. I can't for the life of me work out what is going on with Elizabeth and Her Parliaments. Everything seems like a lead weight and I can't revise – nothing stays in my head. I sit at the kitchen table with Elton's 'The Tudors' before me and I am tucking into the box of sticky figs and 'Eat me' dates. I hate myself for my weak self-indulgence. The truth is that I have been brought down by the desperate babyish way I behaved with my Israeli beau. How could I have shown myself up like that with my baby neediness? He still loved me but something had changed. Nobody likes a clinger.

Coat dresses were the latest thing and it was nice to ditch the school uniform (actually this had been the case when you reached the sixth form) and wear my own clothes. I showed up in my black linen coat dress from Wallis and another creation in light grey stone. My best coat dress had a pattern of red and white Arabic swirls and big red buttons. It gave me some hope, did this dress because I was more or less dead. My essays were confused rubbish and, of course, you were judged to be a lazy failure. Exam time was approaching. I was lying on my bed and I felt like I was sinking. I must have called out (did I?) because my mother came in with a look of panic on her face and she went to the phone to try and get hold of my brother who was at Southampton University studying Law. She reckoned that I needed to speak to someone I knew. I can't remember if I spoke to him or not. The dying sensation passed but I was still stuck fast.

In the Easter holidays the Israeli boyfriend had saved his shekels and flown over to see me. He had arrived at '25 Fos' – as my mother always referred to our address – in a taxi. My parents were out. I was wearing a short skirt and a pale blue and navy patterned nylon blouse, tightly buttoned up. I'd actually slept the whole previous night in red bristly jumbo curlers so that my hair would be dead straight. I was proud that I'd actually slept normally and survived this masochistic exercise. See what will-power can do! He'd bought me Yemenite silver earrings and a necklace which weren't to my taste.. As he kissed me he murmured, 'the same smell' which was a surprising but nice thing to hear. He kept his own counsel but he was obviously put out that my father wouldn't allow him to stay in the house; he had to stay up the road in some drab anonymous boarding-house. As we sat round the Friday night dinner table I observed him looking at my father with a look of dislike. I'm sure he was comparing him to his own father who also sat at the head of a much smaller table where I had lunched the previous summer. We'd eaten stuffed aubergines and other Sephardi food and his father had smiled on me kindly and was obviously wondering about the future of this romantic affair. He worked in the Haifa docks and thus, according to my 'Sabra' uncle who also worked at the docks in the 'Zim' shipping office, this wasn't the right family for me. David and I lay on his bed in his B@B and he wanted – finally – to make love to me. When I resisted he said, with real scorn and disappointment: 'Are you a child?' It was also his desire to go to Soho on Saturday evening. I drove him in my mother's car and got lost. I lost my temper and angrily blamed him for dragging me out that way. He kept quiet. He was no fool. It would have been unwise to do anything else in the vicinity of my father's house. Later on, when we were travelling across the U.S.A in his pale blue mustang he told me that he resented the American Jews who sent their money to Israel and weren't involved in the real fighting. 'Do you know what real life is like – you who are so "mefuneket" ('spoiled, pampered, indulged')?' Warren too had once got a bit angry with me – the only time – and said that he didn't want to be lectured by a schoolgirl. David reckoned that my mother, in her youth, must have been more independent than me and, in gratitude for her ironing his shirts, he bought her a big bouquet of flowers, all wrapped in cellophane. 'What's that all about, I wondered?' She's a middle-aged woman whose eternal place is in front of the ironing board. He played with my younger brother; my elder brother kept out of the picture and probably hid his 'chest expanders'. Poor lad had his mother's figure.

Father did his best to prevent me meeting up with David in Cleveland, Ohio where his elder brother was marrying the daughter of a dentist. I'd originally gone out with this brother, Moshe, (Moses) who'd been working as a swimming instructor, at the swimming pool of the Dan Carmel Hotel, a lovely spot on the top of the mountain (where the prophet Elijah defeated the prophets of Baal) dotted with pine trees. A trusted psychiatrist entered the picture. He was the guy I'd been sent to at the age of ten when I'd been so distressed by my parents' 'going out' and whom I'd telephoned when I was eighteen and distressed by my compulsive eating: 'What's happening to me – I should be working!' He replied, shockingly, that I probably missed my boyfriend making love to me. I visited him in his Paddington Day Clinic at Royal Oak – driving there in my mother's grey Morris 1000 with the dark red upholstered seats. When I was crossing the road at the traffic lights one of his colleagues, a man in his forties who was also an amateur sculptor, tried to chat me up. I was wearing a black ribbed 'skinny' and tight white trousers. He probably thought I was very sexy. Little did he know. Anyway the trusted psychiatrist persuaded my father to let me make the trip. He told him that I needed the experience. My father wouldn't have really understood this reasoning but he consented because he feared an external authority.

Off I flew on July 4th (my 'A' levels done and dusted although my mother had made me thirty minutes late for my English Literature Shakespeare paper because she was jabbering on to me and the au-pair, no doubt gossiping/ complaining about someone or other) with £50 in my purse.

From the word go it was a disaster. Due to torrential storms the plane had to land in Chicago and I had to travel the five hundred miles back to Cleveland by coach. David had been up all night phoning the airport not knowing when to set out to meet me. No wonder he was pissed off when he saw me. He was chewing gum and wearing a striped T-shirt which I didn't like. He was smoking a lot.

The plan was for us to make a road trip across the states in his pale blue Mustang, after spending a few days with his brother's girlfriend's parents. The dad was a dentist and was very nice. I had trouble relaxing at night. They all went swimming and I sat and watched. David's brother told me that David didn't love me any more and David told me that he really wanted the girl next door to accompany him. She was tough and capable and fun. She wasn't 'mefuneket' like me. He drove, smoked and I sat by his side, reading Voltaire's 'Candide' and Nabokov's 'Lolita'. Stevie Wonder singing 'Ma Cherie Amour' was always on the radio. We used to drive five hundred miles a day and he hated dragging my big white case out of the boot of the car into the motel where we slept and had sex.

There was no lack of pretty dresses; pretty dresses be damned! There is a photo of me in a black lace short-sleeved dress in San Francisco, my arms clenched tightly around myself trying to keep warm. I hardly recognised myself with my round cheeks soft as butter and smiling inwardly, for myself. As far as he was concerned persecution was the name of the game. Apparently he wanted to toughen me up – transform me into an Israeli girl. He'd pour his bottle of coke into my lap and say that an Israeli girl would laugh – taking it as a joke. As he drove at 100 m.p.h. he made me climb up onto my seat in order to button down the convertible roof. Driving through the Rockies I was aware of happy families going on their holidays – maybe they were off to the famous Jewish resort in the Catskill Mountains, kin to the 'Normandie' Hotel in Bournemouth.

He despised traditional Jewish observance and when we stayed for a week in Santa Cruz, California and made friends with some locals he enjoyed tricking me into eating non-kosher meat. The girl, Sandy, who had long, thin sandy hair ran up cotton dresses on her sewing-machine and her boyfriend told me about my boyfriend's betrayal. In Las Vegas he drove round the city in ninety degree heat, presumably looking for a motel, in order to give me a hard time. He liked 'Caesar's Palace' and hated me because I didn't know how to play. I don't think he much enjoyed practising 'coitus interruptus' every night in bed. I couldn't even enjoy his virility. What a terrible waste! He tried to make me jealous by flirting with young Mexican girls who were a backdrop to the cacti in the desert states of Arizona and Nevada. We had a quarrel somewhere round there and I reported him to two burly policemen who were standing nearby. I told them that he had stolen my money. They didn't know whether to take me seriously; he, David, looked serious and surprised, wondering whether I was mad. I bet he wanted to throw me out and leave me at the side of the road. I remember Denver as a beautiful white city.

I loved the fine silky sand of Malibu Beach. We'd come to an arrangement whereby he dropped me at the beach whilst he went off on his own. He wanted to learn to surf. I sat by myself in my emerald green bikini purchased at 'Galeries Lafayette' in Regent Street. I wasn't so keen on it because it didn't have shoulder straps but tied up around the neck. A nice male came and sat next to me. For some reason he tried to encourage me to paint. David was always surprised that I hadn't been yearning for him but had enjoyed my time alone. Cars hooted me as I walked along the sidewalk; a guy asked me where I came from with a follow-up of 'are all English girls as pretty as you'. It was nice to get some sweet attention. David told me that I was someone who'd never be able to sleep on my own and that it was no good to be one hundred and fifty per cent woman; you had to be one hundred percent woman.

I had a beautiful silky sundress in colours of pastel green, blue, turquoise, pink, and mauve and I wore it to a party in the most beautiful villa in Santa Cruz, or was it Carmel? There were a lot of attractive guys around. Some political question was being discussed and I came out with my weird fascist views. They'd make me feel tense in the head as I uttered them. They all looked really shocked and horrified and surprised at me. David was dancing cheek with Sandy in order to make me jealous. He was wearing his horrible bright green T-shirt. I wasn't jealous. He was jealous of me when I spoke up (probably spouting a load of pretentious rubbish) when we attended some local political meeting. Women belong in the kitchen and do what they are told. Having lunch with his family in Haifa I don't remember his mother or sister uttering a word.

We went to 'Haight Ashbury' – the hippy place in San Francisco – but it was July '69 and nobody was there; they'd all disappeared. There wasn't a daisy in sight – just dilapidated buildings and barren sidewalks. I am resigned to the fact that a guy with long silky dark hair and the whole paraphernalia of beads and jeans and open sandals isn't going to appear around the corner. I am with the Israeli soldier in his bright green T-shirt and cigarette to hand. We make our way to some old deserted ship on the quai and he tries to play hide and seek with me, or some other such game which ends in victory or defeat and is downcast, demoralised and frustrated because I can't play. What are the rules – I'm not exactly sure? I remember gazing at 'Alcatraz', the famous prison, a misty island in the distance, far out at sea. Are the people within, isolated beyond belief as they trudge around with their ball and chain? Do they know how to pray? Somehow – somewhere – he'd befriended a guy who ended up sleeping on the floor of our bedroom. David told me that he was gay or whatever the term was in those days and this was something which scared him and caused him to lie very close to me through the night.

We return to our brown, drab hotel room where the climax of the trip occurs. He must have done or said something which prompted me to say and I remember saying it: 'If all Israelis are like you they are a pack of Nazis'. This utterance was met with stunned silence. Following a long pause he says: 'I can't spend any more time with someone who says such a thing; you could say anything you like in the whole wide world but not that. We're going straight to the travel shop to change your ticket; you can go home on the next flight'. This abrupt decision came as a bit of a shock but maybe it was also welcomed; I'd had enough of him as well. We went to the travel shop and he changed the ticket. The funny thing was that when we knew we were going to be rid of each other we both lightened up and had a bit of a fun evening. The following day we returned to the shop and the ticket was changed again so that we gained an extra day.

So it was goodbye San Francisco or rather goodbye David Zion. His plan was to drive back to Cleveland, Ohio in record time. I sat in the window seat of the plane and saw him turning away and heading for his pale blue mustang. I cried a little. When I returned home five days short of the month that I was meant to be away, my mother, struggling, as usual, with the washing machine in the kitchen, turned to me and said: 'I was expecting you to walk in at any moment'. Maybe she needed some help.

I caught up with my friends and was relieved to forget all about him. But I couldn't understand why he had treated me so badly. My psychiatrist told me that he was jealous of me. 'Well, that's the answer then', I thought to myself. Must have been on account of me speaking up at the political meeting in Santa Cruz. He certainly had looked most uncomfortable. The 'A' level results came through and I sat in my father's chair in front of his bookcase, dominated by a great volume entitled, 'Hitler and Stalin' and cried timidly, almost silently, with real tears. My grade in History was a sad 'E' (my revision programme had been overtaken by the box of figs and dates) and for French I'd only received an 'O' level pass in spite of my passion for literature. Something must have gone severely wrong with my French grammar. The only positive note was a 'B' grade in English Literature and that was in spite of being half an hour late for the exam; I'd had to launch into an essay on Iago's destructive envy as soon as I picked up my pen. But in that predatory area I was on home ground. Funnily enough, although not so funny, my elder brother hadn't been able to pick up his pen when he sat his end of second year law exams. He'd worked so hard that he was overwhelmed by the pressure of the moment and had to drop his pen and leave his desk. Nothing felt real. Actually as a youngster he had walked around the house on a Saturday afternoon chanting 'I feel unreal'. He had to come home. Our family psychiatrist did so much for him that he was able to retake the exams in September. He gave his services free of charge. My brother, on his way out to see the noble doctor, and seeing me so upset came out with: 'You take my place. You need it more than I do'. (I wondered if that was really the case). Dr Newton told me that I should take the exams again. 'How could I', I thought to myself, 'school is over and done with.'

Passing the time during the long summer holiday I got a job as a filing clerk in a local firm. Waiting my turn to be called at the DHSS I almost failed to respond when my name was called as I'd sunk into a most unpleasant and soporific torpor. The boredom star was in the ascendant. In 'The Daily Express' the paper my mother read or was it my father's newspaper 'The Times'? I came across an advertisement for a 'library assistant' at the London School of

Economics' in Houghton Street, WC2. My mother tells me what satisfaction I'll get from earning my own money; my wage is £11 a week. So, with my own money, I purchase a dusty pink 'pure new wool' kaftan style dressing-gown in which I am totally zipped up and a Dusty Springfield LP. These purchases, especially the dressing-gown, with its black embroidered border, fail to provide the anticipated 'high'. However, that autumn I had purchased a lovely soft grey boucle coat from Wallis which was trimmed with light grey fur all around the hem. I don't remember how much it cost. It was a soft swinger of a coat, that's for sure. Soft grey is almost my favourite colour and what I see gives me the satisfaction I need. As regards earning her own living my mother had excelled as a shorthand typist in 1940. She seemed totally indifferent to the war – she was busy being 'Tondeleo' in 'White Cargo' at Unity Theatre. There are photos of her looking dark and sultry, sitting at the feet of a white colonial master. There is also a photo of her in her A.T.S. uniform complete with cap; she was at home in this functional attire. En route to the L.S.E. I wear a red wool turban and red patent shoes and my swinging grey coat, of course. I take the underground to Charing Cross tube every morning and walk up the Strand, enjoying the crisp autumn mornings. I take my place at the check-out desk in the 'Teaching Library' and learn the mechanics of the job which even a thick person like me can grasp. There were two other girls of my own age; one had a fiancé and wore a lot of 'panstick' and face powder and the other was living with her boyfriend and knew what she wanted – letting the world go to hell. (My parents were always sending people to hell but it didn't seem to do them any good.) The former, with her big blue eyes, was incredibly sweet and cheerful saying 'Hello Mrs Badcock' as she made her entry punctually every morning. We were all punctual. Mrs Badcock was fat, old and ugly and heavily lipsticked but she didn't seem unhappy. In those days all women wore lipstick, like the queen. There was a porter, Denis, who lived in the Old Kent Road with his dad. He stood by the door in his long grey overall coat and round glasses checking that everyone who came in was 'au fait'. He enjoyed his position. He observed my marching through the teaching library to replace books in my knee-high black suede boots and asked me about my forebears, where they came from. 'Russia,' I answered confidently, although this, unbeknown to me, wasn't the case. (Our forebears were from Poland and Lithuania). 'I thought so,' he replied, totally reassured.

At my place behind the desk I could see my reflection in the glass door opposite. I had a red and black brushed wool dress which was similar to the 'bee dress' which I'd worn to the 'Danescroft' youth club when I was twelve. Apparently the youth leader had told my mother that her children never joined in anything (oh dear!) but apparently this comment was followed by, 'but then they look so good they don't have to!'.

These reported comments never struck one as completely reliable although one always hoped for the best, attempting to stave off confusion. My brother, unlike me, was well into sports and thus always joining in. At home he was Jonathan but to all his friends he was 'Johnny' and couldn't have been more popular. He was generous, friendly and rosy-cheeked, as natural as they come and for this reason he was brutally attacked by his father on a daily basis.

Every day I wore a different outfit to work. (The psychiatrist humorously called me his 'little Narcissus' but the full implications of this label were lost on me). There was a pair of black trousers with turn-ups which I wore with an emerald green tabard thing or a lightly patterned smock, bordered in black. (The grim reaper's gear is black and this stalker is always around, night and day, afflicting us with terror. I am tremendously fond of a small black leather pouchy bag, bought in Riccione, and I lovingly caress this soft breast with its polluted milk). But, on the surface, I am enjoying myself on account of getting so much male attention. A proper trainee librarian gives me all her history notes – I must have told her about my poor 'A' level grade – and I read her concise clear essays but the thought of becoming plain Jane when I'm so into my glossy lipsticks is like being faced with some home growing kit when you can simply bite into the juicy apple on the plate.

A New Zealander, who is doing an M.A. in international relations, is next to me in the lift and sees me in my red and black dress, black eyes and red lips, as the apple of his eye. Stepping out of the lift he tells me that he is taking me for lunch. He is much shorter than me and has ginger hair and always wears a brown suede jacket. He smokes a pipe which completes the reassuring picture. He lives in Barnes. His wife teaches French and is still in New Zealand. He takes me under his wing in an avuncular fashion and I am sold. We sit together in a reading room in really comfortable armchairs and he tells me that I should write. I tell him that I have nothing to write about other than the return journey from the LSE to Hendon Central, walking down Foscote Road alone and in the dark. He says that I must write about that. He seems to care about me and comes to see me every day in the Teaching Library. One day he takes me to the Playboy Club for lunch. The girls at the gambling tables wear black costumes and their flesh is pure cream but how silly they look in those silly bunny ears and fluffy white scuts as they walk around in rabbit pairs. He tells me to read Ecclesiastes. All is vanity. I don't speak to my older brother much – he's now living in a flat on Haverstock Hill, between Belsize Park and Chalk Farm but he tells me that he sees Mark on the underground and he, Mark, unnerves him with his continual staring. My brother is known to have film-star looks, satisfying his mother's expectations.

There is a crowd of American students who are also reading for an M.A in International Relations and they come by and invite me for lunch. They seem to want my presence in spite of my 'E' in 'A' level History. The 'leader' of the American group is known as 'Thatch' on account of his short tight blonde curls and he gives me a lift on his motorbike back to Hendon through a deserted central London. I don't wear a helmet. I get so many dates that I have to keep a diary. Wednesday afternoon is my time off and a nice Jewish guy from the Jewish society takes me to the theatre. There is another Jewish guy who invites me to his lodgings and I am knocked sideways by his liveliness and wit. How did God make such mortals? I invite an Israeli guy, Avi what's his name – the only one who tries to pin me against the wall at some party or other – for Friday Night Dinner at the Hendon abode. He certainly doesn't arrive bearing gifts. I am wearing a lovely dress in the softest grey wool, from Polly Peck. It has a white crepe flouncy ruff around the collar and sleeves. We all sit in our separate chairs and my parents don't know what to say to him. He wasn't and isn't a proud Israeli nationalist, convinced of the necessity of 'us' and 'them' – the wall which keeps you separate but not safe. As an Israeli professor with radical views he is interviewed on television whenever the hurt and the hate erupt into violence. Wounds remain wounds even when they're on the back burner.

I go out with a gentile undergraduate who lives at Clapham Common. He's blonde and bright. He can't get home for the night and is not too pleased at having to spend the night in the back seat of my mother's Morris 1000. I just can't let him into the house and allow him to sleep on the sofa. Poor boy – what an ordeal! He's already gone when I go out to the car in the morning. Another blonde gentile in a white suit invites me back to his digs and I am impressed as to how easy-going these guys are – it's not the end of the world if the milk goes off and they don't seem to be endlessly fretting about what they're 'going to do' with their degree, let alone what they are going to eat and what they're going to wear …

All of this time, as per usual, I have another boyfriend on the go. My fellow trainee assistant who lives with her boyfriend tells me that doesn't know what she'd do without him and the sexual satisfaction he provides. I look into her face, feel affection for her, and wonder why this freedom is denied me. In our place the word 'sex' or 'love' is never mentioned although my mother says that I am loaded with sex appeal. On a Saturday afternoon, years earlier, I once asked her for help with something. She told me to 'F… Off'. I took the same problem to my father and he answered in identical fashion. I was truly shocked. They spat out this charming phrase with real bitterness and venom. On a Sunday afternoon, after a delicious dish of roast lamb accompanied by a mint sauce sharp enough to tear off the skin of the roof of your mouth and by my mother's cursing of

Lesley Man, the local kosher butcher whom she blames for giving her bad meat, I am pleased to be meeting my mates, Tina and Philippa, en route to the Kenco in Golders Green Road where I'll go into ecstasies over a toasted slice of butter cake and a glass of steaming hot chocolate. We are crammed together on the red plastic seat and our eyes scan the door, seeing who is coming in. Oh please, please, please God let it be Michael Kelsey. Let me die in the arms of Michael Kelsey, let me kiss him until the end of the world … This is about an eyes closed state of love and longing which is far world's away from the kitchen table and the vocab of home. 'Her' favourite word is 'Ugh' followed by a spitting curse and her favourite phrase is 'shit and sugar' whereas 'He' lives by the three 'Ps' – 'power, pressure and punishment. He also says: 'Those who can do; those who can't teach'. Why don't I punch him on the nose or tear off his genitals? After all, he likes a good fight. But, like a snail, I am already hidden inside my shell; I am part of this world and dependent on it. I am only truly put-out and upset when he comes between me and a sparkling new boyfriend, an Israeli poet with whom, every evening, I walk the quais of Paris, absorbing him and the beautiful city. Father is demanding that I annihilate myself in order to sit with Mother, and carry her load because that's what a daughter is meant to do whilst he is out in the world. But I am not truly aghast; parents have total power and it is my destiny to be pulverised. My mother has the memory of me as a very loving child whom she could push every which way she wanted. 'You're following me round the house like a little lamb', she said sharply, as she went from room to room, making the beds.

The new boyfriend on the go is actually the aforesaid Michael Kelsey. He doesn't speak much, unlike yours truly, but he tells me how much he likes my father. Neither of them can dance. For some reason, one Sunday morning I had found myself in a pub in St. John's Wood (or was it Kenwood) packed with young Jewish males. I hadn't seen him for about three years. He is now a medical student at Barts Hospital; it is all to the good to have a doctor in the family … I shared my first kiss with 'drop dead gorgeous' Richard Morrison on my 13th birthday. He also liked my father and was training to be a doctor. Kelsey, as we call him (in those days chaps were often referred to by their surnames) seems to respond to me in a new way. He tells me I make him feel happy. His father is a doctor and he, the son, doesn't seem to be very close with his siblings. He comes round for tea and my mother is continually thrusting a plate of piled-up toast and jam between us. The toast keeps coming but we just want to be quietly alone with one another. It's a nice feeling to belong to yourself and not give a damn about Mother and her toast. When there is no one in the house we lie on the sofa and he goes further than he should. I wasn't aware that my own flesh was so soft and spongy. He's putting pressure on me to leave the abode and rent a flat somewhere so that we can sleep together. My loving psychiatrist has also told me that 'I've got to get out of that place' – the barren abode where no one talks, nothing gives. I find a flat at No 5 Strathray Gardens, Swiss Cottage and put an advertisement in the Jewish Chronicle seeking flatmates. One young lady answers the ad. and I drive to meet her, one dark evening, at Golders Green Station. No sight of the flower lady who used to sit on the pavement on the corner of Golders Green Road, outside a lingerie shop opposite the station. As I come down the stairs from my bedroom, I espy my mother in the lounge watching 'Perry Mason' on the 'box'. She is always saying how much she loves 'Perry'. She doesn't see me. My father only comes home at the weekends; he's up in Gateshead, trying 'to get production up' in his menswear factory. As I make my way out of the house courage leads the way but I am scared. All is darkness. I also know that without Kelsey's constant 'pushing' I might not have been able to make the move. I knew that I needed to separate myself from a mother who enjoyed telling me that she was my obstacle.

The relationship with Kelsey isn't so great. We lie together on the single bed and he tells me off because 'I don't know the positions'. I tell my friends about this and they all think it's very funny. They visit me on a Sunday morning, and I can see that they are contemplating their own avenues of escape. Carole is plump, sexy and intelligent whilst blonde, blue-eyed Phyllis, whose parents have the dress shop in Queensway and devotees of the Hampstead Theatre Club, dresses with real originality and style. They are doing secretarial courses and, likewise, my father recommends that such a course should replace my little job at the LSE. A year's course is the norm but he reckons that one should do an intensive version in three months because this is best for your brain. Or rather – pressure is good for you. I have discovered the works of the great French writer Colette and, once again, I emerge from my room high and excited at finding a soul mate. Reading 'The Rainbow' by D.H. Lawrence (he was part of the 'A' Level English Literature course) my father had responded by saying with real disdain (as if I'd picked up a pebble rather than a pearl): 'That's not what life is all about' and maybe I said that I'd to be like her because the look I received was withering in the extreme accompanied by a real put-down of: 'You, Colette?' ('Get back in the typing pool; wave your yellow duster out the window'). Of course I'm not her but she wasn't God either. His tone is clenched and mean. He has large hands which make a tight fist. My mother is always on about having been top of the class in English, French and Maths; on occasion, before she goes out to dinner, she stands by the kitchen door and recites Caliban's speech beginning 'this isle is full of noises, sounds and sweet airs that give delight and hurt not'.' She is Caliban indeed. She goes nowhere near James Joyce or T.S. Eliot, let alone

George Herbert or John Milton or classical music. My father reckons she has the personality he lacks.

In my first year at secondary school I got 94% in Geography – the highest mark ever recorded. I did like the subject and the teacher but mainly this mark was due to will power and the desire to be noticed. She is having her tea at the kitchen table when I announce the news. Her flat, indifferent reply is – 'who cares?' – as she takes a bite of her slice of matzoh, loaded and lashed with butter, 'Philadelphia' cream cheese and 'Robertsons' blackcurrant jam. She likes to say, repeatedly, with a sideways shake of the head, suggesting no hope, 'Judy can't keep the beat'. My father never criticises her. He never tells her to get a job or 'to put a sock in it' when she moans about her clothes (everything she buys she returns prompting a letter from Mr. John Lewis who is upset that nothing is to the lady's satisfaction). Yet even she wants to live, to be blessed, because when I emerge from my room having worked on a 'poetry appreciation' essay she says, almost joyously, that my face is full of light. But the default position is the curse of womanhood and my failure, not only to 'keep the beat' but to read and obey instructions and 'get in line'.

My brother and I dance together in the lounge to the latest Merseyside melody and she rushes in from the kitchen, literally gets between us, and starts her tap dance routine, big breasts bobbing up and down. We mutely watch and admire; it doesn't occur to us to push her back into the kitchen and her place at the grey kitchen sink. In the summer my brother is forced to mow the garden lawn – up and down in straight rows. On one occasion, however, in the hall, he has his hands around her throat and she is yelling that he'll give her 'a cancer'.

I love going out with the boys, as is natural. I love the New Zealander, Mark Oberg-Browne most of all because he sees me as a daughter although he is only about five years my senior. When his wife finally arrives in the UK they rent a basement flat in Church Row, Hampstead. She tells me that I remind her of a Maori and Mark will be thrilled to have me over for dinner. My birthday is approaching, coinciding with the release of the Beatles' White Album and I throw a party inviting all my American LSE pals. Before I make my entrance I admire myself in my bedroom mirror; I am wearing a red wool maxi-length skirt and a tight-fitting, synthetic chiffon blouse which is all flame colours on a black background. I love it. One of my flat mates has the same blouse and she's also at the party – with her bald boyfriend. Everyone is relaxed and fine although I am aware that the music isn't loud enough. Kelsey has already told me that he has no idea what to get me for my birthday and seems concerned by his lack of generosity. My father sent me a potted 'shocking pink' azalea which I place on the grand piano in the living room, which prompts a joyous response. What impelled him to do that? He was happier digging up the fruit trees and starting fires. How he laboured over the mauve lupins in one corner of the garden. Kelsey, the father look-alike, dances cheek-to-cheek with a platinum blonde American student with a square jaw and pock-marked cheeks, resembling his own. They are also sitting together on the sofa. The aim is to make me jealous but I'm not. After all, he too doesn't 'know the positions'. My psychiatrist tells me that he is 'a cold fish' and his verdict is always accepted. He knows all and I trust him unthinkingly. It's just nice to be able to throw a party – something I could never do at home because my mother (if around) would criticise everyone. Height is the main point of contention (terrible to be too short or too tall) followed by girth. A fat man with a round fat face has to be thrown overboard, to be eaten by the sharks. Academics are useless; men of power are to be flirted with and gratified, whatever their size.

Through me she has a job volunteering at the Hampstead Theatre Club. Of course this isn't the next best thing to being a great actress (her father loved to watch her performing tap dance routines) but it gets her out of the house. Before her marriage she was the 'bees knees' of 'Unity Theatre' – an experimental left-wing theatre in N.W.1, East London, (she was, she said, even better than Maxine Audley who was, unlike her, R.A.D.A trained) and she was always on about the people she knew who became stars. These included David Kossoff, Ted Willis, Edmund Purdom, Roger Woddis and Alfie Bass. Alfie took her to the theatre and they got thrown out because he took her to front row seats that hadn't been paid for; Roger Woddis offered her the key to his flat; Edmund Purdom said that she was 'a mass of emotional protoplasm' and they all wondered why she was marrying my father; 'why HIM'? they said incredulously. She couldn't have had less interest in left-wing social concerns and politics. Looks were everything. On a Saturday afternoon I receive a telephone call from her telling me to attend the evening show at the Theatre Club – which is just round the corner from Strathray Gardens. It is Roc Brynner's last night of performing Jean Cocteau's 'Opium' and all his entourage are going to be there, including Yul Brynner, his dad. I'm not madly interested, but make an appearance as requested. She has also told me that Roc Brynner has really taken a shine to her because she's the only person who makes him sandwiches. I don a yellow/green tweed maxi skirt and a synthetic satin blue/green shirt. My hair is now long – for the first time in my life I can feel it half-way down my back – and I put it up in a kind of bun on top of my head. It must have been the fashion. I watch the show from the back row and his rendering of Cocteau's opium addiction is pretty gruelling. After the standing ovation all his retinue walk onto the stage including the bald Brynner senior who has real presence. I look nice with my hair up. His gaze alights on me and he stares and stares, without blinking, as if he's suddenly seen the woman of his dreams, the goddess/mother/fairy queen who offers total security. He's not embarrassed by his sudden detachment from all those he is with, including his wife. I can't quite remember what happened next but I receive a written note to meet him around the side of the building. I turn up as he's getting into a white Rolls Royce. His son is highly embarrassed. As he gets into the car he tells me that he is off back to New York so he won't be getting in touch. I am a bit surprised by the discrepancy between the intensity of the stare and the offhand approach by the car.

Well, Kelsey is out of the picture and concentrating on his medical studies. I don't miss him. I think that he became a pathologist. Well, dead bodies certainly don't know 'the positions'! It is the Christmas break at the LSE and everyone has disappeared. There's no one to take me for lunch or ask me out. I am plunged into loneliness which is picked up on by Denis the porter in his long grey overall coat. He lives with his old dad in the Old Kent Road, the cheapest property on the Monopoly Board. I have nothing to do with my flatmates; Thelma from up north works at M&S and there are two French Jewish girls from Toulouse. Can't remember what they do except that they all eat and cook together. I don't eat because I'm on amphetamines. I feel high all the time and, praise be to God, I've lost all my horrible tummy fat. I have my own small room for which I pay £5 a week. The other girls share a double room. I am the landlord since I took out the lease on the flat. Landlords are often bastards. Landladies likewise. At the same time, in my room, I play the newly released Simon and Garfunkel L.P 'Bridge Over Troubled Water' over and over again (principally the title song) and sadly think of my brother.

I am enrolled in Pitmans Secretarial College in Southampton Row. I take the underground to Russell Square station. It's all go in the typing room and the noise generated when everyone starts clacking away is something I don't like. I do my best to learn the skill but I'm a bit slow. I make a lovely new friend – Rose Einhorn – who is of mixed race (although this term didn't exist in those days) and I am impressed by her unruffled calm and quiet elegance. What a panicky creature is yours truly! There are girls from posh boarding schools who speak posh and are always late for shorthand in the afternoon and always 'calling out' to the strict grey-haired teacher from a bygone age. She seems to enjoy their uninhibited friendliness. We have to learn our new forms every evening and are tested the next day. I am quite good at this. There are a couple of clever girls who are really fast and never make a mistake. We go to a matinee performance of Agatha Christie's 'The Mousetrap' and, on a Saturday evening, the big night out, we go on a boat trip together down the Thames. Everyone needs fun and play. Every lunch time the others pop into Lyons Corner House (Pret a Manger hasn't appeared on the scene) and sit at brown tables whilst I make the short walk to Endsleigh Court in Upper Woburn Place where my grandmother lives. She cooks for me and takes pleasure in doing so because it gives her something to do and she knows that I adore her food. From a kitchen the size of a small bathroom she produces 'Wiener Schnitzel'; mushroom 'vol-au-vents' and 'French' potatoes – all of which have a depth of flavour which is as strong and determined as my mother's food is watery and insipid. Her cheese cake – all rich, thick cheese – bears no resemblance to what is called cheesecake these days – even in the best culinary establishments. Once in a while, on her fortnightly visit, taking the tube from Euston to Hendon Central, she'd trudge along, carrying a dish of carp in jelly. Nobody thanked her. My parents resent her controlling ways. I asked her what it was like to live alone and she replied, in no uncertain terms, 'Horrible'. She told my mother that she preferred visiting her other son in Wembley because his two children showed her more affection. (Did my mother accept her new gentile sister-in-law? The fact is that she nearly murdered her with a tirade of fish-woman abuse). In her later years my grandmother suffered from 'black-outs' and dropped dead at a bus stop, waiting for a bus on a dark winter late afternoon. My father sobbed his heart out after the flat clearance because 'everything was so miserable'. My mother turned away to look at the thick gold velvet curtains. I spontaneously put my arms around his neck to comfort him in the same way that I'd spontaneously put my arms around his neck when he was bullying my young brother before he went to school. The words that came out on the latter occasion were: 'I'll kill you if you don't leave him alone!' I helped my brother off to school and watched him make his way up the road, a little boy with a big briefcase. He has no memory of the incident.

But here I am in my sweater dress with a pale blue background. My mother has the same dress with a charcoal grey background. My grandmother doesn't like my mother but has no choice but to tolerate her. She didn't want her son to marry someone from the East End of London and a fat family to boot. When she opens the door to me – I can smell the cooking aroma as soon as I emerge from the old-fashioned lift – she notices my heavily blacked-out eyes but makes no comment, telling herself that that is what they do to their eyes these days – although I must have looked to her as if I'd been in a fight. She serves me cauliflower cheese, bubbling hot. I wonder what she does for the rest of the afternoon. The thing is that we never speak. No one speaks. I know that she entertains the gratifying thought of seeing me married off to the son of my father's 'boss'. When I get back to Pitmans my friends can't wait to hear what I had for lunch.

I get my certificate although my shorthand is better than my typing. What now? It's been a hard, cold winter and my psychiatrist friend tells me to get the money out of my father for a trip to Israel – I need some sunshine. I will stay at my uncle's house in Kiryat Motzkin, a suburb of Tel Aviv. This is a modest dwelling (apparently financed by my father) but it's the perfect villa with a raised rockery at the front of the house and a garden round the back – which they ignore. Their eldest son, Yair, has serious health problems – an inherited Jewish disease which involves his spleen. My uncle and aunt (we show off about the former because, somehow he happened to be on the famous ship called the 'Exodus' which attempted to carry European Holocaust survivors to Palestine in July 1947) don't blah, blah, blah interminably because they're too busy earning a living although he, Gerald, a warm-hearted, good-natured guy, devoid of greed, avarice and ambition, is always telling interminable stories about nothing. Sitting on the sofa he moves around in a fidgety way as if he seriously lacks something ... but his wife listens to him with happy respect; he is someone she loves. I share my cousin's room and waking up to warmth and sunshine and the smell of camels is deeply satisfying. And what do I do every morning? To the mild disapproval of my austere aunt I take the bus to the Sheraton Hotel in Tel Aviv where I don my beautiful brown bikini with the purple, acid green, and lemon yellow splodges and hang out around the pool. How good it is to be away from grey London and the typing-pool. I am aware that my aunt takes in typing in order to make ends meet. My mother rates her as beyond the pale because ... because she is someone else and has thick grey short hair although she's only in her forties. But she draws a map for me and tells me where to get off the bus.

It's spring 1970 and I have such great clothes. I have my beautiful daffodil yellow midi linen coat from Wallis and a silky dress with horizontal rainbow coloured stripes set off by a shocking pink patent belt. I have a mauve gingham check Mary Quant dress with embroidered pads on the elbows and my favourite dress of all is a flimsy pink and brown tight-fitting 'gypsy' dress from 'Fifth Avenue' in Oxford Street. It has a square neck and leg-of-button short sleeves. I love 'cup sleeves' – all cutesy for a little girl. My shoes are two-tone cream and brown patent; they are ultra chic, from Bally in Bond Street, and, miracle of miracles, they fit my poor Jewish feet. Obviously most of these clothes have stayed in my wardrobe, being unsuitable for the Holy Land where everyone runs freely along the beach, picking up beautiful shells and kissing the earth which God gave so freely unto them in perpetuity.

I stretch out my limbs at the side of the pool and delight in 'catching the sun' and becoming a bronze statue. Suddenly a very thin, dark-haired Italian man appears beside me. He tells me that he is a journalist from Rome, covering the goings-on in the Golan Heights. He was working in his room, surrounded by cameras, but seeing me outside, by the pool, he was impelled to ditch all that in order to come down and make contact. His name is Marcello and he's very attractive. He becomes my boyfriend, sort of. When he comes back to the hotel in the evening, a giant rucksack on his back, a call comes out for me to come to reception. But I have already seen him, tired and weary, and make my way towards him in my 'gypsy' dress and ginger shawl. All the weight of work falls from him as his face lights up in a smile. He changes into tight black trousers and a fancy black tight shirt – it has a sort of raised floque design. Could he be any thinner? We have kebabs for dinner in a tiny Arab restaurant in old Jaffa (totally to my taste – the smell of grilled meat is heavenly) where the proprietor nods his approval of me. Back in the car I don't think Marcello is so impressed when I can't tell him how to get back to Kiryat Motzkin 'Does she float around on a cloud, or what?' Nevertheless he kisses me and the verdict is: 'Beautiful'. On a Saturday morning I meet him in the hotel cafe for brunch – which consists of cream blinis and suchlike; Mandy Rice Davies, of the 'Profumo' case (as a ten year old I avidly read all about this scandal in high places) is already there waiting. Marcello tells me that the plan is for them to open a nightclub together in Tel Aviv. She announces that her child has been unwell during the night. Marcello says that I am 'also English' and she replies curtly that she isn't English but Welsh. She has big blue eyes. In the afternoon Marcello and a Jewish lawyer from Lille who lives with his mother almost come to blows because they both want me to accompany them to the hotel disco. They quarrel as to who knew me first. I like the Jewish lawyer because he listens to all my neurotic problems and seems to understand. Mother is a succubus on my back. Marcello never mentions his mother nor the fact that he has a wife and two children back in Rome.

Back in London the date of my younger brother's bar-mitzvah is approaching. They've decided on a friendly affair – a marquee in the garden rather than the formality of the Orchid Suite at the Dorchester. At the synagogue service I wear a pinky/mauve jersey suit from Wallis, my Bally shoes and a white silk turban. I am still very brown from my recent trip to the Middle East and feel the part. Generally speaking, a house of worship is where you go to pray, not show off your clothes, but old habits die hard. Sunday morning I have my hair done by a talented young Jewish hairdresser so that I look like a glamourous nineteen year old not an old woman. I wear a black crepe trouser suit which I consider cool because it has a bolero top and all the way round are little gold coins. I don't wear a bra. My father looks slightly concerned and disconcerted but my mother's subtle look of approval overrules him. For the first time in her life she looks nice in a pink chiffon dress with a flowery print. Her pearls are loosely worn. I see her in cahoots with a young man with jet black silky hair and beard to match. They look as if they are plotting something as indeed they are. The man approaches me and tells me how to get to Thorn House in Upper St. Martins Lane in order to have an interview with his boss concerning a job as his assistant copy-writer at K.M.P. advertising agency. It all seems like a done deal. (The guy, Mike, is the husband of their friend's daughter; the friend has a hairdressing salon in Wembley where my mother goes every Saturday afternoon. She told my mother, when I was about fifteen, that I was a Mediterranean type and she even composed a letter for me to send to 'Petticoat Magazine' in order to get on the journalistic ladder. The blank stare from mother equalled the death of the soul and all dreaming. I could have had a brown paper bag over my head). It's all a bit out of the blue but I know the area because on my Wednesday afternoons off from the L.S.E. Teaching Library I loved to wander around Soho. There was a fishmonger where you could see the salmon being sliced and Old Compton Street had an atmosphere to die for. I had a special fondness for the Church off Trafalgar Square at the beginning of Upper St. Martin's Lane because it somehow breathed Christian Charity not brutal control and superiority.

Sit on the steps and you will be given bread.

This is all to the good because obviously, having graduated from the secretarial college, I need a job. I meet the bosses and I am hired as an assistant to the aforesaid Mike, one of their senior copy-writers. I like the open-plan office. No poky little rooms. I walk through the centre aisle to get to Mike's desk, which is at the very end of the room. He invites me to dinner at his home – somewhere green and beautiful along the river – and at Victoria Station he's intensely pointing to all the giant advertisements. His wife, pregnant with their third child, has cooked a lovely salmon dish and eyes me with some suspicion. She is as silent and restrained as he is funny and exuberant. The next day I am plunged in at the deep end when he asks me to write the 'How do I enjoy myself' section of a travel company's guide to India. I am paralysed; I want to fall down a well or jump off the nearest cliff. How can I do that? I wail inwardly. Where do I start? Extremely tense and scared I go to the cafe opposite, sit myself down surrounded by all the necessary information, and manage to produce something which makes India sound like a wonderful place to visit, what with the elephants on your doorstep and luscious mangoes and guavas on the thick leafy trees. My boss is very pleased with my effort and is telling everyone that he shouldn't have hired me because soon he'll be out of a job. I love him because he's ceaselessly funny. He's also tense and highly-strung. Linda, the forty two year old art illustrator at the next desk has become my bosom pal. She tells me that they had a brief affair but no longer speak. She's in an unsatisfactory co-dependent relationship and is also in therapy. She knows about everybody and I hang onto everything she says, swallowing her insights whole. Mike tells me not to have anything to do with her. She has long fine fair hair and wears floaty dresses. I share a table with Nick, a middle-aged ex-public school guy who is working on a play rather than writing copy. He finds me a bit of a nuisance and nicknames me 'Joodles' – a nickname which Mike finds amusingly apt. One day my father visits the premises (why?) and as he walks down the concourse Mike freezes as if the grim reaper has made an uninvited appearance. There's a young Scottish art illustrator with a shock of wonderful black hair who is as thin as a rake but attractive in his figure hugging gear. Him and his co-workers are always having a laugh but obviously they also come up with the goods. Coming up in the lift with him and another art guy Jimmy says; 'this is our chance – it's now or never' … later telling me that the plan, his plan, was 'to hijack Judy'. He wonders how I can afford to wear expensive clothes. Is he referring to the silky rainbow dress and the Bally shoes? This was the period when hijackings by 'terrorist' gangs were the headline news. I wish Jimmy had hijacked me. I write a piece about 'Nairn flooring' and the head designer is at pains to find out who wrote a piece which so discreetly and elegantly matched his artwork. He is well pleased – this pale tense man manages a smile – and I am mightily filled with wonder and surprise at being appreciated and admired. With Linda I go to a hat shop in Soho and she looks great in a big floppy affair which matches her flip-flops.

Dark clouds, as always, are on the horizon. The lease on the flat has expired and I have to find somewhere to live pronto. I ring my grandmother and ask her if I could temporarily lodge in her spare room. It was usually let out to a student at London University. When my brother got angry (with them) my parents always threatened him with 'the dark room' referring to this back room which was hideously uninviting. It had a massive lumpy old bed with a dark red faded satin coverlet, an oppressive wardrobe and a desk and looked out onto an enclosed courtyard, evoking some ghetto in central Europe. The corner window let in next to no light. I was taken aback when she said, brutally; 'You've got a mother – go to her'. I never spoke to her again. One of the business guys/market managers, a Jewish guy, Martin, who is always hard at work and never eyeing the girls and gossiping, tells me that his cousin is leaving a flat in West End Lane and he'll tell her about me, my need for a room. He is tall and thin and has thick dark wiry hair and a big, loose mouth. Unlike the art guys he doesn't wear skinny jeans or a pink T-shirt. You can tell that he is a thoroughly decent, ethical type and he probably comes from a good, decent, ethical Jewish home where people don't beat each other up. He is always on the phone or running around on some errand, totally absorbed in his work. No rock'n'roll for him! I move into the flat which is above an electrician's shop. Everyone is friendly and leads their own lives. I am surprised to find one of the girls, on a Saturday afternoon, making soup for her granny. I am reading Colette's 'The Captive' and am spellbound by her style; such passion under so much control. I also read Albert Camus' 'L'Etranger' and am struck by the first line; 'Yesterday mother died' or words to that effect. Everyone loves their mum – she's the sweet familiar air they breathe daily and if you don't it must be your own monstrous fault because mothers are sacrosanct – holy cows producing lush quantities of life-giving milk, full of everything you need … Mersault, Camus' anti-hero, has had a different experience.

I no longer see the Israeli guy I used to visit, after 'work', at the Falafel House in Finchley Road. This was the venue for Israeli drop-outs – those who had been expelled from the Land of Israel. But didn't you merit prison if you refused to do your army service? They were probably into drugs. I was attracted to Ronnie, – he was probably illiterate – because sitting with him was like being with a bear. He sat with his arm around me, paid for my falafel in pita bread and then we went back to his place – a large house in Finchley Road – which he shared with all these other strange drop-out guys. I was surprised when he asked me, eventually, if my father could get him some kind of job. I ran for my life, all the way down Finchley Road, when he told me that he had VD and that I should get myself tested. At least, I guess, he had the decency to tell me. I wondered who else he could possibly be sleeping with and why?

What was happening at K.M.P.? Mike was having secret meetings with two short-ass slimy guys with the intent of setting up their own company. I was no part of this drive whatsoever and he'd only hired me to offset his tax returns. I sat at the desk, on my own, and wrote to myself. One of the three big bosses who were stationed on the floor above, visited the floor below – a hive of activity – to see how everybody was getting on. He came to me and the embarrassment was mutual when he saw that I had nothing to do, no one to work for. You can't have someone on the payroll who is a piece of furniture. (I received £14 a week; Linda, my friend, was paid a whopping £40) No one else needed an assistant. He had to let me go, gently. In fact I irritated people because I was always messing around, in their business, when they were trying to work. Like a child. I even tugged Mike's beard. I wasn't upset at leaving because I was 'Nowhere Man' really, bobbing along on a cloud whilst chained to the prison floor. Mike gave me the gift of a free holiday in Mallorca, in September, courtesy of '4S Travel', for whom he worked. I should have been a bit angry with him for leaving me high and dry. But I felt nothing other than the shame of being caught at my desk doing nothing. Mallorca was a revelation – the most beautiful place on earth.

It was also lovely to receive a phone call, whilst I was still at K.M.P. from Gigi, David's best friend, who was captain of a ship and stationed at the East End Docks. I made an appearance in my daffodil yellow midi linen coat, a copy of a Chanel or a Dior creation, on the docks and as he came towards me, he said that he was blinded by my 'brilliance'. How lovely he was, full of warmth and loving-kindness with his great brown eyes and long dark eye-lashes. He could easily have been an Arab and was probably of a Sephardi background. We'd exchanged letters throughout the year following the 'Six Day War' – David had taken me to meet him at the local bowling club in Haifa. He was as bright as

David was dumb but the expression on the latter's face was: 'look at my find and she's all mine'. He, Gigi, says: 'I never understood how you two could get on since you're into ideas and he never was – we were in the same class at school. He had no ideas about anything'. In his cabin on the ship I chat enthusiastically and suddenly he stops me by planting his mouth on mine. How good that feels – the best thing in the world – 'kisses sweeter than wine'. No wonder that the dried up prune from grammar school made me read from 'the Song of Solomon' in Jewish Assembly. She'd been to the 'Slade' and had probably known Jewish artists ... for some reason she didn't kneel in the hall with all her fellow Christians. She chose to be with the noisy Jews. Her teaching got no further than constantly mumbling the injunction to 'look at the spaces between things'. She was a terrible teacher – unable to communicate at all. She asked us what we discussed at the dinner table and told us that we and our parents were the type of people who started wars. We didn't know what this meant. She called me 'a lazy slug' because I didn't move around the model who was posing as 'The Thinker' but sat like a fixture. She got even angrier when I didn't respond: 'Don't you know that I'm being rude to you – why aren't you getting angry with me?' She liked those who had a voice, who could answer her back.

She had another go at me on account of the tree on my desert island: 'She's going to blush when I say this because she's very sensitive but she's just returned from a holiday in Israel – at great expense – and she can't even draw a fig leaf!' Too true. Others were too frightened of her to titter. In the 6th form she told me that she had rooted for me to be a prefect ('it would give her some confidence') – going against the general consensus of opinion that I was unsuitable material. I wonder what my parents' reaction to her would have been if she'd met them at a parents' evening. She probably would have made a personal comment and they'd have had to run to the safety of the car. 'No one in our family is in a bad state – we're on top – anyone can see that.'

Gigi feels a bit guilty because I am with him now but also he knows that David is a thing of the past. David is now working as a security guard on 'El Al' airlines. He knows about weapons and surprising the enemy. Why can't I embrace Gigi, love him and stay with him forever? In the past it was normal for girls to get married when they were nineteen and at the height of their attractiveness. I also have purple linen trousers and a bright yellow shirt. Why – a million times why? It's because I am in a box not of my own making. How can this be is the question any sane person might ask? It is because we do not trust – the world is our enemy and always has been. We prefer to buy our fruit rather than take it from the tree. We prefer to keep people at a distance because we don't do honest to God nakedness or eat vegetables covered in earth. Who wants to get into all that fleshy mess of disgusting secretions? Didn't grandfather Max get angry if someone coughed? Life is for show. People are judged. And there is always something better around the corner. On the ship my 'rocky' Israeli rings go missing. Gigi has the crew in for questioning. Nobody pleads guilty. The poor lads stand silently, heads bent in shame.

Gigi is off to the far east and gives me his itinerary. Thailand, Japan and China are another planet as far as I'm concerned. I enjoy my holiday in Cala Bona, Mallorca, although the small hotel is a ghastly new build and the food is rubbish. Nobody is trying. There's a young fair-haired guy in the group (this was a package holiday affair) who doesn't set fire to the hotel but, next best thing, cuts off the electricity supply. I delight in his anarchy. His girlfriend is the mute, passive variety. There is a slightly older lady who is on her own and us four go out to dinner together, to escape the paltry hotel food. I am wearing my beloved Gypsy dress. A Spanish guy at a distant table catches my eye and raises his glass of purple wine to me. I do likewise. Next thing is that he's sent over a messenger (poor fellow) asking me to join their table. Off I go. He tells me that he'd like me to represent his chain of hotels in the forthcoming 'Miss Mallorca' competition but he needs to see me in a bikini. 'No problem there', I think to myself, 'I have my brown sludge affair from Monte Carlo.' The problem is that I am due to fly back to Gatwick Airport in a couple of days. 'No problem there', he assures me, 'one of my guys will sort that for you and generally look after you'. The flight is changed, his guy comes to the hotel and doesn't know what to do with me. I hang around waiting for I don't know what. I never appear in my bikini.

Back in N.W.3 I no longer have a job. Sitting in a cafe in Finchley Road I overhear some girls (one of whom I recognise from Saturday night clubs – she has long red hair which goes completely grey after marrying my brother) talking about having been an au-pair in Paris. This idea tickles my fancy and I look into it and make all the necessary arrangements. Things were more straightforward in those days. I buy a massive black tacky case (was it made from cardboard?) from a luggage shop in Finchley Road – some of these shops always have stuff on sale – and my father drives me to Victoria Station. He tells me that no au-pair who came with a case like mine ever stayed for long. Indeed, Anne-Marie Chretien, Christian in name and spirit and with her pink cheeks, pale blue eyes and bonny smile was a real hit with my parents and stayed for a long time. She didn't complain about the fact that her bedroom was the only one with linoleum rather than carpet and she wanted to become a nun. My mother talked her out of this 'insane' move. Vieda Shmidt, the Austrian girl knitted thick cardigans and Nelly Kuhn from Zurich and Maria Tzites from Yugoslavia went bananas over my baby brother who was cute as cute, with a big chubby face. My elder brother too has a new mate. My new game is to frighten him, baby brother, with 'ghost faces' when he's in his play-pen. As soon as he stops smiling and starts to cry I laugh and all is well again. Mother is in the kitchen at the grey aluminium sink pretending to do the washing-up. I watch cartoons on TV which I don't take to; their disembodied facelessness fills me with gloom.

But hey, here I am at the 'Gare du Nord' and I am excited beyond belief. This is the Paris of Colette, Andre Gide, Marcel Proust et al. It's the fact that all is bustle and colour and living faces. Young people in berets are sitting at an outdoor cafe. I take a taxi to my new address in 'Arts et Metiers' and my employer helps me drag my big black case up to my attic room. I love its slanting wall. The next day I don my red ribbed sweater and my brown flared jersey skirt with its pinafore top. I am thrilled by the massive coffee cups – milky coffee is a meal in itself and the housekeeper runs up the stairs yelling 'De Gaulle est mort, De Gaulle est mort,' obviously shocked and upset. Was De Gaulle for the French what Churchill was for us? I feel at home in this old top-floor flat with its views across the rooftops of Paris and the street below is a hive of activity – well it is very different from the Finchley Road with its stream of roaring traffic.

Little three year old Thierry is my charge and he's a sweet little thing. Madame Beaurepaire, his mum, is busy filming TV adverts and is very proud of her acting credentials. She has short dyed blonde hair, very dark monkey eyes and eyebrows. She looks a bit like Coco Chanel. She tells me all her stuff – the fact that she still has to rock herself to sleep in her single bed because her mother never hugged her enough. (Her mother is invited to her birthday party and the daughter, very chic in her black trousers and white floppy shirt, is 'on edge' trying to please her …) Her lover comes to visit her in the afternoon and they retire to her tiny bedroom and her single bed. He is tall and stooped and around sixty. He doesn't speak to me. Mme tells me that he is writing a history of the Jewish People, entitled 'The Passionate People' and he's a journalist and a famous playwright. (He must have witnessed the round-up of Jewish families in Nazi-occupied Paris. Who hasn't witnessed a bang on the door at 3am if not at 8am; 'get up you lazy, hostile, selfish bitch' screamed Mother.) Mme is very concerned that I will run up a phone bill and says that I have to leave money by the phone after every call. I never use the phone and am insulted that she'd suspect me of taking advantage of her in this way.

All I want to do is explore. Mme writes Thierry's menu every morning and my job is to buy the stuff in the market. I've never experienced such a market – it's as if the world has become real. People laugh, smile, and communicate. It's normal to have brains for lunch (how tasty they are cooked in butter) and how can you not buy celery, radishes and endives on a daily basis or not return from work with a crusty Baguette under your arm.

I have fallen in love with this city. I want to eat it whole. Everything appeals. On my first full day off I go everywhere on foot, taking in the parks, the bridges and the quais, the Place de l'Odeon (metro stop Chatelet) where, outside the theatre is a stall where oysters, on piles of ice, are for sale, graced by lemons, cut in half. The 'Jeu de Palme' art gallery is an impressionist paradise and how easily you can pass from the conservative grandeur of the 'right bank' (where people have servants) to the messy intimacy of the left bank where men have beards and unkempt hair and are far more intelligent than those who boast of their smart property on the Bvd. Haussman. I choose a nice-looking cafe at the top of the Champs-Elysees. Here I can sit, enjoy my coffee and see the world go by. And all my inhibition with the language seems to be falling away. Who cares if you make a mistake with your reflexive verbs! A guy in a black coat, good-looking, with very fair hair passes by the cafe. He's obviously on a Sunday afternoon stroll down the 'Champs Elysees'. He must have seen me sitting in the window because he abruptly turns round, walks through the door and asks me if he can sit at my table. Is this a pick-up? If it is, it doesn't feel sordid, degraded and vile. He is lovely. He is from Yugoslavia and is working as a translator for some company or other. He has his own flat in Paris. He knows Brigitte Bardot and she'll probably be at a dinner he's been invited to. I am also invited to the dinner and she's not there but the other French people are as chic and stylish as the French used to be before technology put them in an iron brace, a grey uniform. The Gauls are 'red, white and pale blue' whereas the English are brown – dull to their bones. Nicola takes me to see a painter friend of his in Montmartre; I am wearing the mauve jersey suit that I wore at my brother's bar-mitzvah and the friend tells him that he has good taste. We don't sleep together because he gets cold feet. Or maybe we did and there were no Roman Candles, just a damp squib. He buys me Frank Sinatra's 'My Way' and writes on the record sleeve, 'avec un coup de feu …' The relationship falters; did he imagine that I was 'eyeing up' someone else? Men know how to get into a jealous stew. He tells me that I have too much life for him.

Back in the flat I am in trouble. Mme can't understand why I didn't take Thierry into a sausage shop or a patisserie when he needed the toilet; why did I make him wait until he got home. I don't know; natural functions are such an embarrassing performance – they interfere with one's reverie.

But worse still is the fact that I forgot to place the plastic mat in the bath so that he wouldn't slip. This seems to me like a minor offence but Thierry senior has told her that she has to fire me. She pleads my cause, saying that I am 'sympathique' but to no avail. The passionate young jewess with her 'Mary Quant' make-up must go. Or, what is more likely, she's obviously more interested in big boys than in little ones. I have to leave in the morning. I am paralysed with terror. Where will I go? The terror subsides – surprisingly – and I go to the agency who fixes me up with a new post – pronto. Mme then changes her mind and says I can stay after all but I stubbornly refuse to do so. She tells me that she is Catholic and humble (actually she strikes me as somewhat highly-strung and neurotic) and I am Jewish and proud. This doesn't mean much to me nor the fact that my Catholic friend Barbara from St. Paul, Minnesota, whom I met at the Alliance Francaise where I am meant to be having French lessons but drop out because the fusty old teacher tells me that my written French is 'les mauvais affaires' (appalling) invites me to the flat where she is caring for an eighty year old woman. This invisible woman, on being told that I am Jewish (why would Barbara tell her that?) says that no Jew is allowed to enter her flat and I'll have to sit on the stairs. I love Barbara. She wears no make-up, speaks French well, and wears a long fawn-coloured suede coat. She laughs when I speak and tells me that I remind her of 'Jean Brodie' in Muriel Spark's novel and the wonderful film with Maggie Smith in the lead role. She prays for me at night. Her idea of bliss is to be able to serve someone, a beloved mate, every day of her life. She comes from a big family.

My new placement is in Rue de Grenelle, as dull, plain and conventional a 'quartier' as Arts et Metier was 'bohemian'. My new madame is a small dark-haired lady, an optometrist. When we go to the supermarket I follow her around meekly with the trolley and she pops in the same stuff, week on week. No more shopping in the open market. In order to bond she gets me to put on one of her big floppy hats. Doesn't work. It seems that everyone in Paris has a lover. Hers is a small Jewish doctor and he visits in the afternoon. I can hear them at it, the moans and the heavy breathing, in the room next door. Mme has a little three year old daughter who refuses to eat 'la soupe' because she doesn't like to eat 'tout seule' (all alone). On an evening she, he and his two teenage children, play cards. They look quizzically in my direction as I leave the flat but I don't like this part of town, near the Eiffel Tower. I keep away from this tourist hotspot, on principle. In the morning I am greeted by a sink piled high with their dirty dinner plates.

This job, too, doesn't last and my next post is at Villa Boissiere, in a lower-middle class area on the right bank. Madame is appalled that I don't know how to iron shirts – the housekeeper at arts et metiers had also voiced her amazement at my incompetence: 'Didn't your mother teach you how to do anything?' – and sets out to teach me with more firmness than kindness. I have never forgotten how to iron a shirt. I am only allowed to have a shower once a week and my breakfast consists, not of a steaming bowl of coffee, but two dry 'biscotti' on a plate. She is also shocked that I don't see the point in ironing sheets. I never meet her husband or her two teenage children. She is a very correct and proprietorial sort of person. One morning she tells me that a young man had called at the flat asking for me. She didn't seem too pleased about this invasion of privacy, this stranger on her doorstep. The person in question turns out to be David Zion whom I meet one evening at the newly opened 'drug store' in the Champs Elysees. He got hold of my new address from Gigi. Working for 'EL AL' as a security guard he's on a stop-over in Paris. He tells me that he's proud of me in my newly-found independence. I'm pleased that he's proud of me but his viewpoint is limited. Gigi writes to me, telling me that he is concerned about my constant changes of address, saying that this isn't the life for me. I receive a stupid letter from my mother telling me that I'm not a lady. I take satisfaction in the fact that I can tear it up; this is how I feel so take that!

So independent am I that my parents fly over in order to drag me back to the ghetto. They stay at the elegant Hotel Lotti in the Place Vendome, near the Place de la Concorde. It's a nightmare scenario and I feel that they are killing something soft inside me. It really feels as if they are killing my baby. I hang on by the skin of my teeth. They return home and let me spend a night at the Hotel, sleeping in their large vacated room and lush bed. At Villa Boissiere I was in the attic and had to climb six flights of stairs to my room – which wasn't exactly torture. Standing in the centre of the bedroom, a big woman, she harps on about being a lady and other crazy fantasies which spell death to my soul.

My father grants me a small allowance which enables me to rent a room in a flat near the Bois de Boulogne. Madame Charles is divorced and has an utterly lovely three year old daughter, Carole, who smiles sweetly at me when she sees me in the street. Her mother tells me to remember to take off my beautiful brown suede boots when I enter the flat. As if I'd want to dirty her abode. I don't like the mother with her pale pointed nose. She's always decrying others for being 'mal elevees' (badly brought up). Indeed people are divided between the well and the badly brought up. Maybe she is right. I espy her on her chaise longue of an evening, half-naked with a glass of wine in one hand, watching TV. She has many friends round for dinner and is very particular and demanding as regards domestic stuff, speaking to me as I am the very unwanted lodger. In my room I read Jean Cocteau's 'Les Enfants Terribles', Saul Bellow's 'Dangling Man' and 'Seize the Day', Bernard Malamud's 'The Fixer' and Nietzsche's 'Thus Spake Zarathustra'. This last book fires me up exceedingly because it's all about flying high using their own wings. Those poor Nazi people twisted his ideas so that they could be, not free, but on top. Every top dog with his clean coat is still a mangy cur deep underneath. I also read 'The New Testament'. The latter makes absolute sense to me and I don't know why Jewish people are so scared of it. When Jesus appeared, in his floating white gown, in the film 'Barrabas' my father turned his face away from the screen. I bet he regretted taking us to see that one. The usual run was 'Ben Hur', 'Spartacus' and 'The Fall of the Roman Empire'. He loved the spectacle of Roman might; I was transfixed with the 'leper colony' in 'Ben-Hur' (the devoted heroic son searching for his mother and sister) and loved to act out the line spoken by Judah ben Hur's mother in her raspy voice, to her lovely (Charlton Heston) son, after a suspenseful pause: 'We are lepers …' She and her daughter lie all day on their bed of rags, their skin a sea of suppurating sores. Finally, as Jesus dies on the cross, atoning for the sins of all men, their skin is cleansed and they are 'triumphant' with relief and delight. I read a lot of Goethe. Jean Cocteau's 'Les Enfants Terribles' brings real delight as I remember an early closeness with my brother. With Saul Bellow comes Bernard Malamud and in this latter writer there is a deep enveloping sadness. I keep my camembert on the window-sill. We are now in the throes of winter but I find the snow deeply romantic. Every day I eat my bread and cheese and yellow green 'Golden Delicious' apples, and read my books dressed in my below-the-knee wine coloured wool dress and long brown and beige knitted cardigan which keeps me very warm. I have my emerald green velvet trousers and the beautiful brown dress which prompted Mark's wife to say that I reminded her of a Maori. Mme Charles doesn't sanction my use of the central heating and I have my own shower room. I wander around Paris in my heavy dark brown great coat with its gold buttons, belt and epaulettes, visiting any place that takes my fancy. One night I have a nightmare in which a hand is on my neck, clutching it. In the morning my neck is so stiff that I can hardly walk and it takes days for me to recover. This is the hand that takes and does not make.

Outside the 'Louvre' a guy wants to take my photo for a fee. A guy with black hair and beard asks to see the film in the camera. He doesn't sound rude – just curious. The photographer moves away and the bearded guy is gazing at the goldfish in a pond and he expresses the thought that goldfish don't need a 'head' – they just swim round and round in their container. I reply with some thought of my own and he asks me to walk with him. He is wearing a navy blue reefer jacket and has longish black hair and green-brown eyes. He is an Israeli poet travelling through Europe and his name is Simeon Zamereth. He has an ulcer so he has to avoid certain foods and he sleeps in a different hotel every night. Thirteen francs used to be the going price for a room. He steals books in order to pay for his accommodation and shows me how it is done. The big jacket can accommodate a lot of crime. He is twenty nine. He writes poems for an Israeli newspaper. I must have said something to annoy him on the metro because he turns to me and says with real anger: 'I asked you to walk with me because you were intelligent but I can't stand you in your big HEAVY coat and I don't want your company … I don't need anyone's company and I don't need you – I have a beautiful woman back home in Israel, who is an artist … and I hate all those

Israeli women who tout their daughters around, looking for a husband'. I take all this in utter silence, somewhat stunned of course, (if she is beautiful then I am second fiddle) and walk along the underground corridor considering what to do next. He is following me. I am then told that he is really impressed that I didn't crumble under his verbal assault ('most girls would') and he's decided that he wants my company after all. We eat at a left bank cafe and he has a go at the proprietress for being so preoccupied with money. His lack of inhibition amuses me. He tells me that the army in Israel were angry with him because he fell asleep at his post. He couldn't care. Leaning on the old, romantic 'Pont Neuf' bridge (my favourite) he writes of the glimmering reflection of the moon on the water …

I am mesmerised. I just want to follow him, listen to him. He describes most people as zeros and calls me his 'little number'. The fact that he is a thief doesn't repel me; I see him as a brave, bold, fiercely independent individualist. He shakes his head in wonder at the fact that I'm so psychological. Every evening we meet at 8pm in the Place St. Michel, under the clock tower and walk the quais of Paris. Here is someone I can follow – whose will is greater than my own. I love the fact that he is so free – that every night he finds a new thirteen franc hotel room. He tells me that I remind him of James Joyce in my intensity and continually chides me about taking everything so seriously; 'it doesn't matter' is his constant refrain. He tells me that I will have a hard life because I want the truth. (No leafy bowers from whence I came but locks on every door and iron bars across the windows. It was the Indian poet Tagore who said that one should carry one's life as lightly as a dew drop on a leaf).

But one night I wait and wait and, as in the Sandy Shaw song 'boy don't come'. I am as disappointed as hell and make my lonesome way back to my room, suffering from bronchitis. Of course I have no way of finding him and have to come to terms with the fact that he is gone. But you never know what is around the corner and one evening I espy him in the far distance walking along, hunched into the navy blue reefer. He is very pleased when he sees me and opens his arms wide in the middle of the road, ignoring all the cars. He too had been ill with bronchitis and on the night in question he'd fallen asleep and when he woke went to meet me although it was the middle of the night. We walk and talk and eat in one of the small left bank restaurants. He observes my black eyes, red lips and white 'gaulois' cigarette. I even smoked a pipe. I loved its dark brown woodiness. He drops the bombshell that he has met an English girl, a teacher who has a car and she has offered to take him to London for a few days. Before coming to Paris he was in Rome where he was knocked out by the beauty of the Piazza Navona. Hopefully in London he'll be bowled over by Trafalgar Square with its stone lions and statue of Nelson on his plinth. What hurts is him telling me that he can't let her down because she couldn't take it whereas I can.

I move out of my room and deliberately leave the shower room in a horrible dirty mess. Ha! I'm getting my own back on this cold white woman with all her petty rules and regulations and total lack of friendliness and empathy, although in those days I'd never heard of the 'e' word. With my friend Barabara I travel to Amsterdam where it's also cold and blanketed in snow. I get a very potent sense of roots that aren't Anglo Saxon. In a bookshop I discover the journals of Albert Camus and he says things which speak to what I've always felt and this is like finding an oasis in a desert or a diamond on a pebbly beach or hearing God speak! I hug this book to my chest as a starving man hugs his baguette. Barbara corrects my French – apparently I make the same mistake over and over again – but she does so in a spirit of humour rather than angry foot-stamping exasperation or cold contempt for one's inferiors.

On our return I move into an old-fashioned cheap hotel in the Pantheon area, a very old part of Paris now inhabited by students and the like. Maybe it was recommended to me by Simeon. Coming in out of the cold and getting my key from the brown, wooden reception area I espy a tall guy with a wispy beard and big brown Jewish eyes – the eyes of central European Jewry. Are they the eyes of sadness and defeat – never getting your own way or imposing your will on anybody – or the eyes you get from too much introspection and reading. Out of the blue – which I like – he, Tom, tells me that he's been having very strange dreams and that when he returns to Delaware he wants to see a psychoanalyst to help him sort out their meaning. He's a philosophy student and he becomes my boyfriend. We visit the Jeu de Palme art gallery – an afternoon to remember – and he tells me that I remind him of Manet's 'Femme aux eventails' – her hands, or was it the fan, in constant movement, dissolving into transparency. He buys a bag of chocolate truffles and puts one in my mouth – urging me to accept a good thing when it falls from heaven and not to resist EVERYTHING. But I have to protect myself! (The ogre and the witch are always behind me). He says that with what I've had to put up with from my parents I should try to get some money out of them. He says this as a sober fact. For himself he longs to see Chartres Cathedral. I know that he wants to go on his own.

There are some jolly American guys staying at the hotel and breakfast, which consists of baguette and butter and coffee is a funny communal affair. Why does the American guy Bill call me 'le voleur du beurre'? (the butter thief). He calls Tom 'Thomas Aqinas' – that famous sleeper; he is bewildered by Tom's ability to sleep ad infinitum. Tom visits me in my room where I have my trinkets and wear my red Chinese slippers and I visit him in his bare austere cave where he sits on the prison type bed, reading. He tells me that I should carry on being 'fertile' and that the only emotion he ever recalls his mother expressing was anger. He also tells me that I have an ego and don't listen properly to what he is saying; always one step ahead thinking of what I'm going to say next – that my thoughts are more important. 'I don't know if I want to spend any more time with you', he says, reflectively. Shame on me! I don't like it if he farts; nothing like bodily functions to shatter a romantic illusion. Barbara visits and cannot understand how someone like me can be with someone so quiet and retiring. She reckons it's a bad match.

But we move in together. We find a hotel on the Ile de la Cite and it is cheap because it is damp. We have a view of the beautiful Notre Dame Cathedral. I tell him I love him and I mean it. He is uncertain about 'consequences'. We visit 'BelleVille' the old Jewish quarter, still inhabited by Jews, and have dinner in a little restaurant. We are both struck by a sense of shared ancestral memory and on the metro, going down the escalator, we are both gripped by passion and, just as with the Israeli guy, we can't break the spell, we don't want to break the spell, we want to hang on to it and physical expression might well spoil it, degrade it, reduce it to common mud. But maybe we should have touched one another and gone for ecstasy. I love him with every last fibre of my being. We also eat in a Vietnamese restaurant where the food is so bad that we decide not to pay and we just run for it. I relish not having to pay. Theft is about getting your own back on others. However, exasperatingly, I leave my brown cashmere gloves on the table.

We have dinner with the American guys in an old restaurant in the Pigalle district which, with its mirrors and chandeliers and old school waiters, brings to mind a Toulouse-Lautrec painting. This is my sort of place – I have travelled back to a former time when people lived more ... Bradley tells us about his run-of-the-mill sightseeing. He beckons to the waitress, addressing her as 'garconette'. I like him because he is so friendly and open but Tom is not amused. We get back to the hotel and hear moaning from the next room and it's not sexual. We are impelled to investigate and discover a poor girl who is in the throes of a drug overdose. We call the hospital. Tom is appalled that he is the only one who really cares and he can't stop thinking about her. Indeed I don't really care – it's as if there is an inner disconnect; I don't belong to this sad world of mishap and misery. Who is she anyway?

Maybe Tom is getting fed up with my prison of ego. I am getting fed up with the vain superficial French. And the long, cold winter is taking its toll. I have a place to study English Literature at the Hebrew University in Jerusalem. They had no qualms as regards accepting me on my rotten grades. Maybe at the back of my mind I realise that this is an absurd decision but somewhere is better than nowhere. Bill and his friend want me to accompany them on a bike ride through

France. This sounds like an attractive prospect but my place in Israel is set in stone so that's that.

Ten years after my first trip I am back on an EL AL jet in my fancy clothes or rather my blue and grey jersey suit from Betties in Golders Green Road, under the bridge, has been replaced by a red key-hole T-shirt and snazzy striped flares from Galeries Lafayette which are imprinted with figs on a soft goldy-beige background. My aunt by marriage was probably not overjoyed to see me again. She's not the type to start shouting and screaming when things turn up on your doorstep that you'd rather do without. Within days I am off to Eilat on the Red Sea to soak up the sun and see what's around. The toilet at the bus station is in a truly filthy state. I'm wondering if the hippie community has fouled it up. I see a guy on the beach who is lying on the ground with his feet up and seemingly nursing a bad shoulder or back. I inquire about his ailment and he tells me about a muscle injury which leads into his personal history. He came to Eilat when it was just about on the map and established himself with his glass-bottomed boat – taking people out on trips to see the exciting underwater life. He told me that nobody helped him or gave him any encouragement – the clever Ashkenazi Jews lord it over the North African jews who don't play the violin or study Physics at University – but now that he is successful everyone wants to be his friend. I go for a swim and hear him yelling at me from the beach and waving his arms frantically because I am swimming too far out and it feels good that he's on my case. He asks me to drive him (on account of his strained back) in his jeep to a special beach where no one goes. I say I can't and he says I can. I get behind the wheel and do the job. We sit on the beach and gaze at the jewelled stones and the deep blue sea. It is magical. We don't speak. He is aware that most people don't come to see and appreciate but to get something for themselves and when this becomes the norm they'll be nothing left to value, to enjoy. (Einstein said that a man should strive to be, not a man of success, but a man of value). He, Raffi, buys a load of groceries for his simple-minded Arab servant who lives in a tent. I am jealous; God knows why. It is because I have never experienced the give and take of daily life; you help me and I help you. I stay with Raffi for a few days. He gets very annoyed when I decide to take myself off for a walk round the town without even leaving a note attached to the fridge door. 'Are we now in America?' he asks – 'where selfishness is a virtue'. He hosts a wonderful meal with a group of French Jewish tourists. The men are nice and the women are beautifully dressed and all warmth, allure and attractiveness. A feeling of security comes over me, the likes of which I've never experienced. Raffi refers to me as his little something or other. The next day we go out on the glass-bottomed boat. These people are warm and friendly. Raffi confides to me that his 'bonhomie' is something of an act – he doesn't really like people. He chides me for 'letting everything in' taking life too seriously. He wants me to marry him. I take the bus back to Tel Aviv.

I show my aunt the photo of me and him on the boat (probably not a wise move); I am luscious in my brown velvet bikini and he has an arm around me – a gold medallion on a chain ornamenting his hairy animal chest. My aunt says that he looks like 'a Jewish wideboy'. There was a whole contingent of those in Golders Green and my father called them 'low lives' (because, no doubt, they had no sexual hang-ups, nothing held them back from making merry with the ladies, holding them and loving them and swearing eternal fidelity) as if they were bad dogs. To be labelled 'casual' was also to have a cross by your name. My uncle says nothing but cannot ignore my allure. But, in the photo, I look relaxed and happy.

'So she's back – eating our delicious Israeli cheese and yoghurt which she pinches from the fridge. My aunt is stupefied by the empty shelf but says nothing. They have a day job invigilating at an exam centre and they suggest that I also come along and earn a bit of money. I am surprised to witness my easy-going whistling uncle shouting at the poor students. He tells me that he sometimes feels this rage arising out of nowhere. I am visited by Arieh, the son of a next door neighbour who is an El Al airline pilot. This suburb of Tel Aviv, Ramat Hasharon, is a quiet, relaxed place where women love to invite people round for coffee and cake. Even Golda Meir treated foreign dignitaries to her pale yellow sponge cake. Everyone bakes. Arieh has a flat in Haifa where he is a student and invites me to stay. My aunt comments that she hopes I pay my way and remembers Arieh as a little boy who was decidedly two-faced. He does seem to be a bit of a lapdog. As for me I am getting more and more depressed and mental. I don't feel good at all. I don't belong anywhere. My cousin Ruth is also in the Holy Land working on a kibbutz and she arrives for a visit, speaking Ivrit and full of beans. My aunt is really pleased to see her, delighting in the fact that she has learnt the language. I sit glumly in a corner and am ignored by all. I am in a place of introverted mayhem. (When I went to an art exhibition in Tel Aviv I met an attractive ginger-haired kibbutznik who invited me to his kibbutz. This was an open door, an invitation, a way out which I failed to take. With a cross on your back you are far, as far can be, from living in the present. Or do I have a perverse, self-punishing masochistic tendency? I am always scribbling in my little green notebooks and, on the bus, curious Israeli guys press me to tell them what I am writing about.) I must have mentioned suicide to my aunt (she is actually enrolled at the university in Tel Aviv undertaking a part-time English Literature degree; she proudly reads me one of her essays and I am surprised that it's not that good – banal and unoriginal) and she says sternly: 'And what would I have to say to your mother?'. Mother indeed. (They always want to send me back to her). This dire influence is uppermost because, instead of having a good time on a kibbutz with people my own age I have found a job in the doll shop in the Tel Aviv Hilton. Yes, this shop is a haven of mute dolls with staring eyes and rigid dressed-up bodies and my job is to dust them every morning. My time inside this place is a trial of endurance. I finish at lunchtime. I don't remember ever making a sale. I just 'stand there' aware of the passing minutes and hours. The little Jewish lady, whose shop it is, is very neat and correct, sprucely dressed. She tells me that her son said, when he heard me on the phone, that I have the nicest voice in the world. Receiving this compliment feels like a blessing. On a hot summer's day, emerging from the hotel, I see the Tel Aviv skyscrapers and they appear to me as dark grey matchbox edifices which are blocking out the sun and the blue sky. I feel that these things are a menace, a blight on life, cancelling out the soul. I feel that the sky has fallen in and there is no way forward. In hell nothing grows.

 I go out with Arieh and his friend Ami, a bespectacled young man who is very pale with lots of fine, light brown curly hair and training to be an architect. He is canoodling with his Israeli girlfriend. We stop at a petrol station and I observe some natural phenomenon involving ants or some other insect and comment that they only have power en masse – they are nothing on their own. Not a great thought but enough to cause Ami to break up with his girlfriend and want to be with me. He is also an amateur photographer and he takes really good nude photos of me, very tasteful. My head is bent and I am facing the wall. I was amused by the fact that his hands were shaking so much that he could hardly set up his equipment. He is a lovely intelligent lad, with a muffled voice possibly due to sinus problems, who isn't particularly close to his parents. Obviously he broke off with his girlfriend for nothing because he doesn't get very far with me. We are on a boat sailing down the River Yarkon on a hot evening. I am wearing my Mary Quant checked purple dress which is like a long shirt. I make out a shape on the bank of the river which I immediately recognise as Simeon. I stand up and wave and order Ami to row the boat to the shore. Simeon greets me with open arms like a long lost friend. Whatever I say is met with a wide, smiling 'goddamn you'! He invites us into his house which he shares with his painter girlfriend who is probably about ten years older than me. She is nice, plump and her self-portraits are on the walls and litter the floor. They all chatter together in Hebrew. She loves her mum. She eyes me all over and says pointedly: 'And who is this young lady?' Simeon chuckles and replies that he met me in Paris. She stares at me and says nothing. When we leave Simeon comes out of the house and writes down my address.

 The next afternoon finds me sitting at a table at the Hilton Hotel in the company of my father. He was on a business trip in Cyprus and flew over to see me. I am wearing a black polyester dress with little sprigs of flowers and puffed sleeves. This seeing me involves him wretchedly talking about my mother and her therapy (she has the most expensive guy in London) and the fact that nothing he does has any effect and I can feel my head being whacked in the implicit suggestion that a daughter should be with her mother in order to take the load off his back. He fails to ask after my welfare. He sounds like a whining dog. He takes me out, in grim fashion, to buy a fancy waistcoat which is a patchwork affair recalling Joseph's coat of many colours. But it's a square, boxy design which feels like a straightjacket and I can't inhabit its brilliant purple and emerald green. Sadly, I never wear it; I feel dissociated from its lovely colours – I only see the boxy squares. Similarly, when he left my brother and I at the ghastly holiday camp ten years earlier, he presented us each with a small Japanese transistor radio, the latest thing. It was like being given a stone. I never listened to it. My heart was in my boots and I cried all night until they came to take me away. 'Judy can't rough it' is my mother's verdict. Any problem or difficulty is a matter of blame. She was also aware that I didn't want to go in the first place. It's Saturday lunchtime and before the cold meal my father hands us each a small piece of (chollah) bread sprinkled with salt. Salt is memory, its bitter tears. There is also the 'kiddush' wine, thick and sweet, which I love. I ask for another glass. My mother jokingly says that I should drink it before bedtime, to help me sleep. I am only ten and I can't sleep and I have my very own pill box in which I have inscribed my name, address and telephone number – HEN 0381.

Back at 1 Vitkin Street my aunt tells me that a man came to see me. She had no idea who it was. I have never been so disappointed in all my life because I could have spent the afternoon with Simeon, my fun friend, rather than with this father who was making me responsible for his marital relationship and metaphorically tying me to the wall. I write to my Harley St psychiatrist who writes me encouraging letters back but he also tells me that my depression could hold me forever, become a lifelong infirmity, if I don't take action, risks etc (which he knows I know). He also adds that most people lack courage and never break out of their tight little traps and will 'split their sides with envy' when others do.

I have a new job in the Hotel Sharon in Herzliya, (the inferior sister hotel to the 'Accadia' where we used to stay on family visits, which is not much better than the last. I am in a back room in front of a whiteboard where I have to keep a tally of rooms occupied and vacated. I'm not sure what I'm meant to be doing. How weak I am on the technical side of things! The manager of the hotel tells me that I am pretty when I smile so obviously he's taken note of my screwed-up frowning face. Paul McCartney sings 'It's Just Another Day' and this melancholy song speaks to me bigtime. His voice suits a sad theme. The weather gets hotter and the first of July approaches – the day when I start my Hebrew language course at Jerusalem University. My cousin, whose bedroom I share, has long been asking for her room back. She's a few years younger than me and my aunt tells me that her daughter is grateful for the fact that she can always talk to her mother. Everybody has experienced my mother's rudeness but nobody gives her a taste of her own medicine or puts themselves in her daughter's shoes. Ah, but this is how religion works – people only open their mouths in songs of praise and refuse to incriminate one of their own. What is sacred is time-honoured tradition and belonging to the club. Opt out and you may fall by the wayside.

I am assigned a run-down shack which I share with an Australian girl who seems quite a bit older than me. I don't really understand why she wants to settle in the land of Abraham, Isaac and Jacob. Is she fleeing persecution in Melbourne? I surprise her in her narrow single bed frolicking with her Arab boyfriend. She'd forgotten to lock the door. She, and others, are always asking me about my 'mishpucha' (family) and I arouse suspicion because I don't launch into a rhapsody of praise for mummy and daddy or talk of them with normal and natural heart-felt affection. I like the Hebrew teacher – Deborah – who tells us about her experience on the eve of the Six Day Way, getting more excited as she recalls her movements. The trouble is that the class is too advanced for me but I am too proud to enrol as a beginner. Of course there is no shame in being a beginner but there is in my world. If you are a beginner you are already a failure – making mistake after mistake. The golden rule is: 'Thou shalt not make a mistake because God is watching'. I come down in the world and join a new class but the teacher is no good – she gabbles galore and I can't keep up with her. I've had enough of this lark and drop-out. I get a job in a posh dress shop in west Jerusalem and pretend I can speak Hebrew when I can't. When someone comes into the shop I hide behind a rail of dresses. I soon leave and try to fill my time as best I can. I have a little Arabic coffee pot which is my sole comforting possession. There is an American girl on the canvas who resembles my mother and when I see her something comes over me and I am internally reaching out to her and filled with a truly terrible anguish. The dark-haired female turns away. One afternoon, prompted by I don't know what, I get the sensation of being buried alive and a voice is telling me that, logically, I'll never be able to rise to the surface. This is awful. I write to my London doctor in despair. But something else creeps in – a sense of nature and bright life that is stronger than or as strong as the other. I write again to my doctor assuring him that I am ok and that the crisis has passed. He is relieved. I survey the 'Via Dolorosa', Jesus's road to his execution and it is bathed in an atmosphere of peace and serenity. A basketball playing Palestinian student invites me to a Palestinian wedding where we eat rice with our fingers. He's nice, friendly, with no evil intent whatsoever.

I also meet a lovely blonde-haired Israeli guy who is arranging a tour of the land for a party of Norwegian students. He invites me to come on the tour free of charge, no doubt because he fancies me. To my everlasting shame I accept his kind, generous offer and then ignore him. I enjoy sleeping in the same room as the Norwegian girls; they are quiet, controlled, and rational. In unbelievable heat we traipse round the walls of Jericho and early in the morning climb the stronghold of Masada, walking in single file. There is a young guy whose girlfriend is quietly not feeling well. I sit next to him on the coach (on some other trip) and struggle to keep myself sitting upright. He looks at me and inclines his shoulder, allowing me to lean on him. No words are spoken. The Israeli with his thatch of blonde hair sits at the front of the coach and when he catches my eye appears a trifle perplexed and upset and maybe disgusted.

There is also a noisy American group – on some kind of course – who have taken over one of the residence buildings. I run into a young nineteen year old who looks so feminine in his hippy gear and thick long hair. He is the son of a film director and his mother was nineteen when he was born. He tells me that I am packed with power. Or does he mean anger? I arrive at the shack I share with the Australian girl and he is outside, sitting on the ground with a pile of velvet dresses that he bought for me in the old city market. I am not a small-boned Arab – I am a hump-backed Jewess – and I will never wear them. We lie together and then he wanders off. I write a poem about him comparing him to a bird and talk of desolation. I am left with warts in a private place and the kindly Jewish doctor on the campus heals them and, surprisingly, asks no questions and passes no judgement.

But this country is not for me – I feel that I'm being recruited into a Zionist programme. But It's an effort to magically disappear – to get to a travel agency to book a ticket back to London, city of my birth. Indeed I was born just up the road from Kings Cross Station, not on the street but in the Elizabeth Garrett Anderson Hospital, adjacent to the fire station. For some reason or other I make my way to Cromwell Road and get a dingy room in some small hotel. My father comes to see me, looks around and bids me return to his castle. It's as if he's been presented with the dog's dinner: 'How can you stay in a place like this?' he asks incredulously.

I find myself back In the parental abode. I protect my young brother from the bullying father. He suggests that I go into the typing pool at 'Conrad Ritblat' – a property company with whom he has ties. This suggestion strikes fear in my insides – it's as if he wants to put me into a cardboard box. But I know not what else to do and am not able to kick up a rumpus, protest my innocence … I dully go into the typing pool which is in the basement of some massive building block and the little plump friendly Australian supervisor is surprised by my bad typing but her tongue is tied because she's probably been advised that I am the daughter of the boss's friend. It's clearly an embarrassment for her – and for me too. The other typists are two happy-go-lucky Australian girls, Tweedledum and Tweedledee, who are always having a laugh with the supervisor and a poor overweight girl who suffers from bad asthma and whom I visit in her bedsit which is so messy it is as if the roof has fallen in. There is another young Australian who lives with her boyfriend. I read her one of my poems and when I've finished she looks at me straight in the face and says with real bewilderment: 'What are you doing here?

Did I leave home following the threatened murder of my father ('If you don't leave him alone I'll kill you', I screamed) because I am back in S.W.5 looking at adverts for rooms in the window of a confectioner/newsagent. (In the weeks to come the pallid-faced proprietor calmly observes me as I buy packet after packet of chewing gum, not to mention all manner of chocolate products from 'Munchies' to 'Twix' bars to Cadbury's 'Fruit and Nut.' I consume the lot, stuffing it all into my mouth as if my life depended on it and the end of the world was nigh.) I take up residence at 7 Warwick Road, in a large bedsitting room at the top of the house. The rent is £5 a week. A cohort of lorries rumbles past, day and night but I sleep ok, alone in the double bed, with its floral bedcover of huge red cabbage roses. I write poems, one – 'No Exit' – gets published in 'Poetry Quarterly', stuff myself with confectionery until I feel sick and find myself a job in a small hotel in Earls Court Square. It's a cosy place where I feel safe because nobody threatens to beat you up if you make a mistake. After a particularly bad bout of consuming a factory load of confectionery I get myself to the Tate Art Gallery where I experience something wholly spiritual in front of the Mark Rothko maroon and black paintings, the Seagram Murals. I don't know why I love them so much – is it the spiritual glow which is so soft and enveloping? Or is it because I can identify with walls of blood and tears …

Of course there are other people in the house but it seems as if I am the only person who uses the bathroom because it is always, thank goodness, spotlessly clean. There is a bony grim-looking German lady who leaves the house very early every morning. A very sweet fair-haired young man comes into my room to fix something electrical and I am surprised when I bump into him one evening by the front door dressed up in ladies clothing. He's off to the Boltons Pub opposite where I am taken by the New Zealander who has a small single room on my floor. It's a gay, raucous place and I am a bit out of place in my mauve, buttoned-up coat. One can quietly observe. The New Zealander collects old coins, works I can't remember where and tells me that he is screwing the landlady. He shows me photos of his girlfriend back in New Zealand with chocolate bars stuck up her vagina and we play ball across my bed. He's a bit weird. But it's no bad thing when he raps on my door in order to take me to the cheap and goodly restaurant where all the young people go in Earls Court. He knows I've been stuffing myself again and shakes his head in affectionate exasperation. One day he tells me that the previous evening he opened the front door to a man who was asking for me. He was taken by the fact that the man looked like Vespasian on his Roman coins (Vespasian was resurrected!) but none too pleased by the presence of this interloper. Racking my brains, for the life of me, I couldn't think who it could be? Who do I know who resembles Vespasian and why would he be calling on me on a dark autumnal evening?

Earls Court had the reputation of being inhabited by Australian dentists. I meet a tall, blonde haired Australian who persuades me to get involved in the world of selling 'Golden Products' – a range of biodegradable cleaning products which work wonders. I attend a Sunday afternoon indoor rally where the enthusiasm is sky high. How pleased these people are when they find a new recruit. On dark evenings I traipse round Earls Court knocking on doors with my bag of exemplar products. What is the fear that grips before one launches into the unknown? People aren't going to bite your head off, stab you in the back, or kick you in the teeth – they aren't going to string you up, a piece of meat, so that the blood slowly drips out or plunge you into burning oil or sink you down the deepest well; they aren't going to gouge out your eyes or tear out your entrails. They aren't going to whack your head so hard that your brains have spilled out over the pavement … The fear is the darkness of hate; hate attacks and crucifies whereas mankind, at his best, pursues light and healing, guided by grace. Save one soul and the whole world is saved. The desire to do good, to embrace and not to imprison, comes from a lighter, sweeter place. During the day I call on a lady housewife who resides in a smart square in S. Kensington. She cheerfully examines all the products and purchases something. She has a nice friendly manner and the torrent of abuse I am expecting never arrives. She doesn't accuse me of being overweight, selfish, hostile and lazy.

Indeed the chocolate and cake and soft roll consumption becomes so severe that I have to knock on the door of the fusty nurse who lives on the second floor. Was an ambulance called or did I make my own way to the S. Kensington hospital.

All this 'food' is putting pressure on my appendix. Somehow or other my father appears, demands entry and answers, and almost gets into fisticuffs with the Indian doctor who accuses him of being a racist. I am exulting in the effect of morphine on my poor old brain. This isn't the last time I end up in a hospital bed. I have a cyst on my wrist which, I decide, should be surgically removed. I want to know what it's like to be operated on, experience pain and discomfort and have no visitors. My masochist wish of wanting to endure and survive the worst, is granted. At a dinner party in Liverpool the following year a surgeon tells me that he could have simply squashed the cyst with his fist so the surgery was totally unnecessary.

Once again father steps in and we decide that I should retake History and French 'A' level at a crammers college in central London. My god, I only have six months to do a whole new History syllabus and study Camus' 'La Peste' and Sartre's 'Les Mains Sales' for French literature. It is my twenty-first birthday and I walk up Oxford Street. I espy my brother's best mate from University walking along laughingly with a gentile girl. My father takes me to Burlington Arcade in Piccadilly where we purchase a roll neck double knit cable cashmere jumper in dark blue. It is the best quality, the best of the bestest, guaranteed to keep you warm through January and February. Not a word is exchanged between us. I commence the course and work hard. I love studying history. But I still have the weekends to conquer. I take to frequenting the South Kensington public library where there are a lot of Indian men studying hard. I notice an eye-catching advertisement, sporting a blue and black drawing of a peacock, asking for helpers for the Kensington and Chelsea Arts Festival. It sounds interesting and I could be a helper. I make my way to the end of Earls Court Road and ring the doorbell of a grey gloomy looking building. Finally it is opened by a young guy who has long fair hair and is wearing tight rose pink jeans and a grey roll-neck jumper. He has a big bright smile on his face and he invites me up. I feel that I've met a pop star. He is single-handedly managing this festival, getting it on the road, so to speak. He designed the peacock poster – a tribute to the strutting peacocks in Holland Park. He hates the toffs of Kensington, especially Lady what's her name who also has a role in running the show. He curses her behind her back but is perfectly affable in her presence, although not afraid to question her suggestions. He is twenty five and grew up in the East End. He tells me of the boring years he spent in the building trade and running this festival was his ticket out. He is married to Pauline, who is two years his senior and works for the organisation which offers free legal advice to people who can't afford a solicitor. They live in a ground floor flat somewhere in North Kensington which they have painted white. He has known her since he was fourteen and shows me his motorbike photos of his motorbike days.

My job is to try to get local shops and outlets to put a poster up in their windows. I go everywhere I can, from the small local supermarket to the shop run by Indians or Pakistanis selling Turkish carpets. I like trespassing on foreign premises and disturbing people who, in their rightful positions, are calmly getting on with their jobs. I do my best to sell the poster and most are generally happy to display it to passersby. Sometime after I stumbled on 'Golden Products' I had a job selling Afghan jackets in the stifling indoor Kensington Market – stifling on account of being almost buried in a sea of wool lined Afghan coats – just the thing if you live in the mountains. As Sigmund Freud wisely said: 'There is never the wrong weather, only the wrong clothes'. The Afghan boss was always in and out, talking to nobody, unloading more and more stuff. I know nothing of the 'hippy trail' and couldn't be less like a hippy as I stand in the stuffy booth, never speaking, let alone making a sale. God knows why he hired me. He looks at me askance; it is hardly registering that I am totally useless in my job. My workmate is a buxom attractive long-haired blonde who seems more active and engaged. We never exchange a word.

Chris is pleased with the way I am getting the posters up. When he is not organising the festival – there is a lot to do but he is the easy-going type of person who leaves everything to the last minute but for some strange reason doesn't get overwhelmed – he is telling me about his fondness for literature and poetry. I remind him of 'Miriam' in 'Sons and Lovers' but he tells me later that he is bewildered as to whether I am rich or poor or what? I wear my red plaid pinafore dress with its belt that struggles at the waist. I also have a navy blue affair, flared from the high bodice which is too short for words, revealing my long legs in all their shapely glory. How would Jane Austen have seen it? In shame and disgust, eyes open wide with shock, she would have turned away and contacted the 'loony bin' where I would have been disposed of safely. Jane Austen didn't care to walk on the wide side. The electric kettle lives on the floor of the large but dismal office space – it is always the curtains that are a giveaway; these are grey/blue and have absorbed the dust and discolouration of decades – and as I bend over to take it into the kitchen he glimpses my frilly knickers which, he later tells me, amused him. He also tells me that I struck him initially as a 'dim kid' from the suburbs. He has an inkling of the fact that I am 'so wise for a twenty one year old' and so peculiarly passive and dependent. (There's a handle on a door; use it – it won't attack you). As he talks of his taste in literature – he even won a prize for a poem – I am looking at him with desire and longing – probably wanting him to get away from his plain old bossy wife who works at the N. Kensington legal centre. I hate wives and the hold they have over their husbands. Kissing me he feels guilty but I have no qualms at all, no sense that I'm misbehaving. Unlike his wife I can appreciate his love of D.H. Lawrence.

On a Sunday afternoon he calls me at 7 Warwick Road – there is a communal phone in the hallway and you receive a knock on your door if it's for you – and picks me up in his blue van. We sit in a 'Wimpy' Bar somewhere near the river and the waitress realises that we are in love. Look at the way they are gazing into each other's eyes – maybe his big blue eyes are gazing more. Is wifey doing the housework or is she out with her friends? (She doesn't know about my existence that's for sure and when she does a tsunami descends). He visits me in my bed sitting room which, for him, symbolises freedom. But I don't just represent something he aspires to, he loves me and when I am out in the dark buying confectionery he tries to follow me, to find me, to prevent me from 'eating my heart out'. He writes me letters, witty and funny 'there are no lies only liars' and tells me that I am not used to having anyone care about me but he does. I genuinely don't understand the language of care and softness. He's an exciting guy – with socialist principles, of course. We happen to bump into my teenage trendy young brother in Oxford Street and he's surprised that he's nice and doesn't seem to wear the devil's horns of those who grab all and refuse to let others get a slice of the cake. My trusted messiah of a psychiatrist (although I don't see him in a professional capacity and indeed he has never charged me a penny) seems genuinely excited about my new relationship and comments on the marvel of wanting to be part of the other but as time goes on he shakes his head: 'If he was going to leave his wife he would have done so by now'. Chris writes me a melancholy poem which I show my beloved saviour doctor. The last line refers to Mother who is 'always there hiding in the dark', and it is this, indeed, which prevents him from breaking with the past.

One late afternoon we are in the office – definitely not hard at work – when Pauline, his wife bursts in out of the blue. I had already met her at the launch of the exhibition at the Kensington and Chelsea town hall where the grey-haired, middle-aged mayor or MP or whoever he was had taken a shine to me. It was April and I was wearing a caged-canary yellow dress, with its brooch of shiny red cherries and orangey-red clog like shoes which got me from Kensington High Street to 7 Warwick Road with great difficulty. She, a small, plain woman aged twenty seven (which I regard as ancient, over the hill – almost distasteful) with anxious, beseeching dark eyes didn't flaunt herself but kept quietly in the background, protective of her husband. She later told Chris to beware of Jewish girls. She too had a Jewish father, one who had died or disappeared and a goodly Christian mother who carried the can and who taught her how to cook and run a home.

Chris is obviously discomforted by her presence in the office but carries on casually as per normal. He is as casual and easy-going as my father isn't. (Apparently they have a date to see Tom and Jerry cartoons at the local cinema in North Kensington. I think that we too had some sort of date – in my bed at 7 Warwick Road. She is speaking fast in a falsely animated manner. I am glaring at Chris, willing him to say something but he has the look of a frightened child, scared to jump off the diving board. Deep waters beckon. Things reach a climax as she, full of false gaiety, tries to drag him out of the office, totally turning her back on me. Possessive wives enrage me. I too exist and want a bite of the apple. Something has to give and either he or I come out with the fact that we are sleeping together. It's as if she breathes a great sigh of relief saying that everyone in her office knew that he had someone else on account of her description of his behaviour at home over the last few weeks or months. But he had everything at home that he needed and they'd done everything together. (I found it hard to believe that he was still performing his duties in bed – 'how could he?')

Did they or did they not see the cartoons at the cinema? I probably walked back home alone, buying, as always, a packet of nuts and raisins from the 'off licence' en route always hoping against hope that there would be more than one tasty Brazil nut in the mix. (This packet of nuts often served as my supper although I had taught myself to make a proper sauce from Katharine's Whitehorn's paperback 'Cooking in a Bedsitter'). I knew that they were bound together. He'd indeed said that if he was ill he knew that she'd always be there, at his bedside. I listen and remember but can't comprehend all this talk about sickness and dying and bedside vigils. Where I come from you drop dead in the street, if needs be. Or rather you don't drop dead or even faint into someone's arms (there are no embracing arms) – you exercise your will and carry on. Not to do so is to be utterly useless, totally weak. 'I am Spartacus!' is the cry that is needed. In Paris I had been to see 'Lawrence of Arabia' with Tom and was so inspired that I wanted to walk amongst the cars, in the middle of the road, proclaiming that this individualistic destiny was the rightful one for man.

Pauline becomes a bit difficult and annoying with her 'volte face' attitude. She tells me that I'm welcome to him since she's had enough of picking up his discarded underwear. The one and only time he stays the night – he was a bit worried about this and I too had my reservations since daily visits were more exciting and romantic but you have to try things out – things get out of hand when she arrives at around midnight and rings every bell in the house and finally arrives outside my room and bangs on the door, shouting and screaming that I've stolen her husband and that she's just a little sparrow … Chris is wide-eyed with terror – this isn't the guy who is so laid back and competent in the office dealing with all the participants in the festival and who tells me that I should learn to take it easy and go with the flow … Yes, indeed when the truth came out before the 'Tom and Jerry' adventure he sat on a chair crying his eyes out. Oh dear, this relationship is going nowhere. At a screening of a Bergman film, which is part of the festival, I meet a group of travellers – an Iranian student, an Australian art teacher and a fair-haired girl of no fixed origin – who want me to drive with them to Italy. Who would turn down a chance to visit Florence and see Michelangelo's heroic statues? Chris is mortified and is crying once again because, deep down, he'd love to come with … he despairs of simply being able to be himself. My new friends mock him. I now have a small-wheeled bicycle and he and Pauline follow suit. I chain my cycle to the railings on the opposite side of the road – there is no notice saying that this is forbidden – and whilst I am off on my merry way – an attendant approaches with his little black notebook. Chris is watching from the window and sends me a very funny letter describing the scene. He's drawn himself as a Beano character with tears streaming down his face.

Busy with the festival I decide not to sit my 'A' level history exam although I'd completed the syllabus, done all the work. This is a mad act of defiance. I take the French exam however and gain a grade 'B' which is a vast improvement on my sad 'O' level pass. This was obviously the result of living in Paris and having sweet nothings whispered in my ear by my attractive Yugoslav boyfriend. So what is my next move? Through the clearing scheme I get a place at Liverpool University to read Philosophy. 'Why do you want to go all the way up there?' says my saviour doctor friend, scornfully. I expect the north of England is some kind of no man's land.

Between gigs so to speak I stay at my brother's depressing flat in Kilburn which he shares with a fellow law student and an economics journalist. The latter (the guy I saw sauntering along Oxford Street, happily ensconced with his blonde and bonny gentile girlfriend) asks me why I always wear the same old brown dress. I also store some of my stuff with him. Maybe or maybe not he sees me onto the coach going north but he certainly rebukes me for opening my purse so wide so that everyone can see what I've got inside. It's a long journey and in my milk chocolate brown dress I feel quite lonely.

'Salisbury Hall' where I get to reside is a female residence in leafy Upper Mosley Road, on the outskirts of Liverpool; there are two male halls which are predominantly filled with northern guys studying either mechanical or electrical engineering. A bus ferries them into the university every morning; they are off to work. As I am settling into my pleasantly functional room there is a loud knock at my door. Who can that possibly be? It was Caroline Berwick from Northampton who looked at the list of people studying philosophy and since I was one of only a few girls on the course, sought me out. She was my sort of person and I admired her initiative. She seemed to be someone with a mind of her own. She borrowed my long patchwork skirt – a lovely creation – and told me that I'd look good in anything. That's the kind of friend you want. She also thought that I was mentally very split. After some months she left the course and joined an Indian ashram but it didn't seem as if she had found her place in spite of the long loose kaftan and the prayer beads.

I am sitting at the light wooden desk in my room when, out of the window, I see a slightly built boy with very fair hair crossing the courtyard. He is wearing sandals, jeans and a navy blue raincoat and is carrying a musical instrument – in its case, of course. There goes an angel and I call out to him or rather I rush down the stairs and greet him as he goes by. I ask him up to my room and he accepts the invitation. Maybe he was too scared to say no since I was soon to be twenty two – a woman of the world – and he was two years my junior – a kid not long out of boarding school although he'd spent some time in the Shetland Islands as well as working in a metals factory. His age rankles. I introduce him to Oscar Wilde and Dostoyevsky; surely this can't be classed as the corruption of a minor? (My father was outraged when I sent my younger brother a copy of 'The Blind Owl' by Hedayat, a newly emerged Persian writer whom my doctor friend had told me to read). A fat girl with plaits whose favourite dish was black pudding reported Ian to the authorities on the grounds that he was a male interloper in a female Hall of Residence. But I don't remember a night when I wasn't sleeping in the arms of my angel or an evening when he wasn't in my room testing me on my Italian (a very rigorous one year course taught by Dr. Calma, a Jewish refugee from Trieste who told me that she rose every day at 4am to study and her joy at discovering that we were of the same race was immense and I was invited to the 'fellow's restaurant' for lunch ...) Three times a week we are drilled on our grammar exercises; this well-dressed woman looks down on us from the heights of her self-discipline and stability. When the spotlight falls on me, when it's my turn to speak she says, in response to my terrified visage: 'You look as if I'm going to eat you ...' Making a mistake doesn't result in a gun placed to your head.

Unlike the 'mech. eng.' lads Ian and I walked the three miles to the University Campus every morning. Girls would ask him whether his feet got cold in sandals. My doctor friend, to whom I wrote, and visited occasionally, taking the train from Lime Street to London and then the underground to 'Royal Oak' where his day clinic was situated, told me that Ian was far more relaxed than me (hence the sandals) and the relationship wouldn't last because he didn't have a strong enough personality. Oh I wish my Messiah had advised me differently! There was always something wrong with everyone and maybe he was right. When you are twenty one the sea is packed with all manner of fish and the possibility that you'll end up going hungry doesn't exist. And how can you be anything other than young? In the Rodin Museum, in Paris, I looked at a sculpture of an old woman and the caption read: 'Once I was Beautiful'. She looked as if she'd been through the wringer.

Ian is reading Physics but never attends his lectures. There is a pretty dismal basement cafe in one of the university buildings where he hangs out with other nineteen year olds who are trying to be cool but seem like schoolboys. One young bearded guy, however, was kind. For some reason he put his arm around me. I must have been intensely worried about something or other. Ian always sits quietly, doing his 'roll-ups'. He too is a kind person for whom looking after others is natural and normal. He too, like Tom in Paris, sits with a girl who is having a rough night due to a drug overdose. He also sits quietly in my room reading 'The Picture of Dorian Grey' and 'The Possessed'. He is very skilled on his trumpet and flugelhorn and these are his sole possessions. I meet his family when we go to the '100 Club' in Oxford Street where he has a gig. His five brothers and sisters are not in attendance – indeed his elder sister Jonquil, a painter, lives in a caravan, with her partner, somewhere in Australia but his proud mum Sylvia is there with her extrovert engineer husband. Ian tells me that he worked in Saudi Arabia for many years installing freezers/air conditioning and ran up massive debts. He was also in the R.A.F. which is how he, Ian, came to be in boarding school in Germany.

It is the Christmas break and everybody goes home for the holidays except for the foreign students who can't. I am due to stay with Ian and his family in Nutkins Way, Chesham. One evening I am sitting in my room and a young Nigerian knocks on my door. He has a big smile on his face and is looking for some company. I couldn't have been more amazed since I never would have expected a visit in my solitary cave. But the true amazement is the fact that he isn't ashamed of wanting to be human. My brothers and I lived under the same roof and were marooned in our separate bedrooms. We emerged at 9pm to watch the News. Our parents were OUT. Once in a while my elder brother and I would play pontoon and try to laugh.

When I get off the train Ian is standing on the platform waiting for me and this feels like manna from heaven. I get to meet all his siblings. His eight year old brother Leon, skinny as hell, tells me that I am fat. Ian's parents see the same image but, of course, say nothing. I am so because I am still stuck in my habit of consuming a ton of confectionery whenever I am grabbed by anxiety. His mother, a smoker, takes away my long skirt and returns it, beautifully ironed. She likes to talk to me in the kitchen. She tells me how proud she was of Ian, when, as a little boy, he phoned for the ambulance when she was in labour with one of the children. Another was born at home and his dad called him to witness 'the miraculous happening' but he wasn't interested. I can see that she is aware that I have had far more worldly experience than her beloved son. She is pretty and gentle. Ian is very fond of Stacey, his younger sister with the green eyes, who is peeved at having to share a room with the boys. They put a screen around her bed to give her some privacy. Ian is tickled by the Siamese cat who sits up straight with her head under a lampshade. For us some sort of sofa bed has been set up in the lounge. Skinny Leon is curious about us sleeping there but Kirk, with his chipped front tooth, and fourteen year old Lucy who gets up early to do a paper round and resents her folks because they don't have more money to give her, couldn't be more casual as regards my presence. It's a big treat for all when prawns are taken out of the freezer. Ian and I love being in bed together. He tells me to offer to take his parents to the pub and buy them a drink – a gesture of gratitude which would never have occurred to me.

I have to make a duty visit to my parents' house in Foscote Road, Hendon. He sits in his mushroom coloured velvet chair; she sits on the mushroomy sofa – it's a lovely three piece suite actually. Pride of place belongs to the TV set. But the main thing is that they don't speak, let alone do anything. He does his stamps on a Sunday afternoon. Do I detect a look of painful rejection because I have chosen Ian's family over them? This is how it is. No one even looks at anyone else let alone expresses anything in the way of sympathy or kindness.

She, mother, never stops telling us, everybody, about how she had to do all the chores and there were no new clothes (although her mother did make her a gymslip on the sewing machine) and no hot meal on the table in the evening whilst he just whacks the ball even harder never mentioning anything about his childhood other than his parents were on tenterhooks on the eve of the budget in case the price of beer went up by a ha'penny and he didn't like being called on to support his mother in money arguments within the extended family after his father's death. Resentment towards family members seems to last a lifetime. They grind away in the stomach.

The problem is that, in spite of their external sessions with expensive therapists, more so her than him – although he does a two year stint in his early fifties when his mother's passing enables him to get a girlfriend – be with someone who admires him – although this is accompanied by guilt – no one really cares about the other or is carrying their own cross. Better to live in shit together than to be alone. Sylvia told me that in her home county of Yorkshire she had to get on her bike and look for work. There was no option. Poor Shylock sees no option other than that of clutching his bag of shekels. What else can you do in a cruel world that treats people like chattels?

It's the second of January and no one wants to return to work. Furthermore winter has kicked in with a vengeance. One has no choice but to 'get on with it'. Ian is threatened with expulsion if he doesn't attend his Physics lectures. He starts to spend hours in his own bedroom, not reading Dostoyevsky, but working on long abstract equations and says that he's actually enjoying it. I am a bit surprised. In the cafe I see him chatting animatedly with a fellow female Physics student – she has long hair – and is also barefoot and I experience the bitter pang of jealousy. They are enjoying each other's company and I am excluded. However, I am unresponsive when, arriving back late after a trip to London to see my Messiah, he rushes into my room truly anxious as to what had happened to me. On another occasion he also asks me why I am so aggressive and, in response, I shrug. Bewildered, he seeks out a book on Jewish history.

Nevertheless, we decide to move into a flat together – we love to share a bottle of German Riesling wine (a great adventure since in my family there was no wine) as we make the three mile trek back to the Hall of Residence from the University and view some grotty options. I must have informed my parents of this decision because Salisbury Hall received a telephone call that beat all others. On account of my desire to be with Ian and he with me all hell is let loose. My mother is screaming down the phone at me and she also has a go at Ian telling him that he should leave Jewish girls alone – this is the primary thrust of her argument. She won't let go and the switchboard is jammed the whole evening. All the other students are witness to her rage and, when the storm has passed, tell me that they pity someone like that. Her 'outburst' comes as no surprise or shock to me; when my father's brother 'married out' she crucified the poor gentile woman from Rutlandshire who was a dancer at the London Palladium. Margaret was thin, bird-like, raven-haired, and in spite of her nervous apprehension as regards meeting her husband's family she was totally unprepared for the tsunami that came her way. (Years later they spoke together on the phone – commiserating with each other about their husbands' lack of affection. But she, unlike her sister-in-law, sought out new, more fertile pastures). In the end Ian and I decide not to leave the conventional safety of Salisbury Hall. Maybe climbing the wall of hate was too much trouble. My father visits and he and Ian discuss music in his room. (My mother mocks her husband's love of classical music and his stack of LPs are never played). He always seems to enjoy talking to my boyfriends – he is more comfortable with males – other than David, the Israeli paratrooper. This was presumably because the former barred the latter from staying in his house. After my father's visit Ian says, with some conviction, that the difference between his father and mine is that the former puts his family first.

In the Easter vacation there is a conference of psychologists who take over the residence and Ian and I are somehow drawn into their orbit. Suddenly, in the midst of conversation, Ian abruptly leaves the room. What is his problem? What's he running away from? One of the psychologists nearly bends over backwards to get me to share his bed for the night. I decline but am impressed by his insistence and his rationale. He makes me feel that I ought to do what he wills, that only good can come of it and that all repression is harmful. I am beginning to revise for the exams although I am certain that I'm not going to pass the logic paper with its 'Boolean Algebra.' In the lectures I am the only girl surrounded by calm guys who don't seem to have any problem following the stuff on the whiteboard. It's as they're tackling a DIY manual in which everything falls into its rightful place. I enjoy Bertrand Russell's 'Problems of Philosophy' and take to his dictum that there are those who prefer the world of mind, abstraction, pure being and those who go for the active world of sense impressions. Even so, I don't know if I can stand another year of dull professors and useless essays. I pass a note to a fellow student asking them if they want the humanities or the realities. At the end of the autumn term, I espy the logic lecturer, a young guy, on the train to London and I approach him and tell him that I can't do the work. He tells me not to worry so much and concentrate on enjoying my Christmas Pudding. For Italian there is a lot of revision – but I love the major medieval players of Italian literature – Dante, Petrarch and Boccaccio. But what to do next? I am tired of the fact that Ian is my junior. I tell Dr. Calma that I intend to go to Rome, look up the Italian nanny who loved me when I was a baby, and get a job. She is concerned and obviously thinks that I am mad. I AM mad.

She phones me up at the Hall of Residence to tell me how I did in the exam. I am 'quite clever' (not as clever as she'd like me to be, unlike her own daughter) but my result was somewhere between a 2.2 and a 2.1 which was better than I expected on account of all the grammar we had to master. Then it was time to look at the Philosophy notice board where all those who had passed had their names written up. I expected not to be inscribed in the book of virtue, the list of the living, but there I was, my name spelt out in black and white. Must be a mistake but obviously not. Perversely this outcome cements my desire to break free of the institution and fly to Rome. I can leave on a high of pride rather than a low of shame. I make the necessary arrangements and disappear without a trace, leaving Ian to face his heartbreak. Is this hideous selfishness a gene that I have inherited or am I such a mess that I don't know what I am doing, lost and desperate and vainly seeking some sort of escapist 'high'? My brother in N.W. London is ok; he's firmly entrenched in his legal world. I, in spite of my forceful personality, am pretty toothless and fancy-free – you can't exactly get through life on a chocolate bar and a flowery bikini. How are the fallen raised? How do the damned receive the gift of grace? How do the iron bars of self-imprisonment, leading to rage and blame give way to cool mountain pastures and cacti flowering vividly in the desert? How do I get rid of a sense, in the forefront of my mind, that an almighty massive lorry is going to crash into me?

At Fiumincino airport my black patent vanity case is stolen. I only put it down for a minute but probably it wasn't tucked securely between my legs. I stay, in a poor part of Rome, with Bruna, the devoted nanny of my first year of life who told me that I was kind and considerate and that she only stayed in that house because of me, a one year old. The faces of my parents were grim, when they emerged from their bedroom in the morning. 'It was clear' she said, 'that something wasn't going well'. My mother's young sister also observed that something was amiss, when she stayed with them, because 'newlyweds were supposed to be hugging and kissing one another'. When my mother introduced her 'intended' to her own mother the latter commented: 'Well, you can always find a lover'. (Of her own life she apparently said: 'My nights are heaven and my days are hell'). But if he couldn't dance, neither could she. Nor did she have any time for pity. Bruna sits on my bed, gazing at me devotedly, and I find this spooky. We buy delicious little green pears in the market and go down to the beach joined by a pretty dark-haired thin neighbour who is about fifteen and lets her body lead the way; she is free, she doesn't belong to anybody and she is perfectly entitled to ignore me.

I have telephoned my mamma who is going to send me the things on my list – mainly replacement items of eye make-up – dark unguents which turn me into a queen – and luscious lipsticks. The stuff will be sent to the Rothschild's Bank in Rome where my father's business partner works. Such are the communiques that I end up, a lunch guest of his wife, in their luxury flat in EUR, an ex-fascist megalith, on the outskirts of Rome. The cheeses and ham are divinely fresh and tasty and we are served by Paula, the thirty five year old servant, who looks ten years older. She 'takes in' my low cut improper heart-shaped red dress with the cup sleeves and assumes her humble role of serving the 'great and the good'. La Signora buys clothes for Paula's little girl and looks after her as an employer should. This decisive woman is delighted with me and tells me that I must stay with them. She apologises for the fact that I'll be next door to her mother-in-law, in an un-air-conditioned room. This poor old woman is kept out of sight. It's a mystery as to why I am in the poor part of town. La Signora is obviously brainy and she was educated and grew up in Cairo. She married her university lecturer husband and moved to Rome. She speaks Italian fluently with some panache and her children all attend the International School; the youngest 'not as clever as the others' listens to jazz all day now that it's the holidays. He tells me that after a hard day in class he loves to collapse onto the royal blue satin sofa in the 'reception' room. The daughter, who is about my age, is a journalist for an important newspaper and lives with her boyfriend. Henry, about eighteen months my junior, is at Sussex University studying Economics, and is shortly to return home. She tells me, reflectively, that he is 'quite handsome' I overhear the father, not often around, tell his son over the phone that I am a cross between Brigitte Bardot and Gina Lollobrigida. Well, as my mother said, 'she has lovely limbs and you want to take bites out of her'.

I don't take much notice of my new neighbour. The mother-in-law is an old lady with a straggly grey bun and flat breasts which hang above her old grey dress as she shuffles into the kitchen to make herself a hot drink and a bit of something to eat. (Henry tells me that, once upon a time, she used to eat with them and he doesn't like the fact that she is hidden away and disregarded) She stays in the backroom because she doesn't match the royal blue satin three piece suite and the kingly carpets However, of an afternoon she totters over to the phone and speaks to her other son who is in a mental home. I don't know what she says but there's no mistaking the tone of passionate love and devotion. What would she do without him? I am looking at art books and the youngest son, Jean-Simon, is listening to his jazz, rocking forwards and backwards in time with the music.

The stuff that I ordered arrives pretty quickly and Mrs Ergas is imbued with maternal solidarity – 'look at what mothers will do for their children' is writ on her countenance and it's clear that she'd love to meet her London counterpart, so to speak. Henry fills me in on the inside story, telling me that it was she, not their father, who sorted out their schooling and everything else for that matter – including a new car which he drives somewhat haphazardly, to say the least, through the open thoroughfares of Rome, around the Coliseum, but Mrs Ergas, sitting in the back is as cool and calm as a cucumber and has full confidence in his abilities.

When he bursts into the flat on his arrival back from Sussex I can tell that he is curious about the guest but he's not particularly impressed; me neither since he has just turned twenty and I am twenty one and a half. He is 'quite' good-looking as his mother intimated. Every day he sits at the desk in the living-room, the side that is removed from the vast royal blue satin sofa entertaining space, and writes left-handedly in some exercise book. He's working on his dissertation. He never looks up or changes his expression. He's certainly not composing music or writing poetry. It's common knowledge that he was involved with some female at Sussex whom they nicknamed Rosa Luxembourg on account of her strong socialist views and forceful personality. Everything about her was big and challenging. When his friend Matthew comes to stay he never stops baiting Henry about her, and chuckling. In comparison, I am a sad non-political person and probably not as attractive as he was led to believe. Why aren't I continuing with my degree and do I know absolutely nothing about business and politics and the way the world works? It seems as if this is what is passing through his mind. Obviously his mother likes me. I am company for her because her husband is often away and, as Mrs Ergas tells me, he had a mistress to whom she paid a visit asking for her husband back. She also tells me that I would have made a marvellous courtesan. Homely queries about my mother such as 'does she use the dishwasher even when there are no guests for dinner?' fall on a somewhat deaf ear which leave her a bit puzzled.

But I manage to get Henry to kiss me which is a prelude to our friendship. He doesn't seem to rate his sister too highly. She has nicknamed me 'the savage' and when we are out in town on a hot summer's evening, walking around, I tell her that I am a noble savage. She doesn't reply. She and her fat friend are rambling on about Marcello the well-known Roman journalist whose face was blown to bits in the Golan Heights. They don't believe me when it transpires that it was he whom I knew personally in his tight black floque shirt at the lovely Sheraton Hotel in Tel Aviv. The evidence is such that they can't disbelieve me. Mr Ergas is very proud of his daughter and the fact that she has a column in the newspaper. She also has been seeing a therapist, according to Henry. He disapproves of her messy flat – far too many clothes strewn everywhere. Jean-Simon, whose name his mother always calls out fondly, lyrically, when she returns home, is utterly amazed by my passivity on account of the fact that, forgetting the key, I sit outside the front door all day, (or for some hours at least) like a dog. 'Couldn't you have at least contacted a neighbour?' he asks, dumbfounded. This is all the conversation that passes between us. He looks at me with a degree of displeasure no doubt wondering why my stay is so extended and what my function is. I am the alien cuckoo chick who has landed in their nest.

One evening I accompany Mrs Ergas to see an open air spectacle of Flamenco dancing. It is great as Flamenco dancing always is. She says to me: 'it comes right from their guts'. She has a tame looking doctor friend who visits and she takes pains to introduce me in a grand tone – actually a tone of respect – and tells him, positively, that my Italian is really coming on – as if to bring me out of the shadows. Later, we sit down and have a little talk and she reckons that I should be making the best of 'this beautiful country' and could attend the language school in Perugia. Suddenly her mood changes and with an angry inquisitorial stab asks me if I'm frightened of my father, no doubt referring to commands and demands. I am puzzled. In her small bedroom I see a photo of her own father and when I ask her about him she is enraged by the intrusion. (A look of exasperation crosses her face when she goes round her sons' shared bedroom collecting used underpants for the washing-machine). In her bathroom a full array of scientific tools are laid out on a white cloth. God knows what they are for; I can only identify eyebrow tweezers and nail scissors. Apparently she is an insomniac but this doesn't seem to worry her or affect her unduly. (I sleep the sleep of the blessed; as of yet have no inkling of what it is to lie awake all night like a boat abandoned at sea, pounded by grey, angry waves). She has decided that I am very moral – presumably because I didn't want Paula to wash my clothes and because I am always writing in my little book. Paula tells me how hot and tired she is and when she accidentally rests the iron on the front of Mr. Ergas's smart beige suit jacket she is terrified by what she has done and what will happen. I comfort her – making light of the situation. She can confide in me because I am someone who is troubled and to whom she repeatedly counsels 'patienza'. The thing is that no one knows whether I am 'rich or poor'. Mrs Ergas comments that my lovely bolero tops – one pink and the other salmon orange – sent by my mother are suitable for the beach, not for city life. Indeed I love going into Rome and hanging out in the 'Campo dei Fiori' with its open market, its free flow of people and its atmosphere of past adventures. Mrs Ergas drives past the 'Spanish Steps' a beautiful spot – the poet John Keats resided at a house near the top – and there are a crowd of hippies massed together on the bottom steps. Says Mrs Ergas with cold anger in her voice: 'Why don't they clear them away?' I write to the Messiah about her and he replies that she sounds like his wife; plenty of brain but not much heart. 'However, it's good to have someone intellectual to talk to' he says. But how can she have 'little heart' if she tolerates me in her house? Every morning Paula brings up fresh cheese, bread and ham from the grocery below which I avidly consume. But what gets her goat is the sight of a used coffee cup left on the carpet and she also wonders why I need so many hot drinks. When I first moved in my 'godfather' wrote to me that I had certainly fallen on my feet; as time passed he wrote that I shouldn't be in such a place, so totally removed from ordinary life.

My father is coming to Rome, no doubt for a business meeting with Mr. Ergas, but he will also see me. La Signora Ergas seems rather nervous about meeting him and wonders where we should take him. I wonder why she is nervous. She thinks that he'll be a big, important blustery fellow like her husband who will blow her away with his power and authority. In the event she is disappointed. He isn't particularly tall and he is shy. Actually I don't remember him uttering a word; he obviously had other things on his mind. He habitually looks worried. He doesn't know what to do about his indecisive wife who never knows what to wear. Mrs Ergas is all kitted out in navy blue and very pleased with her outfit. 'Now, I'm dressed', she says. She had taken me to a shop near the beautiful 'Spanish Steps' and asked me to help her choose between a long lacey dress which was made in both cream and white (she's preparing for a trip to Venice with some friends, staying at the famous 'Gritti Palace'). She changes from one dress into the other, without getting stressed. It's a boring scenario but I put pressure on myself to weigh up the non-existent pros and cons between the cream and the white. She's not really listening to me but magically floating on air as she envisages her forthcoming stay at the exquisite hotel in the company of her lovely friends.

Money is provided to enable Henry, myself and his friend from University to go to Florence for a few days. Or maybe I paid for myself. I get angry with Henry because he is immersed in the newspaper rather than looking around him. He is impressed by my enthusiastic love of art and genuinely wonders why I'm not reading Literature at University. In those days 'History of Art' wasn't studied much at University but I obviously have a passion for paintings and books. His friend Matthew, also a bright economics student, tries to keep Henry to himself. He ignores me entirely and makes lots of hearty jokes about 'Rosa Luxembourg'. In the flat he had played chess with Henry's father who enjoyed the presence of another male. I am seen as pretty dim and non-intellectual. They all wonder what I am doing and things are approaching a climax, necessitating my departure.

Mrs Ergas is pleased because her husband is around more than usual. He takes the whole family out to dinner to an open air restaurant in Trastevere, a trendy part of Rome, attractively old and atmospheric. We are served with delightful Italian specialities – lots of eggs, artichokes, red peppers and olives – and the ladies are each individually presented with a rose. Mrs Ergas seems to be revelling in the occasion. Mr Ergas, with a big personality, rules the roost. He is so proud of his daughter and likes her quiet, bespectacled, intelligent boyfriend. It's all smooth sailing. Mr and Mrs return to the flat leaving the youngsters to enjoy themselves in town. Maybe Mr Ergas generously handed out a wadful of lira to fuel our revels.

I don't remember any revels – we probably just wandered around aimlessly. But sometime after midnight Henry is in my non air-conditioned room, in my bed and we are enjoying one another's company. We are friends – that's for sure. Henry has told me that he is frightened of his mother and her tight holding of the reins but she, he reiterates, not his father, has been involved in making sure that they get the best education. She herself told me that she doesn't mind what they do afterwards so long as they get their degrees. My mother's ambition for me was a secretarial course at some suburban north London college rather than 'stupid 'A' levels' which don't bring in a weekly wage. But I don't disclose my sordid past – in fact I'm just living from day to day – eating bread I haven't earned and writing in my little notebooks. Suddenly there is a soft knock on the door and the door opens followed by a short gasp as it ever so quietly closes again. It's a 'Jesus Christ' 'Oh my God what happens now' moment. Henry is very calm (maybe he is secretly pleased to be caught 'on the wild side' by his mother) but I am very perturbed as regards facing her at breakfast in the morning.

Morning always comes and I have to make my entrance. Mrs Ergas is beaming at me, cool as a cucumber. She'd wanted Henry to be in love with me but he has assured her that he isn't. Was she envisaging a prosperous match between the big markets of London and Rome? It seems though that the prevailing opinion is that it's time for me to go. As I get ready to leave the old grandmother says to me, in Italian: 'I'll miss you – you were company for me.' Perhaps she just liked it that there was someone in the next room and our paths crossed in the kitchen when she was rummaging in the fridge and I was making my milky instant coffee. Whenever I entered the flat her call of 'chi es?' (who is it) would voice itself drearily. She never went out.

I take up residence in a cheap, not very nice hotel somewhere in central Rome. I must have contacted Bruna, my old nanny, because together we are perusing the newspaper looking for a job. (Mrs Ergas came to visit me and was aghast at my dwelling. Mr Ergas, on hearing about my new abode was perplexed and concerned – how could he tell his mate Cyril that his daughter was now down and out in some grotty pad … maybe we should have kept her after all …) Bruna and I alight upon an advertisement looking for an English conversation teacher at a language school; it sounds as if it could be just my ticket. I attend an interview at a place in a street lined with pink and white oleanders. The director is a lovely attractive man with an open face and lovely kind smile. He hires me because, he tells me later, he really liked me and was prepared to overlook my inadequate Italian. My job is to test 'Alitalia' airline pilots on their English. One by one, in their stone-coloured uniform, they come for their lesson and I'm surprised to find that some conscientiously do their exercises and some do nothing at all. 'Winging it' in a plane is surely not an option. I like the fact that one 'sends over' to the cafe opposite for a coffee. I don't like the fact that an Italian colleague, perhaps a bit older than me, sends me dirty looks. It is very unnerving and I truly struggle to understand what I've done to provoke such hostility. The trouble with envy is that it strangles in its thick coils – it is the snake with its wide open jaws. Destructive force has ignorance at its source and it would turn day into darkest night if it could. The wolf with its salivating fangs devours the lamb. At its stubborn root is not the hymn which begins 'Glad that I live am I/that the sky is blue …' but fear and hate. 'Why aren't I getting what I want and need?' screams the child.

I am still cramming myself with cake and, one day, as I am walking along the oleander-lined street I am stabbed with pain.

I manage to contact Mrs Ergas who gives me the telephone number of their private doctor. In the teeth of jaw-clenching agony I manage to see him and he immediately knows that I need to be in hospital. The hospital in question is a lovely building, staffed by nuns, on the top of a hill. I am seen by a surgeon who operates the next morning to avoid a ruptured appendix. The prodigious amount of stuff that I have been pouring into my gut has pressurised the poor appendix to such an extent that it is screaming out loud and can't take any more. The surgeon tells me that it was very bad and all the surrounding tissue was ulcerated. He's sent the appendix off to serve as a laboratory specimen. This for me is a cause of pride rather than concern. There's no denying that the food in the hospital is of restaurant standard and I tuck in happily. Good food raises the spirits and must always be an aid to recovery. He gets genuinely cross with me when I decide to take a shower without permission: 'Didn't I know that a wound must be kept dry'. After a week I am summoned to his consultation room to have the stitches removed and he can't help but kiss me. I really like him – his informality and, above all, his confidence. He tells me that when I came to the hospital and was lying prostrate in the bed he thought I was about fifteen. I tell him about my mother's forthcoming visit (I am 'wanted' back in London) and he tells me to stay in Italy and escape the maternal clutches – as if this was some easy, everyday task akin to throwing out a worn-out jumper or taking a new route to work. An invasive force nestles into and damages your very being. The nurses seem to be aware that I don't like my mother and advise me to hide my writing from her so as to protect her inherent sanctity. They also know that the surgeon is getting up to his 'naughty' ways and I don't seem to be protecting myself.

Before I went into 'theatre' Mrs Ergas leant over my bed and said, 'Ciao bella', most tenderly. Very nice of her to appear at the scene. MEANWHILE my dear mother has flown over and is sitting in the waiting room with my kind benefactor whilst my appendix is being ripped out. A nun nurse appears and says to Mrs Ergas, believing her to be my mother: 'You can see her now'. An overriding 'I AM HER MOTHER' is what follows as Mrs Ergas is pushed out of the way. The latter humbly capitulates and leaves the hospital. She comes to see me later and relates this episode. She says, 'I like you, you are my friend – but I never want to see your mother again. I couldn't understand you but now that I have met your mother I can.' (She had expected my mother to be someone like herself and was very shocked to see who she was). My mother is in my room after the operation and pulls the bed round so that I can face the window and get a view. This makes me feel sick. I ask her to get me a book from some bookshop in town, (maybe it's that Hedayat book 'The Blind Owl') and she is reluctant to do so, not bothering to control her bad temper. She comes and she goes. A neighbour from Hendon visits and I observe how happy she is; she speaks Italian, has an Italian boyfriend and works at the American Express near the Spanish Steps. She's visiting me out of duty just as Janice did at the Normandie when I was shut away with chicken pox. I remember her in my room, saying nothing, wanting to be outside with the boys, having fun. (Her mother had told her to visit; Mrs Gilbert was a nice woman. Nobody from my family ever showed their face; I listened to P.J. Proby on the radio. My mother took my seat at the Bournemouth Odeon to see the Beatles. I should have been mega furious about this but just told myself that the seat had to be filled). A teacher from the language school comes with my wages and pleads with me to return. How can I? I am defensively closed, too insecure to 'let go' and go with the flow. I'm forced to return to 25 Foscote Road in order to convalesce. A young guy who works for Mr. Ergas comes to the hospital with the loot; nobody can leave before they pay in cash.

This guy has a great respect for Mrs Ergas and considers me ungrateful for all the hospitality I have received. There is a really nice letter from Henry who is back at Sussex and telling me that I have a very beautiful body. The messiah tells me that I was a bit of 'sexual good luck for him' i.e. a gift showing up on his doorstep … I am not so sure about this but concede, as always, to a higher authority. 'N' as I addressed him in my letters was, in my case, encouraging instinct, freedom and fun – but fun doesn't get the work done. Man must create, not a repressive but a protective wall that enables him to rise again and feel safe. An absence of rational thought, control and guidance will result in sleeping on the floor or city pavement, a heap of blood and entrails. Civilisation rests on responsible freedom; if the cart leads the horse you get a sterile freeze, the ship rots in the docks; but if the horse runs amok you get the mob. The thing is that the most repressed people are the most violent.

The Day of Atonement – Yom Kippur – is approaching. One is expected to fast for twenty four hours in order to purify one's soul. And who is thinking about that, I wonder, as they stand en masse, not in the football stand, but in the synagogue. On my arrival back I am instructed that I must rest on my bed. This advice sounds somewhat strange. I'm not in a wheelchair although one was provided at the airport. I have arranged to go down to Brighton to see Henry. The motive is totally innocent; there is no desire to upset the apple cart or tread on anyone's toes. As I am about to depart I observe my mother clinging to the bars of the bannister, asking me pointedly what I am going to do in Brighton … She has already let it be known, in a tone of cold sneering judgement, that Mr. Ergas told them that I was sleeping with their son. (In Camus' 'L'Etranger' the judge talks of 'ma maitresse' but, for our protagonist, the mistress is in his heart and has a name – 'Marie'. This line sticks like glue). She gets more and more worked up and angry and as I get to the phone, (I need to phone somebody!) my father knocks the apparatus to the ground, tearing the socket from the wall. For some reason I run to the windows which have already been locked. As I leave the lounge he kicks me in the ankle, attempting to trip me up and I look at him with profound disdain and disappointment. She is still ranting and raving and he is doing her bidding, as her henchman. I manage to open the front door and, instead of totally barring my way, it's as if he realises that this scenario is descending into total madness and he lets me go. On the street I see a neighbour, an elderly man, at his bedroom window and I ring his doorbell, wanting him to be a witness to the carryings on next door. He probably received an impassioned plea when he answered his door but he said nothing. On my way to the station, all shaken up, I vow that I am going to sue them for 'false imprisonment'. When I was standing in the hall and she was repeatedly interrogating me as to what I was 'going to do' I was literally shaking like a leaf from head to toe as if I was composed of leaves – a silver birch. She could just as well have been beating me with a brush.

   In Brighton, in Henry's student flat, I relate what has transpired. He doesn't really know what to say and is quite nonplussed. His flatmate, a feminist, is full of genuine anger on my behalf – she can hardly believe what she is hearing. His response is a considered one. 'Well,' he says, 'the woman's mad and the man's a brute'. In the flat he generously buys food which mysteriously disappears from the fridge. He says nothing. I also benefit from his generosity when he takes me out for dinner. He's in his final year at Sussex so a lot of hard work lies ahead and I have no choice but to move on. We part on very friendly terms but part we do. In the same way that I found my room in Warwick Road, SW5 I find a basement room in Well Walk, Hampstead. This is indeed the heart of Hampstead; in a house further along the street lived the ex-husband of Frieda, the woman who left all to live with D.H. Lawrence. She wrote a book about her life entitled, 'Not I but the Wind'. The house I'm in, No 4, is owned by a young Jewish solicitor and his blonde, chipmunked-faced wife with small upward-slanting eyes who is a journalist for the magazine 'Mother and Baby'. She changes the plug on my kettle for me and is a bit surprised that I can't do it myself. (Aren't you allowed to touch things?) She is also surprised that I don't get really angry with her boy when he totally wrecks my room. She favours the baby, Barnaby, who is a baby version of her. When they return home, after an evening out, she races up to the bathroom to put in her diaphragm. Eventually the Jewish solicitor starts sleeping with the Israeli 'au-pair', a later addition to the family. I do get on my high horse when, for a second time, I am asked to clear the large basement room so that she can throw a Saturday night party, to which I am invited. Her friends came round on the morning of the first party in order to prepare the place and the solicitor was awed by the efficiency of these women when they got together … how they are liable to take over and run the show. He never speaks to me. On a Monday afternoon I visit the messiah at his clinic at Royal Oak, Paddington. Mrs Well Walk can hardly conceal her amused bewilderment at how odd I look in my heavy winter 'A' line coat when I wear it with a dress rather than trousers. With my slim legs exposed beneath the wide cut of the coat I resemble a big bird – an ostrich too heavy to fly. I wear brown lace-up shoes which hark back to the 1920s. She doesn't know that I am off to see the messiah? She muses that I'd be somewhere in the advertising world if I hadn't gone off the rails. She tells her husband, and others, admiringly, that I am reading Bertrand Russell's 'History of Western Philosophy'. I am indeed but am not aware that this is anything unusual. Chris Bell also noted that I was a girl who 'dipped into Dante'. At Liverpool an Italian scholar visited and read so movingly from 'Hell' that the tenor of his spoken words resonated for ever. What is more powerful than the human voice? Churchill's voice inspired and stiffened the sinews whilst Hitler's harangue was a gun to the head, a hollow volley of live and lethal ammunition. Does the Messiah put an arm around me or hold me tight? Therapists aren't allowed to do that. You are supposed to mine your own pain and change. A quick fix will make you dependent on the giver. You might get to believing that a hug will save you. The Messiah believes in stronger stuff; somebody like me needs a man in their bed, today and for evermore. He himself was sent away to boarding school at an early age because he was always after the girls. Once, after a dietary binge at Earls Court, he put his arms around my waist and told me that he'd spank me if, ever again, I allowed myself to get so depressed ... This was what he did – neither right nor wrong although far more right than wrong.

On account of my refusal to clear away all my stuff to make way for her party I am told to pack my bags. Does my father come to the rescue? Obviously this renting a room business isn't working out very well so it's best that I take up Law studies and Father will pay the rent on a flat. Nothing can be studied other than LAW. Father decrees this in the same way that he believes in single sex schools and is always on about the 'framework'. What do people DO with Arts degrees? They might as well throw themselves off the nearest cliff. My mother likes to joke about a distant female relative who threw herself off 'Beachy Head'. So, the deal is that I enrol at the Lancaster Gate Law School to study for the Solicitor's Qualifying Examinations. We find a flat in Romney Court, Belsize Park, which is as quiet as an old people's home. Maybe it was an old people's home. The rent is £30 a week and this is a fact that I have to keep secret from my fellow students at the Law School because, in 1974, this was a lot of dosh which few could afford. A nice boy, who shares a house in Chalk Farm, invites me round for tea and looks upset when I refuse. He doesn't know that It's because I won't know how to easily interact with him and his housemates. And I'm not feeling too jolly. A hammer on your head grinds you down. Wings are continually clipped and faces mutilated. My nice friend wants to qualify so that he has a job, a function, a societal role – which is utterly normal and above board. I am just obeying orders – pushed down the Highway. Those iron bars are strong beyond endurance. 'NO' to openness, to living, is the final decree – the last will and testament.

I have no interest in Contract Law and can't do it. I don't really take to Mrs Pedley in her long skirt and plimsolls, rolling her cigarettes in the cafe, surrounded by fervent admirers. She is fat, has trembling hands and long dark straggly hair. She is obviously a clever woman. I get to the college early so that I can be first in line for a slice of fresh veal and ham pie and a lovely fresh tomato and cucumber salad. A very thin guy from some Asian/African country befriends me. He is studying for the gruelling Part 2 exams and doesn't think he's going to make it. He is living with a foster family because he's some sort of refugee. On some bank holiday or other he phones me to join him on a family outing to the country but I refuse. I am living alone in this big flat with its depressing decor of mustard and grey. In those days they weren't the fashionable colours that they are today. I take to having a hot bath before bed as this is the only way I can face such a cold desolate place. When I have a cold the messiah, on his way home, appears at my door with a bottle of 'Captain Morgan' rum and a handful of lemons. He loves to please; what a sweet man he is. He tells me that I should leave a note for the Torts Lecturer, Henry Hodge, whom I sort of fancy because he seems so human and because I've seen him ogling me in my close- fitting black cashmere sweater as I energetically make my way along the corridors. I leave him a note saying that I need extra help with 'Animal Law'. He embarrassedly and swiftly drops a return note on my desk which says that, judging from my test results, I don't need any extra help. I can't do Land Law. Criminal law is easier and more amusing.

My neighbour is a Mr. Hewitt from Trinidad who takes his studies very seriously and finds me a distraction. A Jewish Lady, newly widowed, sits next to the boy from Chalk Farm and behind me is a wealthy married lady of Polish origin who leaves her three little girls in the cafe whilst she pursues her studies. She flaunts her fur coat as does a young Sussex University graduate who has a posh Chelsea accent and stomps in late to every lecture. I ignore everyone and am ignored back. Some of the girls are really ugly (and obviously got nowhere at school) but they seem to be ok, chatty and friendly. I observe all the Part 2 candidates in the library who are really struggling hard making huge efforts to master and memorise all the stuff they've been given that day. The sky will turn blue for them when they are fully qualified and established in their law firms. I am snug in my black, figure hugging, cashmere jumper. I don't perform very well in the tests – only in 'Torts' I do well because I like Henry Hodges – who seems human on account of his uncertainties – his self-corrections

I trot down to Camden Market – it's a dreary walk past Chalk Farm and the forbidding outer wall of the Round House – and buy fresh mackerel and green cabbage with the intention of reproducing a beautiful dish which was laid out for me in Albufeira, Portugal where the waiter told me I was beautiful. Albufeira is my father's latest find and my parents seem to be constantly holidaying in some tasteful upmarket complex. He pays for me to go on my own for a week in July/August and I recall a flat which was so white and pure and lacey that its inner message was to look and pray but not to touch. I cook this lovely dish in the open plan Romney Court abode and stink the place out. The Jewish landlady pays a visit – the flat is being rented out by the daughter of some lovely old

Jewish couple – and is not impressed. In fact she is probably horrified. No sign of dusting or hoovering. 'And her father is so nice – such a gentleman'. But the windows don't seem to open! I circle around Camden Market, not knowing whether to buy apples or pears and a working lady in her sixties, fully in charge of her stall, looks at me askance and says that I'm putting the evil eye on her. Now that's not a very nice thing to hear. She is disarmed by my soft-voiced response but not convinced.

I do have a few visitors. One Sunday afternoon as I am wandering around in Belsize Park a guy comes up to me and asks where he can find a pharmacy that is open on a Sunday. He comes back to my flat. He is Jewish, American and a philosophy lecturer at London University. He is living with somebody. We talk about stuff and he suddenly turns a bit nasty asking me if I want to resemble Italians, 'who sit around all day eating'. He asks me if my father can find him a flat. Are these people crazy or what? Do they think that getting what they want is a matter of flicking the switch of the right contact – and that I have some sort of hotline to God. Am I the doted-on daughter of a rich sugar daddy whose open hand never stops giving? Fortunately, getting rid of him is not difficult. Another visitor is a lovely young man whom I met at a party given by a boy from primary school whom I was in love with because of his blonde curls (happy and merry like all those guys who have blonde curls) and he was also the fastest runner in the world and the son of my parents' friends – the 'Findus' frozen vegetables people. Guy Fawkes parties were held alternately in our respective gardens and my mother observed him chasing me as hard as he could and me enjoying the flight when I was about five years old. Was she aware, even in her early thirties, that she couldn't run, that her lifeblood wasn't running through her veins and giving life to her heart? I bumped into him in Hampstead, outside the Everyman Cinema, and his feisty Scottish girlfriend invited me to their party where I re-met the lovely young man in the plum-coloured velvet suit with whom I had danced at 'Danescroft' when I was twelve. Our eyes met across a crowded kitchen and he approached me and asked me if I wanted a drink. It was so deliciously natural and easy. Outside the Everyman cinema I also had the joy of seeing the singer Paul Jones – the sexiest guy in the world – with his girlfriend. They were both wearing Afghan coats. I was impelled to approach him and said: 'I remember you from a long time ago'. He took this as an insult – nobody wants to be remembered as a 'has-been' but I meant the opposite and because he walked off in a huff I had no chance of telling him how fantastic he was in the mid-1960s.

My newly acquired friend is doing a postgraduate degree in creative writing at the university of East Anglia. He's really into the poetry of Emily Dickenson. In my flat he persuades me to smoke dope and dope is the operative word because, the next day, I feel so dopey that I can't do my test at the Law School. I am furious with him and threaten to report him to the elegant, welcoming building in Hampstead, at the beginning of beautiful Downshire Hill, which is the police station. He doesn't doubt that I'd actually do this. He is dark-haired, attractive and quietly thoughtful and he tells me about some unforgettable Israeli woman on a kibbutz, much older than him, with whom he had an affair and with whom he is still in contact. In those days people wrote letters. I am still angry about being doped. The Messiah tells me that this Jonathan guy sounds as if he is a self-centred sort of person and so his loss is no bad thing. He's forty seven years my senior so his pronouncements are indeed holy writ. He also visits me in my flat, lending me the collected stories of the American writer Sherwood Anderson (he's touched that I Sellotape all the loose pages together) and the journals of Lord Hervey, active at the court of the second George. I am somewhat depressed and find it hard to read, to focus; Newton seems animated by the fact that these Kings had such appalling relations with their poor, spoilt sons. (My father forced his eldest son to work in a factory, as a packer, and made sure that his car was mega small and inferior to his own. I can still see my brother's look of pained frustration when in the presence of his bullying dad).

My studies are going from bad to worse and when it comes to Christmas Holiday revision I am sitting at the living room table consuming a whole tin of 'Quality Street'. These vividly wrapped chocolates were always put out by my mother for her 'guests' – friends who'd come over on a Tuesday evening – the men and women chatting together on different sides of the room. It was nice that my parents were at home and not at the theatre or 'Antoines' the fish restaurant in Charlotte Street. Did my mother delight in telling me that she'd seen Paul McCartney get into a taxi with Jane Asher knowing how much I adored him and the fact that it was she, not I, who had seen him in person. When the Messiah alludes to his wife, who is a Jungian psychoanalyst, (he's close enough to her to catch her cold) I don't like it. I hate wives and their refusal to share. I imagine her as being cold, clever and confident. She buys her clothes from a ladies dress shop in Baker Street. He has to tell her that he comes to see me and he's aware that she'll perceive me as a threat because I'm so young. Eating alone in my bedroom I have the deep and terrible feeling that I live to consume. This is a deep and fearful sadness. I feel that I am f… for life. Nobody can escape the truth about themselves.

The advertising guy that I worked for at Thorn House, Upper St. Martins Lane has died of cancer at a very young age and his widow lives around the corner in Primrose Hill. Did I visit her out of sympathy – probably not. (The sad fact of material passing hasn't impacted me). But I am in my house and she is telling me to sew name tapes on her sons' clothes (shades of being called in to my mother's bedroom to 'do her zip') so that she can go out with her nephew who is Scottish – an Oxford graduate in modern languages now studying to be an accountant. ('Is this really me?' he asks himself. He doesn't take to his fellow students. He's a biggish thick-set rugby-playing guy). What is so good about him is that he takes the children out in his sports car and visits Jack, who has a rare bowel abnormality, in Great Ormond Street Hospital and does his best to improve things for everyone, to lighten the sky. He tells me that his aunt jokily suggested they go to bed together. I observe her taking her baby boy into bed with her for company. She has long straight hair and calls to mind the cruel, go-getting and lustful Regan and Goneril in Shakespeare's 'King Lear'. In the kitchen she slices the meat with an electric chopper, jumping back as the blade efficiently executes the joint. It's not nice to watch. She is friends with my mother (although the latter complains that whenever they go out to lunch she never offers to pay) and forever wondering if I slept with her husband. 'Of course she wouldn't do that' says the Mother. And indeed the thought never entered my head. I observe Jonathan's good deeds from a distance. I can't enter into the spirit of his goodness because I am too depressed and because active care for others is truly alien to me.

He takes me out to some restaurant called 'Tiddly Dolls' or something, an annoying place in Soho where everyone is dressed up. He is wearing a white suit and wonders why I couldn't have made more of an effort. He gets really fed up with my constant complaining. For some reason my father, on a Sunday afternoon, is sitting in the flat, with his back to me. My Scottish friend, who comes from a family of mum and dad 'in the dress business' and two or three siblings, says something about me to my father – expressing his exasperation in a friendly way. My father is so embarrassed by this normal, direct intercourse that he turns away just as he turned away when Jesus, in his white robe, appeared in the film 'Barrabas'. It's like running for cover when the sun comes out. My Scottish friend asks me if I think he has enough grit in his personality. He gets me to read one of his European literature essays from University. Decades later I hear that he got married (as people do), emigrated to Canada, and had four children. Most people manage to get what they need for themselves.

The Messiah knows my parents – everything he says about them is totally true – and tells me that he was sure that my father tried to run him over when he was crossing the road outside Kent Terrace – overlooking Regents Park – on his way to his office in another terrace overlooking this landmark London park. It's a beautiful part of London, that's for sure. He tells me that I should 'get the money' out of my father in order to buy a flat since I 'suffered from his cruelty throughout my childhood'. One hears things that are true but one doesn't grasp the full extent of their meaning. And is what anyone else says the whole story?

He says that my father has sadistic lips and that he's probably a latent homosexual. But remember him listening, with real pleasure, to Eartha Kitt on television, as my mother shuffled around nervously and then brought him a cup of tea. He does perceive however, that the poor, worried man is split between wife and daughter (and deceased Mother). His telling me to 'get your father to take you out to dinner' was advice of the highest necessity. He also tells me to show up for the Law exams otherwise the family will think that I just haven't bothered. I do show up but after looking at the paper on Constitutional Law I walk out. I'm surprised at how easy the paper is and probably if I'd done some work I could have passed. Why did I think that it would all be so impossibly hard? I see my fellow students applying themselves assiduously and chatting heatedly afterwards about the questions. I take myself off to a Greek restaurant in the vicinity of Alexandra Palace and dimly feed my face, sadly aware of old ladies around me, lunching together. When the results were published in 'The Times' my elder brother told me that he kept on searching for my name in the appropriate column and couldn't understand why it wasn't there. 'Search again and it will appear', he said to himself. I speak to my father on the phone and he says sharply: 'Can't you stick at anything?' I have no reply. My thin Asian friend fails every 'head' of his Part 2 exams and wonders what he is going to do next.

What I am going to do next is move into a top floor flat at 19 Parkhill Road. I'd visited a couple of other flats with my father – we are both wearing our raincoats (indeed a fellow student at the College – a conspicuously Jewish lad from Golders Green told me that my 'gold' Aquascutum raincoat was something his father would wear and then wrote me a letter of apology when he realised he'd upset me) and I am aware of his response towards the heavily pregnant occupant of a Steeles Road, Belsize Park, property. It's as if he's disgusted by this image of 'Mother Earth' with all its associative paraphernalia of bloody mess. It's different with his own wife because he saw her as the most sensual beast ever to cross his path and was never not attracted to her. He himself is as sensual as an iron club. Tragically her natural attributes were at odds with her damaged interior. It was as if her God given body was an easy 'yes'! whereas her fear and guilt screamed a defensive 'NO'!

He gives me a fixed amount of money in order to furnish the flat. This is perceived not as a warm open gesture but a sharp twist of the wrist – ha! – see what you can get on that – I'll crucify you a bit. We annihilate the soft flesh. 'Power, pressure and punishment' is the driving force and he pronounces these words with force and conviction, as if they come from his very source. But he's no fool. With equal conviction he repeatedly quotes Oscar Wilde's assertion that every man kills the thing he loves. He damns all teachers by saying: 'those who can do whilst those can't teach.' He observes that within me there is both a fat man and a thin man struggling to get out. (I can see that my friends are frightened of him; or rather they shy away defensively and are happy to return to their jovial dads). In any event I am the proud owner of the most expensive bedsitter in the world. It is a two-bedroomed flat with a large living room but I solely inhabit the larger bedroom overlooking the garden which belongs to the landlord who lives on the ground floor. He is a music master, old school, and perhaps the ugliest man in the world. For the small bedroom I buy a cupboard in which the ironing board is kept. For all the world it resembles an upright coffin. In my bedroom wardrobe I keep a beautiful Mary Quant dusty pink coat that I bought for 28 guineas and which is never worn.

For my bedroom curtains I choose fabric that recalls a Monet painting; it is all pink blossom and pale green foliage. The Frenchman who works in this Baker Street upholstery shop mistakes my surname for 'Matisse'. My brother's wife's father is 'Relyon Beds' and he gets me a double bed at a discount. He is always jokingly asking me when I'm going to go out with him and his daughters humorously, lightly, tell me to take no notice of him when I'm not sure what to reply. My brother is now married for life, much to his father-in-law's joy. His daughter develops some kind of skin disease and sobbingly laments the fact, in the kitchen of their Haverstock Hill flat, that my brother shows her no affection. Thirty years later, on being asked what she got from the marriage she replies 'Grief'. All that beautiful red hair turned to grey. In the synagogue, as we wait for the bride to walk down the aisle on her father's arm, my father's aunt observes that I have 'missed the boat' since I am almost twenty four (and also a bit overweight). My mother looks as if she wants to say something 'au contraire' but doesn't dare. Her own parents also were of the opinion that twenty five was the cut-off point for tying the knot. She was happily engaged with Unity Theatre, near Kings Cross, where she wanted to stay. Her fellow actors ogled her curves, her powerful physicality but she never slept with anyone, or fell for anyone. She's in her own self-admiring world. She met my father at the 'Jewish Men and Women's Ex-Servicemen Club' where she played 'footsie' with him under the table. Studying to be an accountant he's a good choice for lifelong security and he isn't fat, bald and funny but lean, muscular and purposeful. I am very surprised when the rabbi's daughter tells me that she's crazy about him. (What a poor girl she is in her threadbare winter coat and 'falling down' socks but she knows what God said to Abraham, Isaac, Jacob and Moses, our father). At my brother's wedding reception I wore my long red imitation silk 'Ossie Clark' dress which disappeared into the ether. Maybe I danced with my younger brother who always keeps me at a distance totally forgetting that I cared for him and saw him on his way when his father reduced him to tears at 8am on a school day. Did father and son both forget that I got my arms around his neck and said: 'If you don't leave him alone I'll kill you'. My father's boss tells me that I am a vamp. He also says that, in life, one chooses either love or money.

My bedroom walls are painted pink by Mr. Martin, my father's decorator and the green carpet is an offcut from their old living-room carpet. It looks worn. My father is feeling mean. Mr. Martin sits perilously close to the edge of my bed and talks of his ex-wife who had 'a hundred pound of clothes on her back', paid for by him or her new man, I forget which. I always forget the complicated details of people's stories. He tells me that my teenage brother is always in his bedroom. He, the brother – a nice, friendly boy – would like to be a teacher 'but I don't think your father would like that because there's no money in it'. He also observes that we do nothing together as a family. I don't know what he means. (Yes, we were all in our separate rooms doing our homework and I'd also be listening to Beatle records played on the lovely blue and grey record-player that my father bought for me as a birthday present). What kind of things? Do they play board games or go to the cinema together? Do they sit around the television watching 'Hancock's Half-hour' or 'Hugh and I' pronounced by my brother, sitting alone, as 'Hug and one' – much to my mother's amusement? Do these normal families go fishing together or set off to climb Mount Everest? Mr Martin, the painter and decorator from Wembley, tells my parents, in their front hall, that their daughter has the most beautiful eyes he has ever seen. Really? I thought they were small and ugly. They don't know what to say. My mother confirms his statement but refers my dark inherited eyes back to her own poor mother who used to say that her days were hell but her nights were heaven. Well, she wasn't such a poor woman, after all. I never again set foot in my mother's house and she never visits my flat. My brother and his wife move to Muswell Hill, opposite the house where a terrible murder took place and where they start their own family. Their first child is still born but, luckily for them, they know how to move on and forget things. Or do they? The next three are born live and kicking.

I make my own bread and frequent a greengrocer in Belsize Park and a health food shop on Primrose Hill Road where I buy kilo bags of dried figs and dates. The figs are my favourite so my diet consists of bread, dried figs, assam tea and apples. Sometimes I walk to the Sainsburys on Finchley Road and buy a subtly tasty hunk of Irish cheddar cheese (staring with hard, frozen eyes at the varying sizes and not knowing which one to choose). There's also a shop near Fleet Road, run by a Sri Lankan family who sell solid blocks of dried dates from the Middle East. I am a frequent visitor and the young wife, with her long black plait who serves me, says curtly: 'Well, it's better than sweets'. She has a lovely little girl who stands by her side behind the counter or is round the back with her grandmother. The young working wife no doubt internally raises her eyebrows when she sees me coming.

There is a building site down the road which I pass every morning. One day the foreman rings my bell and asks me out for a drink. He is young, attractive, fair-haired and friendly. I am so taken aback (who is this interloper?) that I utter a shocked 'No' and he turns round, looking humiliated and abashed, to descend the steps he had so bravely climbed. But my door is well and truly open to the Messiah who visits of an afternoon, three or four times a week. On a Friday he goes down to Fulking, Surrey, where he and his wife spend the weekend in her inherited cottage. He loves to dig in the garden whilst she prepares papers for her learned society. I always write to him, addressing him as N (N = God) or RDN – his initials. Writing to him is what I do. He is a collector of second-hand books and, with me, he shares his vast library. Fosco Maraini's 'Meeting with Japan' is a wonderful unforgettable book and he introduces me to Freya Spark and her fascinating autobiography 'Traveler's Prelude'. I love reading the 'Pasquier Chronicles' by Georges Duhamel as much as I used to love reading Enid Blyton's adventure books. I am introduced to the great rambling works of John Cowper Powys and those of his younger brothers Theodore and Llewellyn. These were saintly men indeed – of a different breed to those who are spawned today. I read and read sitting against the radiator to keep my back warm. I am an avid fan of the works of Colette. If only I was her! 'N' tartly remarks that she was brought up to look after herself and that she was an extrovert: 'She'd have had to be in order to tolerate the music hall for so many years'. When the roof leaks he remarks that I've never had to deal with all that stuff implying that it's about time I did. 'Your father took care of everything'. When he comes round we stand up, facing the garden and I complain about my fate. He listens and He always says: 'You weren't encouraged' followed by 'Shall we go bed', as he begins to disrobe. This is my cue to do likewise. I probably don't want to but this is expected of me. I love him, he's everything to me and I know he loves me so that's the way it is. Just as he loves the smooth silky skin of my tummy I feed on his insight and experience. He says that Colette had remarkable insight into herself. My parents, of course, weren't real people and they'd turned their backs on one another years ago. I like to hear about his life, his loves, his sons and the world as it was when every village had its pond. He is totally committed to his opinions which I swallow whole. But they are expressed in contemplative humility rather than arrogance and pride. He says that science and technology have pushed out art and literature – or rather 'they've won' and our society is totally fragmented as a result. Every year (and we are in 1975) things get less real. He blames medical science for keeping everyone alive and says, 'better off dead' concerning the plight of someone or other – some poor bugger who is unable to function. He also says, softly, and with genuine scornful amazement that I have no idea how dependent most people are. And that very few people really live. How true this is and brings to mind the words of Jesus Christ about the very small opening into life that few find. To have the killer instinct is also to be able to cut out one's own offending parts. His name for me is Lilith. Apparently she was the first wife of Adam and ran away to become a demon. She had a special power over children.

When I first moved to the Earls Court bedsitter I got a job with 'Lund Humphries', the Publishing House on false pretences since my typing was dreadful and the nice, gentle boss didn't enjoy having to fire me. In the lunch hour I visited Newton and sobbed galore on account of the shame and despair at my uselessness. He makes me return to the office in the afternoon, in order to keep my head up, although this is a very difficult thing to do when you want to simply disappear.

Newton's main belief is that people are sensual – which is the way to be – or a pain, stuck in their heads and their cold, robotic bodies. (He, of course, belongs to the former category. His wife isn't sensual although she thinks she is because she likes to go out and buy cream cakes from 'Lindy's' or 'Sheratons'.) My mother is as sensual as I am, 'pure animal' and so is obviously with the wrong man. He also says of her, in an undramatic, matter of fact way, that she has no genuine feeling at all. With conviction he describes my father as one of 'life's unfortunates'. He buys me an LP by the opera singer Victoria de los Ángeles; her voice is like mellifluous honey, devoid of all shrillness or dark notes. It expresses love, gaiety, sweetness. She sings a beautiful love song 'Damunt de tu nomes les flors' (the words are by Jose James, a !9th century poet) about the kiss of flowers, the kind of love that is no more. I know that he loves me as you'd love a pearl and would come crawling on his hands and knees to see me. The record cover, picturing the artist's lovely face, a living Madonna, is forever facing my room. She has a false hair piece to give herself height and is wearing a black lacy and velvet dress, like the one my mother had. My beloved doctor gets fed up with seeing this 'picture'. Even if he is aware of my motivation he believes, with all his heart, that now he is with me all my troubles are far away, gone for good', never to return. 'Didn't your mother wear a lot of black?' he suggests, with almost a twinkle in his eye. He has spoken to her, face to face, and his major impression is of her dissatisfaction. (It's not as if she has to worry about paying the bills – ha!) In later years, a rant of blame directed against me, her daughter, provokes the following response from her analyst: 'You can't blame someone for wanting to live'.

He's always telling me to get out more – with the intention of finding a lover, someone to un-repress me – to make my blood boil. He also says that he wishes that I had more friends. I've certainly put all my eggs in one basket. In April 1975 Tangier in Morocco seemed like a good place for a 'spring 'break'. After all, I'm used to taking off to the Middle East at this time of the year, getting my quota of sunshine and palm trees. I stay in a lovely hotel – 'El Rif' – and am surprised to see a guy in a djellaba walking past outside as if there's no such thing as Monday Morning blues, the London Underground, or clocking in at the factory. He walks erectly, with dignity, as if he belongs to himself. In the hotel I meet a nice Moroccan architect who speaks English perfectly and says lovely things to me. I am rude to him and find myself enthusiastically chatting to a Lebanese businessman called Charles who hardly responds. God only knows what I was telling him but he replies that it sounds to him as if my doctor friend has a hold over my soul which is not good. I 'pooh pooh' this ridiculous assertion; it is my mother who has the possessive hold ... I see him again before dinner and I am wearing my red imitation silk Ossie Clarke dress. He is plump and has a sensual semitic look – he is forty five (age means nothing to me) and has three sons and is in Tangier in order to try and sell his rotten trawler boat. We have dinner together along with some other men and he tells me that he didn't like me in my 'pantalons'; when I gracefully descended the staircase in my long red dress he thought it was a different person. The 'other men' are Moroccan friends and when I dance for them, one of them says, thoughtfully, that I am 'a good demon'. We make our way to someone's home and the wife makes an appearance from the kitchen. She is upbraided because she hasn't got more to offer other than some little cakes and I am embarrassed for her sake. Her husband actually says, in front of me, 'Is this all you have to put on the table'? Wordless, she retreats to the kitchen where she stays with her daughters whilst the men talk business.

Late that evening he says goodnight to me as I withdraw into my bedroom. Our rooms are on the same corridor. Silly fool that I am, lacking all boundaries, I enter my room, shut the door and then open it again, inexplicably. Am I playing with him? In short he forces his way in and, after kissing me, pushes me onto the bed and asserts his rights over me. Frightened – I have to ask permission to go to the toilet to insert my diaphragm (provided by Newton's next door neighbour at Kent Terrace, a gynaecologist, who told me that I had a beautiful long cervix) and he hardly believes me, reckoning that I might be attempting to escape. I tell him that he's a thoroughly weak man and he agrees. He'd imbibed a lot of alcohol during the course of the evening. But he gets his way and it's not such a bad thing (is he a big, bad teddy bear?) – it's worse to be punched in the head and verbally abused. What is more shocking is the fact that, at breakfast, he ignores me and looks ashamed, concentrating on his breakfast. I approach him with a smile and he knows that he is forgiven. He must have felt himself to be a very lucky boy! With an English farmer friend called John, a guest at the hotel, we have lunch at a beautiful hotel called 'El Minzah'. It exudes wholesomeness and tranquillity. The waiter decorates the plates with flower petals and smiles at me. Indeed, when I walk down the street I turn round and a crowd of Arab boys are following me, laughing and smiling and calling out 'habibi' (darling). A waiter tells me that I am beautiful and there is a photo of me with him in my red 'Ossie Clark' dress holding the key to my room in one hand, and, in the other a packet of 'Gaulois' cigarettes in their sky blue packet. With Charles I swing gently on the hammock but padded swinging chairs make me feel sick. I manage to dissuade him from the idea of sending his sons to 'Gordonstoun' the rugged school in Scotland which Prince Charles allegedly hated with its cold showers, rugby in the cold mud and rain. (Cold, cold, discipline was the name of the game. A German Jew founded the place) He is not totally convinced. Charles doesn't care to talk about his wife who has been severely ill – probably with the big C disease that invades like the devil.

    Back in London Newton tells me that he, Charles, is a man with nothing other than a penis and wonders if he wipes his own bottom. He reckons that he 'probably has a string of prostitutes all over Europe'. Charles the Lebanese sends me a postcard from Andorra telling me how much I'd love this little state in the Pyrenees, sandwiched between France and Spain. He comes to London and we meet at the Playboy Club and I am wearing a dress the colour of the 'rinse out' drink at the dentists which has a sash around the back such as would befit a little girl. Indeed there is a little girl of nine in the next door house in Parkhill Road. Her single mother travels to the states and leaves her in the care of the cleaners. I see the little girl confidently walking to school in the morning. I also see her with her mother having a picnic in the garden and I am so stunned by the sight of them happily chatting together that I have to leave the bedroom window and remove myself into the large empty front room in which there was only a bookcase containing all my paperbacks of French 20th century authors, a brown corduroy sofa which opens up like a coffin and the leaves of the acacia tree dancing against the window pane. There are purple and red petunias in the window box. Newton bought me a child's (red) fork and trowel and we collected leaf mould on Hampstead Heath for a window box which has produced the biggest, most robust petunias in the world. What a show of red and purple. It gives the lie to the sweet love-making that is taking place inside. It is more like the eternal flame of defiance.

    As a very small child I am sitting on the boiler in the kitchen and my father forces me to take the travel sickness pill crushed into a drink. 'Drink it' he commands, with white lips pursed. I have to swallow the bitter brew and its bitterness is a killer. Ten years on I am sitting on the boiler reading 'Lord of the

Flies' on a Saturday morning whilst they are at the synagogue. Sitting or standing next to my mother in the garden after school when I am thirteen she tells me that 'some women are fat 'down there' and that 'once you start you can't stop' – something she'd observed amongst the theatre crowd ... I am also periodically told that I 'grow low' (to my distress nothing seems to be growing at all on my flat chest) and, first and foremost, accompanied by a side to side shake of the head: 'Judy can't keep the beat'. She's always in Selfridges or Upper Marylebone Street buying lamps for the lounge. At night she must have heard the animal whimpering from my bed, and, in her pale blue nylon nightie she gets in and lies by my side. Not a word, let alone a cuddle. After a bit she says, 'Are you feeling better now?' I reply in the affirmative and she gets out, returning to her own cold mattress. (She struggles with the brocade bed cover every morning and I am called in to help: 'Can you come and help me with my bed?' And in I trot.) She mocks women who have flat chests and if you can't conceive or have a difficult pregnancy well ... God has certainly turned away from you and put you on the rubbish heap. Her inability to say a kind or a true word, to see the person who is before her eyes (after all she's not blind) must, no doubt, be traced to gender issues and heart disease. But there are pills for everything – sleeping and waking, eating and drinking. The cold emptiness must be a defence against living and loving, and all sorrow. I stand alone, heart-broken and resistant.

The woman next door, at Parkhill Road, is some sort of political scientist and a nice woman. When my heating breaks down she says that I can have some of theirs and she tells me not to fret. She also complains of the fact that she's made her daughter a great birthday party and the little girl has behaved in a way that hardly expresses gratitude. 'Perhaps only children are spoiled?' the mother ruminates. Dr Newton reckons that this woman is thirty seven or thirty nine and his surmisal suggests that she's 'had it' – she's 'over the hill'. No man will ever look at you again. She has spots of brown on her teeth and a big 'Afro' hairstyle.

I have a lot of trouble with noisy neighbours. The couple below me are horrible – as if there is something rotten about them, especially the guy. They enjoy their noisy get-togethers with friends and always slam their doors. They don't give a thought to me upstairs; my existence is probably too strange to even warrant a thought. They ask me to feed their cat. The woman gets pregnant and as Newton rightly predicts: 'That will probably shut them up for a bit'. An Irish lady, Mrs Geoghegan, comes to clean the 'common parts' and sometimes I espy her in Mr. Anderson's ground floor flat, sitting on a high stool reading the paper. On one occasion she has to pass Dr. Newton on the stairs and looks as if she was praying to become part of the wall. She is the quietest, most modest woman in the world. She smiles at me and says something about my 'father's visits'. Is she mad or what? (She also addresses me kindly as if I am someone who lacks a mother). My real and actual father phones occasionally and asks me if I'm doing the dusting.

I see something of my old mates. Philippa, my buddy from my mid-teens, visits the flat and I show her round. 'I'll buy it' she says humorously and it was her humour and insight which I loved. Most people are chronically serious and painfully intelligent or stupid. But she is married now and has a house in the suburbs. People think that I went off the rails. My wonderful witty friend from my 'A' levels, Kate Denby, phones the Hendon address and asks about me. 'Is she still the same, like uncorked champagne?' she inquires of my mother. This inquiry falls on deaf ears. Kate is training to be a solicitor and doing it properly. She was wonderfully bright and witty. (Her father wasn't a business man but a poor tailor). She's also engaged to be married to a nice Jewish boy called 'Stew' who owns a garage. She'll wear the trousers, that's for sure. She comes round to visit and I can see that she is taken aback by my inhospitality – I don't offer anything in the way of food. My young brother, now about eighteen, also visits and sits with me in the cold kitchen. He says that I remind him of Jane Eyre and states that 'it's impossible to love someone who is so full of hatred'. He also tells me that 'parents' are always watching him and expressly says that 'father' should find friends of his own. We never call them 'mum and dad'.

On a Saturday afternoon everyone is out and about and I am stuck in my room. I am wearing a stripey dress that is like a long T-shirt. It has bows on the shoulders and I feel that I am 'strung up' like a side of beef or lamb. My mother too had a thing about bloody meat, pricking the roast beef with her fork and watching the blood seep out. The raw meat would be laid out on an aluminium plate, doused in salt, for three hours although the strict religious practice said that six hours was needed for the bleed. I can no longer be in this room. It's July 1976, the hottest summer on record (everywhere the green grass has become a brown wilderness) and my room, under the roof, absorbs all the heat making it difficult to sleep. I am aware that I have no intelligent company and this needs somehow to be remedied. I note that my favourite play 'Othello' is being staged at the Regents Park open-air theatre and a well-known British actor is in the lead role of 'Othello'. I am sure I could somehow get to speak to him.

I sit at the back of the tiered seats and, at the interval, I dare myself (and it takes some daring) to approach the stage door and cross the line, overstepping the 'PRIVATE. DO NOT ENTER' sign. All is quiet on the home front – no sign of anyone. No snarling monster has emerged from one of the tents to order me OUT. A blonde-haired smallish guy, barefoot in shoes, looking tired, is walking along the path between the tents. I recognise him immediately and tell him how much I am enjoying his performance. 'How kind!' he replies and then asks me, somewhat pointedly, whether I act. I have to reply that I don't. Do I make some comment about the nature of evil or do I ask him what he thinks? He stops in his tracks, stares at me, and asks me if I have a few minutes to spare and whether I'd like an ice-cream. (My mother always had a little refrain/ditty about ice-cream: 'I scream, you scream, we all scream'. She had a retinue of similar ditties). Together, we leave the vicinity of the backstage dressing room and walk around Regents Park. We stand on the bridge and look at the black swans with their red beaks. We talk softly together and there is agreement in our souls. He doesn't want to go back to the theatre for the second half – he wants to stay with me in the park. He tells me that 'I am far more eastern' and, under his breath, he murmurs, 'very sensitive'. In an exultant moment of pleasurable madness he takes off his shoe and writes my telephone number on the sole and then strides, with a deliberate effort, back into the arena.

But he doesn't phone. I cry all day. Newton, by way of comfort, tells me that I don't know 'what he has on his plate' and that he is having contacts all day whilst I am having none. I am 'a poor little rich girl.' Obviously he doesn't like to see me so upset. He'd love to hand me over to the blonde gentleman, whose photo he has seen outside the theatre. I write to him, (including some sort of sketch – copied – in order to impress and prove that I'm not 'a good for nothing') although heaven knows how I got hold of his address. Eventually I receive a reply which is almost a love letter, a soul letter, in spite of the fact that he has a family. Married! It ends with a quotation from 'Othello' as regards the dog Iago: 'more fell than hunger, sadness, and the sea.' I dwell on this line obsessively, not fully getting it. He says that I 'have a sense of the tragic, which stirred in him'. I re-read the letter until I memorise it. Eventually he comes to the flat and it's clear how uncomfortable he feels at crossing this line. He's probably only there because he has been moved by my entreaties. He comments on the fact that I don't seem to have any friends and there is no difficulty in categorising my parents, simply, as 'punishers'. I am 'down' – probably he didn't realise this when he met me in the park. Sensitivity has become eccentricity. He tells me that I should get away from the pink walls but in a burst of real passionate feeling says, 'I wish I could stay'. He's a caring, lovely man, and this genuine care for others isn't something I can relate to as a basic component of being human. A Christian soul should belong to us all.

Adolf Hitler was our dear friend. 'Hitler and Stalin' was the big book on the bookshelf behind my father's armchair and where I cried on receiving my poor, disappointing 'A' level grade in History. (Surely no one, besides my father, has admitted that they love war? Too busy fighting, I guess). I was at the top and ended up at the bottom … 'What now?' is the question. Survival is hard and made of stone. Help, support from others, is as weak and tepid as tap water. It interferes with your sense of self, your identity. It befuddles and makes things worse. Don't hold my hand; I am braced for an amputation and will face the pain, if not invite it. But what kind of masochistic martyrdom is this? A self-punishing perversion indeed. But can you survive if you are soft as the dawn and blind to the approaching storm, the ever-present tsunami on the horizon? 'Meals on wheels' are for those who can't get out, have lost the use of their pins. Why aren't they foraging for mushrooms in the woods or learning, in proud defiance, to live off three beans a day. Pain is nothing; what is truly scary is the thought that you will die – be annihilated – (by the monster in the shadows) and will no longer be here to fight and suffer another day.

He sends me a postcard from the Edinburgh film festival and notes that a theatre/film director tells him that he is looking 'as gloomy as ever'. 'What he doesn't realise', says the actor, 'is that I'm thinking'. The postcard picture is of a painting of a rosy-cheeked (peasant) girl selling apples. He mentions the poet Robbie Burns in connection with this painting and says that Burns 'would have liked me for sure.' He promises that we will meet again. Another postcard arrives – it is Van Gogh's portrait of the postman's son – and he addresses me as 'Dear darting glance'. He wants to meet for lunch. This never materialises. Finally I receive a long, somewhat anguished letter in which he said it was all about sexual attraction (the way I moved and yet was trying to put a stop on myself) and wanting to wade into me as he licked his ice-cream on a very hot, working day in Regents Park. I am a 'poor sweet' who had no idea as to what was really going on his mind ... Newton dismisses him as a 'write-off'. He says that 'they' – meaning other people – 'lack the feeling and the sensuality; His wife is probably as inhibited as he is'.

Decades later I once again boldly go backstage to say 'hello' (actually it was in the reception area that I asked, somewhat embarrassedly, if he could come to the front of the house). He comes because he has good manners but he's in a hurry to catch the last train back to Kings Cross. I receive a postcard saying he hopes my hard times are over and that he can't believe that I can't embrace happiness and that even seeing me for such a short time was as delightful as ever ...

After a long weekend on my own I find that I have difficulty actually forming language and this is a bit disturbing. I take my pink duvet covers to a launderette in Haverstock Hill where they are beautifully laundered. There is a mouse in the flat who comes up the pipe and ends up in the rubbish bin and the rustling sound it makes causes high alarm. Newton suggests that I befriend the little creature, 'it probably just wants to sit next to you' but instead I get in the vermin killers and write a story entitled 'The Story of the Mouse'. It was an excellent story. There are two mice; one is timid and afraid and brown; the other is lively and sweet, pink and white. But the timid one is full of need, and keeps travelling up the pipe ...

When you're in your twenties, the day is young and there is always another guy around the corner. I travel to a little town called 'Tyrennia', near Pisa, in Italy. I have no idea why I chose this small town although it's near the sea and seems pleasant enough. I check into a pleasant looking pensione. I walk along the beach. I am eating my dinner in the modest hotel restaurant when a very Italian looking guy, albeit sensitive and soulful, comes in, accompanied by workmates. He looks tired to death. He literally can't take his eyes off me. It seems I have to do something about this so I beckon him to follow me to the telephone so that he can help me call someone – something to do with a trip to Siena. Or maybe he just appeared at my side when it was clear that I was in trouble. The help with the Italian language is useful since I'm mangling it to death and then he grabs me by the hand and takes me to his car and we drive around for ages, in the dark, going nowhere. He is saying my name over and over again as if it's poetry or bedecked with sparkling gems and I wonder why we can't stop somewhere for an ice-cream, at least.

We communicate somehow and he tells me that he is a labouring man and compares the palms of our hands; his are rough whilst mine are smooth, delegating me to the class of people who do not work. I gather that he and his workmen travel round the region repairing ornate plaster ceilings; it is skilled artisan work and the phrase that keeps on coming up is 'soffitti ingesu'. I never find out his name – in my mind it's 'soffitti ingesu' now and forevermore. I catch a glimpse of their dark communal room – full of beds. He shares my bed for the night and I am in love with him. But when I wake in the morning he is gone and it is as if I've been knifed in the heart. There is a letter by my bed.

From whom can that be and how did it get there? Oh my Lord it's from an English couple whom I'd met a day earlier; they were planning on starting some business in this part of the world. They were subjected to a big splurge about my background and my parents which obviously made them feel very uncomfortable. This letter is a reprimand, rapping me on the knuckles for laying into my blessed forbears – and to COMPLETE STRANGERS. This is what shocked them and prompted them to put pen to paper to vent their disgust.

At reception I ask about the Italian crew and the proprietress tells me, with venom, that I am extremely immoral and must go. A near relation, emerging from his room, is exclaiming, 'E brutto, e brutto' because she has rapped on his door, destroying his sleep. A look of spiteful satisfaction crosses her face. She tells me that I didn't pay for the telephone call I made and this lie is infuriating. I always pay. Everything about her is indicative of a small-minded person, the worst sort. I pity the guy whose sleep she profoundly disturbed. Once on the road, on the bus, I run into a group of American soldiers serving at a nearby base. One of them befriends me but although he is pleasant and friendly enough he seems like a boy, a child. I make it to Siena, which is a wide, open place. Who wouldn't marvel at the gigantic medieval square. I have lunch at a tiny restaurant, the hole in the wall variety, and the waiter places fresh cherries on my plate for which I'm not charged. Cherries are plentiful and fall from the tree into your open mouth.

Of course I am heart-broken by the loss of 'soffitti ingesu' and am kicking and hitting myself on account of the fact that I failed to get his name and address. I remember him showing me on the map the small village in Tuscany where he lived but I wasn't interested in insignificant screwed-up dots on the map. I should have listened better. For years I go to sleep saying his 'name' or rather as I do so I am bathed in liquid comfort and peace. On the plane returning to the U.K. a nice lady asks me if I don't find it lonely travelling on my own and I'm not sure what she means. Dr. Newton has also referred to me in terms of 'appalling loneliness' but this is like telling a hunchback who manages to get around that they are disabled or someone with a smile that their life is blighted by a birthmark that has obliterated their face and will make any love life an impossibility. Back in my flat Newton says that he was a 'masochist' on account of the look of deep feeling and tiredness on his face. I am told that most of life is practical and superficial and that's the run of it. I was unaware that I was something nice that appeared on the road as he made his way between jobs. He was simply aware of the 'Hard Day's Night' common to all men.

It's a Saturday night and you're supposed to go out. I have no idea about the social scene post 1975; what comedy shows people are watching, the pop music that teenagers are dancing to and the pop idols they are drooling over. In my book the music I loved ended in 1972. Both melody and meaning are dead. Punks and Goths be damned; they are ugly with their spikey hair and black lipstick. I go to a marquee somewhere in Chelsea to see a ballet. I'm hardly a Chelsea girl – that is, someone who attended the 'Elysee Francaise', speaks posh and has barons and earls in their ancestry. I know Hendon, Golders Green and Hampstead. I get bored watching the ballet and leave early. I am wearing a lilac-coloured jersey trouser suit and it's pretty odd because the jacket is new, hardly-worn whilst the trousers are so worn (I wear them around the flat) that they're baggy, shapeless and faded. My mother always made a rigid distinction, subconsciously, between clothes worn 'around the house' and 'glamourous gear' that is worn for show. I walk along the streets and am attracted by a place that looks lit up and inviting. It turns out to be the 'Polish Social Club' in South Kensington and I like the look of the guy who is manning the coat cupboard. I tell him that I've just, by chance, alighted on this place. He seems pleased to talk to me and his English is … totally English. His name is Greg and he's from Katowice in Poland. His mother is a florist and I forget what his father does although he does say that he no longer has any contact with his family. What he wants is to gain a place at an English Art School. He is very thin, very short-sighted and has the look of an East European poet. He talks eloquently about his dreams and his feelings, something that is so un-English. He is highly strung so all his movements are abrupt and jerky. He tells me that his English girlfriend has become very controlling and domineering and he wants to get rid of her. No doubt about that in his mind. We arrange to meet in Regents Park and, when we do, I tell him my story. Chuckling to himself he says something about 'beauty and the beast'. How simple that is, like Henry's definition of my parents as the 'the brute and the madwoman' but I am tormented by their legacy; there are two opposites within (north and south) which are separate and miles apart and impose on my brain. How one feels in oneself can never be measured and is all that matters. Walking in the park I espy my father's boss who is with his mother and, playfully or rather mischievously, I trot along beside them saying repeatedly: 'I bet you don't know who I am.' He, the boss, is very confused, trying hard to remember who I am (he danced with me at my brother's wedding and told me I was a vamp) and becoming more so as his mother says, repeatedly, 'she's trying to pick you up … ' He later tells my father, all composure regained, (the armour is back on) that he saw me with a guy who looked as if he needed a good meal. One of Greg's visits to my flat clashes with a visit from the Messiah and the young guy looks as if he wished the earth could swallow him up. Why does he look so uncomfortable? Newton tells him, sincerely, how grateful we were in WW2 for the actions of the Polish Air Force, who helped in the fight against the Nazis. Greg smiles uneasily. Newton has told me that in 1940, during the Blitz, he felt real fear that we would go down. Throughout this time he kept his London clinic open, seeing children in need. On another occasion my father shows up at the flat (he, apparently, had had a 'passive' war stationed in Burma – something about which he never spoke a word – as was his way) when Newton is there and the look on the former's face is one of concerned bewilderment. 'Should one speak as a father or should one bite one's tongue in the presence of a superior power?' The psychiatrist is friendly, deliberately trying to be 'inclusive'. No further action is taken.

What excites me about Greg are the letters he sends me. He uses daffodil yellow paper, folded in a way that dispenses with an envelope and they are addressed to 'Your Majesty'. His pen line drawings must have impressed the postman too. He gives/lends me an LP of Polish songs which are melancholy and mournful and beautiful and stand in direct contrast to the fundamentally joyous notes of the collection voiced by Victoria de los Angeles. He has something 'nihilistic' about him which is very un-British. He talks yearningly of the Polish Mountains. But Poland has been through a lot. He has a bit of a Jewish look and he tells me that he and his friend were once thrown off a train and had insults thrown at them as 'yids'. He lies in the bath for a long, long time. He is desperate to get into art college. Something goes wrong with the relationship and I turn out to be not sweet, loving and supportive but angry and domineering. I can't remember what Newton's verdict was – thumbs up or thumbs down? No relationship is without its irritations and devoted to me as he is he probably gets fed up with my complaints. All he can say, over and over again, is: 'They never encouraged you'.

Mr Anderson has sold the house and I have great trouble with the new owners. Newton observes that the little Irish wife, who works as some kind of secretary up at the Royal Free Hospital is like my mother. She has short, black dead straight hair, small green eyes and a big ugly mouth and is always racing around in her little mini. She is Irish and 'terrifically emotional' with 'great mood swings'. Her husband is tall and pale and plays the guitar, when he is allowed to. She bangs on my door calling me a 'bitch' because I won't pay my share towards the cost of renovating the common parts which are in perfectly good nick. 'We are the landlords now' is her constant refrain. Her husband knocks politely on my door and, a bit flirtatious, tries to win me over. The couple in the flat below have moved on on account of their baby and have been replaced by a Swedish girl called Lina who is at some sort of dance school and is noisier than her predecessor. She gets a boyfriend who gives up his boring job in an office furniture company in order to sit in his girlfriend's flat, no strings attached. I too can hear the monotonous 'thump, thump, thump' of his music. He has a very fine face with large blue eyes and Newton, who has obviously seen him, 'en passant' says that he is a very sensitive guy and that I should keep my claws off him. He also says that he'll get depressed through not having a job and calls him 'that wretch.' He smokes very heavily. I do have a chat with him; I can't see what he sees in the cold pale girlfriend who neither appreciates him or cares for him. He replies that she can be OK sometimes. Her well dressed mother comes to visit and I complain about her daughter's noise. Her look of long sufferance and disappointment says it all. (Wasn't buying a flat for her in London meant to be all to the good?) But at least she can accept criticism of her offspring. There is real war between myself and the new landlady. She has two young children; the little boy seems, in Newton's words 'not quite right' – he's about three or four years old and still has a dummy – and she's always calling on the poor little girl, who is tall and thin and fair like her dad, to help her. She screams too for the dad's help with whatever job is defeating her and he runs willingly to the slaughter. She and Swedish Lina seem to be buddies and they have ganged up against me. Dr. Newton can see what she's like and is also aware of the fact that she has two young children to look after – a fact which I don't take into consideration since I am consumed by loathing. And I am very, very frightened of her because she is so irrational and small-minded. Without a moment's reflection she will run upstairs and thump my door. Sunning myself in the garden she chases me out and I cut my leg on the rough iron bar of the sunbed and the scar is forever visible. One Sunday afternoon her parents visit; they look like the type of godly people you'd want to run away from and, indeed, I observe her tearing down Parkhill Road, en route to God knows where.

I am en route to the Greek island of Crete, although it's mid July and don't I know that the heat will be insufferable? Don't I know that it's folly to prostrate myself beneath a fiery southern sun? Newton tells me that I am hardly an adventurous person and that I am hiding myself away, avoiding contact with others.

(Oh dear, oh dear! – what is so wrong with me?) He wishes that I had more friends and reckons that I should be married, with a couple of kids. I meet a guy at the Round House who has a devious way of getting into a show without paying – I am as flummoxed as the ticket checking guy by his 'spiel' – but he is thoughtful and intelligent. I talk about myself and he bursts out of himself, declaring, with real incredulity, that neither parent related to me. I proceed to tell him about Dr Newton ('see – there has been someone in my life') and his almost daily visits and he is even more shocked. He wishes I was making it up but it's clear that I'm telling the truth. When I tell Newton about my disclosure he is furious with me – at my stupidity. Do I intentionally want to put people off?

I land with a bump on the island of Crete. The place is thronged with Norwegians and it seems that I am always seeing girls with their mothers sitting at cafes and walking around the harbour. The colour of the sea is so wonderful, so vivid, that it brings to mind the story of the Greeks – Newton leant me an acclaimed book about their brilliant civilisation. I have nowhere to stay and traipse from hotel to hotel seeking a room. In one place the kindly son of the owner, or maybe he was just a daring employee puts me up in a kind of broom cupboard which is excruciatingly hot. I sit in the port and make friends with two guys, one of whom says that I can sleep in his motor home. His girlfriend is back in Norway, visiting her family. I am impressed by how someone can live so neatly in such a restricted area. (My paternal grandmother – from a kitchen in which there was only room for one person let alone gadgets – produced food that was the salt of the earth, finger lickin' good). Everything is put away; everything has its home. But he turns funny – what did I do to upset him? – and I run away. Men hate 'easy' women. Shakespeare's Hamlet is furious with his mother Gertrude for messing around with men. Women are supposed to be blue-robed

Madonnas, radiant and pure, forever holding the male baby. But we are all born into the sinful world.

I visit a mediocre sort of restaurant – the sort that spring up like mushrooms in tourist resorts – and the proprietor (a friendly, fatherly sort of guy) sees me outside, scanning the menu on the window. He approaches me and tells me that I have a good heart and that I can eat for free in his restaurant. I am genuinely surprised. Is he crazy? But he does indeed mean what he says. I am embarrassed by this offer but don't take it up because the food isn't much to write home about. One afternoon I find myself sitting next to him on the beach or maybe it is the other way round and I can see that he has noted, sympathetically, the surplus rolls of fat around my middle – something that is disguised when I'm fully dressed. Maybe he's thinking that I'm not as free as I appear and have hidden troubles.

I see a pair of wonderful sturdy brown sandals in a shop and hum and haw so much over the cost that someone gets there first and I am left teetering on the edge in strapless mules. I sit at a cafe in the port and mull over this lost opportunity. I espy two guys at another table who are undeniably attractive. One is handsomely Greek looking whilst the other has blue eyes, long blonde hair and the femininity which I always seem to go for. I befriend them and we make a nice threesome. The blonde guy tells me that his mate told him that he sussed from the way I was looking at him that I wanted to sleep with him but that was a lie – I was simply admiring him. They tell me that they had been working on a Greek ship but the continual noisy thud in the bowels of the vessel had proved insufferable and they'd decided to look for work elsewhere. Where am I sleeping? I can't, for the life of me, remember. The blonde Greek and myself decide to go away together and we are waved off by the handsome friend. We get on a bus and alight at some deserted place near the sea where we find a room together. He tells me that his father murdered his mother and that his sister is a nurse. He says: 'Some days I feel like Adolf Hitler and on others I feel like Jesus Christ.' He tells me, 'truly, madly, deeply' that if I don't return to Crete, as I have promised to do, he won't be able to bear it. He gives me his sister's address and I really believe that, on my return to my flat, I will write. How could one betray such sincerity? He is a real lover but I am useless. Do I have too much iron in my soul weighing me down? I should be splashing in the shallows, enjoying life, not lying on my back at the bottom of the ocean – a poor, drowned girl.

In my red cotton print dress with the puffed sleeves I flip back across the seas and at the airport I absent-mindedly pick up an identical suitcase (soft and brown) to my own without looking at the name tag. Bloody wrong case! I phone my father who helps me out – perhaps driving me back to Gatwick. He strides out to collect the rightful suitcase but the uniformed staff hold him back since the label is in my name. He protests – to no avail. It is July/August in the UK and the weather is grey and wet. I eat bananas and get on a number 13 bus to some dismal part of London. I pointedly say to Newton that I don't know what I'm doing here and he asks me – in no uncertain terms – why I don't return to Crete. I slap him round the face. He says, 'I don't care if you hate me.' So I fail to fulfil my promise to contact the far-away nurse whom I've never met. But I decide to learn Greek and put up some sort of notice at London University. A guy responds and Newton drives me to my lesson. The Greek guy sets me to learn the alphabet and is amazed at my progress. One day I arrive for my lesson to find the curtains drawn and the table set with loads of tasty Greek fare. Maybe this is the time to make my escape. I have trouble finding his car and – there he is – sitting at the wheel – the very picture of long-suffering patience. He is still a working man, shouldering responsibilities, and shouldn't be waiting on me. He has told me about the patient who phones him every evening reporting on the progress of his bothersome 'wind'. What on earth do psychiatrists have to put up with … If only 'play' (the sweet communion with others) was the order of the day.

It's not the first time that he has taken me to the country in his dark green Volvo. I am so surprised that it's such a short drive to England's green and pleasant land. Newton tells me that every village had its pond and I love to hear stories of life in the time of previous monarchs. He tells me that he used to play the piano for returning WW1 soldiers so he 'must have had some confidence in himself'. He believes that shyness comes from a sense of inadequacy. For years he was the superintendent of a mental hospital and lay awake at night wondering if he'd ever get out. It was a chance meeting with the 'Official' Solicitor which saved his bacon. 'You can't get through life lying on your back', he tells me. He also says that 'sex is life's fun and the excitement in a relationship wears off after a couple of years.' He knows about relationships and maybe the fact that women tend to never forgive and forget. He's not so thrilled about the fact that he still has to support his first wife, a nursing sister, with whom he had four sons, one of whom, Chris, is 'a sailor in the Caribbean'. He has the best relationship with his youngest, David, who was rejected by his mother but is now a headmaster – 'he even managed to get some 'O' levels'. Paul is a solicitor, 'always running back to retake exams' and the eldest, close to his mother, is headmaster of a boy's boarding school. He, Newton, lived with Pat, an occupational therapist – 'I got her the job' – in a flat in St. Albans overlooking the gas works for ten years before she poured some hot liquid or other over his bed. He had an affair with Joy, a Jewish woman, a feisty single mother, who came to him looking for work. 'She was the best social worker I ever had,' he said. (Before she'd had her children she'd actually lived on a desert island with one other.) He loved her four clever children who all attended St. Paul's School. She wanted him to move into her house in Golders Green but he is married to Kate, the Jungian psychoanalyst, the aunt by marriage of the up and coming celebrated violinist Nigel Kennedy who lives with them and has the heating on all day whilst he is practising. Kate has taught him, Newton, a lot about music. She is still in love with him. She wakes up in the night crying 'because her patients aren't getting any better' and he tells me, decidedly, that I have more insight than her. He also pities people in analysis, saying 'that being in a room with a listening other is the only smidgeon of happiness that they'll ever experience'. The Jews are his favourite people on account of their culture and intellect. He's a great admirer of the philosopher Isaiah Berlin and gives me his book 'The Hedgehog and the Fox'. I read the books and listen to the bedtime stories. I write about my parents and then paint the page black and rip it out of the exercise book. I am 'them' and the eternal jewel of me is polluted, besmirched and buried beneath the rubble.

It's the summer of 1980 and weather wise things aren't so great. Nor are the crowds in the streets. It seems that London is becoming the 'Wasteland' of T.S. Eliot's prophetic poem. I used to tell Greg that London was 'a dark dirty hole' and I wanted nothing to do with it. (You could tell that he wanted to believe me but was unconvinced). Newton has commitments in court, rescuing children from warring parents, but wants to take me to Kew Gardens. I haven't been out for yonks other than a habitual constitutional march around the roads of Belsize Park. I nurture a fantasy of stealing all the cheese from the continental delicatessen in England's Lane run by a dark-haired and capable Jewish lady who has turned her shop into an Aladdin's cave of tempting foodstuffs. I also make a beeline for a greengrocer in Primrose Hill run by a man and his rosy-cheeked, fair-haired wife who is active and busy and has a young daughter who also helps in the shop. Maybe I buy some token oranges or maybe I just stand there staring. One day she turns to me and says out loud 'WHAT DO YOU WANT?'

Dr. Newton wonders if I'm ok to be left on my own at Kew Gardens and whether I'll find my way back. His paternalistic concern is touching but unnecessary. Kew Gardens, of course, is a treasure trove of plants but I don't remember seeing anything much other than the Japanese Pagoda. As I'm wandering down some path or other I espy an attractive original/artistic looking male lying at full stretch on a park bench. He's wearing blue trousers, a sort of teal colour, and a pale blue shirt. I call out, 'I wonder if you could tell me where I can find some refreshments' and in a single bound he leaps off the bench and is at my side, saying 'I'll join you'. Here is the fox rather than the hedgehog. With an internal shudder I say to myself: 'I've picked him up – a day labourer'! But he tells me (and this turns out to be a cock and bull story) that he's been working in Australia in cybernetics or some other strange computer operation. He is even speaking with an Australian accent. He's presently living with his mother 'but it's not what it seems.' At thirty six he's seven years older than me and I am more than impressed by the fact that he's been working, out in the world, looking after himself since the age of sixteen when he left Dulwich College. He joined the Navy and sailed the seas, living an unsuitable life for someone so young … a fact which is later remarked on by Newton. Basically, he didn't get on with a father who sold his school prizes to buy presents for his mistresses, hating his love of jazz clubs in Richmond and generally resenting his going out, his youth. His mother was goodly, submissive, a Cheshire girl whose father, a builder, left her lots of houses which his father acquired and sold. During the war he'd been a bomber and his mother had been attracted by the uniform 'but they were never in love or anything' . He left her with a council flat in Ealing (where he is now living) and after a long liaison in Oxford with a jeweller he buggered off to Mallorca where he met his present wife. His son declared that he ripped off Oxfam when he was treasurer to the Bank of England. The worst thing is that his father prevented him from going to art school and wanted him to work in a bank, like himself. His recitation of all the different jobs he's had – 'Heavens', I tell myself, 'what wonderful, brave initiative he has' – establishes him in my mind as an individualistic hero and above all or equally my sympathies are fully aroused by the fact that he was prevented from attending art school and becoming the artist that he is. He talks of himself – oh with such gay optimism – as 'the new Picasso'. I tell Newton all about him and everything sounds great except for the cybernetics. 'What on earth is all that about'?

I was amused and a bit shocked when he picked flowers for me from someone's garden; they were just grabbed in one risky swoop. At Kew Gardens, he guided me out of the mud as I was talking about my mother and not heeding where I was going. My neighbour in Parkhill Road had done likewise. The Greek guy telephones me since he wants me to continue with my lessons but that is all past history since I have met someone new, someone lively and talented.

I don't hesitate to let him stay the night but find the story of his dream, about birds, somewhat weird. He does tell me the true story of what has recently happened to him. In Cambridge, working as an English teacher, (I am highly impressed by his self-training) teaching English to foreign students, he met an Italian girl from Cosenza, Calabria, with whom he fell madly in love: 'All of Cambridge were after her'. He even paid for her to have extra English lessons. They had a plan of returning to Cosenza where they'd set up an English school together. He said goodbye to his two children, packed a load of books and made his way south. (He was divorced from his wife whom he'd married at the age of twenty four and they'd always lived in rented cottages in South Cambridgeshire).

Once there her ancient Calabrian repressions kicked in and she returned to a former boyfriend. He returned alone, heartbroken, just managing to hold himself together. After the Calabrian disaster he returned to his mother and found himself a job in some company in dreary west London and described himself as 'a wage slave'. He was always on about being some sort of pioneer in the world of 'computer aided design'. He has a lovely friend who is a travelling salesman for a wholefood firm and with whom he shared a house in the Cambridgeshire village of Whittlesford. This guy is funny, generous and knows that he has to get on the road and do a job that is less than inspiring because he's a responsible adult male. Under his breath, in a give-away aside that speaks the truth, he says to me, apropos the intended move to Corsica (where, finally, he can develop his art), on a note of scorn: 'He'll be in every bar ...' One wonders about this thing called friendship and the criticisms that are always there, deep down, and never expressed. Keith, the friend, gives me a scarf and this prompts a fit of crazy jealousy which was a red warning sign about this guy, if ever there was one. MONEY was the other one.

His lovely kids, and they were truly nice, prove to be a bit of a sticking point. Every other weekend he rushes off to see them and I am jealous of the loving, affectionate relationship. To my shame I truly am. He quits his job because there had been some kind of 'break-in' where he was employed due to the fact that he was working for MI5 and someone had gotten wind of this and tried to steal documents. He was in a real sweat about this, literally, and felt he was being pursued. He moved in with me in order to hide. I was asked to contribute to the alimony he had, by law, to pay to his ex-wife and it was a bit grating to have to cough up for Easter Eggs and a school trip. He was into Eastern philosophy and his project on 'Lao Tsu' necessitated the purchase of rare books. In 1980/1 thirty pounds was a lot of money for a book. He pleaded and I gave in. It was at this point that any sane, self-respecting individual would have politely shown him the door – put in some boundaries.

Newton, ridiculously, almost whiningly, asked me why I couldn't sleep with both of them. I didn't want to see him any more or rather it was inappropriate for him to come round. However, he did come round to meet my latest beau and told me that he thought he was very unself-centred and a true artist. Robert couldn't understand how, after knowing Newton for so long (he was indeed puzzled by my relationship with 'loverboy') he'd never invited me over to his flat. We were consequently invited over one evening and sat with him and his nice wife in their spacious lounge. He later told me that she thought he, Robert, was mad. (She said, authoritatively, that I was a 'lover'). He, Robert, doesn't approve of my non-activity: 'You can't sit around reading all day' and makes me get a job on the road as a lollipop lady, standing by the zebra crossing outside the local primary school and wearing a horrible industrial coat. I eventually get the sack because I don't wait at the zebra crossing for the late kids but pack up promptly, and depart the scene at nine o'clock. He sells all my paperbacks, all the works of Dostoyevsky, Gide and Colette and the diaries of Franz Kafka. I also get a job as a waitress in a Richmond cafe and the Jewish owner takes pity on me as a poor girl because my shoes are so down-at-heel. His own daughter bangs the drums. If a fried egg falls to the floor it is returned to the plate. And the dishcloths are never washed. I am suffering from repeated bouts of cystitis which tests R's patience and which he blames on my enforced chastity.

On a Sunday afternoon we go to the 'Marine' cafe at Chalk Farm where they sell delicious ice-creams. I pay for our ice-creams and then another. When I say 'no' to the third or fourth I am branded as mean – mean beyond belief. As we walk back up the hill the 'meanness' tirade morphs into a political tirade about the labouring classes, poor underdogs who are told what to do and have no way of getting out of the rut they're in. Dare I say that they could try to think for themselves? But they are so beaten down, so victimised, that this is an impossibility. They are a tribe who need saving. 'Am I really so mean?' I ask myself, full of self-blame.

He can't understand why I'm still in the flat – rotting away – what with the awful landlady and the noisy neighbours. His great grief is that he was prevented from becoming an artist and his big idea is for me to sell the flat in order to buy a place in Corsica where he can paint and sell his works. He convinces me that there's going to be some sort of nuclear holocaust and the main thing will be to have access to a source of freshwater. If you have fresh water you'll be ok. If we don't get away we won't survive. The decay of the west is on its way. He makes a trip to some art establishment in Soho and buys boxes and tins of beautiful pastel chalks, his chosen medium. He buys everything he needs for the venture. I pay because he has no money although he constantly reassures me about the tax rebate that is coming his way which will enable him to repay the loan.

He's also a talented craftsman and used to make wooden walking sticks, one of which was used by the Queen Mother. He draws a picture of my dusty pink velvet chair, lodged in a corner. He doesn't doubt his talent. Newton says that he's not nervous about living abroad because he knows he can cope. The former is a bit dubious about the financial gifts/loans. He reckons that his kids must miss him loads. He says that I will be his 'emotional anchor' which is what he needs and this will be a good thing. Newton knows that I am a slave to warmth and comfort – it holds me back – so the outward bound exposure to God knows what (we've bought a load of good quality camping stuff) will do me good – force me to shape up).

When I tell my father on the phone that I am pregnant his response is: 'Are you married'? Newton asks whether R is pleased about the fact. As for myself I had a deep and real desire to have a baby. It was more in the nature of a profound visitation rather than a mere desire. I meet R's mum who asks me kindly whether I really want to have a baby in a foreign country. She's never been abroad. She's a cheery lady who used to work for the council at Acton Town Hall and was very tough on scroungers. Does she still nurture her disdain for her ex-husband, who stole so much from her? She loved her window cleaner boyfriend, Bill, who was warm and kind and, unfortunately, died.

We visit my father in his office and as we walk down the corridor R murmurs to himself, under his breath: 'God, it's so right-wing'. Apparently, in my sleep, I sometimes stop breathing and this genuinely frightens him. His nickname for me is 'cosy' and he also calls me Molly. We eat off the same plate. When he was working at the place in West London I washed his shirt every day. He tells my father about his plans who, years later, also revealed to me that he thought he was mad: 'How can you say that if things don't work out you'll go south to Sardinia in order to raise some cash …'

My father, quietly, tenaciously, digs in his heels and attempts to put a stop on the sale of the flat. He never told me that it was mortgaged, in part, and that I owed him 'X' thousands of pounds. Eventually the flat is sold, at a loss, to another single young lady and I have to leave behind my velvet tub chair, my silk shaded lamp and my pink and green Monet curtains. She got a good deal – that girl. It is snowing – in late April – when my father drives us to Victoria Station. My father is never late but R is. It takes him an age to pack all his art materials. We also have the camping gear since we intend to camp until we find a permanent abode. My father's advice has been to rent rather than to buy – in case you change your mind – but we are both desperate to burn our bridges and flee the UK. He still believes he is being hunted. When we arrive in Paris he gets off the train to buy croissants and only just makes it back in time. When we arrive in Nice he leaves me in the hotel room in order to buy provisions. He doesn't return. I get the receptionist to phone all the hospitals and thus he is located. They return him. His face is smashed up and his smart jacket is covered with what looks like egg – and blood. He'd been drinking in a bar (he loves to drink) and a gang had come in and ordered everyone out. He had refused to leave and so got beaten up and thrown in the gutter. We manage to make the crossing by ferry to L'ile Rousse where our twenty month adventure begins in earnest. I wouldn't have survived without the correspondence between myself and Newton but that's a story for another day.

Printed in Great Britain
by Amazon